THOMAS BETTERTON

Restoration London's leading actor and theatre manager Thomas Betterton has not been the subject of a biography since 1891. He worked with all the best-known playwrights of his age and with the first generation of English actresses; he was intimately involved in the theatre's responses to politics, and became a friend of leading literary men such as Pope and Steele. His innovations in scenery and company management, and his association with the dramatic inheritance of Shakespeare, helped to change the culture of English theatre. David Roberts's entertaining study unearths new documents and draws fresh conclusions about this major but shadowy figure. It contextualises key performances and examines Betterton's relationship to patrons, colleagues and family, as well as to significant historical moments and artefacts. The most substantial study available of any seventeenth-century actor, *Thomas Betterton* gives one of England's greatest performing artists his due on the tercentenary of his death.

DAVID ROBERTS is Professor and Head of English at Birmingham City University. His previous publications include *The Ladies: Female Patronage of Restoration Drama* (1989) and editions of Defoe's *Colonel Jack*, *A Journal of the Plague Year* and Lord Chesterfield's letters. His articles and reviews have appeared in leading journals including *Shakespeare Quarterly*, *The Review of English Studies*, *ELH*, *The Times Literary Supplement* and *New Theatre Quarterly*.

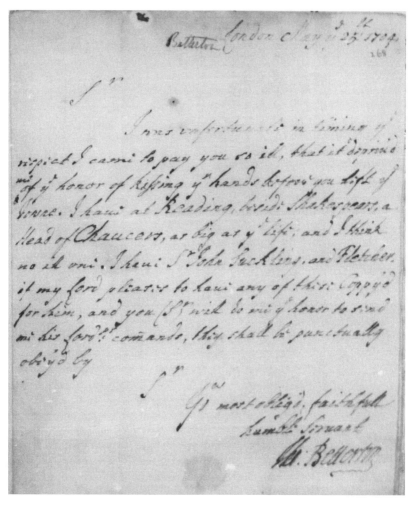

Letter from Thomas Betterton to Colonel Finch, steward to Thomas Thynne,
Lord Weymouth, in Longleat House, Thynne Papers, vol. XXV (1700–9), f.268
The letter reads:

Sr

I was unfortunate in timing ye respect I came to pay you so ill, that it deprived^me of ye honor of kissing y^r hands before you left y^e [*word unclear; perhaps 'Donne'*]. I have at Reading, beside Shakespeares, a Head of Chaucers, as big as ye life, and I think no ill one. I have Sr John Suckling, and Fletcher, if my Lord pleases to have any of these Coppy'd for him, and you (S^r) will do me ye honor to send me his Lord^ss commands, they shall be punctually obey'd by

    S^r

        Yo^ur most oblig'd, faithfull
            humble Servant
              Tho: Betterton

THOMAS BETTERTON

The Greatest Actor of the Restoration Stage

DAVID ROBERTS

CAMBRIDGE
UNIVERSITY PRESS

CAMBRIDGE UNIVERSITY PRESS
Cambridge, New York, Melbourne, Madrid, Cape Town, Singapore,
São Paulo, Delhi, Dubai, Tokyo

Cambridge University Press
The Edinburgh Building, Cambridge CB2 8RU, UK

Published in the United States of America by Cambridge University Press, New York

www.cambridge.org
Information on this title: www.cambridge.org/9780521195843

First published 2010

Printed in the United Kingdom at the University Press, Cambridge

A catalogue record for this publication is available from the British Library

Library of Congress Cataloguing in Publication data
Roberts, David.
Thomas Betterton : the greatest actor of the Restoration stage / David Roberts.
p.   cm.
Includes bibliographical references and index.
ISBN 978-0-521-19584-3 (hardback)
1. Betterton, Thomas, 1635?-1710.   2. Actors–Great Britain–Biography.   3. English
drama–Restoration, 1660–1700.   I. Title.
PN2598.B6R63 2010
792.02′8092–dc22
[B]
2010009140

ISBN 978-0-521-19584-3 Hardback

To Fiona, Joe and Maddy

Contents

Illustrations

Acknowledgements

My gratitude goes to those who have read and commented on part or all of this book throughout its evolution: Maureen Bell, Claire Cochrane, Jackie Gay, Robert D. Hume, Ian Marchant, Derek Paget, Gail Kern Paster, Alison Shell and Philip Smallwood. I owe a particular debt to Barry Turner for his generous interest in the project. Peter Holland and Peter Thomson deserve special thanks for their invaluable comments on the draft manuscript. The faults that remain are mine.

Specific enquiries were answered promptly and informatively by Henry Paston-Bedingfield, York Herald at the College of Arms; Philippa Smith, Principal Archivist at the London Guildhall; Christine Reynolds, Assistant Keeper of the Muniments at Westminster Abbey; Marcus Risdell, Archivist at the Garrick Club; Philip Fisher, Administrator at the Birmingham and Midland Institute; Professor Shearer West; Dr Kate Harris, Curator of the Longleat Historical Collections; Gudrun Muller, National Portrait Gallery; and Lisa Spurrier, Archivist at the Berkshire County Records Office. Staff at the British Library and the libraries at Birmingham University, Birmingham City University, the Birmingham Central Library and Newman University College have been unfailingly helpful.

No one working in this field could fail to acknowledge the heroic labour of making the contents of *Early English Books Online*, *Eighteenth Century Collections Online* and the Burney newspaper collection so readily available and searchable. My debt to the triple peaks of Restoration Theatre scholarship – *The London Stage*, *A Biographical Dictionary of Actors* and *A Register of Theatrical Documents* – is set out in the Introduction. Without the work of that peerless Bettertonian, Judith Milhous, some of this book could not have been written.

Part of Chapter 2 appeared as 'Shakespeare, Theater Criticism and the Acting Tradition', in *Shakespeare Quarterly*, vol. 53, no. 3 (Fall 2002), 341–61; part of Chapter 4 as 'Thomas Betterton, Bookseller's Apprentice', in *The Review of English Studies*, New Series, vol. 58, no.236 (November 2007), 473–81; part of Chapter 5 as 'Caesar's Gift: Playing the Park in the Late Seventeenth Century', in *ELH*, vol. 71 (2004), 115–39; part of Chapter 11 as 'Thomas Betterton, Private Tutor', in *Notes and Queries*, N.S. vol. 54, no. 1 (March 2007), 56–7; and a section of Chapter 12 as '"I Think No Ill One": a Letter from Thomas Betterton Sheds New Light on the Chandos Portrait', in *The Times Literary Supplement*, no.1550 (14 August 2009). My thanks to Oxford University Press, Johns Hopkins University Press and the *TLS* for permission to reprint this material.

Ruth Page, Stuart Robertson and Philip Smallwood helped cover my Head of School duties at Birmingham City University when this project started to gain momentum, while Pamela Taylor and colleagues generously allowed me space to finish it during my tenure of the John Henry Newman Chair at Newman University College. No author could hope for a more considered and professional commissioning editor than Sarah Stanton, while Rebecca Jones has overseen the production process with exemplary understanding. Because there has never been a more considerate and loving family than Fiona, Joe and Maddy, this book is dedicated to them.

Note on dates and texts

New-style dates are used throughout except where otherwise indicated. For performances of plays, including Betterton's, the date of the premiere or first performance by Betterton is used; dates for printed texts are indicated separately where appropriate. The availability of *Early English Books Online* and *Eighteenth Century Collections Online* means that first editions are generally used for play citations. Where page references are missing in such early texts, the relevant EEBO or ECCO image number is given as (for example) 'EEBO 12'.

CHAPTER I

Introduction

From the Restoration of Charles II in 1660 to the rise of David Garrick in the 1740s, Thomas Betterton was widely regarded the greatest of English actors. Long after his death in 1710, his name was a by-word for precious commodities: emotional logic over barnstorming effect; substructures of feeling not superficial reactions; the ability to transcend age and physique in search of a character's passions. Appreciating Betterton as a performer and a person also meant suspending conventional judgements about his profession's social status, so high were the standards he observed when dealing with fellow actors, managers and writers.

'Fellow', because Betterton himself was all those things. He created well over 100 roles, some of which help constitute today's core Restoration repertory.[1] He was a great exponent of Shakespearean tragic roles, encouraging future generations to conceptualise an English theatre tradition. The most successful theatrical manager of his period, he adapted plays and commissioned much of its best work.[2] An innovator in stage technology, he earned the friendship of major writers and arbiters of taste. Restraint, intelligence and mastery of the repertoire made him, in the richest sense of the term, the first *classical* actor. Early in his career he received the ultimate accolade from those discerning playgoers, Samuel and Elizabeth Pepys: 'he is called by us both, the best actor in the world'.[3] For three generations it stuck, and as late as 1756 he was cited as the 'English Roscius'.[4]

Yet Betterton remains the least written about and recognised of the male actors who constitute the 'great tradition' of English performance. Garrick, Kean, Kemble, Macready, Irving and Olivier have been amply served by modern biographers.[5] By contrast, while there have been essays on his acting, an expert study of his managerial career and an unpublished thesis on his influence, the last time anyone attempted a biography of Betterton was in 1891. Even then R.W. Lowe's study was commissioned by William Archer as part of a series on 'Eminent English Actors', as if tradition were at issue rather than the man.[6] From sketches of that tradition Betterton often gets excluded. Albert Finney once said that he 'wanted a great career, like Garrick and Kean and Irving, in that tradition'.[7] His mentor Laurence Olivier described as 'great volcanoes' the quartet of 'Burbage, Garrick, Kean and Irving'.[8] Quartet becomes trio of 'Garrick, Kean and Irving' in the hands of Anthony Holden, and even academic critics are prone to citing the same holy trinity.[9] In 1712 it was otherwise: an unspoken prologue would by the delivery of an unnamed actor 'have equall'd *Roscius, Allen, Burbage* or *Batterton*'.[10]

The reasons for Betterton's relative neglect merit a separate chapter, but they start from who he was and what he left behind. Physically unremarkable and staunchly respectable, he justifies Judith Milhous's memorable verdict: 'an obstinately shadowy titan'.[11] Unlike his successors, he left no Flaubert's parrot of a wig, sword or chair that might connect us to him; a solitary letter has recently come to light to take its place alongside a few legal documents as witnesses to the private man.[12] So shadowy is he that he is hard to accommodate not only in the acting tradition but in the art of biography, at least as defined by one of its finest contemporary exponents. Richard Holmes detects the origins of the form in the 'calm, noble culture of Augustan Enlightenment' which declared the proper study of mankind to be man.[13] Biography accordingly affirms 'the possibility and the desirability of knowing our fellow man and woman – how we "really are" (beyond the masks of fame, "success", obscurity, or even ordinariness) ...'.[14] Holmes's intellectual godfather is Boswell, whose 1791 *Life of Samuel Johnson LLD* has both 'epic scale' and 'relentless, brilliant intimacy'; the Johnson who emerges from it is at once titanic and sunlit. Titanic, shadowy Betterton wears every mask in sight over and above his myriad performances – fame and success, ordinariness and obscurity, all rolled in together. He offers the epic scale of tragic art but combines it with fleeting chinks of intimacy. Nor is he ripe for what Holmes calls 'anti-hagiography' or 'polemics as unreliable as panegyrics'. No student of Betterton can be 'a type of predator, grave-snatcher', or 'gossip driven by commercial instincts'.[15]

But the elusive, private centre of Betterton's life should encourage curiosity about why his life really mattered – why, that is, he was such an important figure for those who knew and watched him. As Guy Davenport observed of Picasso, his '*life* is there on the canvas; all else is lunch'.[16] Knowledge of Betterton does not comprehend much that could be called 'lunch', although Milhous's work on his managerial decisions discloses a much sharper sense of the man's mindset and nose for business than any other study. His extensive collection of books and paintings, catalogued in 1710 by Jacob Hooke as *Pinacotheca Bettertonaeana* but ignored by most previous studies, tells its own array of stories. But the most significant narratives lie elsewhere. While Betterton left no archive of letters, journals or personal reminiscences to complement his library, there is the enormous, oblique, still more inviting treasure chest of raw material constituted by the 264 manuscript plays and parts in his possession when he died.[17]

Few other subjects allow such certainty about the words they spoke professionally. Betterton's roles occupied a huge portion of his life. Some he learned and dropped in a matter of weeks, some he may not have learned very well at all.[18] Others were successes at key points in his career or in the nation's history, while a few, like Hamlet, he returned to over several decades. Some roles engaged palpably with national or company politics: as well as Hamlet, Henry VIII; an early and defining success, Marullo/Pisander in Massinger's *The Bondman*; the succession of libertines diplomatically overlooked by early biographers. It is a risky topic, naturally. Actors merely act their roles; his Bondman might masquerade as the evidence of the Bettertonian self it is supposed to reflect. But Betterton worked in a tightly organised repertory system where casting patterns both reflected and generated layers of 'text' that went beyond the published word: a system geared by commercial imperatives to catching and redefining the mood of the moment. Old plays were as likely as new ones to generate subtexts in the act of performance.

One thing about Thomas Betterton is certain. He lived through the fortunes of late Stuart London just as surely as he acted them. If biography 'offers a shapely doorway back into history, seen on a human scale', Betterton spent his days creating images of history's grandest chambers, formed by the period when Britain killed its king, restored one of his sons and then banished the other, and finally settled on a form of government in which the theatre, having been an arm of royal policy, became a form of bourgeois entertainment.[19] A boy in Interregnum London, Betterton owed his career to the Restoration; he helped stage the capital's changing landscape, planned his first major project as a manager in the wake of the Great Fire, acted for the signatories of the Treaty of Dover, mounted political plays during the Popish Plot crisis and survived the Glorious Revolution. He played figures from ancient history that allowed dramatists to disguise reflections on the modern state.[20] A famous man at the refracted centre of public life, his burial in Westminster Abbey was a minor public event, as much the interment of a real king as his actor-imitator if we are to believe his friend, Richard Steele:

While I walked in the Cloysters, I thought of him with the same Concern as if I waited for the Remains of a Person who had in real Life done all that I had seen him represent ... I could not but regret, that the Sacred Heads which lie buried in the Neighbourhood of this little Portion of Earth in which my poor old Friend is deposited, are returned to Dust as well as he, and that there is no Difference in the Grave between the Imaginary and the Real Monarch.[21]

The exact location of Betterton's grave, probably beneath one of the worn stones between Aphra Behn and Anne Bracegirdle in the East Cloister, has not been precisely determined, and any visitor can puncture Steele's encomium by observing that his friend shared his final resting place with musicians, painters and the church plumber.[22] But the symbolism is more important than the topography. For a cognate thought, see the photograph of Laurence Olivier's admission to the House of Lords. Flanked by the squat figures of the noble members whose task it is to present him, Olivier *wears* his robes; the rest are smothered by them.[23] The difference is that Betterton, actor of kings in an age wary of them, impersonated ideals his culture struggled to accommodate.

This book has two aims: to reconsider Betterton's significance for Restoration London, and to show how his public profile was rooted in the particulars of his personal life. Like any biography it has to tell a story; like most stories, it blends the uncontentious with the unfamiliar. It draws with critical gratitude on the three peaks of Restoration Theatre scholarship: *The London Stage*, *A Biographical Dictionary of Actors* and the *Register of English Theatrical Documents 1660–1737*, as well as on Milhous's invaluable studies of the actor.[24] But because a biography should interpret facts, not list them, there is no attempt to chronicle every known moment of a long career, and there are necessarily occasions when inference and circumstantial evidence feature. While this study is organised according to phases in its subject's life, and while it does find a place for every one of Betterton's known roles, chronology often defers to themes.

A theatrical biography can do an actor no greater service than to help readers understand what it was like to watch him at work, so this study begins by evoking Betterton's performance of a role which, for five decades, he made his own. He played his first Hamlet in the aftermath of Charles II's 1661 coronation, his last well into the reign of Anne, in 1709. The performance was a landmark in the formation of an acting tradition, not only a bridge with the Renaissance but a normative interpretation for the future. Chapter 3 broadens the question of Betterton's legacy by examining the development of his biography and representation in popular culture. While early studies served, especially in the wake of a work assumed to be by Charles Gildon, to restrict interest in the real range of his achievement, they succeeded in capturing his social background and trajectory.[25]

Just how is outlined by linked chapters on Betterton's upbringing in Civil War and Commonwealth London. Chapter 4 pieces together the clues that explain why and with whom he became a bookseller's assistant in post-regicidal London; Chapter 5 highlights changes to the environment in which Betterton grew up, their representation in some of the comedies in which he later appeared and their impact on his contribution to the newly fashionable comedy of manners. The working environment of his early career, from 1659 to 1663, is the subject of Chapter 6. It takes in his first two theatre companies, the social backgrounds of his fellow actors including the first generation of English actresses, and management styles and repertory in the wake of the Restoration. For all their success, the early years of the Duke's Company saw tensions arising in the shape of Betterton's fellow leading actor and later co-manager. Henry Harris was a painter by training whose social habits suggest aspirations more elevated than Betterton's, and Chapter 7 reads the Duke's Company's repertory from 1661 to 1664 through their contrasting stage and private identities.

Harris's grievances dissipated and in 1668 he and Betterton assumed joint managerial responsibility after the death of Sir William Davenant. Chapter 8 considers their different duties, their relationships with actors and playwrights, and the opening of the new Dorset Garden Theatre in 1671. This was the setting for a show that exemplified a new breed of spectacular entertainment, the 1673 *Macbeth*. The chapter takes in recent work on the nature of Restoration rehearsal methods, so offering an opportunity to take a close look at the working conditions of Betterton's life while focusing on a performance that had a distinctive significance in the 1670s.[26] For the best part of his career Betterton worked in the service of the man who became the country's most prominent Catholic: the heir to the throne, James, Duke of York. Chapter 9 explores the implications of the Duke's public profile and wider Catholic politics for the company repertory in the 1670s and early 1680s.

When, in 1682, Betterton assumed control with William Smith of the united Duke's and King's companies, he led London's only significant theatre company at a time of successive political crises. He worked with Dryden on the acme of Stuart spectacle, the last court masque of the seventeenth century, *Albion and Albanius*, which served in 1685 as both a

memorial to Charles II and a paean to his newly crowned brother. Chapter
10 reviews the circumstances leading to the performance and the development of new repertoire in the wake of the Glorious Revolution. The
most difficult period of Betterton's career saw him in conflict with United
Company shareholders and forced to form a new company in 1695, all in
the context of a personal financial crisis. Returning to the Lincoln's Inn
Fields Theatre which Davenant had first occupied in 1661, he attempted
to match older working methods to a younger generation of performers
and writers. Recent work has attempted to diminish Betterton's centrality
to this new company but it sits uncomfortably with the evidence superla-
tively mined and explained by Milhous, to whose work Chapter 11 is particularly indebted.[27]

Four months after Betterton's death his books, prints and paintings
were auctioned by Jacob Hooke, whose sale catalogue offers an invaluable
glimpse of the late actor's interests. Surprisingly for a man widely held
to be a link in the chain that connected Restoration performance to the
practice of the King's Men, there are barely any Shakespearean items. But
the Longleat letter provides almost certain proof that Betterton owned
the celebrated Chandos Portrait for a period of up to forty years after
Davenant's death, and Chapter 12 examines its significance for the actor's
life and career. With a career high point for Shakespeare and Betterton
alike, this book begins.

CHAPTER 2

Look, my lord, it comes: Betterton's Hamlet

Saturday 24 August 1661 was for Samuel Pepys a day of two prodigies. In the morning he was called away from business 'to see the strange creature that Captain Holmes hath brought with him from Guiny' – 'a great baboone', so uncannily human that Pepys doubted it was 'a Species' rather than 'a monster got of a man and a she-baboone'. He thought it understood English and 'might be tought to speak or make signs'. After a liquid lunch he went 'straight to the Opera' for a second epiphany. He saw '*Hamlet, Prince of Denmark*, done with Scenes very well'. But the novelty of stage pictures was not the highlight when 'above all, Batterton did the Prince's part beyond imagination'.[1]

It was no commonplace adulation. Pepys regularly mulled over the difference between stage and page, sometimes attempting both at once – disliking Shakespeare's *1 Henry IV*, he reflected that 'my having a book I believe did spoil it a little'.[2] Peter Holland has shown how his viewing habits improved with exposure to live theatre, and Betterton's Hamlet was a milestone on the journey.[3] '[B]eyond imagination', it was less *foreseeable* than hours with the text had suggested. Illuminating previously unseen meanings, it compelled reassessment of what any performance could achieve. Opposed in linguistic competence to Holmes's 'baboone', Betterton's Hamlet helped transform Pepys's appreciation of another suspect 'Species', when a mere actor could out-do the best efforts of the gentleman reader. By 1668, Betterton's Hamlet was so impressive that it collapsed any taxonomy that distinguished text from performance: 'mightily pleased with it; but, above all, with Betterton, the best part, I believe, that ever man acted.'[4]

So what was it like? Any answer is risky in terms of medium and selection. Hamlet was one role among at least 183, and Milhous regrets the 'natural ... tendency to stress Betterton's Shakespearean parts', as if they were his best vehicle.[5] The best evidence creates the agenda; it is only the rich accounts of his Shakespeare that allow us to understand his life's

7

work. Yet such may have been his own preference. In his last complete
season, four of the six known roles he forced his gout-ridden body to play
were cornerstones of the modern classical repertory: Hamlet, Macbeth,
Othello and Lear; the latter three he had also played the previous season,
with Falstaff.[6] The great fringe roles such as Timon and Angelo also interested him, as did less significant parts: Edward IV in *Richard III*, Duke
Humphrey in *Henry VI* and Bassanio in George Granville's adaptation,
The Jew of Venice.[7]

   How to write about past actors is a less tractable problem. Even if there
somehow existed a film record of Betterton's 'best part' it would generate
'a misplaced confidence that [could] actually block our understanding',
such is the inadequacy of film in representing theatrical impact.[8] Written
records, alternatively, preserve the observer's wonder, but all theatre criticism is subject to the paradox John Carey detects in its parent genre. The
writer of reportage attempts to bring us close to lived experience with a
set of tools that encodes our divorce from it, so that he or she is forever
battling the 'inevitable and planned retreat of language from the real'.[9]
Jane Milling turns the screw even tighter. What evidence there is represents only the 'rhetorical and declamatory' Betterton of his twilight years
evoked for a genteel readership, not the 'exacting, physical' actor who in
August 1661 had played Hamlet 'beyond imagination'.[10] When Alexander
Pope characterised Betterton's style, it was as the 'grave Action' of someone who 'dignify'd' the least blotted lines of Shakespeare; Steele recalled
him behaving 'with suitable dignity' even during scene changes.[11] Judith
Milhous puts the problem differently. The 'concentration of very late evidence' for his acting style means that the best accounts are tainted by adulation of the 'Living Legend' that was Betterton at seventy, when he would
give one-off performances after handing the roles on to younger men.[12]
Overall, there is insufficient data about Betterton to support a study such
as Holland's on the sound Garrick made.[13]

   It is possible, Milhous adds, for the modern scholar to over-compensate
by assuming that for more than just his benefit show in 1709 Betterton was
the 'feeble old man tottering through a gallant but embarrassing performance ... with the literal support of his two leading ladies', since to do so
would be 'a grave injustice to a man of remarkable energy and durability'.[14]
Replacing declamatory old Betterton with vital young Thomas might even
betray an historically insensitive prejudice against the style he had always
practised. He did, after all, scale down his acting commitments later in life
in order to perform signature roles with something of their original shape
and force.[15] For his last known appearance as Hamlet he still managed to

appear through the force of 'manner, gesture and voice' as 'a young man of great expectation, vivacity, and enterprise'.[16]

After the performance archaeologies of Joseph R. Roach and Dene Barnett, such talk may seem profoundly mistaken. Roach's Betterton is the last major performer to act to the tune of classical rhetoric and Galenic physiology, with its motley science of the 'bodily incarnation of the inward mind'.[17] Even his legendary self-discipline was calculated to keep humours from thickening. His capacity for swift mood changes groups him with Burbage and Alleyn, while the custom-free and rational style of Garrick condemned to obsolescence his 'oratorical' stylistic legacy.[18] Barnett similarly stresses the eighteenth-century science of gesture as an external embodiment of passions.[19] Besides recycling the pre-determined judgements of theatre history, such categories sit ill with the best evidence of Betterton's acting – not rhetorical or medical texts, but the eye-witness records left by Colley Cibber which outline an act of critical embodiment beyond biomechanics. Galenic Betterton is historicised only in the paradoxically abstract, sub-structural way that often characterises readings of the body, reducing the actor to an amalgam of redundant discourse, the thespian double of an author re-buried. It cannot explain how the actor performed in time, in individual roles, for his times and with the full range of theatrical resources at his disposal (performance wasn't just about *his* body, after all). That is as much as to affirm that the meaning and value of the canon of acting should be susceptible to the same questions that have been asked of the canon of literature. An institutionalised selection determined by prevailing genres and social practices? Or, despite all the evidential problems, a discourse of value underpinned by shared observation and judgement that might just inform future interpretations? The truism that every age experiences its best actors as astonishingly natural does not authorise the fallacy that its conceptions of what is natural are doomed, like actors, to expire.

How to write about such acting can be answered pragmatically. Even the sceptical reporter must combat the retreat of language from the real and attempt, in Carey's words, 'to isolate the singularities that will make his account real for his readers – not just something written, but something seen'.[20] Early accounts of Betterton's acting yield that quality enough to overcome even the misplaced confidence of film and to sketch, in Stanley Wells's words, 'not simply what [his Hamlet] sounded like, or what [it] looked like, but what it meant to be present at [it]'.[21] Accordingly, the following account takes the measured risk of blending academic analysis with a discourse his Hamlet helped initiate: that of theatre criticism. It starts with an impressionistic, present-tense exposition designed to evoke live performance while respecting the evidence of it; to understand why Betterton's Hamlet was beyond imagination, we must imagine for a while. But the performance was also a cultural focal point, a means of crystallising social and political questions as well as aesthetic ones, so the ultimate purpose of evoking it here is to indicate the manifold worldly contexts it helped illuminate.

In imagination, then, it is mid-afternoon on 24 August 1661, four months and a day since the coronation. Thomas Betterton, leading man of the Duke's Company and just turned twenty-six, waits for his cue:

> But now, my cousin Hamlet, and my son.[22]

It is a long wait. After the tension of the first scene, centre stage is taken by Claudius. I.ii takes its mood from the reception he gets, but the spectator's eye is drawn to the figure in the corner who flaunts his inky cloak.

The audience of the Lincoln's Inn Fields Theatre can see him up close. There are perhaps 600 squeezed into the former real tennis court, squinting in candlelight one scholar reckoned equivalent to a 100-watt bulb; later that day, the August heat will break into a storm.[23] In Hamlet, the 600 see someone not naturally cut out for heroic roles: a shortish, stocky young man with an imposing chin and nose, and resolute, bold eyes – among Hamlets of recent times, a Simon Russell Beale rather than a Samuel West.[24] 'Not exceeding the middle stature' is how Cibber would remember him; 'inclining to the corpulent' but with 'limbs nearer the athletic than the delicate proportion'.[25] Anthony Aston was even less flattering:

Mr Betterton (although a superlative good actor) laboured under an ill figure, being clumsily made, having a great head, a short thick neck, stooped in the shoulders and had fat short arms which he rarely lifted higher than his stomach ... He had little eyes and a broad face, a little pock-fretten, a corpulent body and thick legs with large feet.[26]

But as with Russell Beale, the unromantic physique draws eyes to the intensity and intelligence of the performance: beyond imagination partly because it is in excess of immediate sense impressions.[27]

His look disarms caricature – 'a serious and penetrating aspect'. Eyes have been upon him since Claudius began to speak. 'Upon his entrance into every scene,' continued Cibber, 'he seemed to seize upon the eyes and ears of the giddy and inadvertent.'[28] He is, as the text demands, clad in a customary suit of solemn black; if a Boitard illustration in Rowe's

1709 edition of the play can be relied on, he wears black tights, coat and breeches, and he sports a novelty in the history of English dress, one of the full-bottom wigs which had become *de rigueur* among those anxious to follow the latest in royal – and French – fashion.[29] He is sure to look the part: as he would supposedly tell Gildon, the actor 'must know how to give the proper Graces to every Character he represents, those of a Prince to a Prince ...'.[30] Betterton has learned his 'Graces' by working at them, the 'athletic' in pursuit of the 'delicate'. Already they have been assessed by the restored king. The week before, Charles II had descended with his brother, James, Duke of York, and sister-in-law to see an old play of his loyal servant Davenant's: *The Wits*, in which Betterton had played the leading role of the Elder Pallatine.[31]

If this Hamlet cuts a robust figure, he is also an ambiguously topical one amid the 'uneasy relationship of stage and court'.[32] No evidence has come to light that Charles II would see a performance of the play until the safer distance of 1674, when its edge had been dulled by time and dancing Danes.[33] According to Evelyn, this 'old play' failed to measure up to new aesthetic priorities forged by the king's exile in France.[34] In 1661 there is a more palpable incongruity. Betterton's Hamlet may be royal to the buckles of his shoes, a study in learned graces, but as the man apart at a time when everyone else is celebrating the new regime there is something of the black-clad puritan about him. Yet it is the old king he mourns, the one whose ghost still stalks the palace, as the presence of the royal martyr Charles I was remembered in books and woodblock prints. Audiences of the 1660s, writes Nancy Klein Maguire, were offered plays that dwelt on 'a restored king with a decapitated father', tragicomedies 'mirroring the double vision and the ambiguity of the Restoration'.[35] Maguire does not mention *Hamlet*, but it is the missing piece of her puzzle, a perennial favourite that enables the audience to revisit the contradictions of a time recently 'out of joint' (I.v.188). To Betterton falls the role of the prince in internal exile, deprived of his birthright by the scheming but competent serpent who, having deprived his father of his life, now wears his crown.

This is Shakespeare not only for a healing body politic but, in Pepys's view, 'done with Scenes, very well'. Around Hamlet, painted shutters and a backcloth that can change with the scenes of the play, depicting settings fit for later productions: for *Hamlet*, logic says, a stateroom, a more intimate space for Polonius's family and the 'closet scene' with Gertrude, and an outdoor scene for the ramparts and the graveyard. Steeped in the contradictions of recent history, the production also marks a break with the past, a declaration of the new production values of an improved age.

It is a new kind of theatrical space the actors must learn to use, half-way between the inclusive, open platform of the Elizabethan theatre and the illusionistic proscenium stages of Victorian London. Upstage, 'in the scenes', they are a visual attraction, pictorialised in their surroundings, objects of the nascent 'gaze' that eagerly embraced the novelty of actresses, Hester Davenport and Mary Saunderson as Gertrude and Ophelia; down-stage, pacing an area the size of a living room, they remain cheek by jowl with the audience, trading on the boundaries between fictional, social and private selves.[36] The cramped old tennis court with its forestage meeting the audience chin to chin is the perfect vehicle for intimacy, and after that facility has been swallowed up by managers eager for more seating, Cibber will remember its gift to performers and spectators: 'A Voice scarce rais'd above the Tone of a Whisper, either in Tenderness, Resignation, inno-cent Distress, or Jealousy suppress'd, often have as much concern with the Heart as the most clamorous Passions.'[37]

Betterton prepares to speak, visibly. Aston says that his 'left hand fre-quently lodged in his breast between his coat and waistcoat, while with his right he prepared his speech' (it was Kneller's way to paint delicate fingers, but the ones he gave Betterton suit a gestural art). Hamlet's first words require the intimacy this theatre offers:

> A little more than kin, and less than kind.[38]

It is a gesture of companionship, a sign that Hamlet will share his troubles not with his mother or stepfather up there amid the scenes, but downstage with the audience. To share Hamlet's joke is to be taken to a different, edgy level of thought – a mix of teenage grumps and querulous nit-pick-ing. Betterton has the knack of drawing people into those moments when he speaks directly to them. In his soliloquies, Cibber will recall, 'the strong intelligence of his attitude and aspect, drew you to such an impatient gaze, and eager expectation, that you had almost imbibed the sentiment with your eye, before the ear could reach it'.[39] Beyond the intimacy of the space, Cibber testifies to the modernity of the style. To communicate to the audience's impatient gaze a feeling which precedes words is the skill of a film actor. As his first biographer claimed to hear him say, 'you adjust all the Lines and Motions of the Face to the Subject of your Discourse'; only then can the audience begin to imbibe with the eye the sentiments of the role.[40]

A little more than kin? On this occasion, less than 'kind' by a slender margin, because the line Shakespeare wrote is not what the audience of August 1661 has just heard. Restoration theatre managers attempted to 'improve' Shakespeare by dressing the plays in painted scenes, but also by simplifying his language. Betterton's manager, Sir William Davenant, has produced an acting version of the play which will not be published for another fifteen years.[41] The original, says the first edition of 1676, was just too long to perform, much of its language too dense and unpredictable. Davenant could not see Hamlet descend to the particularity of 'inky', so he substituted an epithet which does the work of 'cloak' before the line gets there: 'mourning'. Such clarity was symptomatic of a broader desire for social and religious conformity. Among the aims of the Royal Society, said its first historian, Bishop Thomas Sprat, would be to 'reject all the amplifications, digressions, and swellings of style'.[42]

So what the audience hears is not Shakespeare's line but something plainer: 'A little more than kin, and less than kin.' Claudius is too close but not as close as he thinks. The pun on 'kind' has gone, and the sound of the line has changed, with perhaps a new pun that chimes, like Hamlet's morose presence, nervously with the times – more than king, less than king. But on 24 August 1661 the actor's sound puts to distance the ironing out of meaning. Thomas Betterton has just spoken and it is the most resonant, musical voice anyone has heard on the stage, its musicality aided by the filtering of verbal texture. Whatever feeling the audience had imbibed with the eye a split second earlier seems incomplete now that the ear has reached it. 'In all good speech', Gildon records, 'there is a sort of Music', and music is what everyone hears from Betterton.[43] Remembering his voice, Cibber will speak of his facility with the 'flowing numbers' of verse and liken the effect to listening to the 'celebrated airs of an Italian opera'.[44] Theatres of the 1660s are noisy places where people chatter while trading fast food and flirtation.[45] But when Betterton speaks, says Aston, chronic talkers listen; he gets 'universal attention, even from the fops and orange girls'.[46] That is his own index of success. He knows that an actor can 'deceive an audience into a loud applause' with rhetorical tricks, but he thinks no applause 'equal to an attentive silence'; 'to keep them hushed and quiet, was an applause which only truth and merit could arrive at'.[47]

A little more than kin, and less than kin – Betterton, who will befriend John Dryden and Alexander Pope, perhaps modulates Hamlet's riposte into an Augustan arc, rising with 'more' and falling with 'less'. The actor who has learned the graces of the prince's part must speak the language of the restored court and its self-conscious polish.[48] But just as Betterton's corpulent body has trained itself towards grace, there is another dimension to the voice, something grittier; if it is operatic, it is the tenor of a Vickers, not a Pavarotti. Aston says that although it is sometimes 'low and grumbling', he can 'tune it to an artful climax', as if blending speech and music, earth and air. It was a voice that 'gave more Spirit to Terror, than to the softer Passions'.[49] The music Betterton finds in Hamlet and other roles makes him the first actor to be remembered for speaking Shakespeare as poetry rather than metre, the antithesis of the 'strutting player' evoked by Ulysses in *Troilus and Cressida* who measures 'wooden dialogue' with his 'stretched footing'.[50] To speak is, after all, the actor's highest dignity: in this Cibber is consistent with Gildon, whom Betterton allegedly told that 'Mimes and Pantomimes [do] all by Gesture, and the Action of Hands, Legs, and Feet, without making use of the Tongue in uttering any Sentiments or Sounds'.[51]

The sound of that first musical arc may be Betterton's alone, but there are some there who believe its contours have been shaped in another age, for during the summer its embodying 'ill figure' has been submitted to a regime of ferocious discipline. Nearly half a century later, in 1708, a memoir of the Restoration stage will appear under the title *Roscius Anglicanus* – the English Roscius, Betterton, the actor whose name signifies both a person and a history. The memoir is that of the man who is sitting offstage that August afternoon with a copy of *Hamlet* in his hand, waiting for one of the actors to dry. His name is John Downes and he is relieved to be where he is; two months earlier he had a part in *The Siege of Rhodes* but panicked at the sight of the audience, which put him 'into a great sweat' and 'spoiled him for an actor'.[52] Downes believes that behind Betterton's Hamlet lies a trail of performances going right back to the only begetter himself. Davenant, so eager to prove his literary credentials that he claimed to be Shakespeare's illegitimate son, had worked for the King's Men before the Civil War.[53] As a boy, he said, he had seen Hamlet played by Taylor, 'who had been instructed by the author, Mr Shakespeare'. Over the summer of 1661, Davenant has taught Betterton 'every article' of Taylor's performance.

The story is famously flawed. Of the two known actor-Taylors of the Renaissance, Joseph did not join the King's Men until Burbage's retirement three years after Shakespeare's death, while John was a boy actor in a junior company with no known connection to the author of *Hamlet*.[54] True or false, Downes's genealogy of Betterton's Hamlet is ripe with possibility, and its pattern of hearsay is repeated in tales of a portrait of Shakespeare and of his first arrival at a London theatre.[55] This is a time when actors learn by imitation, and Joseph Taylor had almost certainly studied the part of Hamlet with Burbage, who must have had conversations about it, at the very least, with Shakespeare; or Shakespeare may have been involved in training the boy Taylor. For all its flaws, that Davenant and Downes so want the tale to be true is revealing enough. Betterton's Hamlet connects them to a seamless tradition of performance, eliding the inconvenient truth of the Interregnum.

After the court scene and the reunion with Horatio, another wait, as if Shakespeare knew that the intensity of what was to follow needed the tragicomic interlude of Polonius's family. Next, Hamlet is on the battlements, and Betterton does something which will help future actors and readers recognise a different kind of performance history. Early modern actors played towards the 'points' of a role, the moments of maximum emotional intensity where some extraordinary gesture or inflection proclaims a special quality and lives in the audience's collective memory.[56] Kabuki supplies a living parallel: at key moments – *mie* – an actor will freeze and, disturbing the flow of dialogue, give a slow motion repeat of a pivotal gesture or reaction. Audiences applaud and call out, complimenting the actor on his resemblance to some past master.[57]

The defining 'point' of Betterton's Hamlet happens now, in Act I, Scene iv. Perhaps it is something he has learned from Davenant's memory of Joseph Taylor. Shivering, Horatio, Hamlet and Marcellus lament the drunken celebrations at court – here again, Hamlet is the man in black at the Restoration party – and then the ghost appears.

> Look, my lord, it comes. (I.iv.38)

Shakespeare prescribes a wish for self-protection: 'Angels and ministers of grace defend us' is Hamlet's first response (I.iv.39). But it is one of those moments where text gives way to performer. In Olivier's 1948 film, Hamlet barely sees the ghost at all. Its presence is extra-sensory and the actor's eyes roll upwards as if he is already communing with the dead; dizzy, he falls into the arms of his friends before daring to say a word. According to Hazlitt, Edmund Kean eschewed such spectacle; surprising, perhaps, for an actor noted for his extremes of passion.[58] Seeing the ghost, wrote Hazlitt, Kean's Hamlet showed a 'surprise' which modulated into 'eagerness and filial confidence', an 'impressive pathos of his action and voice'. Kean sought an alternative to the pyrotechnics of his great predecessor in the part, David Garrick, the first English actor to be noticed for characterising a role from the feet upwards: 'Garrick turns sharply and at the same moment staggers back two or three paces with his knees giving way under him; his hat falls to the ground and both his arms, especially the left, are stretched out nearly to their full length, with the hands as high as the head …'[59] In turn, Garrick cast an eye back towards Betterton that was both critical and appreciative. Rowe's 1709 Shakespeare includes a Boitard engraving of the second ghost scene that probably recalls Betterton – arms stretched out, one leg bent, the whole body pushed back by some superior force – in a way that fed Garrick's imagination. At the same time, this is a moment of baroque display, the characteristically 'clumsy' and 'fat' body of Aston's description contorted beyond its limits, taken to the edge of nature in the face of the supernatural. We see the same 'point' that Cibber would describe: the actor, his artist or both quoting, as if in leitmotif, the excitement of the first encounter with the ghost. Shearer West doubts whether, the signature gesture of knocking over a chair apart, Boitard's engraving represents Betterton's performance at all, but it is hard to dismiss the fact that it shows a feature of it to which critics were repeatedly drawn.[60] As the texts of Shakespeare's early editors attempted to lend consistency to what the playwright had written, so portraits of actors created a complementary authenticity to records of performance, creating a canon of great acting even as the canon of English literature was beginning to embrace Shakespeare as a national poet.[61]

Colley Cibber was not born until ten years after Betterton's first night as Hamlet and did not publish his *Apology* until nearly thirty years after his death, but if that diminishes its status as an eye-witness account, it magnifies the significance of Betterton's performance for later generations of actors and theatregoers. Cibber begins by recalling a barnstorming performance by an unnamed actor, and in his familiar, unctuous way, lets the reader know that he was sitting next to Joseph Addison at the time, sharing his disapproval:

You have seen a Hamlet perhaps, who, on the first appearance of his father's Spirit, has thrown himself into all the straining vociferation requisite to express rage and fury, and the house has thundered with applause; though the misguided actor was all the while (as Shakespeare terms it) tearing a passion into rags – I am the more bold to offer you this particular instance because the late Mr Addison, while I sat by him to see this scene acted, made the same observation, asking me, with some surprise, if I thought Hamlet should be in so violent a passion with the Ghost, which, though it might have astonished, it had not provoked him? – for you may observe that in this beautiful speech the passion never rises beyond an almost breathless astonishment, or an impatience, limited by filial reverence, to enquire into the suspected wrongs that may have raised him from his peaceful tomb and a desire to know what a spirit so seemingly distressed might wish or enjoin a sorrowful son to execute towards his future quiet in the grave?[62]

Illustration 1 Hamlet sees the ghost again. Engraving by
Francois Boitard in Nicholas Rowe, ed., *The Works of
Mr William Shakespear*, 6 vols. (London, 1709)

The text provides the actor both with an opportunity and a set of restrictions, based on his observation of what was natural in the circumstances described. According to Cibber, it was Betterton who had best understood its contours:

This was the light into which Betterton threw this scene; which he opened with a pause of mute amazement, then rising slowly to a solemn, trembling voice, he made the Ghost equally terrible to the spectator as to himself, and in the descriptive part of the natural emotions which the ghastly vision gave him, the boldness of his expostulation was still governed by decency, manly, but not braving, his voice never rising into that seeming outrage or wild defiance of what he naturally revered. But alas! to preserve this medium, between mouthing and meaning too little, to keep the attention more pleasingly awake by a tempered spirit than by mere vehemence of voice, is of all the master-strokes of an actor the most difficult to reach. In this none yet have equalled Betterton.[63]

Betterton's skill in the scene is to convey the radical naturalism for which Shakespeare was in the process of being discovered by a generation of poets and critics; he understands, to anticipate Dr Johnson, the innumerable modes of combination which life brings, the way one state of mind might be counter-pointed by another in 'adherence to general nature'.[64]

Milling contends that he 'specialized in parts offering opportunities to transform suddenly from one believable and highly-strung emotion to another';[65] but that diminishes the restraint and emotional complexity that emerge from Cibber, where Betterton's Hamlet is shocked and afraid, yet respectful and devoted. He tries to govern his feelings when his feelings might govern him; restraining passion is the best way to show it. Above all, he must make us see the ghost not for ourselves, but as he sees it. The two qualities are related, for his command of the complex play of emotions is the means by which we can enter his consciousness, to transform what we see into what he sees. Cibber may have had in mind the 'straining vociferation' of George Powell when he recalled the ranting princes he had seen. According to Aston,

Powell attempted several of Betterton's parts ... but lost his credit, as in Alexander he maintained not the dignity of a king but out-heroded Herod, and in his poisoned mad scene out-raved all probability; while Betterton kept his passion under and showed it most (as flame smokes most when stifled).[66]

Aston is drawn to Hamlet's own dislike of over-acting in citing his warning not to 'out-herod Herod', moderated by the neo-classical imperative of 'probability'. Betterton's skill as an actor is completely self-absorbing: 'from the time he was dressed to the end of the play [he] kept his mind in the same temperament and adaptness as the present character required.'[67] It was a tribute he shared with Burbage, who according to Flecknoe 'so wholly transform[ed] himself into his part, and put ... himself off with his clothes, as he never (not so much as in the tiring house) assumed himself again until the play was done'.[68] Like his predecessor's, Betterton's temperamental immersion is an index not just of professionalism but of the way he used the discipline of his own imagination to awaken the audience's.

He brings the same quality to Hamlet's second encounter with the ghost. Reading Cibber's account of I.iv might lead us to suppose Betterton a cerebral actor, his voice doing the work his unpromising physique could not, but a contemporary of Cibber's thought otherwise. Although, according to the Boitard engraving, Betterton reminds his audience of the moment in Act I, he also differentiates between seeing the ghost for the first time and sensing that it has returned to caution him:

I have lately been told by a Gentleman who has frequently seen Mr *Betterton* perform this Part of *Hamlet*, that he has observ'd his Countenance (which was naturally ruddy and sanguine) in this Scene of the fourth [sic] Act, where his Father's Ghost appears, thro' the violent and sudden Emotions of Amazement and Horror, turn instantly on the Sight of his Father's Spirit, as pale as his Neckcloth, when every Article of his Body seem'd to be affected with a Tremor inexpressible; so that, had his Father's Ghost actually risen before him; he could not have been seized with more real Agonies; and this was felt so strongly by the Audience, that the Blood seem'd to shudder in their Veins likewise, and they in some Measure partook of the Astonishment and Horror, with which they saw this excellent Actor affected.[69]

Such intense physicality of emotion Betterton brings not simply to the body language of performance, but to the body of the text, the two joined in the utmost exercise of imaginative power. *The Laureat* continues:

And when Hamlet utters this Line, upon the Ghost's leaving the Stage (in Answer to his Mother's impatient Enquiry into the Occasion of his Disorder, and what he sees) – *See – where he goes – ev'n now – out at the Portal:* The whole Audience hath remain'd in a dead Silence for near a Minute, and then – as if recovering all at once from their Astonishment, have joined as one Man, in a Thunder of universal Applause.

The effect was the all-enveloping emotion of astonishment – in Roach's words, 'one of the most desired effects' of Restoration performance.[70]

It is the discipline and inner intensity of the performance which allows Betterton to go on giving it into his seventies with the same degree of credibility. In the account given by *The Tatler* on 20 September 1709, there are the familiar high points, but they are part of a performance which embraces general principles of human nature realised through 'the force of action':

he acted youth; and by the prevalent power of proper manner, gesture, and voice, appeared through the whole drama a young man of great expectation, vivacity and enterprise. The soliloquy, where he began the celebrated sentence of 'to be, or not to be!' the expostulation, where he explains with his mother in her closet; the noble ardour, after seeing his father's ghost; and his generous distress for the death of Ophelia, are each of them circumstances which dwell strongly upon the minds of the audience, and would certainly affect their behaviour on any parallel occasions in their own lives.

Without reference to portraits or emerging theatre criticism, that is a tribute to Betterton's acting which shows its most profound permanence: in
the minds of those who had seen it. 'He was a man', concluded Aston in
Hamlet's own words; 'I shall not look upon his like again'.[71] The power of
his Hamlet turns him into a ghost who haunts the minds not only of his
audience, but his fellow actors. Barton Booth, a colleague of his later years,
remarked, 'When I acted the Ghost with Betterton, instead of my awing
him, he terrified me. But divinity hung round that man!'[72] Terrifying but
divine – the contradictions of a baroque intensity which, drawing its principles from an emerging category called 'nature', skirts in the minds of its
spectators the edges of the superhuman.

Across its forty-eight year history, Betterton's Hamlet was a source of
wonder for those who saw it but also a miniature cultural history. While
Downes makes Betterton a simulacrum of Taylor and so of Shakespeare's
own intentions, Cibber turns the actor into a species of critic who has
studied the text and divined the shape of its passions. No longer an imitator, Betterton has become an interpreter who rejects the crowd-pleasing
display of his fellow actors in favour of a considered, inward reading. Those
are not mutually exclusive alternatives, any more than the rhetorical category of 'invention' – the arrangement of existing materials – precluded
originality: it is the discipline of art that allows any performer to do both.[73]
His performance proves to be a model for future attempts which none
have yet equalled; although definitive, it is by an enduring paradox not the
last word. Instead of looking to the past to keep tradition alive, it looks to
the future, gainsaying Richard Cumberland's tribute to the agile Garrick,
whose performances in conventional theatre historiography dispel 'the
barbarisms and bigotry of a tasteless age, too long attached to the preju-
dices of custom, and superstitiously devoted to the illusions of imposing
declamation'.[74]

  Betterton's 'mechanical reproduction' as an ideal text also challenges
Walter Benjamin's famous analysis of the impact of technology on tradition. Benjamin saw in the 'mechanical reproduction' of film and other
modern media an assault on the 'aura of the work of art' which would lead
to a 'tremendous shattering of tradition'. When art is no longer 'authentic'
it can be based not on ritual but on politics. The antithesis of mechanical
reproduction in Benjamin's argument is that chronically ritualistic, charismatic event called 'the stage play'. So stark is that antithesis that for
Benjamin the arts of screen acting and stage acting are mutually exclusive: where the stage actor creates an organically consistent role with which

he and the audience can identify, the screen actor's creation is 'composed of many separate performances'.[75] Benjamin's modernist fervour assumes a restricted understanding of screen acting, but it is the assertion that stage acting is somehow immune or opposite to the forces of mechanical reproduction that seems, in Betterton's case, misguided. The reputation of Betterton fed and gained from a public appetite for the mechanically reproduced records of performances represented by printed words and pictures. These were palpably not 'the real thing', but their effect was the opposite of the one predicted by Benjamin: not the shattering of tradition but its creation and affirmation; not an assault on authentic presence but a celebration, even a mystification of it. Remembering Betterton's Hamlet in the words of Ophelia, Cibber wrote, 'To see what I have seen!'[76]

The shift in the critical consciousness of Betterton from reproductive imitator to reproductive originator places him in the realm of another cultural process: the invention of the idea of the author, situated variously in the book trade and in progressive definitions of plagiarism.[77] Paulina Kewes traces the evolution of plagiarism out of an older practice of collaboration, seen by the 1680s as a sign of failure or outright dishonesty. But theatre people know that no dramatist is an island, so the capacities of the newly discovered author remain shared among those, like Betterton, whose job it is to articulate them to the public. Cibber put the case rhapsodically:

Betterton … was an actor, as Shakespeare was an author, both without competitors! formed for the mutual assistance, and illustration of each other's genius! How Shakespeare wrote, all men who have a taste and nature may read, and know; but with what higher rapture would he still be read, could they conceive how Betterton played him! Then might they know, the one was born alone to speak, what the other only knew to write! … Could how Betterton spoke, be as easily known as what he spoke, then you might see the muse of Shakespeare in her triumph, with all her beauties in their best array, rising into real life, and charming her beholders.[78]

In 1732, the theatre in Goodman's Fields featured 'the Heads of Shakespeare, Dryden, Congreve and Betterton'.[79] One consequence of the association was that Betterton was, over the course of the early eighteenth century, credited with the authorship of numerous plays and stage histories, and soon after his death a friend of Pope's thought it a pity he had not written more and acted less.[80] If Gildon is correct, however, he was content to see actors sharing the poets' crown for 'lay[ing] down those Signs, Marks and Lineaments of Nature, that you may know when she is truly drawn, when not'.[81] The argument would flourish and be repudiated long into the eighteenth century.[82]

Facsimile copy to critical reading – this was also, obliquely, a change of political colour. In August 1661 Betterton's Hamlet represented continuity between pre-Civil War culture and the post-Restoration 1660s, analogous to an unbroken royal succession, yet alive with the ambiguities of the tragicomic plot. By the time his legacy was being defined by Cibber, he had come to represent the new bourgeois gentleman with a taste for moderation: from succession to politeness, from authenticity to reason, from Stuart glamour to Hanoverian trimming. If in 1661 the performance had summoned Stuart ghosts, by 1740, with Culloden five years ahead, it was remembered in order to exorcise them. Betterton-Hamlet's dealings with the ghost, Cibber said, were 'still governed by decency, manly, but not braving'. He had become a model for the social and political present and future, not for the past.

To the extent that Cibber tried to define the sort of tradition which Betterton's Hamlet might initiate, then it was a particularly English one, the embodiment of the Kit-Cat values promoted by Addison.[83] Robert D. Hume has said that '[s]tarting conspicuously with Dryden, English writers aspire to be independent, to establish themselves as *English*'.[84] Among the canon of English dramatists there had to be a benchmark for such a project. The mix of vulgarity and classical poise that was Jonson's work disqualified him, while Fletcher's plays owed too much to the atmosphere of French romance; it was Shakespeare whose range, expressive variety and engagement with English history best celebrated what Hume calls 'English separateness and individuality'. Paul Langford has similarly shown how many conduct books and other treatises of the period focus on the inculcation of distinctively English manners.[85] Betterton's performance is a model of gentlemanly virtues: manly, but not braving, without outrage or wild defiance, governed throughout by decency; 'it was their want of Ability to speak which made them have Recourse to bellowing', as he is alleged to have said of Cicero's rivals.[86] He enquires into suspected wrongs with the sympathy of a sentimentalist, his enquiry replicating the critical distance of the true connoisseur of performance. If we are to learn from him, we should learn, like him, to refuse the easy 'clap'.

So Cibber offers not just a means of appreciating the distinction of Betterton's performance but a map of what it means to be a person of distinguished taste. This is the world described by the French sociologist Pierre Bourdieu, whose seminal study *Distinction* charts the rise of cultural capital among the bourgeoisie of eighteenth-century Europe.[87] If Betterton occupies a pivotal place in the great English acting tradition, he is also the first actor to be the subject of appreciation by a self-appointed connoisseur. His Hamlet raises the transient, disreputable world of theatre performance to the official status of art, in the service of a broader social discipline. Reflecting on the first biography of Betterton, Cheryl Wanko invokes not Bourdieu but Foucault. The actor's is 'a life well disciplined through the public gaze of performance and print, an internalized set of rules to create roles that maintain rather than disrupt "Appearance" and social order'.[88] Betterton's response to the ghost of old Hamlet is, therefore, not just the highest 'point' of a performance but a signpost to a new set of cultural objectives underpinned by a new kind of theatrical culture: professionalised, circulated through the publicity of print, thriving on a self-conscious understanding of its obligations both to the past and to the living text of the national playwright, distinguishing its truth with the category of art.

It is in the nature of the evidence available that the study of Betterton's Hamlet speeds from performance analysis to cultural criticism. Faced with early sources that produce for an admiring public what Cheryl Wanko calls 'a life well disciplined', the student of his biography must learn to slip into reverse: to locate the individual amid the rules and the roles. There are substantial points of symmetry between the purpose of Gildon's *Life* and the imperatives of Betterton's life, which was nothing if not well disciplined. At the same time, Gildon's work makes limited sense unless it is understood as an attempt to fuse contradictory patterns and tendencies, to reconcile – for one thing – the old Stuart with the new Hanoverian. Its presiding theoretical genius is therefore neither Bourdieu nor Foucault but Bakhtin, for whom 'a plurality of independent and unmerged voices' were the key to Dostoevsky's novels.[89] In Betterton's case, this was not the commonplace multiplicity that comes of acting for a living, but of the daily realities of a changing business and political environment. There was much more to the life well-disciplined than *The Life of Mr Thomas Betterton* could accommodate, and the effects of Gildon's economy have been felt throughout the strange, intermittent history of the actor's biography.

CHAPTER 3

An obstinately shadowy Titan: Betterton in biography

That history began in earnest, so Charles Gildon claimed, with a social call. Summer 1709 or thereabouts, and Gildon is travelling through Berkshire with that hardy signifier of narratorial unreliability, a 'friend'. They reach Reading, with its remnants of a wool industry, farmers coming and going, and churches still under repair after the Civil War, when the royalist garrison had fought bitterly.[1] It is cheap, at least, for the famous couple who keep a 'country house' there, ruing an investment which had devoured their savings years ago, but enjoying the contrast with Covent Garden.[2]

'Being hospitably receiv'd', one day after dinner Gildon follows the semi-retired Thomas Betterton into the garden. They talk theatre; Gildon has written plays and shared the acquaintance of Steele and Dryden, Wycherley and Behn. It is a warm evening. Betterton has long suffered from stones and gout – a particular trouble in recent performances – so they sit in the shade and grumble.[3] Ignorant audiences, incompetent managers, wretched playwrights, but above all, showy, lazy, greedy, vain, ill-disciplined actors: 'Much was said by my Friend against the present Players, and in praise of those of his younger Days.' What was to be done?

On cue, Betterton goes into his house, and 'after a little stay return'd'. He is clutching some papers. The wine goes round and the excitement mounts. Betterton says that another 'friend' has written out the manuscript for him but he is being typically modest: Gildon recognises the handwriting as Betterton's. It is a view of 'everything necessary for the Action and Utterance of the Pulpit and Bar, as well as on the Stage'. This is how he has supposedly spent the quieter months that have come since 1707, when he began to hand over roles to younger actors 'systematically, not casually'; his summer breaks were lengthening.[4] He still had sufficient involvement in the theatre to write from first-hand knowledge. On 7 April 1709 he had resurrected for a benefit performance a favourite role, Valentine in Congreve's *Love for Love*, fresh from appearing as Othello.[5]

Former colleagues had returned to the stage to honour him, ticket prices rose, 'unusual Encouragement ... was given to a Play for the Advantage of so Great an Actor', and although so 'lame with the gout' that he 'burlesque[d] the Part of the youthful Valentine' propped up between two actresses, Betterton collected the equivalent of about a year's salary before continuing to perform for the rest of the season and beyond.[6]

He had the more leisure for writing the textbook to set all actors straight. In time, others would enter the field, offering from less experience to define the essentials of the performing arts.[7] What greater service could any friend undertake than offer to publish it? Berkshire does not abound in booksellers, and Betterton lacks the energy and ego needed to see the manuscript into print. The loose papers made such an impression on Gildon that they could be recalled with some accuracy and rolled in with other attractive items – a few pages about Betterton's life, one of his plays, sundry writings on the dramatic arts.

So appeared, in 1710, *The Life of Mr Thomas Betterton*, thanks to the energy of its real author, against whom, for once, the charge of self-publicity could not be laid. Playwright, poet, essayist, journalist, grammarian, biographer, historian, editor, theologian and pen for hire, Charles Gildon had grasped his opportunity. To lend his name to the book would undermine its authenticity. This was not, readers are assured, the work of a 'plagiary'.[8] But it could not be passed off as Betterton's alone, with its biographical narrative and reprint of St Evremond on music and opera. Such deceit would have to wait until the high point of Betterton's posthumous fame. A year after Cibber had celebrated his Hamlet, the 1741 *History of the English Stage* exploited the idea of the lost manuscript less subtly: announced as Betterton's, never before published, and with a furtive dedication by Edmund Curll. The habit was infectious. When Lewis Theobald published *Double Falsehood*, the play allegedly based on Shakespeare and Fletcher's lost *Cardenio*, he could think of no better proof of authenticity than to refer to a manuscript copy 'in the Possession of the celebrated Mr. *Betterton*, and by Him design'd to have been usher'd into the World'.[9] Betterton's fame was exploitable for charitable ends too. In 1712 Pope is reported to have published his own translations of Chaucer in Betterton's name so that the proceeds would help his destitute widow.[10]

At least Gildon could say that the world knew him for Betterton's friend, and the actor did keep what was evidently a decently furnished house in Reading, where tradition says 'he was honoured and respected like the prince he had so often and so justly personated'.[11] Nine years earlier Gildon had acknowledged his assistance with 'the Fable' or plot of his tragedy, *Love's Victim*, while the *Life* was dedicated to Steele, a mutual acquaintance.[12] Gildon's way of attributing the words of published rhetorical treatises to Betterton means the biographical plausibility of the *Life* is easy to overlook; it is largely, not exclusively, 'a pastiche of French elocution texts'.[13] Glaring lapses abound, of course. By his own admission ignorant of Greek and Latin, Gildon's Betterton reveals a wide knowledge of Graeco-Roman oratory, sometimes for pages on end. Betterton's scribe had supposedly been a man of greater learning but Gildon, who had the benefit of the classical education afforded by the Catholic seminary at Douai, was there to tidy up.[14] His point, Cheryl Wanko observes, was to invest Betterton with 'classical authority' and 'other accoutrements of gentility' in order to show how he reconciled the fashionable debate of ancients against moderns.[15]

By the time the book came out it would be hard for anyone to establish how far Betterton had helped Gildon with this fable. *The Life of Mr Tho. Betterton*, goes the impressive title, *the late Eminent Tragedian*. For his death on 28 April 1710 Gildon blamed the prescription. 'Gout, by repellatory Medicines, was driven into his Stomach, which prov'd so fatal as in a few Days to put an End to his Life.'[16] On 2 May he was 'bury'd with great Decency at *Westminster-Abby*'. Cibber blamed his determination that the show must go on, explaining his death with a fancifulness equal to Gildon's but with less chronological accuracy. April 13, 1710 saw Betterton's last known performance, as Melantius in Beaumont and Fletcher's *The Maid's Tragedy* (movingly, a columnist of 1764 speaks of it as 'the first play I remember to have seen', Betterton's performance 'a living picture').[17] He wore a slipper to relieve the pain of gout 'rather than wholly disappoint his Auditors' and showed the 'more than ordinary Spirit' becoming an actor receiving yet another benefit performance; too much so, for 'the unhappy Consequence of tampering with his distemper was, that it flew into his Head, and kill'd him in three Days'; on the eve of his death, Wycherley had told Pope that 'Gout being gotten up into his Head', he would be making 'his Exit from the Stage of this World'.[18] Grieving a fortnight on, Pope proposed an epitaph from Tully in recognition 'as well in his Moral as Theatrical capacity': *vitae bene actae jucundissima est recordatio*. It is a great pleasure to recall a life well acted.[19] 'Gout' signified many kinds of painful swelling. Purges, baths, jellies and plasters were prescribed to cure it and so far as his friends identify Betterton's symptoms, kidney failure is likely to have caused his death.[20]

Unsurprisingly, the *Life* did not appear for sale until late September 1710. Betterton's life having ended, Gildon set to work on his *Life* and on the recollections and documentary fictions that would lend it authenticity. As a playwright he had seen the man at work, talked to him about plots, rehearsals, blocking, gesture, vocal delivery; he could share notes with Steele, the dedicatee, whose *Tatler* essay on the cloisters of Westminster Abbey had been Betterton's first obituary.[21] But he and Steele had been Betterton's juniors by decades. What of his childhood, of his early years as an actor when Charles II had been restored to the throne? Here was a piece of luck, for Gildon had been preceded by the man who had made his living from following Betterton's every word and move. In 1708 John Downes had given the world a prompter's eye view of the Restoration stage and bestowed on his old master the eminently repeatable title of the English Roscius, subsequently to enjoy a less merited attachment to Theophilus Keene and Barton Booth.[22]

It was an ideal source for Gildon partly because it stole little of his thunder. He sharpened Downes's focus and offered the world *the* life of Mr Thomas Betterton. Others had started to write the lives of actors. The anonymous and exhaustively entitled *An Account of the Life, Conversation, Birth, Education, Pranks, Projects, and Exploits, and Merry Conceits, of the Famously Notorious Matt. Coppinger* had appeared in 1695, and Tobyas Thomas's *The Life of the Late Famous Comedian, Jo Hayns* in 1701, while Edward Alleyn had featured in Aubrey's *Brief Lives*.[23] Still, Gildon's work embodied a startling idea. Those squalid creatures, actors,

> A pack of idle, pimping, sponging Slaves,
> A Miscellany of Rogues, Fools and Knaves,

as Robert Gould had called them, could merit the attention of a 'life' on the same terms as any nobleman.[24] The lives of Coppinger and Haynes belong to the rogue or picaresque tradition that inspired Defoe and Fielding; their nascent theatrical celebrity was widely construed as a 'threat to social stability'.[25] But they were far from mainstream theatrical figures, minor 'comedians' not major 'tragedians'. In the cloisters of Westminster Abbey, tragedian Betterton lay in the company of kings, symbolically apt for Steele but an exception to a rule nonetheless. A French visitor captured the paradox well: 'by his Merit [Betterton] made his Profession be forgot and dispens'd with, and … was welcome to Persons of the first Rank, and as agreeable in serious Conversation as on the Stage.'[26]

Wanko argues that Gildon's *Life* is significant not as a lone example of the 'gentleman-actor' biography, but as part of a contrast with the 'rogue' biographies of Coppinger and Haynes, those 'famously notorious' comedians. Such a contrast created the 'ambiguous, contradictory presence' that later becomes 'a defining element of celebrity' in eighteenth-century theatre culture. The celebrity subjects have no say in it, since 'the emergent capitalist order is not yet prepared for figures on the margins of society to control their own presentations'.[27] But Gildon's *Life* projected an 'ambiguous, contradictory presence' of its own, regardless of the rogue tradition; in doing so it refused to collapse Betterton's value to the status of 'celebrity' so far as that is understood as the triumph of the cult of personality over that of character; and it is far from certain, for all Gildon's borrowings, that Betterton played no part in the telling of his story.

An advertisement in *The Post-Man* of 16–19 September 1710 trod cautiously in describing the new book:

This Day is published, *The Life of Mr Tho. Betterton, the late Eminent Tragedian*. Wherein the Action and Utterance of the Stage, Bar and Pulpit are distinctly consider'd (useful for all such as Speak in Publick) with the Judgment of the late Mons. de St Evremond, upon the Italian and French Musick and Operas; in a Letter to the Duke of Buckingham. To which is added, the *Amorous Widow, or the Wanton Wife*, a Comedy written by Mr Betterton with his Effigies prefix'd, curiously engraven from an Original painting of Sir Godfrey Kneller.

Yours for 3s 6d; individual copies of the engraving and the play were also available for 3d and 1s 6d respectively – everything the Betterton souvenir hunter could want.

But the reassurance that the subject is suitable for well-bred readers is tendered too nervously to be taken for granted. Glossing the grandeur of the life on offer, 'Eminent Tragedian' passes over unseemly details in favour of public utility, yet because it would not do to suggest that the demands of the stage, bar and pulpit are equivalent, they are 'distinctly consider'd'.[28] The judgement of a distinguished Frenchman is brought to bear on the elite forms of 'Musick and Operas' which Betterton had been instrumental in cultivating, so that the life of Mr Betterton can be paraded as a fit subject for the emerging category of continental good taste rather than, as Milling asserts, as 'an antidote to French studies of the art of the stage'.[29] Justice could not be done to this complete man of the theatre without also representing him as an author, but it is unfortunate that the title to hand promises nothing but old-fashioned Restoration rumpy-pumpy: the spot of grime the air-brush cannot conceal.

At least, with his muddled sense of duty to a friend, Gildon can assure readers that Betterton never wanted *The Amorous Widow* in print. In 1676 he had won a mock 'bays' for failing to publish his work.[30] The play was only available because 'a surreptitious Copy visited the World after it had been acted almost 20 Years. He would never suffer any of them to be printed'.[31] That edition had appeared in 1706, to a fanfare of modest professions:

> Were we to reveal the Author of this incomparable Comedy, as that we durst not without a Violation of the Promise made to his exemplary Modesty, which often requested the Gentleman, to whom he bequeathed this rich Treasure, never to divulge its Parent, his very Name would challenge a just Veneration from all the most sensible part of Mankind, as well as strike Terror in the severest Criticks.[32]

From Betterton's modesty could be inferred, in the recently discovered language of sentimentalism, a natural moral rectitude that served society's interest.[33] Well past his death, debate about the play continued. The prologue for a performance in 1758 imagines a 'maiden, antiquated Dame' outraged by the play until it is explained to her that it is the impeccably moral work of 'Betterton – a man of highest note; / In private life, the boast of all that age'.[34] Even so, Gildon could hardly avoid the admission that Betterton had something to be modest about. With a Lady Laycock at the centre of its sex-fuelled plot it is no wonder that *The Amorous Widow* is now seen as a trend-setter for comedy in the naughty 1670s.[35]

The problem extended beyond Betterton's writing. As any owner of play texts and their accompanying cast lists would know, he had not only been a tragedian but an actor of comic libertines, the sort who had started to fall out of fashion twenty years before when Glorious Revolution demanded new heroes. So it was a serious misapprehension by the author of 'The Stage' to claim that Betterton was

> by Religion a Tragedian made,
> Play'd virtuous Parts, and liv'd the Parts he play'd.[36]

As Etherege's Dorimant he had risen from bed after casual sex; as Shadwell's Don Juan he had fornicated and blasphemed his way round Seville; as Dryden's Jupiter he had led Amphitryon's wife to bed; as Nemours in Lee's *Princess of Cleve* he had been a *tableau vivant* of rapacious decadence; he had overseen productions of such riotous specimens as Edward Ravenscroft's *The London Cuckolds*; when Congreve ventured to exorcise the ghosts of Carolean *droit du seigneur* with his duplicitous tyrant-in-the-making Fainall, it was Betterton who had played the part, as he had in Southerne's earlier assault on the ethics of high Stuart comedy, *The Wives Excuse*.[37] He did it with conviction, his stocky form capable of sexual charisma; of *The Libertine*, Downes said that 'Mr Betterton Crown'd the Play'.[38] There is no indication that when playing libertines he could, like his younger colleague William Mountfort, 'wash off the guilt from Vice, and [give] it Charms and Merit'.[39] Yet Gildon's determination to associate Betterton with the buskin rather than the sock worked, aided for his readership by the transfer of key roles to younger men in the early 1700s; it was not long before his range was compared unfavourably with Garrick's, and even today he is often pigeon-holed as a tragic actor.[40]

If the literature of celebrity draws attention to 'personality' at the expense of 'character', then Gildon's Betterton was emphatically not a celebrity; not until 1731 did someone use the slightly less tainted term, 'star', to describe a performer, and not until Garrick did the idea attain currency.[41] Partly this is a symptom of theatrical cultures, a modesty fabricated by marketing style. Even at the peak of his fame in his lifetime, Betterton was not advertised as the main feature of a play; if anything, it was authors who would be singled out.[42] It follows that from a recent study called *Theatre and Celebrity*, Betterton is merely antecedent to the topic.[43] The biographical conventions available to Gildon take their share of blame, for early writers of lives routinely avoided the chronology and domestic detail that bestow individuality rather than a sense of moral attributes.[44]

Although Gildon was, in any case, determined to have Betterton understood as an instance of 'character', the *Life* cannot avoid reacting to facts and events it suppresses. The first item that Betterton read out on that half-imagined summer evening in 1709 was not an essay on Shakespeare, correct gesture or vocal modulation, but on the 'Regard an Actor ought to have to Conduct off the Stage'.[45] When, in the aftermath of the controversy caused by the Reverend Jeremy Collier's *Short View*, drama could best be defended on the grounds of its 'Moral Lessons', the character of the people acting them out mattered:[46] 'to hear Virtue, Religion, Honour recommended by a Prostitute, an Atheist, or a Rake, makes them a Jest to many People, who would hear the same done with Awe by Persons of known Reputation in those Particulars.'[47] He did not pause to explore the converse argument, that a man of 'known reputation' seen acting 'an Atheist, or a Rake' might be brought into disrepute. Still less did he reflect on the experience of appearing before the Justices of Middlesex in May 1698, thanks to the zeal of the Collier army, for 'debauchery and blasphemy' in the presentation of Congreve's *The Double Dealer* and Thomas D'Urfey's *Don Quixote*.[48] By November 1701, when a King's Bench indictment was brought against Betterton and eleven of his colleagues for 'using indecent expressions in some late plays', the assault on his respectability was becoming systematic.[49] When all twelve were convicted the following February, it was in danger of being proven.[50] Such infringements supplied an unlikely context for the assertion that all actors, 'Male and Female', should have 'the greatest and most nice Care of their Reputations imagin-able', and it was perhaps with that in mind that a racy prologue intended for Rowe's *The Fair Penitent* in May 1703 and 'Design'd to be spoken by Mr Betterton' was 'refus'd'.[51]

The Collier crisis did not make it inevitable that Gildon would attempt to erase Betterton's past as a comedian and portrayer of lewd blasphem-ers. Other commentators on the theatre such as John Dennis chose to celebrate the 'fine imagination' and 'sound judgement' of the Carolean audience, qualities which were 'requisite for the judging of comedy'.[52] Permitted such a context, the life of Betterton might have emerged as one suffused, in Dennis's words, with the 'human, gay and sprightly philoso-phy' of 'conversation and dramatic poetry', even if the 'sound and show' that Dennis deplored in modern theatre were substantially Betterton's work.[53] Nor should it be concluded that Gildon invented Betterton's respectability as a belated riposte to Collier. The actor's successive appear-ances in the dock gave him the opportunity to rehearse arguments learned from such anti-Collier works as *A Vindication of the Relapse, and the provok'd wife*, Dennis's *Usefulness of the Stage* and *A Review of Mr Collier*, all of which he owned.[54] Legal technicalities provided some respite, but he would have needed a more responsible argument than the one advanced by his colleague George Bright, who as well as trotting out the usual line that 'profane' plays had already been licensed by the Lord Chamberlain, pleaded that management had forced him to speak his lines.[55] In counter-ing Collier's attack on the theatre, Gildon's approach was in all likelihood Betterton's. It was prudent as well as 'modest' not to publish a play like *The Amorous Widow*.

It is hardly due to the connivance of late Augustan culture, either, that the Betterton described by the next generation of theatre histor-ians remained substantially Gildon's. The 1747 *Biographia Britannica* instated the actor for the first time as a national figure in the wake of Cibber and Curll, although he did not figure in the ten-volume *British Biography* published thirty years later; in 1749, *An Account of the Life of that Celebrated Tragedian Mr Thomas Betterton* drew information from Downes and Gildon while turning up fresh evidence about his childhood. Thomas Davies's 1784 *Dramatic Miscellanies* critiqued the growing body of biographical writing about Betterton, while in 1790 Edmund Malone was the first to reprint their documentary sources.[56] John Genest's his-tory of the English theatre since 1660 helped establish the chronology of Betterton's acting career, work consolidated by Joseph Knight's entry in the first *Dictionary of National Biography*.[57] Even then, however, a rescue

job was necessary. In 1862 John Doran had published an article designed
to reinstate Betterton as a vital link in the acting tradition (there is something to be said for the way its use of circumstantial evidence provides
convincing answers to questions that would otherwise be ducked).[58] The
DNB was partly the stimulus for Robert Lowe's 1891 *Thomas Betterton*,
a Victorian biography written during the heyday of the form in a style
some find irritatingly 'chatty', vague and comically reverential: 'I have not,
in the course of extensive wading through the mud-heaps of Restoration
satire, met with one derogatory allusion to him …'[59] Knight had thought
likewise, adding a Macaulayan distaste not for Restoration satire but, of
all things, Restoration theatre.[60] Arthur P. Stanley went on to question
whether it was proper for any actor to be buried in Westminster Abbey;
still, it was at this time that Brownlow Street, Covent Garden, gave way
to what is now Betterton Street.[61] Betterton, Knight's argument goes,
was exceptional not because he was the product of his age but because he
transcended it. Both Knight and Lowe missed some derogatory allusions
near the foot of the mud-heap, but their work embodies the paradox of a
Thomas Betterton obstinately true to the shadowy titan bequeathed by
Gildon: so great as to demand the first theatrical biography, so respectable
as to deserve it.

Cracks began to appear in the monumental edifice when, amid the sceptical *zeitgeist* born of war and Lytton Strachey's *Eminent Victorians*, scholars
turned from acting to management. With the work of Leslie Hotson and
Allardyce Nicoll in the 1920s, informed by scrutiny of legal documents,
came revelations about the cunning and recklessness of Betterton's financial mind.[62] Great Hamlet he may have been, but he advanced loans to his
own company at twenty per cent interest and blew money on unpopular shows. Joined to murmurings about his problems with younger rivals,
the Olympian actor was smudged into the Augean manager. The strain of
reconciling the two was felt in Betterton's entry in the 1973 *Biographical
Dictionary of Actors*, but a riposte came in that high point of professional
theatre studies, Judith Milhous's 1979 study of Betterton the manager. A
systematic and persuasive defence, Milhous's fine book nonetheless fans
the suspicion that its subject was manipulative to a degree unimagined by
Gildon. Now, fresh reasons have arisen to undermine Betterton's monumental presence in Restoration theatre history, not only because 'celebrity'
was a later invention. Study of the first generations of actresses has more
consciously attempted to deflect focus away from his achievement as an
actor and a manager.[63]

Such work is the welcome result of a theatre history informed by cultural theory, but it is a sign of where it might lead that a new series entitled *Lives of Shakespearian Actors* starts abruptly with Garrick.[64] Does it have to be said that whatever else is signified by the history of celebrity, it is not the history of acting?

Not being a celebrity means that even when Betterton has enjoyed his fifteen minutes of fame in modern culture they have really been someone else's. His most prominent screen appearance, in Richard Eyre's *Stage Beauty*, confuses him with Davenant.[65] Young actor becomes grizzled impresario as Tom Wilkinson's Tom Betterton exploits his licence to cast real women. Poor Edward Kynaston, last of the drag actors, looks set to lose his livelihood until he learns that actresses create a new kind of performance, heterosexually charged and emotionally authentic. Much as one would like to credit Betterton, or even Davenant, with introducing method acting to London – or little as one would like to credit either of them for fuelling the history of homophobia – *Stage Beauty* goes an anachronism too far.

Laurence Dunmore's fine film, *The Libertine*, sees Johnny Depp's Rochester coaching 'Lizzie' Barry in another suspiciously 'method' process: bringing her own experience of love to the stage.[66] It was Mrs Betterton who had 'mangled' the speech they rehearse in hock to the rhetorical pomposity of her husband, who here is as obscure as it is possible to be. Freddie Jones, a success as ageing actor managers in Ronald Harwood's *The Dresser* and the Royal Shakespeare Company's revival of *Nicholas Nickleby*, appears in the credits as Betterton but not in the film. This Betterton is a bad guy, author of poor Lizzie's notice to quit before Rochester shows her the true path. Without disrespect to Jones, imagining the performance on the cutting-room floor is not hard. His Crummles and 'Sir' were comic hams capable of stopping a train with one flex of the vocal chords. The film serves Betterton the ultimate insult of reassigning his roles. It is his co-manager, Henry Harris, who lurks in princely black, but at least Betterton is spared the indignity that befalls Harris when he is scheduled to act three times in a day nude, aroused and satisfied in Rochester's *Sodom*.

Betterton is conspicuous enough as the hero of Baroness Orczy's 1919 bodice-ripper, *His Majesty's Well-Beloved* – a Restoration Scarlet Pimpernel, in fact. Orczy's sensibilities had been multiply petrified by flight from a popular uprising in Hungary and her novel bristles with indignation at Bolshevism. Glamorous royalist actor sets out to foil a

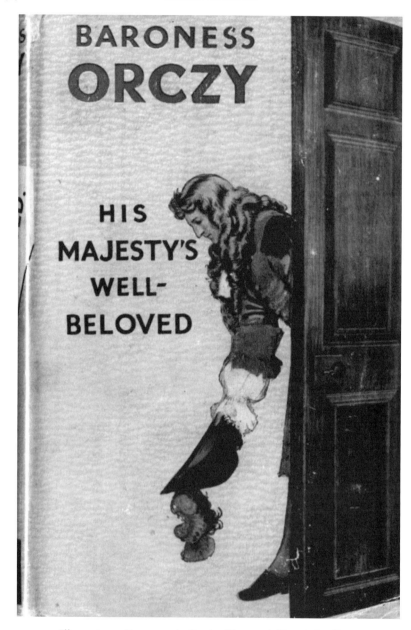

Illustration 2 Betterton the Scarlet Pimpernel. Dust jacket from
Baroness Orczy, *His Majesty's Well-Beloved* (London: Hodder & Stoughton, 1919)

republican plot against the recently restored King and in the usual Orczy manner the narrator keeps us abreast of history: 'Another Regicide! Oh my God! Another era of civil Strife and military Dictatorship such as we had endured in the past decade ... No! It should not be!'[67] The intrepid Betterton, 'his Face striking, his Voice at times masterful and full of Power, at others infinitely sweet', causes the royal mistresses to swoon in their closets: 'the Lady Barbara was trembling so violently that some few moments elapsed before she was able to walk across the room.'[68] For all Orczy's immersion in the historical sources – she appears to have read Lowe's biography – Lady Barbara's trembles are another case of substitution. It was the actor Charles Hart who had an affair with the woman who became Lady Castlemaine.[69] Eyre's and Dunmore's films and Orczy's novel, different as they are, produce the same problem for anyone interested in Betterton: he is sufficiently 'titanic' to demand a presence, but too 'obstinately shadowy' to be recognised for what he was and did. Even a biography is not immune; his professional persona must be reconstructed partly from those of his colleagues, in a search for what he was through what he was not.

The casting of Freddie Jones points to a generic reason for Betterton's absence from the potted English acting tradition. It is the doom of any performance or performer to be one day dismissed as stilted and unnatural. If the technology of film and television has played its part in hastening that process, moulding acting styles to their needs, the technology of painted scenes that helped form Betterton's acting style presupposed, with imperfect accuracy, a grandeur that made him and his heirs an easy point of departure for actors more mobile (Garrick) or febrile (Kean).[70] Betterton suffered in the Romantic reaction against Augustan values, when to be classical even in the richest sense meant something was missing – ostensive emotion, the power to plumb the depths of individual experience. For the Betterton advertised by Gildon, acting started from a very Augustan principle: 'the Government, Order and Balance, as I may say, of the whole Body.'[71] Seeing Betterton act, Francis Manning could not decide 'whether Nature spoke, or Art'.[72] It was a principle observed by successors and imitators such as Barton Booth, whose Mark Antony was noted for its 'dignified action and forcible elocution'.[73]

The reaction had begun in Betterton's lifetime. Even house playwrights might joke about his waning stamina, his longevity collapsed to antiquity of style and physique.[74] In 1698, a rival actor, George Powell, heard as a 'grunt' the 'low and grumbling voice' which Aston said could be 'tuned to an artful climax', and Powell doubted whether 'a Child of sixty-five' could convincingly 'make Love'; Sir Car Scroope had mocked

> florid *Roscius*, when with some smooth Flame,
> He gravely on the Public strives to sham.[75]

The Female Wits, a rehearsal play of 1696, parodies the grand Betterton effects: the 'long strides', the 'voice big' and the 'eyes terrible'.[76] If those were commercial ploys by a rival company, other aspersions sprang more obviously from a disdain for Betterton's commercial origins. An anonymous poem of the 1680s, conferring on him the soubriquet 'Brawny Tom', belittled the 'formal stiffness' and 'awkward grace' that were the outward marks of his drive for gentility.[77] The shop, not the stage, was the right place for him. Such comments informed debate over whether 'the genteel middling sort and urban gentry' could be reconciled 'to the theatre as a site of civility and reformed manners, rather than courtly decadence'.[78] They also speak of the fragility of Betterton's social aspirations; the body even of the age's most skilful actor was easy prey for those who read in it his origins. In that sense too Gildon's *Life* did not merely invent its subject for a civil audience but drew on Betterton's most profound aspirations and sensitivities.

Although he became renowned for reproducing the performances of the presentational stage of the Renaissance – another reason to deny him the personalised aura of 'stardom' – Betterton's career signals the end of the era when actors depended on word, intonation and gesture to convey space and mood. His audience had discovered the delights of total theatre formerly practised only at court, with elaborate musical interludes and visual effects. He became the supreme actor and manager of the baroque, in which acting, music and visual splendour combined to transport the audience to the higher consciousness described by Pepys, who swooned at the sound of an oboe playing in the theatre as he had when first falling in love with his wife.[79] Betterton's alleged descriptions of the research an actor should undertake refer to the visual arts: 'that the very same Passion has various Appearances, is plain from the History Painters, who have followed Nature'; the actor 'ought not to be a Stranger to Painting and Sculpture, imitating their Graces so masterly, as not to fall short of a *Raphael Urbin*, a *Michael Angelo*, &c'.[80] For all Gildon's cutting and pasting, the idea is not fanciful. Betterton owned paintings of historical characters he played, while his collection probably gave him ideas for scene designs; for his final benefit performance there appeared 'Three Designs,

Representing the Three Principal Actions of the Play, in Imitation of so many great Pieces of History Painting'.[81]

With his fellow managers, Betterton sought ever larger spaces in which to practise baroque theatre; when he succeeded, his acting style developed to fill them. Present at the birth of English opera, his way with words would come too readily to be dismissed as operatic, and the very success he enjoyed as a manager of spectacle would for future generations diminish his claims as an actor. Even Gildon recorded the murmurings: 'Others have laid it to the Charge of Mr *Betterton* as the first Innovator [of scenery] on our rude Stage, as a Crime; nay, as the Destruction of good Playing.'[82] He helped trigger the stage's own dissociation of sensibility, the lapse into the visual at the expense of the aural which Walter J. Ong encapsulated in the formula, 'sight isolates, sound incorporates'.[83] As the practice, history and critique of Shakespearean performance turned its back early in the twentieth century on the excesses of Shakespeare according to Irving and Tree, so the man who had helped start the trend seemed less appealing.[84] The first actor to be prized as an aesthetic specimen, the subject of a discriminating choice, Betterton suffered the corollary of such distinction, that of being an acquired taste. It was a sign of the times when, in 1754, his claim that the actor's greatest satisfaction was in having a silent audience was reprinted in the journal, *Connoisseur*.[85]

Measuring the history of Betterton's biography against the known facts of his life suggests that when Gildon fashioned his genteel English Roscius he may have failed to chime with much that constituted a professional repertory career, but succeeded in capturing its motives and trajectory. A quest for the security and dignity of a prosperous metropolitan existence runs through every decade of Betterton's life. If an anecdote of 1717 is to be believed, he was the first to demonstrate the standards of taste Cibber thought requisite for an appreciation of his Hamlet. Betterton is taken to a puppet show, sitting 'some Time with a World of Gravity, and Pleasure, to see the Motions of the little Wooden Performers'. Revelling even in miniature stage technology, he 'admir'd how well the Wires, and artificial Mechanism supply'd the Offices of Life'. But when it came to a presentation of the death of the Duke of Grafton ('his Head shot off in the Siege of Limerick') and the puppet Duchess offering to dance a jig, Betterton's mood changed. He

started in some Disorder, and turning on his Friend with a Look of Accusation for dragging him to such an Entertainment, 'Sdeath! Sir, says He, the Duke's Head shot off, and the Dutchess coming to present us with a Jig? What Indecorum!

What Intolerable Absurdity! In short, all the Persuasions his Friend could urge, were in Vain to engage his Stay; and he immediately with Dissatisfaction quitted the Theatre.[86]

By background, association and professional habit, Betterton bore many hallmarks of the upwardly mobile petit bourgeois craving the decorum of cultural capital, and by the same criteria was also a dyed-in-the-wool royalist. As his squat figure laboured to imitate the graces of a prince, so he strove to master and disseminate the discipline required for successful enterprise.

It was a striking combination of attributes, but one that a recent study of gentility and theatre struggles to accommodate. Mark S. Dawson has argued that the reputation for licentiousness enjoyed by many Restoration actors gave genteel audiences an excuse for dismissing the subversion of their performances, 'reinstating the social distinctions that their genteel performances were about to disrupt'.[87] If that is true, Betterton's eminent respectability could not be so easily placed (Dawson's fine book duly contains only two passing references to him). Social conflict is not the whole story of the stage's representation of gentility any more than it captures the audience's sense of itself; in his chapters on the Restoration audience, Dawson allows sporadic outbreaks of violence to stand for the daily reality, the 'everyday' signification of discourse annihilating what actually happened every day. Betterton gained his eminence through the exercise of bourgeois virtue, becoming accepted as the foremost impersonator of royalty on stage because he produced the task as, conspicuously, a profession, a job. He lent stability to the term 'gentility' by reconciling the values of royal service with the virtues of bourgeois industry. He showed that it could, with a little effort, extend to actors, and the nature of that effort is clear from what we might now dare to envisage as the real life of Thomas Betterton.

CHAPTER 4

An actor of London: early years, 1635–1659

Betterton was a discriminatingly well travelled actor. He visited Dover, Oxford, Warwickshire and Windsor, and France perhaps twice or more. We might expect to find him touring the provinces in time of vacation or plague; instead, what survives is an idyll of him performing later in life in the Hampshire home of Kit-Cat member Richard Norton.[1] When it came, semi-retirement meant the country house in Reading. But it was his home town that dominated his life, with good reason. Restoration theatrical seasons usually ran from late August to early May, with an average of 210 acting days and perhaps thirty different plays, in the vast majority of which he appeared.[2] Outside six performances a week and constant rehearsals, the actorly disciplines described by Gildon probably filled up the time: studying, memorising, practising in front of a mirror. In time, he would even live over the theatre. For most of his long career, then, Thomas Betterton inhabited an area not only less than the two square miles of Restoration London, but in the two neighbourhoods of Lincoln's Inn Fields and Dorset Street.

He was born in the summer of 1635 and baptised on 11 or 12 August in St Margaret's Church, at the eastern end of the street where he would spend his childhood. Going west from Westminster Abbey, Tothill Street was the main thoroughfare separating St James's Park from Tothill Fields. Two years earlier, Ralph Agas's woodcut map of London had judged it too marginal to be fully represented, for it was semi-rural.[3] Cattle grazed in Tothill Fields; vegetables and herbs were grown. It was a miniature leisure quarter, with horse-racing, archery, the occasional parade, bull or bear baiting and a maze, drawn by Wenceslas Hollar with some strolling, preening ladies in the foreground.[4] The highlight of the year was 13 October: St Edward's Fair, named for Edward the Confessor, founder of Westminster Abbey. Like Bartholomew Fair, its value to local businessmen meant that it survived the Puritan restrictions of Betterton's later boyhood. More conventional violence did intrude – duels, muggings and justice. A year after

Illustration 3 Tothill Street, where Betterton grew up, is shown on this map
running west from Westminster Abbey. From Richard Newcourt, *An
Exact Delineation of the Cities of London and Westminster* (1658)

Betterton's death the fields witnessed one of the last known resolutions by
pistol of an affair of honour; highwaymen lingered there; since 1618 there
had been a prison. Come the horrors of 1665, specially built houses accom-
modated the parish's plague victims, Tothill Fields their corpses.[5]

The area would develop fast. To compare Agas's 1633 map with John
Oliver's of 1676 is to see Tothill Street succumbing to that very Restoration
phenomenon, the spreading West End.[6] Between them stands Richard
Newcourt's map of 1658, its attractively sharp view showing every house
to best advantage, if not more.[7] But it suggests mixed social credentials.
The north side signals past aristocratic possession through spacious formal gardens bordering St James's Park; bishops, lords and knights had
lived here. At least one still did, by an appealing coincidence: Sir Henry

Herbert, Master of the Revels, licenser of plays and impresario for court theatre. The south side, formerly as grand, is skirted by new buildings and an industrial yard.

Like much else in Betterton's life, Tothill Street saw nobility and high fashion bumping up against the disciplines of trade. Betterton grew up in a house owned by and possibly shared with his maternal grandparents, Alice and Thomas Flowerdew. A monument on the south wall of St Margaret's describes Thomas Flowerdew as a vintner, its prominence an index of success. Tothill Street was a natural place to be. On the north side, the Swan with Two Necks Yard had been named after the insignia of the Vintners' Company, while a plan made in 1612 by Ralph Treswell indicates a 'Brewehouse' next to a large plot of land owned by 'the Lady Graye'.[8] Flowerdew's monument also declares him 'free' of the haberdashers' company, and such flexibility would prove a stubborn feature of his extended family.

To this respectable trade background, Betterton's father Matthew brings something more glamorous but less dependable, an air of failure in a former life. He worked in King Charles I's household as an 'under-cook', yet described himself in his will as a 'gentleman', although no coat of arms exists for a Betterton until the nineteenth century.[9] Tothill Street was a few minutes' walk from Whitehall Palace, and Matthew could spend them consoling himself for whatever mischance had led him there – a bereavement, perhaps. Thomas Betterton's mother was Matthew's second wife, and she was the vintner's daughter. Her name, fragrantly, was Frances Flowerdew, and she had married Matthew in October 1630, a good match for the gentleman under-cook.

Newcourt suggests that on both sides of the street were substantial three-storey dwellings, big enough for Betterton and his five siblings. There was an older boy who may have been a stepbrother, sisters Mary and Frances, and two younger brothers: William, born in 1644, who against the odds for such a family would also be an actor, and Charles, born in 1647, who took the safer course of following his father into royal cooking, for the restored court. Charles and Thomas would celebrate the Restoration by serving their king through the stomach and the senses but it would hardly be surprising if it was Charles's choice of career that met with greater encouragement. When Matthew made his will in June 1663, Frances and Mary got the money and half the moveables. Charles would give his mother his earnings in return for maintenance while Thomas was to receive nothing but the symbol of his father's precarious claim to gentility: a seal ring that had belonged to Matthew's grandfather.[10]

The solid foundations of the Flowerdew household were shaken early in Betterton's life. Thomas Flowerdew died when Betterton was only two, on 15 September 1637. The Tothill Street house was bequeathed to Matthew.[11] In a further setback to the family business, Flowerdew's eldest son William followed at the age of twenty-four, on 28 May 1641. It was Alice, the 'loving and sorrowful' widow and mother, who paid for their monument, which speaks of a devout family bringing up their four children as good Christians and taking comfort from their devotions. William had 'departed this life in the true faith of Christ' after his father had 'rested from his labours', which adds to the feeling of incongruity in the family: the down-at-heel gentleman Matthew amid the god-fearing vintners, two of their grandchildren seduced from trade by the intoxication of the stage. In the circumstances, however, the Bettertons probably supplied the material comfort of lending hands to the business. At the end of the next century, a Betterton would still be in the London wine trade.[12]

By Thomas Betterton's seventh birthday in 1642, Matthew could feel grateful in turn. Servants of the royal household were used to the changes entailed by the tours of the realm, which contributed to the high level of debt incurred by the household. In 1641 Charles I was in Scotland for the entire autumn, attempting to suppress the rebellion ignited by his introduction of the Laudian prayer-book, and did not return until 25 November.[13] The civic banquet that followed may have been Matthew's last big occasion in the household, for on 10 January 1642 the King escaped from London in secret for Hampton Court and did not return. What was left of the royal household at Hampton broke up as the queen and princess departed for Holland. From Christmas 1641, therefore, the Betterton family was looking about for material comfort. Personal safety could well have seemed precarious too. Convenient for Matthew's employment, Tothill Street also abutted the scenes of unrest that ushered in war. On Christmas Day 1641 Westminster Abbey, convenient symbol of Laudian policy, was attacked by a mob. Once Charles I's escape to Hampton Court was discovered, parliamentary troops marched down the Strand and around Westminster, now a neighbourhood under occupation.

Some 100 years later, it was claimed that Betterton fought for the king during the first conflict of the Civil War, the Battle of Edgehill, when he was just turned seven.[14] It is the easiest to ignore of the fog patches in early biographies. Dismissing it, however, should not obscure the link between Betterton and Stuart family fortunes, which assumes particular importance in the next stage of Thomas Betterton's life, his apprenticeship. Boys of his station in life could expect to enter into articles when they were about twelve, and in Thomas's case that meant a year or so after the Civil War had been won and lost, and just over another before the trial and execution of Charles I. In such times, what did a family like the Bettertons do?

The death of the Flowerdew men ruled out an apprenticeship close to home; the presence of Betterton's shadowy elder brother or stepbrother in any case diminished that opportunity. There may have been other financial pressures: after years of protection under Charles, the Vintners' Company was being squeezed for money by Parliament.[15] It was a familiar position for a second son, and the family had to look further afield. Beyond their means was the nearest school, Westminster, where John Dryden and Robert Hooke were studying, although at least one other actor known to Betterton would go there.[16] The wide reading in English and French that struck Gildon were the result of Betterton's own efforts.[17] Not surprisingly, an attraction to the theatrical trappings of academic life persisted; his collection of prints included the 'Habits of the University of *Oxford*, in 12 Sheets'.[18]

If Matthew and Frances Betterton had any regard for their son's future security, it is safe to assume that the theatre did not enter into their reckoning – fanciful for a respectable family at the best of times. A very young Thomas Betterton might have seen theatre in pre-war London, either at a public playhouse or from behind his father's apron in a corner of the Court of St James; he might have heard of the performances given down the road by the boys of Westminster to get them 'accustomed to proper action and pronunciation'.[19] The possibility that he saw plays as a teenager in republican London is less remote than it once seemed. But performances were both unpredictable and prone to interruption by zealous troops. Actors risked public flogging while audiences might lose their admission money, a five shilling fine, or personal possessions. They might even be pressganged.[20] A simpler course for the soldiers was to pull down the theatre buildings, as happened to the Globe in 1644 and the Fortune in 1649. Even if there was plenty to see when Betterton was approaching the age for apprenticeship, as a career the theatre promised as much in rewards and risks as a life of petty crime.

A more sober option emerged. In Gildon's words, Betterton's father 'bound him Apprentice to ... a Bookseller'.[21] Apprenticeships were not undertaken lightly; they could mean an almost complete break with the family for seven years, and the Statute of Artificers gives some idea of their rigidity and even cruelty. Behind the decision, says one source, lay an atmosphere of good will: 'he had a very good Education, and when he was come to Years sufficient, by his own Choice' was apprenticed to a book-seller.[22] Here, the family acquiesces in Betterton's determination to follow a path that lies well within his capabilities – a quiet life for the studious boy, if that is what he wants. But the author of *An Account of the Life of That Celebrated Tragedian Mr Thomas Betterton* (1747) thought the family had swallowed their disappointment: he 'received the Rudiments of polite Learning in several Schools; and shewing a great Propensity to Reading, it was proposed he should have been brought up to some learned Profession, but was, at his own Request, bound apprentice to ... a Bookseller'.[23] That sounds odd. The church, the law, even medicine gave opportunities not just for more advanced study but for the very thing that would bring Betterton success – oratory, the shaping of words in the air referenced to the motions of the face and the hand, sentences made living in the ears of an audience. He started, in this account, from what he knew and stayed there: cautious, wary, shy of his abilities or of special favour.

The 1747 *Biographia Britannica* sheds a different light. Thomas had been intended for a learned profession, but 'the violence and confusion of the times [put] this out of the power of his family'.[24] Lone though this evidence is, it does have a named source in the playwright Thomas Southerne, who had worked closely with Betterton in the 1690s.[25] It also chimes with the known misfortunes of the royal household and the Vintners' Company. Nothing in it gainsays the sequence of events in the other narratives. Thomas's abilities suited him for something more literary than the Flowerdew business or another comparable trade and an oppor-tunity had to be found in difficult times. Bookselling, fortunately, was one he was happy to pursue.

To be a bookseller in the seventeenth century meant combining publish-ing and general retail of books and other stationery.[26] In Betterton's case, both the candidates for his first master were publishers who subcontracted their printing and kept a shop, so he was spared the routine of the printer's apprentice, which ran to six seventeen-hour days a week in cramped prem-ises. Instead, there were long hours helping in the shop, running errands to the printer and maintaining stock. Eventually, he would be taught how to proof-read, keep accounts, deal with other publishers in a syndicate and negotiate with authors. There is a relationship between some of these tasks and the trustworthy professional actor and manager Betterton would become; the handwriting of the Longleat letter embodies the accuracy, clarity and deliberation of someone used to keeping records. But it is the 'great Propensity to Reading' noted by the early biographer which catches the eye. His Hamlet, Cibber would note, was itself to be considered as a species of critical reading, not just empty display, and throughout the 1660s in particular, when he and his master Davenant needed to develop a core repertory for the Duke's Company, pre-war plays would need to be located and assessed. A systematic knowledge of book stock would be useful.

Who would be Betterton's master? Bookselling in the 1640s and 1650s was a highly political business and many booksellers had distinct profiles and market shares, but the identity of this one is the most persistent puzzle of Betterton's early biography. The primary sources disagree while the standard reference works report the confusion without attempting to resolve it. Scholars have juggled two names – John Rhodes and John Holden – and opinion veers periodically in each direction. That is probably a mistake when the truth, although it requires serpentine proof, may be very simple: he worked for both.

Stationers' Company records contain a single piece of information which proves only that ever since people have started wondering about Betterton's apprenticeship, the identity of his master has been in doubt. The court books show the following entry dated 5 March 1704/5: 'Q. If Mr Batterton the Player bee Free of the Company. he was Apprentice to Mathew Rhodes.'[27] Most likely the second sentence is supplementary information offered by the person asking the question, but it could also be the answer he received. Either way, whether Betterton ever completed an apprenticeship is at issue. The only known bookseller called Matthew Rhodes gained his freedom in November 1619 and last published a book in 1642, when Betterton was only seven.[28] Matthew Rhodes was, however, the elder brother of John Rhodes, and records from 1653 indicate a friendly, semilegal trade between them in copyright. Lodowick Carlell's *The Deserving Favourite* was 'assigned' to the publisher Humphrey Moseley by Matthew Rhodes, its original owner; the play had also been 'for the use & benefit of … John Rhodes'.[29] Perhaps the friendly relations extended to apprentices. No other indication exists that anyone called Betterton was legally bound during the actor's lifetime.

The unusual form of the entry – a question about Betterton's official standing that was never followed up – does not mean that no conclusions can be drawn from it. In the five years afterwards, Gildon and Downes would go to print on the subject of Betterton's career, and perhaps one of them sought clarification of this detail but didn't get it. In the absence of any other records, that commonly indicates procedural irregularity.

Betterton described himself to Downes and Gildon as an apprentice but officially was only, in the common parlance, a 'boy' – a venial fib that lent respectability to a difficult period in his life.

Downes and Gildon describe him as working for John Rhodes at the sign of the Bible at Charing Cross, near enough to the Betterton family home. The advantage for his biography was Rhodes's theatre connections; a John Rhodes is listed among the 'Hired Men and Assistants' of the King's Company in December 1624.[30] In that year he had become free of the Drapers' Company after a thirteen-year apprenticeship.[31] Perhaps the court connection brought him to the notice of Betterton's father; he was probably among those who dodged the troops in the theatre of the 1640s and 1650s. In 1659 he would respond to the relaxation of prohibitions against public entertainment by setting up a theatre company at the Cockpit Theatre in Drury Lane, and in his company appeared a twenty-four-year old Thomas Betterton, transformed in the wink of missing evidence from bookseller's boy to leading actor. The draper had four other apprentices, Edward Kynaston, Edward Angel, Christopher Williams and John Nash, who would end up as actors.[32] Why not his 'boy' as well?

Rhodes was used to moving fast and understood the value of connections. By late March 1660, he had obtained a formal licence to perform from General George Monck, temporary protector of the nation, who used Drapers' Hall as his headquarters after entering the city in February. Once Rhodes obtained his licence, the Drapers' Company spent more than £400 on an entertainment for their new patron.[33] In the line-up were Rhodes's thirteen actors, including Betterton and his brother. Two of Rhodes's actors had also been King's Men, and the motley combination of the former printer's boy, his brother and some old friends from before the war suggests a company thrown together to seize an opportunity, for all Rhodes's care in bringing on young drapers and turning them into actors.

But until Rhodes got his licence from Monck, performing at the Cockpit and Red Bull blended danger and antiquarianism – an organised attempt to revive a threatened culture whose legal status remained unresolved until the autumn of 1660. As late as 4 February 1660, when it was already clear that the King would be restored, Rhodes and two actors including Betterton's first Claudius, Thomas Lillieston, were arrested for their pains.[34] Some spirit of adventure must have possessed Betterton in giving up his chosen profession for one so uncertain. Rhodes's arrest also speaks of a faith shared with thousands of other Londoners that with the King's Restoration would come the theatre's. If Betterton's upbringing had taught him the virtues of honest industry, he had also learned the over-arching necessity of loyalty to the crown. Any nervousness in the Betterton household that arose from Thomas abandoning bookselling for acting, and taking his younger brother with him, might be calmed by the prospect of their working, like his culinary brother Charles, in the royal service.

Unfortunately, Rhodes's prominence in the theatre gives only so much help in assessing his role in Betterton's life because so little is known of his activities as a bookseller. The British Book Trade Index lists a John Rhodes, but only as active from 1631 to 1632; moreover, a search of *Early English Books Online* reveals not a single occurrence of Rhodes's name among title pages from 1632 until the end of the century.[35] If Rhodes was operating as a bookseller in the late 1640s and 1650s, it was as a second-hand dealer and outlet for other publishers. Probably he operated as he did running a theatre company – taking his opportunities, relying on friends and influence over young minds, risking the odd skirmish with the law, hiring and firing as the need arose. On the face of it he was not the kind of man to whom the Flowerdews and Bettertons would readily entrust their son.

John Holden looked a steadier option in the late 1640s. Later accounts, including the *Biographia Britannica* and *An Account of the Life of That Celebrated Tragedian Mr Thomas Betterton*, propose him as an alternative to the shadowy, unproductive Rhodes. Their chief source is an unlikely one, Jonathan Richardson's *Explanatory Notes and Remarks on Milton's Paradise Lost* (1734). According to Richardson, Betterton had told Alexander Pope that he 'was 'Prentice to a Bookseller, *John Holden*' at the Blue Anchor, out towards the Tower.[36] Holden started publishing when Betterton was fourteen – a plausible age to start an apprenticeship – in 1649, the year of the regicide. The thirteen publications bearing his name suggest a man of royalist leanings concerned to offer comfort to fellow travellers. Recently there had been a substantial increase in the number of booksellers and printers working in London; civil war had made it a boom industry.[37]

Holden's thirteen titles, most of them printed by Thomas Newcomb, indicate a distinctive ideological environment. The second issue of *Lachrymae Musarum* went on sale at the Blue Anchor in 1650. Poets including Herrick, Cotton, Denham and Marvell mourned the King obliquely through elegies on Henry, Lord Hastings, son of the Earl of Huntingdon.[38] In Marvell's coded words,

> All he had tried, but all in vain, he saw,
> And wept, as we, without redress or law.[39]

Abraham Cowley's *The Guardian* also appeared in 1650 in a commemorative issue harking back to happier times: the comedy, says the title page, had been 'acted before Prince Charls, His Highness at Trinity-College Cambridge, upon the twelfth of March 1641'. Christopher Elderfield's *The Civil Right of Tythes* (1650) mounted a rational defence of the Church of England, while Joseph Hall's *The Balm of Gilead* (1650) offered 'Comforts for the distressed, both morall and divine' for 'these woful times'; Quarles's *Gods Love and Mans Unworthiness* (1651) had a similar purpose. A first English translation of Sandoval's *The Civil Wars of Spain* (1652) reflected on recent events from a covertly royalist perspective, while *Sir Walter Rawleigh's Ghost* (1651) was more pointed in its attack on the 'atheists and politians of these days'. Such texts might shape interpretative habits as well as political orientation. Reading the royalist literature of the period is an exercise in what Betterton became famous for: separating layers of meaning, discerning the permanent, underlying code when the uninitiated see only the noisy surface; locating the scarcely visible stream of affiliation to the natural and the good. Royalist writing was, in Lois Potter's formulation, the exercise of secret rites.[40] When Betterton began to collect books himself, the fortunes of the House of Stuart were a constant preoccupation.[41] The social colour of the bookseller's life also clung: forty years on, an adversary would describe him as a '*Hawker*' who 'sold *old Books, Gazets and Votes*', a glorified newsagent steeped in the political corruption for which his connections qualified him.[42]

Holden had no theatrical pedigree to recommend him as a way of easing Betterton's graduation from bookselling to acting, but he did have something equally persuasive: a business association with Sir William Davenant, Betterton's manager after the Restoration. The best-known of all Holden's titles was Davenant's epic royalist poem *Gondibert*, which appeared in 1651. Jonathan Richardson claimed to know not only that Betterton had never completed his apprenticeship, but the precise reason why: 'persuading his Master [Holden] to Part with him, [Davenant] brought him first on the Stage.'[43] The date in question is usually taken to mean 1656, the usual term of seven years on from the date he probably started. That year Davenant introduced to English cultural life the medium of dramatic opera, with its mixture of heady rhetoric, musical set-pieces and awe-inspiring painted scenery: '[Betterton] began to act in 1656, or 1657, at the *Opera-House* in *Charter-House Yard*, under the Direction of *Sir William D'Avenant*, and continued there till the Restoration,' says the *Biographia Britannica*.[44]

To bring it off Davenant needed all the expertise and prestige he had gained in the pre-war theatre. He had begun writing plays in the late

1620s; as Ben Jonson's successor to the yet unofficial post of Poet Laureate in 1638, he tied his fortunes to those of the royal family, and was knighted for his valour at the siege of Gloucester in 1643. His association both with the court and the King's Men had been much more glorious than John Rhodes's, whom he almost certainly knew, and he would have been a persuasive presence not just in arguing for toleration of his entertainment, but in assembling an unprecedentedly diverse group of acting, musical and designing talents to mount it at a time when the traditions which should support them were under severe threat. Milhous is attracted by the idea of Davenant visiting his publisher and overhearing the rich tones of the young man in the stock room, but justly suspicious of Richardson's suggestion that Betterton was instantly whisked away to perform in dramatic opera: 'If Betterton's [apprenticeship] ended at twenty-one, he should have been released in 1656. While he was old enough to participate in Davenant's earliest unlicensed performances, they were too intermittent to support him.'[45]

Indeed: the young Betterton would need to have been smitten blind to accept any such offer, his famed sobriety masking a desperate recklessness. Whatever the novelty of a few private performances of a new and elite theatrical genre, the stage itself scarcely had a bright future, and the list of principals for Davenant's show does not include Betterton. But there is a more straightforward reason to be sceptical. The thirteen title pages bearing Holden's name were all published between 1649 and 1652, and in the latter year only two new titles appeared. Holden's health was probably fading, for in May 1652 he died. Add this fact to the mix of contrary claims, and the idea that Davenant paid off Holden in order to take Betterton under his wing starts to look ridiculous. It clearly could not have happened in 1656, when Holden had been dead for four years, while Davenant's activities make an earlier date just as unlikely. In May 1650 he sailed from Jersey to take up – it is assumed on Queen Henrietta Maria's orders – an appointment in Virginia or Maryland, but he was intercepted and imprisoned first at Cowes and then in the Tower, only to be released on bail in October 1652, at least four months after Holden's death.[46] Some time in 1653 Davenant was arrested again, this time for debt, and he was not released until 4 August 1654. This is not, however, grounds for excluding Holden altogether from the story.

R.W. Lowe proposes, albeit in a brief parenthesis, that Betterton may have been apprenticed to both Holden and Rhodes; *Biographia Britannica* entertains the idea but gives up on it.[47] The circumstantial evidence is strong, however. The year 1652 is an almost impossibly early date for the end of Betterton's 'apprenticeship' if it went its full course. Davenant's circumstances rule him out of any intervention at that time, so a move to Rhodes in 1652 is plausible. In all likelihood there was no apprenticeship at all, just a move from being Holden's 'boy' to Rhodes's. The lack of information about Rhodes suggests he was not a very prominent or desirable alternative except geographically, for Charing Cross was substantially closer to the Betterton family home in Tothill Fields, Westminster, than the New Exchange. The old court connection made him at least a friendly alternative.

The following chronology, therefore, accounts for most of the inconsistencies as well as the key events of the early biographies. Betterton worked first for Holden in the late 1640s until his master died in 1652. He then transferred to Rhodes, for whom he worked first as a bookseller and finally, from 1659, as an actor. Davenant spotted his talented leading man in the auspicious setting not of a bookshop near the Tower of London in the 1650s, but of the Drury Lane Cockpit Theatre in the spring of 1660. In the autumn of that year Davenant secured Betterton's services not from Holden, as Richardson reports, but from Rhodes, who continued to operate a fringe theatre company for the next few years. In this account, Betterton's early years look yet more fraught, and more improbably exciting: employed out of the family trade, in desperately uncertain times for anyone with connections to the royal household, his first master dies perhaps halfway through his term, and an alternative has to be found. But that alternative, by sheer chance, plugs the young apprentice into the new connections which will make him one of the most famous men in London. In the circumstances he would need the qualities a later commentator attributed to him: 'naturally of a cheerful disposition ... [with] a very high confidence in providence.'[48]

In the company (in either sense) of John Rhodes, he could keep stock of something even more alluring than books, plays and their promise, one day, of performance. The cultural memory of print ran seamlessly into anecdotes of actors, narrations of scenes – the materials on which theatre tradition is built. To dismiss entirely as legend the notion that the Hamlet Thomas Betterton gave in August 1661 reproduced Shakespeare's intentions via Joseph Taylor and William Davenant is to risk forgetting that before he so much as met Davenant, he had access through Rhodes to the oral history of the King's Men. Studious and youthful Thomas Betterton, child of two decades without theatre, did not need to see a play to fall in love with the theatre when he could listen to an old wardrobe keeper talking about it.

A final piece of evidence slots neatly into this narrative. Gildon and Downes mention Edward Kynaston, born in 1640, as Betterton's 'under-apprentice', and Kynaston was formally apprenticed to Rhodes as a draper in 1654. By then, a Betterton aged nineteen and with previous experience could be trusted with the boy. Perhaps the Betterton and Kynaston families enjoyed an old friendship that led to their children being twinned in this way; the names 'Thomas Betterton' and 'Bryan Kynnaston' appear in the London subsidy rolls of 1 October 1599 among five residents 'Adhuc St Magnus Parishe', on the north bank of the Thames next to London Bridge.[49]

When the opportunity to perform plays arose in 1659, Rhodes had in Betterton and Kynaston two contrasting, willing and pliable young actors for his company, and the two he needed most: one to play male leads, the other female. Often they would play lovers. The professional relationship between the two actors would go through many different phases. In 1660, Davenant recruited Betterton but not Kynaston, who joined Killigrew's company, and there he continued to play women. He was ideally cast in Jonson's *Epicoene* as a boy masquerading as a woman for reasons which Pepys, on 7 January 1661, well appreciated. Kynaston's protean sexual attraction – the prettiest woman in Pepys's view only when dressed as a fine gallant – made him a collector's item both in the theatre and in society. Downes even doubted 'whether any woman that succeeded him so sensibly touched the audience as he'; some years later, Cibber asserted that he had been 'so beautiful a youth that the Ladies of Quality prided themselves in taking him with them in their coaches to Hyde Park in the theatrical Habit after the play'.[50]

His relationship with society men was correspondingly troubled but largely stemmed from his resemblance to Sir Charles Sedley, who knew what it was to live on the edge.[51] Kynaston took to dressing like him. For once in an actor's life, accurate impersonation proved disastrous and the indignant baronet had him beaten up by someone fooled into thinking his victim was Sedley himself. Kynaston was too proud to submit, and brought his imitation of Sedley to the stage – a mistake, since Sedley was a frequent and noisy member of the theatre audience who continued to have no difficulty in hiring thugs when he needed to. On 1 February 1669, the Pepyses expected to see a play at the King's Theatre but found the performance cancelled because, again, Kynaston was nursing his wounds.

The more cautious among Kynaston's colleagues and rivals probably agreed that he should bear some of the blame. A day's lost takings meant pain for everyone. More broadly, the success of the theatre depended to a significant degree on its ability to maintain harmonious relationships with the court and the higher reaches of society. Kynaston's example reveals something about Betterton's: where his former 'under-apprentice' demonstrated recklessness and vanity in his dealings with high society, Betterton remained a model of discretion who scrupulously avoided offending anyone.

There is a twin coda to the narrative of Betterton's early life. When the new King's and Duke's companies were in their infancy, he lost one former 'under-apprentice', Kynaston, to the rival house, and another to a fatal accident. William Betterton, seventeen years old, perished while swimming in the Thames at Wallingford in 1661. His death came at the start of the summer when Thomas began to reach far back in English cultural life to learn Hamlet, and it is no strain to imagine that a more personal retrospection also preoccupied him. William's death loosened one of the links which bound his brother's new profession to the very different world of his origins, and accentuated the solemn ambiguity that came of performing *Hamlet* to a Restoration audience.

   The young actor had other complications to manage in the aftermath of the Restoration. Two poems by John Crouch were published under his imprimatur. The titles are revealing: *A Mixt Poem ... upon the Happy Return of His Sacred Majesty Charles the Second* and *The Muses Joy for the Recovery of that Weeping Vine, Henrietta Maria*, of 1660 and 1661 respectively. Even in the first flush of his success as an actor, had the vicissitudes of his youth told Betterton that he needed something to fall back on? If so, what better than the trade he had learned with Holden and Rhodes? There is no certainty that the publications were Betterton's work, but it seems futile to object to the idea on the grounds that he was reluctant to publish his own work.[52] He operated close to his family home – the title page of Crouch's *Mixt Poem* gives the location of Betterton's shop as 'Westminster Hall'. Perhaps these one-off exercises were done for a friend in the hope of securing royal notice, and the contrast with Kynaston is plain. Of Rhodes's two apprentices, Kynaston embraced the theatre and high-society life for all he was worth, while Betterton went on steadily accumulating, insuring himself against future changes of fortune. It had, after all, been the way of Thomas Flowerdew, the haberdasher-turned-vintner, of Matthew Betterton, the gentleman under-cook, and John Rhodes the draper, bookseller, costumier and theatrical impresario: a mentality hardened by adversity and the experience of rapid social change.

If reconstructing much of Betterton's early life is, finally, a calculated matching of sparse facts and contradictory claims to rich contexts, it seems clear that he belonged to what might be termed the royalist cultural underground of London. His business and education were with people who worked for the royal household, published royalist literature, who embodied the old days when theatre companies were patronised by royalty instead of being hounded by parliament; people who took every opportunity to beat the ban on public performances or get those in authority on their side. A sense of being on the political ropes was enforced by his physical surroundings. Poised between Tothill Fields and St James's Park, the family home in Tothill Street looked out over two urban Edens that bore all the marks of civil war. In the autumn of 1651, 14,000 parliamentary troops mustered there; Scots royalist prisoners taken at the Battle of Worcester were held and in as many as 1200 cases buried in Tothill Fields, while others were 'driven like a herd of swine through Westminster to Tuthill Fields and there sold to several merchants, and sent to the island of Barbadoes'.[53] To the north, St James's Park had a complex political history of its own which would silently inform many of Betterton's apparently most carefree roles. A child of war, Betterton learned to transform his experiences not only in Shakespearean roles such as Hamlet, but in the self-regarding form we know today as Restoration Comedy. To appreciate how, it is time to digress by taking a walk in the park.

CHAPTER 5

A walk in the park: Betterton and the scene of comedy

Betterton is often thought of as a tragic or heroic actor, yet roughly a third of his known roles and nearly half his new ones were in comedy.[1] It was an inclusive genre. He played schemers such as Maskwell in Congreve's *The Double Dealer* and Goodvile in Otway's *Friendship in Fashion*, boorish drunks like Sir John Brute in Vanbrugh's *The Provok'd Wife*, and characters who could be both: Toby Belch and Falstaff.[2] Towards the end of his career came creaking patriarchs such as Morose in *The Silent Woman* or Heartwell in Congreve's *The Old Bachelour*, and when the chance came he even switched from Troilus to Thersites, but generally he avoided farce.[3] As a rule, says Milhous, 'he did not appear in Mrs Behn's lighter plays, or in Ravenscroft's frothy concoctions', and the most enduring farce his company performed was written with another actor in mind.[4] The rapid physicality and humiliation of farce were not for Betterton, nor its mockery of 'the intellectualism and verbal wit of higher forms of comedy', his preferred comic territory.[5] Observing 'nature' was still paramount; in his Heartwell was 'the Reluctance of a Batter'd Debauchee to come into the Trammels of Order and Decency: He neither languishes nor burns, but frets for Love'.[6] As with Hamlet, Betterton found a tension between contradictory states that defined his character's progression. His Heartwell was the more powerful for exploiting his stolid private self, showing him alienated from yet striving towards his immense reputation for 'Order and Decency'.

As much as inward 'nature', central to much of Betterton's comedy was the outward impersonation of gentility, to be found in what Nicoll calls 'the character of the contemporary gallant, easy, graceful and debonair'.[7] But in an age when grace was proved from the floor upwards, gracefulness did not come easily to a physique like Betterton's. He had large feet and struggled to dance, although Gildon has him recommend it as a way for any actor to improve an already 'active, pliant and compacted Body', in addition to fencing and vaulting.[8] Thanks to his astonishingly mobile ghost scene in *Hamlet*, it is Garrick who is thought to have been the first to act with his feet, and it is no surprise that when Cibber looked for actors who had succeeded in all types of roles, tragic and comic, Betterton's was not the first name that came to mind. William Mountfort had 'acted low humour' as a younger man, 'and when he was in great Esteem, as a Tragedian, he was, in Comedy, the most complete Gentleman that I ever saw upon the Stage'.[9] To do Betterton justice, Cibber added that he had been 'as eminent' as Falstaff as he had been as Othello. Although Charles Gildon asserted that Betterton 'excelled in both *Comedy* and *Tragedy*' the actor himself was in Gildon's words typically modest: 'tho I have attempted two or three Comical Parts ... yet Tragedy is, and has always been, my Delight.'[10] The numbers do not add up, and Gildon's Betterton has forgotten the inconvenient truth for neo-classicists that comedies sold better than tragedies, but the resemblance to Cibber's evaluation cannot be dismissed.[11]

Learning to become a complete stage gentleman was for Betterton a matter of study, diplomacy and personal history. His own remote claims to gentility crystallised in the seal ring bequeathed by his father. Edward Kynaston was the bruised epitome of how not to go about mimicking good deportment; Richard Braithwait's *English Gentleman and English Gentlewoman* of 1641, part of Betterton's library, may also have entered the equation.[12] At one with his classical instincts, his natural caution would have led him to ponder the essence of gentility rather than its individual manifestations. Where in tragedy he was guided by the 'passions' of a part, in comedy his studious attention would turn to the domain the Restoration made routinely comic: manners.

The term 'comedy of manners' has long fallen into disrepute. Jonsonian, Fletcherian, French and other distinct styles told Nicoll that 'Restoration comedy is by no means a thing wholly of the manners style'.[13] That style, however, is no aggregate of plot types, language or psychology. It comes of locating the comic in the upper reaches of its audience's social world, then returning it reshaped, not just through acting but scenery. If the new scenic technology risked rendering the first generation of actresses as objects of desire, it gave to the 'manners style' an infectious authenticity. Playwrights made repeated use of stock scenes depicting fashionable locales: the New Exchange, the Mulberry Garden, Westminster Hall, Covent Garden and the Royal Parks.[14] To the comedy of manners they were as integral as individual performances of gentility, uncannily convincing like the actors who paraded in front of them, a thrilling if potentially unnerving simulacrum. Nicoll thought park scenes were popular because they were 'taken from those very places where the audience loved to stroll and preen themselves',[15] but more fundamentally they served narrative ends, providing the occasion for misunderstandings, surprises and counterplots, as well as for exhibitionism. Schemes dreamed up in the security of a private lodging could be unravelled in the open spaces of the exchange or the park.

A good instance is one of Betterton's most significant comic successes: Dorimant in Etherege's *The Man of Mode*, performed in 1676. By then he was approaching forty-one, and his physique must always have made him an unlikely piece of casting compared with either Harris or the younger William Smith; he had never been 'the chief lover of the Duke's Company'.[16] Yet something about the performance lingered in the memory: when, in June 1711, a benefit was held for 'the Widow of the late Famous Tragedian Mr Betterton', it was on the insistence of 'several Ladies of Quality' that *The Man of Mode* was performed, even though Betterton had yielded Dorimant to Robert Wilks some time before his death and Mary Betterton had always played the slightly ignominious role of Belinda.[17] The play concerns a young rake trying to cast off one mistress while toying with another and chasing an heiress. Dorimant largely gets what he wants and disposes of what he does not, except for a humiliating public reversal when his ex-mistress Loveit joins forces against him with a clothes-horse just back from Paris, Sir Fopling Flutter. When Dorimant is at his lodgings or visiting, he is in control, forging plans and furthering his own ends. Out in the open spaces of the Mall, he falls victim to counterplots which dent his heroic self-assurance. The part demands something more than being an obvious candidate for 'chief lover'; Dorimant is as much philosopher as philanderer, given to summarising the textbook of Restoration libertinism, Thomas Hobbes's *Leviathan* of 1650.[18]

The play's success lay partly in the way its hero's three objects of desire tapped into profound concerns of the period and its royal dynasty, with whom it was popular: the restless desire to discard or reformulate the past; the toying with current pleasure for its own sake; the quest for a final settlement in which desire, finance and succession could be reconciled. The heartless elegance of Dorimant's language wins out over the ranting of Mrs Loveit, just as the social project of politeness responded, in Amanda Vickery's words, 'to the uncompromising religious fanaticism of the civil war years, and the political hatreds which lingered afterwards'.[19] Tradition links Dorimant with the real philosopher-libertine, the Earl of Rochester, but with Kynaston's fate at the back of his mind, Betterton would have been wise – and attuned by temperament – to conceal the association, even if the King sometimes encouraged satirical portraits of his courtiers.[20]

The performance in any case required the greater symbolism that came of the interplay of actor and scenery.

What was for playwrights a narrative opportunity was for Betterton an exercise in the craft of performance. The Duke's Company, the next chapter shows, was young and relatively inexperienced, and Davenant probably had this in mind when he recruited them. Their malleability as performers included a willingness to be upstaged by their manager's devotion to new technology, or at least be compelled to blend into it. Scenery and multimedia production carried with it the danger that all the actors would be swallowed up 'to the destruction of good playing', as Gildon put it.[21] Modern classical actors are notoriously suspicious of productions where spectacular designs dominate rehearsals and performance. Davenant's skill was in persuading his young actor-shareholders that their financial interest was best served by moving with the times and, whatever stories were told about his links with the great tradition begun by the King's Men, making a decisive break with the actor-centred production values of the pre-war years.

More agile, individualistic performers might have been stifled, but for Betterton's style and temperament the new scenic stage was the perfect vehicle. To get the most out of scenery in what were still relatively small spaces there would need to be greater discipline in blocking; with the higher degree of physical discipline would come a greater focus on the expressiveness of the voice and the control of gesture. With good reason did Gildon's Betterton recommend the study of painting and sculpture – in the new scenic theatre actors would form part of the coherent, organised vision of the masque which everyone would play their part in creating and sustaining. In time, Betterton would be credited with providing the 'Soul' that informed the 'Motions' of scenery: only his 'Genius', according to Francis Manning, 'could control / Each rude Machine, and cultivate the Whole'.[22] The result was neither artificiality nor the eruption of naturalism imagined in *Stage Beauty*, but a quality Betterton was uniquely prepared by upbringing, physique and ability to supply: craftedness, the projection of performance as a discipline, a visibly mastered skill that strove to chime with its surroundings whether they were a painted version of St James's Park or the real thing.

It was a quality often scripted by the playwrights whose plays he commissioned and performed. Park scenes in particular demanded not just stage pictures but a distinctive form of stagecraft, based on appreciation of the semiotics of the feet and their place in an appropriate pacing, so to speak, of scenes. For all his clumsiness in dancing, he allegedly said to Gildon, 'A constant and direct Foot is the Index of a steady, certain, constant and right Study and Aim of our Designs'.[23] Drawing Fopling aside in the Mall, Dorimant urges him to 'Walk on, we must not be seen together, make your advantage of what I have told you, the next turn you will meet the lady'.[24] In the same idiom, Mirabell and Mrs Fainall from *The Way of the World* exchange notes on the whereabouts of Fainall and Mrs Marwood:

> MRS FAINALL: They are here yet.
> MIRABELL: They are turning into the other Walk.[25]

Such scenes depend on a precise interlocking of speech and footwork, so that walking itself is highlighted not simply as a fashionable pastime but a narrative ploy. In Elizabethan drama it had been common to represent walking by report: either as an easy means of securing an entrance or exit, or as the reported occasion for some reversal of fortune, which any good Aristotelian would have learned to identify as the plot feature *peripateia*; witness *The Comedy of Errors*, *Twelfth Night* and *The Jew of Malta*, where the lone man walking the streets is a source of untold confusion. By contrast, Restoration plays show the use of walking as the most visible way of advancing the plot: that is, by showing how the manipulative protagonist seeks to exploit the 'turns' of the park for his own ends.

   Such behaviour was familiar to Betterton's admirer, Samuel Pepys, who was constantly exchanging significant news or observing significant happenings among royalty or aristocracy while 'taking a turn' in the Mall or St James's Park. As in the theatre, walking is the structural underlay of talking in these exchanges: conversation hinges on 'overtaking', on the quantification of 'turns', on the intimacy of walking 'together' rather than with the company, so that the park, with its manifold ecological gifts, also bequeaths a means of communication distinctive in being both public and private, both open-ended and measurable by pace and extent, both theatrical in its display and dramatic in its pursuit of plots. A form of discretion masquerading as exhibitionism, Pepys's own 'turns' in the park supplied both occasion and cover for an exchange of information either confidential or scandalous, which in turn underwrote his right to be there at all, tracking the company about the King and the Duke. In 1668 he 'walked together in the Pell-Mell' with Wren, 'here talking of several things: of the corruption of the Court'; in 1666 'two or three turns of the Pall Mall with the company about the King and Duke' encouraged discussion of the latest Navy crisis; later that month Sir Philip Warwick of the Treasury complained during a turn 'in the Pell Mell' of 'the melancholy posture of affairs, where everyone is snarling at one another, and all things put together look ominously'.[26] When Nicoll wrote that park scenes were taken 'from those very places where the audience loved to stroll and preen themselves', he underestimated the importance for both participants and spectators of being in on the plot as well as merely admiring the costumes, for the royal parks were places where concealment mattered as much as showing off. For Pepys and his circle that plot was generally a political one, comprising the fortunes of Restoration government which unfolded ceaselessly in their own walking commentary on it.

Park behaviour, then, joins outward display and narrative logic – not just the political and civic ceremonial of street pageants and the rest, but political and civic soap opera, a place where plots and policy are in motion, where the seams of public and private life are unpicked and reassembled. Lewis Mumford just misses the mark when he eloquently describes the royal parks as a theatre whose audience beheld a 'daily parade of the powerful' in order to feed 'a vicarious life of dash and glitter'.[27] The park did not offer only the illusion of participation but also the substance there beneath the feet; its spectators, whether in the theatre or the Mall, could always murmur that here, by the grace of God, go I. Watching actors imitating a walk in the park engaged a complex set of what Eduardo E. Lozano has called the 'associations' and 'reinforcements' which help citizens make sense of the spaces they inhabit.[28] Actors and playwrights had after 1660 established their royalist credentials but were subject to double vision on the part of their audiences, the person and the role living in a state of uncertain truce, and as such their performance of walking the fashionable, restored spaces of London both accentuated and (for those who still despised the actors' social pretensions) challenged the self-image available to upwardly mobile playgoers like Pepys. Here too were rising professionals on the fringes of the court circle semi-fictitiously treading the paths laid down for it. No longer wandering – whether as the vagabonds of Elizabethan statute or as royalist exiles – the actors of these scenes gather as Pepys and his acquaintance did to impersonate the new values of leisure, authority and confidential membership embodied in the royal walking spaces of London. Where Edward Alleyn's Tamburlaine had in Dekker's imagining stalked the suburbs, Betterton's Dorimant strolls in the park – literally and metaphorically a scene of arrival.[29] In the park scenes of Restoration comedy the royalist, once the exiled rover of Aphra Behn's famous play and its source, Thomas Killigrew's *Thomaso, or the Wanderer*, reclaims the cultural centre for and with his own feet. It may look like leisure on display, but it is a kind of triumph.

An anonymous painting depicts Charles II strolling along Horseguards Parade in the company of his court, a role model for Pepys, Betterton and any other park strollers by virtue of embodying a de-ritualised court at ease with itself.[30] Anna Keay has recently challenged such a view of the restored king by enumerating the ceremonies of power he deployed in a vain attempt to re-establish the mystic potency of his position.[31] The argument depends, perhaps, on the insecure distinction made by performance theorist Yi-Fu Tuan, who differentiates between 'ordinary activities' and those of 'ritual and theatre' on the basis that in everyday life 'we are not usually aware of how our bodies form patterns and rhythms or command space'.[32] Whatever else they did, parks collapsed that distinction. They were sites for the ordinary business of walking and talking which produced the sharpest consciousness of bodies in space – a social theatre whose imitation by actors borrowed from and returned to it a demonstration of true gentility. So, whatever else Betterton did to learn the body language of gentility, one of the easier routes to success was to do just what his father had done when he had left the Tothill Street home every day to go and cook for the King at Whitehall: take a walk across St James's Park. Anyone could take home their findings and do what Gildon's Betterton recommends to any actor or statesman: 'stand and repeat his Orations' in front of 'a great Looking-Glass'.[33]

From the start, the new scenic technology had conveyed political as well as social messages. Drawings of Davenant's first set of scenes shows how his Rutland House audience saw not just an early English opera but a political showcase. In 1656, to a country at war with Spain and uncertain of its own constitutional basis, *The First Days Entertainment* offered unsettling images: the righteous knights besieged in the walled town, the royal pavilion of Solyman, and the general assault with 'the greatest fury of the army being discerned at the English station'.[34] Later playwrights would exploit the shock value of visual theatre. The gorily sensational scenery Betterton commissioned for the 1673 production of Settle's *The Empress of Morocco* was, Jean I. Marsden has written, 'designed to startle the audience into recognizing the potential ramifications of topical problems'.[35] When Betterton traversed parks in character, as Dorimant in *The Man of Mode* or Fainall in *The Way of the World*, he helped sketch in the scandalous under-belly of Gildon's respectable Roscius, highlighting libertine excess and failure. Rochester's poem, 'A Ramble in St James's Park', suggests that the place should be prime territory for a man like Dorimant, a semi-rural, open-all-hours knocking shop, the complement of Simon Schama's brilliantly characterised New York Central Park, whose verdant spaces 'shelter a savagery at which even Pan himself might have flinched'.[36] Writing of such a space, Betterton's own Lovemore attempts to entice Lady Laycock with the prospect of the 'Wilderness' adjoining the Mulberry Garden, of the 'Evening' delights of St James's Park.[37] Dorimant's failure to establish himself there, to find his superiority dented by the counter-schemes of Mrs Loveit and the francophile Sir Fopling, compounds his humiliation: the libertine, seeking to exert control in the public domain, finds trouble in his own backyard.

A different version of pastoral emerges from the fine work of Cynthia Wall. Parks are both significant and popular in Restoration comedy precisely because they had been unaffected by the cataclysm of the Great Fire.[38] Where almost everyone else is obsessed with the 'names and shapes of the lost topography of the City', Restoration playwrights devote themselves to these pastoral settings that 'need no reinvestment of meaning'. At the same time – this Wall demonstrates with great skill – as urban renewal proceeds, everyone pays more attention to topographical detail, whether writing about parks or anything else. The motive for this retreat into the park, then, is part social exclusivity, part trauma; a pastoral alternative to a city no longer there, a species of spatial nursery food. Yet the park scene also implies, in Henri Lefebvre's words, the '*obscene* area to which everything that cannot or may not happen on the scene is relegated', that 'obscene' being in this case 'the silenced, excluded, or metaphorized City, that would only gradually re-enter the dramatic spaces, more or less when the Citizens entered the gentrified cultural spaces of London life'.[39] In this reading, parks are the pastoral made true: a green world preserved for those who can afford it, transforming the actor who traverses them into a latter-day Strephon or Dorcas.

But for Betterton, Dorimant or his audience, the parks were sites crossed by the memory and symbolism of royal power. When Inigo Jones drafted garden scenes for the court masques of the Jacobean and Caroline period, his stage pictures were, as Roy Strong puts it, 'images of the King's peace'.[40] The period which saw the parks rise to such heights of popularity in the theatre, from the novelty of James Shirley's *Hyde Park* in 1632 to *The Man of Mode* in 1676, was also the period in which they changed hands, were pillaged, and then were made new in a startlingly different style (so Lefebvre's 'obscene' is not in park scenes a half-acknowledged world elsewhere, but integral to the scene itself). The actor who, like Betterton, walks the fictitious park space also goes for a walk with history, even as he acts out what seems to be the most contemporary kind of comedy – he paces out what it means to be part of the Restoration generation. The earliest mentions of urban parks are alive with royal or imperial mythology. There was no more potent story for seventeenth-century Englishmen than that of Julius Caesar, and it spoke to people across the political spectrum, whether republicans, royalists or constitutional monarchists.[41] Among other things, it explained how royal parks came into being. In Suetonius, Antony discovers that Caesar 'left the general public his gardens on the banks of the Tiber for use as a recreation ground'.[42] *Deliciae populi, quae fuerant domini*, wrote the appreciative Martial: what had been the delights of the lord are now the delights of the people.[43]

The episode lived in English dramatic history. In Shakespeare's *Julius Caesar* the people of Rome are whipped into murderous frenzy not (as in Plutarch) by the sight of the imperial corpse, but by the promise of Caesar's

> walks,
> His private arbors, and new-planted orchards,
> On this side Tiber: he hath left them you,
> And to your heirs for ever: common pleasures,
> To walk abroad and recreate yourselves.[44]

Shakespeare's exchange of corpse and arbour goes further. When Calphurnia had dreamed of Caesar's statue running 'pure blood' (II.ii.76), Decius turned the omen to favourable account by interpreting it as a sign that from Caesar Rome

> shall suck
> Reviving blood, and ... great men shall press
> For tinctures, stains, relics and cognizance.
>
> (III.iii.87–9)

Caesar, of course, prefers the metaphorical reading even though Decius is lying like the truth. Decius's residual Catholic language of 'stains' and 'relics' substitutes for Calphurnia's imagined murder not the security of metaphor but the metonymies of martyrdom. But his linguistic sleight of hand will rebound with interest. When Caesar's blood is really spilled, and Antony announces the final bequest, we hear the retributive proof that Caesar was indeed a martyr – not of stains and relics, but of walks, private arbours and new-planted orchards. No 'great men' pressing for 'tinctures' here: all Rome now has 'heirs' and the freedom to 'walk abroad'. In 1599, celebrating the arrival of the Globe on the south bank, Shakespeare was sharing a joke about the new quarters. 'On this side Tiber' sat the new theatre, and it allowed its patrons the chance to 'recreate themselves' – both to have fun and to fantasise at being a notch up socially by watching actors playing gentlemen. The puritan Stephen Gosson warned of 'privat men' taking to the stage in order to 'walke gentlemen-like in sattine & velvet'.[45]

Shakespeare's prescience seemed greater in the early 1630s, when Hyde Park was opened and the King endorsed the people's right to lawful recreation on Sundays. James Shirley capitalised with the first park play: his *Hyde Park* of 1632 makes the space symbolic of a peaceful realm, so that the park is both scene and agent of a typically Caroline fantasy of political harmony, in which 'court and country are brought into a mutually respectful, mutually beneficial relationship';[46] the environmental paradox of the park, the pastoral amid the urban, serves this wishful resolution. The nightingale's song, later the motif of a ravished crown, symbolises for Shirley fecundity. The parks were closed in the winter months, as if the reign of good King Charles I were as naturally beneficial as the onset of spring.

The image was tarnished when, in 1636, Charles set about enlarging Richmond Park through an aggressive policy of enforced purchase. According to the Earl of Clarendon, the 'murmur of the people' had it that 'the King would take away men's estates at his own pleasure', and those murmurs grew as Charles ordered work to start on a brick wall of 'ten or twelve miles about' to enclose land which he had not yet even purchased.[47] By 1638 the wall, costing £8122 7s 6d, enclosed more than 2000 acres, but its greater effect was in bringing the very concept of royal parkland into disrepute: a symbol now not of the Protestant supremacy which had justified their original formation from monastic lands, but of absolutist contempt for property and common law.

Whatever controversy attended the royal parks in the 1630s was nothing compared to what followed. In wartime Parliament troops used them as camps; in February 1649, number 288 of *A Perfect Diurnall of Some Passages in Parliament* told how the King 'was brought from Saint James about ten in the morning, walking on foot through the Park' to his execution. Soon the scenic backdrop of that parade was as mutilated as the king's body. In 1650, Richmond Park was given to the City of London as an Act of Favour; its royal palace ended up in the hands of Sir Gregory Norton, a signatory to the king's death warrant. In 1652 Hyde Park was, like Marylebone Park, sold off to property speculators; the following year John Evelyn complained of 'the sordid fellow who had purchas'd it of the State as they were cal'd'.[48] St James's Park was retained by the republican government as a rallying point for soldiers, but suffered a fate common to all the parks: its trees were massacred to provide wood for the navy, their stumps a 'terrible emblem of revolution'.[49] Fittingly, a royalist print represents the regicide as

Cromwell and his cohorts felling the 'Royal Oake of Brittaine'; after the Restoration, 'the wanton felling of trees' became a symbol of 'republican politics'.[50] This was the environment of Betterton's youth: his semi-rural surroundings butchered in the name of the new English navy. It would be an apt tribute of John Downes to describe him in old age as the quintessence of English royalness, 'like an old Stately Spreading Oak ... Environ'd round with brave Young Growing, Flourishing Plants'.[51]

Replenishment of the royal parks after 1660 was as charged as their spoliation. In his royalist textbook on forestry, Evelyn figured the replanting of trees post-1660 in the grandest mythic terms. He begins by posing a Homeric tale of exile and return in which Caroline father and Carolean son are interchangeable: Ulysses returned to Ithaca and 'found his aged Father in the Field planting of Trees ... "against my son ... comes home"'. By the end he envisages a work of renewal 'than which nothing so much resembled that tedious Slavery, and Return from it, than did the Restoration of King Charles II'.[52] In contrasting treatments, Waller and Rochester represented the trees of St James's Park in royalist terms. Kings were not, as John Milton and other radicals had urged, 'deputies and commissioners' of men 'naturally ... born free'; rather, they were as ancient to the world's constitution as the arch-royalist Sir Robert Filmer's pastorally monarchic Adam.[53] Turning to those 'aged trees' which, although mutilated, had survived the attentions of the republic, Edmund Waller saw new life in their reaffirmation of a kingship as natural as vegetation itself:

> Bold sons of earth, that thrust their arms so high,
> As if once more they would invade the sky.
> In such green palaces the first kings reign'd,
> Slept in their shades, and angels entertain'd.[54]

In Abraham Cowley's prefatory poem to Evelyn's *Silva*, the Druids, royalists to the man, prophesy 'The Mighty Triumph of the Royal Oak'.[55] Rochester acknowledged fashion by debunking it, tracing the origins of St James's Park to the whoring of an 'ancient Pict' who, in his frustration at being disappointed of an assignation, masturbated on the ground,

> Whence rows of mandrakes tall did rise
> Whose lewd tops fucked the very skies.[56]

Rochester scrawls on the myth rather than seeking to displace it, and it is easy to infer that Charles II's relationship to his parks was as beneficent and natural in its individual style as his father's had been in the golden days of the early 1630s. The painting of Charles II in Horseguards Parade shows him strolling, like the affable fellow he was, among his subjects – a royal walkabout in which everyone gets the chance to walk about. As with the Hyde Park of the 1630s, periodic closure played its part in idealising the royal park. When, in June 1683, St James's Park was closed to the public because of the risk to the King's person presented by the Rye House Plot, it was an ugly reminder of an allegedly more factious, less enlightened age. Four years before that, when it had been feared that there was a Catholic plot to assassinate Charles, it was natural for one illustrator to envisage the scene of this failed regicide as a park through which the king innocently strolled, the satanic incompetents lurking in the bushes of a political Eden there in the middle of London.⁵⁷

But however much Waller tried to idealise St James's Park, he could not help dwelling on the seams of history which crossed it. Evelyn's invocation of Ulysses, fraught with the memory of loss and hardship, gives way to what seems more reassuring: here in the restored park, with its abundance of 'new sprung fowl', 'silver fishes' and other animal life, the 'greedy eye' may see '[t]he choicest things that furnish'd Noah's Ark' (6). Both royalists and republicans represented the traumatic mid-century as the Flood and in merely using the trope Waller raised awkward questions. In his anxiety to justify the King's restored possession of the space, he turns, as Filmer had, to 'Eden's garden'; only Charles's ambitious new canal went one better, transforming him from pastoral monarch to superhero: 'famous cities' have 'founders', but building a river is comparable to the virgin deeds of 'Nature's bounty' itself (9–11). With the same heroic force Charles played pell-mell, leaving his subjects to wonder at this powerfully membered body which, with unintended ambiguity, 'confirm[s] our hopes we shall obey him long' (62). Yet even Waller must end with the recognition that the improved park stands for the still 'divided world' of the kingdom; moreover, that 'these Nations' will need to be improved 'more / Than this fair Park, from what it was before' (135–6).

The cultural provenance of Charles's canal might have given Waller further cause for doubt. This spectacular feature signalled the compromises which built it, for the entire restoration of St James's Park was an exercise in half-baked translation. Charles II employed French principles whose political language was as controversial as the French gardener who implemented them. André Mollet had been employed in 1630 to redesign the gardens of St James's Palace; on the eve of the Civil War he was doing the same for those of Wimbledon House, which Charles I had acquired in 1639 for his French Catholic queen. House and garden were, like the parks, disposed of in the 1650s. Mollet's pre-war designs had meant sweeping aside Elizabethan features to accommodate the new French vogue for *parterres* which are key to the 'immense gesture of power' that characterises the high French style.[58] A set of *parterres de broderie* achieved maximum impact from the centre of the *piano nobile* of the house or palace which fronted it – the equivalent in garden design to the autocratic perspectives of the court masque. Mollet's *Jardin de Plaisir* (1651) was the textbook statement of absolutism for gardeners, so his appointment by Charles II early in the 1660s as gardener in chief at St James's, to be assisted by his brother (or nephew) Gabriel, was both a reinstatement of old personnel and a statement of political ideals. Eventually the French goose-foot canal and avenues combined with English meadows and ponds. The grandiose ambition of the French royal design, with its sacrifice of countryside to garden, was, as the traveller Martin Lister noted in Paris in 1698, 'not English'[59] – for the restored Charles, it was a financial impossibility as much as a political one, a sign of unwelcome constraint.

One challenge of Betterton's role in producing new plays was to ensure that the scenery of the hybrid park of St James's looked like the park itself. When the scene painters of the Duke's Company came to render this restored St James's Park for their audience, they probably used a combination of flats from stock – representing what was described as 'boscage', or shrubs – with a specially prepared backdrop. Sometimes the dialogue in a park scene indicates a precise place, sometimes not, and visual signals and pleasures were expected. Whatever was on a backdrop depicting St James's must have represented the place as it had been restored and improved, not as it was during the republic or before. So conspicuous and politically significant had the changes been that any other approach would have been unthinkable. Presumably, then, spectators from the 1660s onward looked at a St James's Park scene which included the most unambiguous signs of Restoration: replanted trees, the new Mall, and possibly the famous canal which Pepys and other Londoners went out of their way to admire.

In what style? Inigo Jones's sketches for *The Shepherd's Paradise* (1633), *Coelum Britannicum* (1634) and *Florimene* (1635) are an obvious place to start. They are 'stage garden pictures' which, originating in the masque, formed part of a 'visual argument' located in emblems of the garden 'as the image of the king's peace'.[60] Complementary to and derivative from French engravings, such as those by Jacques Callot which give maximum emphasis to the axial designs of the new *parterres de broderie*, they are a synthesis of English and European ideas. Much of the machinery and ethos of the Caroline masque survived in the public theatres of the Restoration, and the principles and ideology of Jones's designs fit the trend.

Jones's sketches are cognate with surviving stage designs from the end of the Restoration period. Sir James Thornhill's 1705 sketches for the Clayton/Motteux opera, *Arsinoe, Queen of Cyprus*, use the same language, and their description by one commentator as giving 'the illusion of a lengthy perspective, culminating in a series of distant views: formal gardens, with an ornamental pond and a river' could easily apply to a generic park scene.[61] However, like Jones's, Thornhill's culminations are uneven – sometimes perfectly in perspective, sometimes so unnaturally steep as to suggest the kind of panoramic, forty-five-degree view which was the vernacular of contemporary garden illustrators such as Johannes Kip and his associate, Leonard Knyff. Kip's engravings of English palaces and country seats, themselves a tribute to the restoration of garden spaces after the revolution, are unambiguous in their topographical exactitude, taking in the whole shape and relationship of house and grounds. His views of parks – St James's included – emphasise the French virtues of line and unity which Charles II had sought to import to St James's. Like perspective theatre, they are oriented towards – without strictly reproducing – the ideal angles of views which their patrons or owners sought and experienced. As culminations to a perspective, such views would have had the virtue not only of exactitude (no one could miss Mollet's goose-foot so represented), but also of flexibility, underwriting rather than undermining the actors' claims to move around the park. In addition, their strong, axial lines would have given substance and perspective to the 'turns' or walks being acted out in front of them.

The realism of the new scenography, therefore, lay less in a naturalistic portrayal of a familiar landscape than in a painstaking reproduction of details seen to best advantage: an advantage which was at once perceptual and political. Officially, park scenes imprint the Restoration principles of indemnity and oblivion on the theatre, producing a verifiable account of the new London which excludes visual citation of its recent political past. Unofficially, they specify the ideal locale for the examination of that leisured, accessible, manipulative model of behaviour identified as late Stuart masculinity. Parks, like Davenant's besieged Rhodes, were spaces where values were inscribed under threat of erasure, and the mishaps which occur in front of them in the theatre show how far their representation had indeed been discredited as an image of the King's peace. It is no surprise, then, that it is in the open spaces of the reformed park in *The Man of Mode* that the alpha male English Dorimant is embarrassed at the hands of the Frenchified Sir Fopling; the incomplete English gentleman who was Betterton upstaged by the elegant William Smith. It is Fopling who, with his train of Gallic-sounding servants, attracts everyone's attention in the social theatre of High Mall. Betterton's career was dogged by half-successful attempts to cross-pollinate English and French theatrical styles; the most successful playwrights exploited the awkwardness. In one of his best comic roles, scenery and actors combined to exploit something in their audience rather deeper than a desire to see the places where they strolled and preened themselves: an anxiety about what it meant to be English and what compromises had been made in the name of Restoration.

CHAPTER 6

In the Duke's Company, 1660–1663

As an actor Betterton walked in company in two senses: with people of varying temperaments and abilities, and in an organisation with a hierarchy and procedures. John Rhodes's company had a flat structure; pushing for legitimacy while avoiding the law, it might be forced at any moment to pack up and fade into the provinces. When he moved to Sir William Davenant's Duke's Company in autumn 1660, Betterton entered a different world – a stratified, stable operation enjoying the protection of a licence, published terms and conditions and relatively transparent finances. Here, 'lines' of performance – the types of parts for which actors became known – and lines of responsibility could readily be communicated and maintained, and the result was a harmonious working environment well suited to theatrical innovation. Betterton was its product and best advocate, and in deciding to join he had his eyes wide open.

The story of how the Restoration companies formed is too familiar to need repetition here, so this chapter reorients the narrative towards Betterton and explains the choices he faced at the start of his career. While Rhodes was getting into trouble for acting without official approval, Davenant had divined in March 1660 how restored royal policy would move and secured a lease on the old tennis court in Lincoln's Inn Fields.[1] Others, including Thomas Killigrew, William Beeston and George Jolly, had their own plans, and their manoeuvrings meant that Charles returned to London to a reception of adoring crowds and, among legion petitioners, importunate old stagers.[2] If Betterton was there on the streets with John Evelyn and the 'triumph above 20,000 horse and foot, brandishing their swords and shouting with inexpressible joy', his feelings were probably reflected in the poem he is thought to have published for John Crouch in 1660.[3] Its baroque mingling of the spiritual and the erotic foreshadows territory his acting would chart in the 1670s and 1680s, while in coronation entertainments such as John Ogilby's were premonitions of Betterton's

later experiments with lavish multi-media productions:[4] 'Great Charles',
wrote Crouch,

> brought upon Angel's wings, appears,
> The long despair of prayers, of sighs of tears,
> Welcome three kingdoms' love, methinks all three
> Now in my heart's triangle panting be.

Rapture provided cover for uncertainty, since neither Betterton nor anyone
beside Davenant, Killigrew and the king could know how London theatre
would look later that year; erase Davenant from the story of Betterton's
bookselling career and the young actor's position early in 1660 looks more
vulnerable. If Rhodes had said anything about pre-war theatre he would
have spoken of several companies with house playwrights and lesser competition on the fringes – an optimistic tale for a young actor seeking work.
Yet Rhodes's company was performing often enough to be assessed for
substantial poor rates in St Giles in the Fields parish, still under threat
of interruption by troops who did not share the emerging tolerance of
theatre.[5] Although a man called John Rogers duly petitioned for security
rights over the theatres, the danger that had surrounded acting days when
Betterton was a teenager continued long after he had joined the Duke's
Company, indeed for as long as he acted.[6] On occasion, it might spill on to
the stage and even the dressing rooms. The idea of paying for entry to the
auditorium continued to cause offence to some patrons, particularly those
who expected their servants to attend.[7]

Rhodes represented enough of a threat for Davenant and Killigrew to
push through their proposal to maintain two theatres under the King's
authority, orders for which were issued in July 1660.[8] Charles disliked the
idea of theatres proliferating and his political concerns matched the financial ambitions of Davenant and Killigrew, whose manoeuvrings would lead
to Beeston, Rhodes and Jolly being squeezed reluctantly into training junior actors, touring the provinces and playing Norwich.[9] Another awkward
adversary was Henry Herbert, Master of the Revels, who feared that the
new settlement would remove his ancient right to licensing fees.[10] In time,
he would extract his due: £2 for new plays, £1 for revivals and a standing fee
of £4 per week, while further control would be exerted in 1663 when Roger
L'Estrange was appointed licenser of the press with authority even over
the printing of play-bills.[11] Although he pressed hard for money, Herbert
knew that Davenant and Killigrew's position was protected so saved his
most severe scrutiny for the fringe companies and remote pockets of resist-
ance such as the mayoralty of Maidstone; unsurprisingly, he appears to

have done so with the connivance of the new patent holders.[12] On 20 August 1660, one day before the King provisionally granted Davenant and Killigrew their monopolies, Davenant drafted an order for the suppression of all other theatres that, had it been issued, would have driven his future leading man to Norwich and beyond.[13] But he may already have started the negotiations that would bring Betterton into the Duke's Company. By 8 October 1660 Herbert was writing ominously to Rhodes to ask on whose authority he acted; Rhodes's use of the King's name failed to convince.[14] Days later, having ordered the arrest of William Beeston for 'acting stage playes without leave', Herbert turned his attention to Michael Mohun's company, prompting them to appeal to the King as well.[15]

Whatever bad news Rhodes passed on, the company was busy. The excitement of the Restoration and the influx of people into London meant that the theatrical season extended throughout the summer.[16] His repertory included Shakespeare's *Pericles* and Middleton and Rowley's *The Changeling*, and Betterton had the chance to shine early in major roles as well as filling in amid assorted revivals and adaptations. Massinger, Fletcher, Middleton and Chapman, as well as Shakespeare, gave him his best early roles. One success was De Flores, the villain of Middleton and Rowley's *The Changeling*, who agrees to kill his mistress's unwanted fiancé but demands a more intimate reward than she expected. Betterton could exploit the potential of his stage presence to disturb an audience: the 'penetrating aspect', the broad, 'pock-fretten' face. 'Oh my blood', exclaims De Flores as he imagines his fee and the pleasure of hearing Beatrice Joanna 'praising this bad face'.[17] Downes would recall that he was 'applauded for his acting in all these plays' and that his voice was already 'as audibly strong, full, and articulate, as in the prime of his acting'.[18]

If Rhodes worried that his company would defect to theatres better funded and connected, at this stage Betterton at least was still only a prospect, not instantly recognisable even to future admirers. Pepys recorded a visit to the Cockpit Theatre, where Rhodes was mounting Fletcher's *The Loyal Subject*:

one Kinaston, a boy, acted the Dukes sister but made the loveliest lady that ever I saw in my life – only, her voice not very good. After the play done, we three went to drink, and by Captain Ferrers means, Mr Kinaston and another that acted Archas the General came to us and drank with us.[19]

It is a poignant record of one of the last occasions when a woman's part is routinely taken by a 'boy', his deficiency of 'voice' a portent of the imminent change; Kynaston was, to give him his due, no 'boy' but twenty years

old. His companion, 'another that acted Archas the General', was almost
certainly Betterton, since Archas was one of his roles. Pepys catches him
before his fame and recalls the performance, not the person. If Betterton
said anything, Pepys thought it not worth recording and 'another' deferred
to the under-apprentice.

His obscurity suited Davenant. With third choice of actors in the 1660
carve-up – Killigrew and Jolly got in first – Davenant went for youth.[20]
Among the older actors were status-conscious troublemakers, and
Davenant wanted compliant temperaments. There was no place in his
set-up for society darling Edward Kynaston. Personnel went with management style: while Davenant prospered by having a hand in almost every
decision, Killigrew let his senior actors get on with it and suffered the consequences. Davenant's most pressing need in the autumn of 1660 was a
leading male, and he seems to have solved the problem by making sure
that Betterton, the beacon of Rhodes's company, had an offer he could
not refuse: shares in the company, leading parts, knowledge of the latest
in French scenography and – it is hard to believe this did not figure in
Davenant's pitch – a place in the Shakespearean tradition.

The alternative can hardly have appealed: a future with Rhodes of
stark provinciality punctuated by occasional court performances.[21] Once
Rhodes had his own licence from the king on 2 January 1663 his company
would be able to perform 'in any Convenient place w[it]hin the kingdome
... within any Towne Halls Motehalls Guldhalls Schoolehowses or other
convenient places';[22] and doubtless many inconvenient ones too. In years
to come, Rhodes would be pursued by plaintiffs with monotonous regularity.[23] A similar licence issued to George Jolly shows that if Betterton's
acting future had lain in town halls and school houses, it would have
meant exile not just from the centre of cultural gravity but from home and
the insurance of its old business connections. Mayors, Sheriffs and Justices
up and down the kingdom were instructed to allow Jolly to perform any-
where he chose, 'London & Westminster with ye suburbs adjacent onely
excepted'.[24]

Killigrew, not Davenant, was conceivably the first to save Betterton from
that fate; a document dated 6 October 1660 lists him among 'the King's
comedians' alongside the major names of the King's Company, Burt, Hart
and Mohun.[25] If that is more than a documentary error, Davenant lev-
ered him out fast. Opportunity alone was a convincing argument. Had
Betterton joined Killigrew's company he would have seen more estab-

lished actors lay claim to the better parts; his name comes thirteenth out of thirteen on the list.

Leaving a bookseller's career for the stage might have been a daring move, but the stage would have its own hierarchy and system of rewards which made Davenant's company a significant step up from Rhodes's. External investors apart, there were four levels. In the first belonged the patentee, responsible for the management and answering to investors, including landlords. Davenant's style was so direct that he lived in the house adjoining the company's theatre, was landlord and surrogate father to its actresses, and held more shares than anyone else, although he soon began to sell to outside investors as more cash was needed.[26] His rapid, complex dealings and resilience in the face of legal challenges, not to mention the eye for opportunity that had seen him, in November 1660, seek a monopoly over theatre in Dublin, set a standard for his protégés.[27] His example brought out the Flowerdew in Betterton, honed in commerce and capable of adjusting to circumstances with cunning and mettle.

Betterton occupied the tier below Davenant, one of nine senior actors who held stock in the company; who, since they took their share of profits instead of being salaried, had the strongest motive for responding to public taste. The Restoration stage's restless desire for innovation derives from the atmosphere of cut-throat competition between the two companies for what was, at a time of huge urban expansion, a surprisingly limited audience: no more, perhaps, than 30,000 regulars.[28] In the third tier of the company were 'hirelings' – the lesser actors and all the women, who were paid a set wage. By providing board and lodging for four of his actresses in a house adjoining his theatre, Davenant also secured his interest by protecting them, not always successfully, from passing members of the aristocracy. Below the actors in the hierarchy came the carpenters, dressers and other people needed for scenic theatre.

Betterton's memory of the Duke's Company was of a disciplined unit reminiscent of a school:

When I was a young player under Sir William Davenant, we were under a much better discipline. We were obliged to make our study our business, which our young men do not think it their duty now to do. For they now scarce ever mind a word of their parts but only at rehearsals and come thither too often scarce recovered from their last night's debauch.[29]

Success was built on a modern professional ethic. Every performer, in Aaron Hill's words, was 'master of the whole subject of the play'.[30]

Davenant's patent demonstrates the legal and financial clout he had in enforcing discipline and artistic policy, but also the versatility he expected from his performers: 'Tragedies Comedies Playes Operas musick Scenes and all other entertainments of the stage whatsoever' were the order of the day.[31] Existing plays were assigned to companies, so immediately the actors' professional destinies began to be forged; at the same time, the fringe companies' right to individual plays was questioned.[32] Davenant could charge what he deemed reasonable ticket prices 'in regard of the greate expences of Scenes musicke and such new decorations as have not been formerly used'. It is easy to see how theatre-going would be turned into a middle-class, leisurely occupation, ripe for the connoisseurship Betterton stimulated. Davenant was to be in sole charge, with the ability to eject 'mutinous' members of the company, who by a reciprocal arrangement could not then join Killigrew without Davenant's consent; this was a recipe for 'strong, centralized management' with inducements to charge whatever the market could bear.[33] The two patentees were granted hereditary rights of ownership, giving them considerable power to make disgruntled actors fall into line.

When Davenant drew up the articles of agreement with his actor-shareholders on 5 November 1660, Betterton had jumped from thirteenth out of thirteen to first out of nine, ahead of Thomas Sheppey, Robert Nokes, James Nokes, Thomas Lovell, John Mosely, Cave Underhill, Anthony Turner and Thomas Lillieston.[34] Rhodes was put in a precarious position since Davenant and Killigrew had taken over most of his Cockpit Company. A few actors stayed for his occasional shows at the Red Bull, at Court, but mostly in the provinces, and for this rump who had missed out on regular performances to high society, it must have been a bitter pill. Davenant's company started to act at the Salisbury Court theatre on 15 November, a week after Killigrew's had begun at Gibbon's Tennis Court in Vere Street. In the next few weeks there was further unrest, for it was less than a month before the Lord Chamberlain issued a decree forbidding the transfer of actors between the two companies.[35] It may have been Davenant poaching Betterton from Killigrew in October that had sparked the quarrel.

Betterton observed in his new master managerial habits that would stay with him, but the difficult negotiations of the summer and autumn of 1660 left another abiding impression. Hostility towards the Master of the Revels, who continued to press for his old rights, did not dissipate; Betterton felt it so strongly that it would see him indicted for assaulting Herbert's messenger in the next two years, perhaps riled by being named instead of Davenant in one of Herbert's frequent attempts to gain legal redress against the company for not paying their dues.[36] The same hackles would be raised thirty years later in his dealings with another man ignorant of the theatre but determined to exact his dues from it, the lawyer-manager Christopher Rich. It surfaced too, in subdued form, in a legal dispute with a shareholder in the 1680s.[37] The respectable, bourgeois Betterton portrayed by Gildon reserved a special contempt for people who found in the theatre only the respectable, bourgeois opportunity to accumulate money.

As a boy he had been content with the second-best option of becoming a bookseller's apprentice, guided by a father who leaves the impression of mixing kindliness with hopelessness. Having discovered a talent for acting with Rhodes, he jumped at the higher challenge offered by Davenant, and no figure in his life was more dominant or influential. John Rhodes, having rescued him after Holden's death, had given him the chance to perform; bringing him to Davenant's notice meant an introduction to someone much better placed to advance his career. Many writers and historians have mythologised 1660 as a new start in English politics and culture; others point to the array of unsolved problems which did not go away until the Glorious Revolution of 1688.[38] For Betterton, 1660 was the most decisive year of his life, an emphatic step forward professionally and financially. He moved from the fringe that was semi-licensed theatre to being the undisputed leading actor of a fully constituted, licensed business built on royal patronage. The hand that guided him was no longer that of an ex-wardrobe keeper and obscure bookseller, but a former Poet Laureate with a significant reputation as a poet, playwright and court favourite. Whatever else 1660 signified, it was Thomas Betterton's *annus mirabilis*.

The same was true for his fellow actor-shareholders. Although Davenant's troupe was the less experienced of the patent companies, it was a blend of old and new: the majority were of Betterton's generation, born in the mid-1630s, but there were also actors old enough to have performed before 1642. Any repertory company needs a balance of ages and all of these actors would also need to meet Davenant's financial conditions. The oldest were Thomas Lovell, a boy actor in the 1630s, and Anthony Turner, who had played the Cockpit Theatre as early as 1622 in Lady Elizabeth's troupe. Of the remainder, the Claudius of 1661, Thomas Lillieston, was a weaver from Holborn and a father of three by Christmas 1660. Lillieston may have been acquainted with the family of another shareholder, Cave Underhill. They lived in the same parish, St Andrew's in Holborn, and worked in the same industry – Lillieston was a weaver and Nicholas Underhill, Cave's father, a cloth worker; another connection with the Drapers' Company, where John Rhodes had started.[39] Two other Nicholas Underhills of the period are recorded, and it is attractive to believe that they were part of the same extended family since Nicholas Underhill 2 was one of the King's Musicians in the 1620s, and Nicholas Underhill 3 a member of the King's Men at the same time. If that is so, Cave's background has a similar feel to Betterton's: respectable trade, royal connections and a son clever enough to be thought worth educating; Underhill attended Merchant Taylor's School from the age of eleven.

The impression of a tightly knit group with common values and status is confirmed by the presence of the Nokes brothers, James and Robert, who kept a toyshop near the Exchange at Cornhill. Robert was the lesser performer of the two, and the absence of any record of him after 1664 suggests he may have died in the Great Plague. James Nokes was to become the period's greatest comedian, his 'plain and palpable simplicity' as funny in life as it was on the stage. He had begun in women's roles and, even after the introduction of actresses, played comic parts such as the Nurse in *Romeo and Juliet*. His upbringing in the toyshop, which presumably meant making as well as selling, told him what had to happen behind the scenes as well as in front of them if mouths were to be fed. With Betterton and the final shareholder, Thomas Sheppey, he was appointed to oversee the company's accounts. Sheppey was a little too interested in money, defecting to the rival King's Theatre as a building investor and occasional actor after a decade at the Duke's. If 1660 was the opportunity this small band of business-minded men were looking for, they took advantage not only because of their acting talent and business acumen, but because of the balance of expertise in the company. Lists of those affiliated to the King's Company include support staff such as 'scene keepers' and 'house keepers'.[40] No comparable information survives for the early years of the Duke's Company, but Davenant did employ the necessary backstage staff; yet the balance of the two companies in background and attitude was decisively different. The King's Company would founder on the clashing egos of its leading actors but at the Duke's the weavers and cloth workers, toy-makers, the book man, the established actors, joined in 1661 by the painter Harris, brought all they had to bear on the chance to impose themselves through royal service on the life of the capital. A shared background in the disciplines of regulated trade also explains how the nine actor-shareholders were able to bear the financial risk of going into business with Davenant. They thrived not only on strong leadership; this was not entirely, as Milhous argues, 'a motley assortment of inexperienced actors' needing to be shaped into 'an enterprising and innovative company', since enterprise and the innovation required for successful business were already part of their outlook.[41] They were that proverbially English phenomenon, a company of shopkeepers.

As such, they were attuned to a working environment in which women played a prominent role, for the structure of a company like Davenant's was not essentially different from that of any other medium-sized seventeenth-century family business, where mothers and sisters, wives and daughters were accustomed to pulling their weight.[42] Throughout his career, Betterton would show a consistent willingness to work on equal terms with women, knowing that it was not only actresses or any individual performance but ensembles that worked on the audience's imagination.[43] Davenant brought his customary discipline to managing his actresses. Initially there were eight: Hester Davenport, Mary or Moll Davis, Mary Saunderson, Jane Long, Anne Gibbs, and three known now only by their surnames, Holden, Jennings and Norris. The first four lived in Davenant's house adjoining the Lincoln's Inn Fields Theatre. Not much is known about the backgrounds of all these women, but it is certain that where Betterton had taken a risk in acting for John Rhodes, the young actresses had little to lose. As late as 1688, that broad-minded man the Earl of Halifax cautioned against young ladies watching plays too often, never mind acting in them for money,[44] and the little we do know about the Davenant eight suggests that they were generally younger than their male counterparts (James Nokes, after all, continued to play older women), extremely attractive to heterosexual men, and not from the bottom of the social ladder. Mary Davis, whom Pepys referred to as 'a little girl' in 1663, when she had two years of acting behind her, was said to be either the illegitimate daughter of a Colonel or from a blacksmith's family; Holden may have been the orphaned daughter of Davenant's publisher and Betterton's first master.[45] Mary Saunderson too had lost her father. The pattern was repeated among the next generation. Elizabeth Barry, the greatest Restoration actress, was probably the daughter of a barrister with royalist inclinations who had lost his fortune in the Civil War; like so many other actors, Betterton included, she came to the stage with a sense of a lost inheritance that had somehow to be restored through performance.[46] The apprentice system was largely barred to women, and among the many accomplishments they would need to flourish in a busy repertory theatre, one was still rare enough to be beyond the reach of the vast majority of Englishwomen: the ability to read.[47]

Davenant's wish to exercise control over his actresses was justified by the speed with which at least one of them moved up in the world. Hester Davenport lasted barely more than a year before the Earl of Oxford 'presented his flame with a fair promise of marriage'. She refused, but gave in the next day when he reappeared with a minister and witness, who later turned out to be his trumpeter and drummer.[48] But Davenport's case was not typical; racy accounts of the liaisons Davenant's other actresses enjoyed with courtiers overlook not only the women's legitimate wish for social advancement and economic security, but the remarkable longevity of their service to the company. Mary Davies became the king's mistress and gave birth to his daughter, Lady Mary Tudor, in 1673, but she did not quit acting until just after Davenant's death in 1668. Jennings's career lasted ten years and Long's eleven before they left to get married, while Norris was still performing in 1684; for Jane Long, Betterton retained what fondness is implied by keeping a drawing of her.[49] Of the others, Saunderson and Gibbs would marry into the theatre: Gibbs to one of the Duke's Company's most prolific playwrights, Thomas Shadwell, and Saunderson to Betterton himself. Holden left no record after 1662, when a disastrous slip of the tongue in *Romeo and Juliet* may have shaken her confidence:

There being a Fight and Scuffle in the Play, between the House of Capulet, and House of [Montagu]; Mrs Holden Acting his Wife, enter'd in a hurry, crying O my Dear Count! She inadvertently left out, O, in the pronunciation of the Word *Count*! giving it such a vehement Accent, put the House into such a Laughter, that London Bridge at low-water was silence to it.[50]

Count or otherwise, the company was remarkably stable for the first decade of its existence, benefiting from the hierarchy and discipline that would allow an older Thomas Betterton, and his friend Charles Gildon, to construe acting as, plausibly, a respectable profession.

As a business it was highly planned and Davenant straight away acknowledged that a better theatre and bigger company were future objectives. Salisbury Court playhouse was the chief temporary home. There were fourteen shares, with Davenant holding four and one left over for common expenses, and receipts would be shared equally after the expenses of hired actors and other staff, house rent and so on. It was up to the actors to engage 'a consort of musicians' as Davenant directed but the cost should not exceed 30s a day, which was to come out of general expenses. Once a suitable place had been found for a permanent home, there would be one week's notice to quit, and Henry Harris, painter and actor, would join the group of shareholders, 'with other men and women provided or to be provided by the said Sir William Davenant'.[51] There would be a restructuring of the share arrangements to reflect Harris's membership and the increased costs to Davenant of mounting expensive shows with scenery and music. It remained for Davenant to appoint a wardrobe keeper, barber 'and all other necessary persons' out of the general charge; for him, too, to establish wages for all 'hirelings'. The actor-shareholders were to supply their own hats, feathers, gloves, ribbons, sword belts, bands, stockings and shoes, unless they were for the general property box; to offset this was the perk of having 'livery' in return for royal service.[52] As part of a reciprocal agreement, Killigrew would have a box at the theatre for free whenever he wanted it, and Davenant alone was to be 'master and superior' of the company, inheriting the share of any member who died. Every shareholder was bound to Davenant for the terrifying sum of £5000.

It was not a recipe for instant riches. In the 1640s Betterton's family had too little money to secure him an apprenticeship, and he would have earned little under Holden and Rhodes. The flush of theatrical success he enjoyed in the early part of 1660 – combined, perhaps, with a bookseller's business on the side – may have put him in a position to buy his share in Davenant's enterprise but he probably borrowed to do it against future earnings. His own father would live until 1663 and then leave him nothing of financial value. Milhous has calculated the approximate costs and revenue of running a Restoration theatre; her evidence suggests an annual salary of £66 for a stakeholder who, like Betterton, owned a single share.[53] That was about half the salary earned by minor government officials.[54] Pepys, with his steady job at the Navy Office, needed about £7 a month, £84 a year, just to cover his household expenses, so we can assume that Betterton lived in the style of someone a good notch or two lower down the social ladder, like one of Pepys's office clerks. Betterton's £5 10s per month was about twenty times what Pepys's servants made, but it would not have allowed him to announce his status with a fashionable suit and cloak – even if official livery was some compensation – and one lot would have been eaten up by the props and other items he was required to buy for use on stage. It was substantially less than the sum Pepys's office paid to the lowest-ranking ship's captain, who had accommodation and food largely provided, and it depended on box-office takings, whatever the occasional bonus of a share in payments for court performances.[55] So it is a surprise to hear from Pepys in 1662 that Betterton was already 'grown rich' on what he had earned from the theatre; the cause was hard saving rather than high earning.[56] Many Restoration actors and managers – including Davenant, Rhodes and Henry Harris – were pursued for debt at some time in their careers, but Betterton appears to have avoided the indignity entirely.[57] The values of the shopkeepers' company served him well.

The auguries for success were good in the early months. In their temporary quarters, Davenant revived a favourite from Rhodes's repertory, Massinger's 1632 tragicomedy, *The Bondman*. Pepys kept going back, and it was Betterton's performance that persuaded him of the actor's exceptional talent. The association of Betterton and *Bondman* became so strong that an adaptation of the play published in 1719 was – almost certainly falsely – attributed to him.[58] On 1 March 1661, Pepys described it as 'an excellent play and well done – but above all that I ever saw, Baterton doth the Bondman the best'. On 19 March he wrote, 'though I have seen it often, yet I am every time more and more pleased with Batterton's action'. A week later, he went again. The play, and Betterton's role of Marullo/Pisander, dealt with the themes of usurpation and restoration which attracted audiences to *Hamlet*. This company had a knack of finding old plays and commissioning new ones that chimed with their audience's need to revisit the past in order to make sense of the present.

The Bondman is set in Sicily at a time of war with Carthage, and the heroine, Cleora, has been blindfolded by her jealous lover, Leosthenes, while he is away so that she will not be able to look at another man. Marullo leads a slave rebellion against the corrupt court while the army is away but protects Cleora; when the war is over, the army returns and quashes the rebellion. Cleora, feeling a secret bond with Marullo, joins the rebels. Marullo, it turns out, is really her former suitor, Pisander, and she rejects Leosthenes for him. Something in Marullo would speak to any royalist in 1661: the adherent of the true faith cast in the role of a rebel, standing up to the troops and awaiting his ultimate restoration:

> There how I bore myself needs no relation.
> But if so far descending from the height
> Of my then flourishing fortunes, to the lowest
> Condition of a man, to have means only
> To feed my eye, with the sight of what I honour'd;
> The dangers too I underwent; the sufferings;
> The clearness of my interest may deserve
> A noble recompense in your lawful favour.[59]

For the actor of Marullo/Pisander there is the additional thrill of playing two roles, virtuosically keeping Cleora and his audience guessing as to his true identity. For Betterton, as with his fictionalised walks in the park, the role described a political trajectory. When Pisander sheds his disguise at the end and shows himself to be no plebeian demagogue but the secret, long-suffering aristocrat, the moment articulates Betterton's own arrival as the supreme actor of the royalist experience, the vicissitudes of his early life transformed by acting.

The new theatre opened on 28 June 1661 with Davenant's own scenic spectacular, *The Siege of Rhodes*. It was the first time modern scenic technology had been used in a public theatre, and it was enough to bring Charles II to one for the first time. Davenant's trick in mounting the play in the 1650s had been to persuade the authorities that his new theatrical language suited their politics. In the 1661 revival he returned it triumphantly to its royal roots, giving an amazed public a glimpse of pre-war courtly splendour. Dryden credited Davenant with inventing a new dramatic genre called the 'heroic play', which became a significant vehicle not only for Betterton's acting talents, but for propagating and questioning Stuart family values.[60] The Restoration had turned the play's relationship to contemporary history inside out; where in 1656 it vindicated incumbent English knights under siege, in 1661 it acquired the glamour of the royal court's spectacle along with its decadence.

Dryden had reservations about the piece: the 'design and variety of characters' left something to be desired. The part of Solyman the Magnificent was hardly a subtle portrait of the Ottoman ruler, but it gave Betterton an opportunity he was to exploit throughout his career: to play an imperious exotic, a fantasy of what absolute power might look like, its terror and sensuality a means of reflecting from a safe distance on the ambiguous figure cut by the restored Charles II and his hankering after a more continental style of government.[61] The satire of later writers would draw an unlikely parallel between Betterton's line in exotic tyrants and his alleged managerial and sexual proclivities, but in 1661 the resonances of Solyman were less personally charged.[62] At the start of the play, he berates his general, Pyrrhus, for slackening in his efforts to capture the beleaguered city:

> Away! range all the Camp for an Assault!
> Tell them, they tread in Graves who make a halt.
> Fat Slaves, who have been lull'd to a Disease;
> Cramm'd out of breath, and crippled by their ease!
> Whose active Fathers leapt o're Walls too high For them to climbe:
> Hence, from my anger fly:
> Which is too worthy for thee being mine,
> And must be quench'd by *Rhodian* blood or thine.

He gets the response his diatribe merits: '*Exit Pyrrhus, bowing.*' Then he turns a mordant eye on his enemies, who are annoyingly brave for such squalid creatures:

> In Honour's Orb the Christians shine;
> Their light in War does still increase;
> Though oft misled by mists of Wine,
> Or blinder love the Crime of Peace. Bold in Adult'ries frequent change;
> And ev'ry loud expensive Vice;
> Ebbing out wealth by ways as strange
> As it flow'd in by avarice.
> Thus vildly they dare live, and yet dare dye.
> If Courage be a vertue, 'tis allow'd
> But to those few on whom our Crowns rely,
> And is condemn'd as madness in the Crowd.[63]

The moral outlook of the Muslim despot blends with that of the English non-conformist. Disguise served Betterton well. A chalk drawing of him as Solyman by John Greenhill, done in 1663, is thought to be the first picture of an English actor in character.[64] Betterton was surely proud of the distinction: his picture collection included a painting of himself, also by John Greenhill, 'in a Turkish habit' which probably recorded this performance in the more opulent medium of oil.[65] His gift, already, was not only to act the contours of royalist dispossession and restoration, as in *The Bondman*, but to articulate from the safe distance of a different kind of cultural impersonation the strongest possible oppositional voice. Describing this pattern as a set of 'villain roles' or characters who 'come to appropriately bad ends' fails to capture its significance.[66] Betterton may have been the 'symbolic king' who in death would lie in Westminster Abbey, but his equally striking presence was as the nightmare of kingship gone wrong, pushed beyond the bounds of law, a republican cartoon. In years to come he would succeed not only as Hamlet, but as Macbeth.

CHAPTER 7

Equal with the highest: Thomas Betterton and Henry Harris, 1663–1668

The Siege of Rhodes saw the emergence of an actor who features prominently in Betterton's early career as a dramatic and personal foil. The tenth share-holder, Henry Harris, was about the same age as Betterton, Underhill and the Nokes brothers; born in 1634, he was 'of the Citty of London, painter'.[1] That is all that is known about him before 1660; it is even harder to decide than in Betterton's case whether he was ever apprenticed.[2] If he was, the most likely date for his freedom – when he was twenty-one – coincides exactly with Davenant's preparations for *The First Day's Entertainment* in 1656. Whatever his talents as an actor, the Duke's was a company built from trade skills, and it would be useful to have an experienced painter for the new scenes. Harris drove a hard bargain. When actors' shares were allocated he was 'to have a portion equal with the highest', which encapsulates his approach to company life.[3]

Since he was earmarked as a leading actor he may have performed as well as painted in 1656, although he did not take the romantic lead, Alphonso, as he would at Lincoln's Inn Fields in June 1661. Apparently he did not act with Rhodes or anyone else in the months surrounding the Restoration. From the start he was an outsider, his talents vouched for by Davenant rather than proved in the risky, semi-legal theatre of 1659–60, and the situation was ripe for the sort of professional conflict which duly surfaced. Harris initiated it: having come in on a good deal, he pushed for more.

A portrait by John Greenhill suggests an actor unlike Betterton. Here, he is Cardinal Wolsey in Shakespeare and Fletcher's *Henry VIII*, a part the Duke of York thought his best.[4] Other Cardinal roles, such as the Governor of Poland in John Crowne's *Juliana* of 1671, would confirm the impression. With Hampton Court in the background, Harris's Wolsey holds a fateful letter to the Pope, his face lined not with cunning but anx-ious ardour, a Romeo in the College of Cardinals who wears his scarlet with impeccable dignity. For all their indulgence towards wigs in medieval

Illustration 4 Henry Harris as Cardinal Wolsey, engraving after
John Greenhill (*c.*1664). Reproduced by permission of the
National Portrait Gallery

Denmark, audiences were sensitive to costume – in 1664, a Julius Caesar
sent on 'with his feather and muff' was promptly hissed off – and the sight
of this handsome actor in full cardinalia perhaps excited feelings of dangerous attraction to the demonised other that was Roman Catholicism.[5] If
any Restoration actor was born to play the febrile, feminised Hamlet envis-
aged by a later generation of poets and painters – Baudelaire, Coleridge
and Delacroix – it was not Betterton, but Harris.

   Their social profiles were no less different. Betterton was the model professional and bourgeois accumulator while Harris skirted the excesses of
the Restoration libertine. Samuel Pepys would know it to his cost, although
his first encounter with Harris was innocent enough. In 1664 he spotted
him at a coffee house with Dryden 'and all the wits of the town', enjoying
'very witty and pleasant discourse'.[6] Compare this with the diarist's only
social encounter with Betterton, back in 1660.[7] Betterton was 'another',
while Harris shone among university men. Betterton certainly knew what
the inside of a coffee house looked like ('I had spoken with Mr Betterton

by chance at the Coffee house', Dryden wrote in 1684) but he probably cut an unusual figure there.[8] Robert Gould's aspersions about his background and behaviour ring true in so far as they suggest a man who made up in acquired dignity what he lacked in natural charm:

> In whate'er Company he does engage,
> He is as formal as upon the Stage,
> Dotard! And thinks his stiff comportment there
> A Rule for his behaviour everywhere.[9]

Thomas Brown went further, describing Betterton as 'that majestical man' whom no one was to approach 'till the stateliness of his countenance is rightly adjusted, and all his high-swelling words are got in readiness'.[10] Playing kings, Brown thought, had gone to his head. There is no strain in reconciling Gould or Brown's sour impressions with any of the more favourable ones. It was not for nothing that Motraye reported him 'agreeable in serious Conversation'.[11] Like his art, his life was a crafted performance, its studiousness nowhere more obvious than among coffee-house charmers like Harris.

The contrast is emboldened by the friendship Pepys struck up with Harris. In January 1667, Pepys invited him to dinner, judging him 'a very curious and understanding person in all pictures and other things, and a man of fine conversation'.[12] They went on to party at Pepys's office, Harris showing off his singing voice. The fun resumed in May and when Harris came to Pepys's Twelfth Night party in 1668 his charm was irresistible: he was 'a very excellent person, such as in my whole life I do not know another better qualified for converse'. After dinner he and Elizabeth gave him a lift to the theatre.[13] The show was the Duke's Company's *The Tempest*, with Harris as Ferdinand. He joined Pepys and friends for a post-performance party with music, drinking and a cake which, his host ruefully noted, cost him almost as much as the trip to the theatre. Harris left at two in the morning, perhaps with a part to play in the afternoon's performance of James Shirley's *The School of Compliments*.[14]

For months the two would often be in each other's company at the houses of mutual friends and Harris's local, The Blue Balls. On 29 March 1668, Harris comes to Sunday lunch with the composer John Banister, director of the king's private orchestra – 'most extraordinary company both', remarked Pepys, 'the latter for music of all sorts, the former for everything'. They sing and play, and Harris takes a liking to the portrait of Elizabeth by John Hales. He persuades Pepys to have Samuel Cooper paint her for £30. Harris has friends in his former profession, wants to do them a good turn, and is quietly forceful with clients. The next day he and Pepys meet Cooper and Hales at the Covent Garden coffee house and repair to Cooper's studio.[15] Impressed, Pepys resolves on the commission and devises another way of flattering his friend: Hales will paint Harris's portrait, 'which I will be at the cost of'. By 26 April Hales has started work, but by the time Pepys has seen it the truth has begun to dawn:

> there came and dined with me Harris, Rolt, and Bannester, and one Bland, that sings well also; and very merry at dinner; and after dinner, to sing all the afternoon. But when all was done, I did begin to think that the pleasure of these people was not worth so often charge and cost to me as it hath occasioned me.[16]

He cannot keep away, however. Three days later, he goes to see Harris in a revival of Etherege's first play, *The Comical Revenge; or, Love in a Tub*.[17] He visits the actor's dressing-room, 'where I never was', and is reminded of his magnetism: 'there I observe much company come to him, and the wits to talk after the play is done and to assign meetings.'[18] Another fortnight on, he reappears during the interval to ask Harris for the words to the echo song in *The Tempest*, the tune for which Banister had 'pricked down' for him the week before.[19] Harris obliges. For the sake of those free dinners it is worth keeping Pepys sweet, especially when the debt collectors are at the door.[20]

The toxic glamour of Harris's company is fully brought home to Pepys on 30 May 1668. He goes 'to the New Exchange, and there [meets] Harris and Rolt and one Richards, a tailor and great company-keeper'; in turn, they fall in with 'Harry Killigrew, a rogue'. Killigrew is the son of Davenant's fellow patentee and still banished from court for alleging that the king's mistress, Lady Castlemaine, pleasured herself on any device that came to hand, mostly her own. He and his friends are, Pepys reckons, 'ready to take hold of every woman that came by them'. They repair to supper and talk dirty, Harris explaining to Pepys the meaning of the term 'Ballers': a group of 'young blades', Harris included, who had danced naked in a brothel. 'Lord, what loose, cursed company was this that I was in tonight,' reflects Pepys, 'though full of wit and worth a man's being in for once, to know the nature of it and their manner of talk and lives.'

By the time Hales's portrait of Harris is ready on 5 September 1668, Pepys knows the sitter too well to be convinced. The picture is 'mighty like a player', overly so for the charming companion of recent years. How could the suave conversationalist, brothel creeper and leech of the luncheon table appear convincing as the stately Henry V of Orrery's conception,

as opposed to the former Prince Hal of Shakespeare's?[21] Many of Pepys's
books, pictures and other possessions are in the care of his old college,
and the picture of Harris is not with them because he always intended
to pay for it and give it to the actor – 'which I will be at the cost of'.[22]
Harris's vanity was tickled enough for him to treasure this record of one of
the very few occasions when his part in a play was more interesting than
Betterton's, but it would be no surprise either if he sold it to keep creditors – or merely his wife – at bay; at any rate, no trace of it survives. In 1676,
Anne Harris would resort to legal action to extract maintenance from her
husband and had to do so again the following year, but not before Harris
was charged with non-payment of an £8 loan made to Anne by another
woman, Emma Worcester.[23]

Harris and Betterton offered Pepys contrasting models of the actor's
private gentility, a commodity on display in coffee houses and gossip as
much as on the stage. Where Betterton attained respect – and sometimes
contempt – through craft, prudence and industry, Harris coasted on his
connections and charm, behaving naturally like the 'complete gentleman' Betterton laboured to imitate. Neither sits comfortably with Mark
S. Dawson's argument that spectators' knowledge of the actors 'served as
a temporary means of social subordination and placement, reinstating the
social distinctions that their genteel performances were about to disrupt,
even elide'.[24] The private gentilities embodied by Harris and Betterton
challenged preconceptions about the class, behaviour and social networks
of performers before they reached the stage. Whether Pepys saw an actor
among all the wits of the town or heard about another studiously accumulating his fortune, he recognised something worthy not of disdain but
emulation.[25]

The tensions inherent in Harris's deal with Davenant did not so much surface as erupt. It took until 1663, when the delayed issue of the official Duke's
Company patent on 15 January focused minds.[26] Since control of the company was granted to Davenant and his heirs, and Davenant was fifty-five at
the time, succession presented an immediate issue. Unsurprisingly, Harris
had not been charged with superintending the company accounts and he
was issued with an arrest warrant for debt dated 29 June 1663, just as, after
two years of playing second fiddle to Betterton, he was about to make an
illegal attempt to join the King's Company.[27] The edict of December 1660
preventing movement of actors between the patent companies was very
much in force, so Harris's response was to manufacture circumstances
that would gain him greater recognition or allow him to defect.

Pepys heard the news on the street. It was already public that Harris was no longer acting for the Duke's Company and on 22 July 1663 Pepys found out why from Wotton, a shoemaker:

[Harris] grew very proud and demanded 20 *l* for himself extraordinary there, [more] than Batterton or anybody else, upon every new play, and 10 *l* upon every Revive – which, with other things, Sir W Davenant would not give him; and so he swore he would never act there more – in expectation of being received in the other House; but the King will not suffer it, upon Sir W Davenant's desire that he would not; for then he might shut up house, and that is true. He tells me that his going is at present a great loss to the house. And that he fears he has a stipend from the other House privately.

Harris knew his value to the Duke's Company and gambled. Betterton, whose father had just died, knew better than to be provoked. Largely unprovided for in Matthew Betterton's will, his earnings and professional self-respect appear to have eased him through any disappointment at his father's decisions or his colleague's antics.

Harris was pursuing another tack too. Davenant can hardly have been delighted to learn in August that his errant actor was to be sworn in as Yeoman of the Revels.[28] The job entailed stage management and coaching duties for court entertainments.[29] It says something for his profile as a performer, not to mention his political skills, that he was permitted to do such a job less than a year after being fined for assaulting and kidnapping a member of the royal office for which he now worked.[30] Now he could cultivate the networks needed for his tussle with Davenant, although his tortuous path to official confirmation suggests he had enemies too.[31] Now he had endless opportunities to compliment dukes and duchesses on their carriage and vocal distinction, and to learn from them. Now – best of all for a man perpetually cash-strapped – he had a second income. As Yeoman of the Revels he earned 6d a day plus £15 per year for house rent and a further £13 6s 8d for food and attendance; that is, about fifty per cent of a shareholder's salary. Sympathy may have been in short supply when, in 1667, he petitioned for an increase of a further 6d a day.[32] The arrangement suited Harris so well that he was still doing the job forty years later, although the extra money did not stifle complaints from his wife and creditors.

His court connections worked: he returned to the company, triumphant, in October 1663. The king had forbidden him to defect and that, one would have thought, would be the end of it. But at some stage over the summer the matter was handed over to the company's patron. The Duke of York put pleasure above principle and decided that London's foremost acting duo should be kept together. Again, Pepys got his news in the shoe-shop: 'by the Duke of Yorkes persuasion, Harris is come again to Sir W Davenant upon his terms that he demanded, which will make him very high and proud.'[33] Davenant had no choice, and he may well have felt that the risk he had taken in bringing Harris into a relatively stable group of actors had backfired. There is no evidence that Betterton or anyone else asked for a similar increase, however strong the temptation. In that sense the company ethic prevailed, even when Harris displayed none of it: 'He tells me that the fellow grew very proud of late, the King and everybody else crying him up so high, and that above Baterton, he being a more ayery man, as he is enedd.'[34] 'Ayery' – in 1663, the word might mean speculative and imaginative, merry and sprightly, flimsy and superficial, all the things Betterton was not. Dizzy with the adulation, however, Harris had failed to notice that there was also a prize for sobriety: 'But yet Baterton ... they all say doth act some parts that none but himself can do.'

The contrast between Betterton and Harris was not only a source of conflict but a commercial opportunity, and it was part of Davenant's managerial skill that he was able to exploit it; the very success of his casting strategy contributed to the dispute of 1663 by constantly handing Harris lesser roles. After the June 1661 *The Siege of Rhodes* had come a revival of Davenant's *The Wits*, and they played brothers, Betterton the elder.[35] Then the *Hamlet* of August 1661 – the defining moment for Betterton in which Harris was bound to play an inferior role. Not old enough for Claudius, he was assigned Horatio, patronised by Hamlet from start to finish.

After *Hamlet* it seemed natural to pair them again in Shakespearean roles. In any *Twelfth Night* today Orsino would be the natural choice for a romantic lead, but in September 1661 Harris must be Sir Andrew to Betterton's Sir Toby – a disappointed suitor, butt of coarse jokes, and a dupe throughout.[36] Even Harris's flowing locks might be fair game. Had Sir Andrew 'followed the arts', he would have had 'an excellent head of hair' (I.iii.86–7). The stocky, grumbling Betterton, accustomed to playing heroes and manipulative villains alike, against the languid, cavalier beauty of Harris, doomed to be dominated by his more successful partner – one subtext in a performance designed, like *Hamlet*, to appeal to post-Restoration London, for Toby and Andrew join in their baiting of the 'kind of puritan' Malvolio (II.iii.128). The King's Company had started the trend of mining old drama for mob prejudice earlier that summer with Jonson's *Bartholomew Fair*, in which the idiot puritan, Zeal-of-the-Land Busy, was made up to look like Richard Baxter, theologian of nonconformity.[37] Good servant of the old regime that he was, Pepys thought it in bad taste and found little to admire in *Twelfth Night* amid the self-recrimination that came of failing to save money.[38]

In October 1661 the company turned to another preoccupation of Restoration London: royal spectacle. The result can hardly have mollified Harris. Costumes for Davenant's pre-war play, *Love and Honour*, included the coronation robes worn at Westminster Abbey that year: 'This play was Richly Cloath'd; The King giving Mr Betterton his Coronation Suit; ... The Duke of York giving Mr Harris his …'[39] It was a studied distinction. That *Love and Honour* had 'a great run' and 'Produc'd to the Company great Gain and Estimation from the Town' helped Harris manage his debt but not his ego.[40] Pepys saw the production three times in one week without expressing a preference for either Harris as Prospero or Betterton as Alvaro, but by November, when Massinger's *The Bondman* entered Davenant's repertoire, Betterton confirmed his place as the main attraction, the 'best actor in the world'.[41] Harris's contributions did nothing for the experience as far as Pepys was concerned; he thought *The Bondman* less successful in Davenant's production than in Rhodes's. Betterton, on the other hand, was so good that Elizabeth Pepys would name her dog after him.[42] Repeat performances of *Hamlet* in December confirmed Betterton's reputation.[43]

A further Shakespeare revival in the New Year held out more promise to Harris. When *Romeo and Juliet* was cast for 1 March 1662, he may have thought he was making progress. Youthful looks earned him Romeo but the scene-stealing role of Mercutio would go to Betterton. The production was not a success for either as the strain of the repertory system told. Pepys observed of the first performance that 'all of them were out more or less'; he even hinted at an uncharacteristic note of disdain for the company when he wrote that it was 'the worst acted that ever I saw these people do'.[44] He was not impressed with the play either, and again Harris was in the position of acting promising roles dampened by the unfashionable excesses of Shakespearean romance. The company resorted to a tragicomic version of the play, acted on alternate nights with the original.[45]

Amid the emerging quarrel, Thomas Betterton married. He had acted with Mary Saunderson for more than a year before she was Juliet to Harris's Romeo, and the attachment was probably formed early. In December 1661 she had been referred to prematurely as 'Mrs Betterton' in the cast list of Cowley's *Cutter of Coleman Street*.[46] Although portraits of her are listed in *Pinacotheca Bettertonaeana* none has come to light, but if the following description of her character in Dryden's *The Spanish Fryar* is any guide she was a beauty 'of a middle stature [and] dark-coloured hair' capable of assuming 'the most bewitching leer with her eyes, the most roguish cast'.[47] 'Assuming', because Mary is generally taken to be an introvert among extroverts, a melancholic woman who as a wife was 'prudent and constant' rather than 'fond and passionate', unlike her 'naturally cheerful [and] confident' husband.[48] The slender evidence of her background reinforces the description. Like other actresses in the company she had lost her father; when she came to marry at twenty-five, she sought her mother's permission. Like her husband's, her early associations were trade; on her marriage certificate, her mother's first name was proved by a St Pancras grocer.[49]

Two years Betterton's junior, she specialised in tragic roles. As Lady Macbeth she commanded 'those quick and careless strokes of terror' which were the signs of the 'disorder of a guilty mind'.[50] Her role as Thomas's stage lover began with the April 1662 revival of *The Bondman*, when she replaced Hester Davenport in the female lead, Cleora. The play was a safe choice after the failure of *Romeo and Juliet*, and its recasting meant that once again it would speak a private language to Betterton, promising 'recompense' in his leading 'lady's lawful favour'.[51] In September, Saunderson was the Duchess to Harris's rabidly jealous, 'ayery' Ferdinand in Webster's *The Duchess of Malfi* (true to their usual lines, Betterton was the earthier character, Bosola). By October, Betterton and Saunderson were rumoured to be married or living together – hence the name conferred by Cowley's printer – but Pepys's friend Benier, who was 'acquainted with all the players', told him that was not the case. Even so, he proceeded to fill Pepys in on the sort of husband Saunderson could expect. Betterton, he said, was 'a very sober, serious man, and studious and humble, following of his study, and is rich already with what he gets and saves'.[52]

Benier makes it sound as if this actor of careful habits waited for marriage until he was sure he could afford it; Gildon likewise indicates a very deliberate choice. Mary Saunderson was 'no less excellent among the female Players' than Betterton was among the actors,

and in being bred in the House of the Patentee, improv'd herself daily in her Art; and having by Nature those Gifts which were required to make a perfect Actress, added to them the Beauty of a virtuous Life, maintaining the Character of a good Woman to her old Age. This Lady therefore Mr Betterton made choice of to receive as his Wife; and this proceeding from a value he had for the Merits of her Mind, as well as Person, produced a Happiness in the married State nothing else could ever have given.[53]

Did Betterton announce to Davenant his wish to marry, and did Davenant give him the choice of the women in the house? It would have been difficult to do anything without Davenant's permission, but Betterton would surely be at the head of any queue that had formed: regally, he *received* Mary as his wife, and rationally too. 'This Lady *therefore* Mr Betterton made choice of'; he was crafted, measured, formal and proper in everything. Hester Davenport may have fled into the arms of the Earl of Oxford but in Mary Saunderson, Betterton had found a woman who shared his conviction that acting, like marriage, required 'a studious Application of a Man's whole Life'.[54]

The festivities were scheduled for Christmas Eve 1662, near what was probably Betterton's lodging in Islington: shared gifts and provisions (that day the Pepyses exchanged food with their friends and made mince pies, so perhaps the Bettertons' Christmas-baked meats furnished forth their marriage table), and not an acting day. In Pepys's view, it was a marriage not only of serious temperaments, but of beautiful voices; yet his appreciation of her acting, like Cibber's appraisal nearly seventy years later, proves it might be second nature to think of actresses as professionals on a par with their male colleagues, not simply as objects of desire.[55] As for the marriage, it lasted without sign of disturbance until Betterton's death, forty-seven years later, when the sale catalogue of his books and paintings showed how political priorities cohabited with domestic ones: next in the list after his picture of 'King *Charles* the second and his Queen' comes 'Mr. Betterton and his Lady, by the same Hand'.[56]

But Mary understood that even Thomas Betterton could not be proper in everything. On 4 July 1662, just before the company had gone into rehearsal for *The Duchess of Malfi*, Ferdinand and Bosola joined forces. The persistent Master of the Revels, Henry Herbert, arguing that the Duke's Company was defaulting on payments to him, sent one Edward Thomas with a warrant to prevent further performances until the debt was cleared. Twelve members of the company, including Betterton and Harris, assaulted Thomas, 'beat and maltreated him', and held him hostage for two hours. They were tried two weeks later and fined 3s 4d each; the leniency of the fine suggests that the affair was explained – and accepted – as a prank gone wrong.[57] Here, perhaps, was the dash of dangerous charisma that made Betterton the star turn of Shadwell's *The Libertine*.

When Harris returned victorious to Davenant's fold in October 1663, his manager knew better than to sit and grumble. Awkward or humiliating the outcome may have been, but when shoemakers were talking about it there was a commercial opportunity. The play chosen to move the company on from the dispute while exploiting its publicity value was one described by Pepys as 'rare', and it was to be the defining success for Harris that Hamlet had been for Betterton: Shakespeare and Fletcher's *Henry VIII*, which would run during the Christmas holiday of 1663 as a seasonal spectacular.[58] Betterton was the King, Harris Wolsey, and Mary Betterton Queen Katherine. Casting the play was straightforward but required legerdemain. Harris might be returning on his own terms but he would not get the lead. Betterton must be the King because of his physique and position in the company, and while Harris was young for Wolsey it is arguably a more interesting part than Henry, with soliloquies and a tragic arc. The content of the play must have caught Davenant's eye; that he lighted on this 'rare' piece, admittedly part of the original licensed list, says something for the detailed knowledge he and, perhaps, Betterton, the former bookseller, had of the repertory.

The play hinges on the fall of Wolsey, whose circumstances constantly resemble Harris's. Trusted as the loyal first minister, Wolsey turns out to have been in secret correspondence with the Pope; he is also notoriously greedy. The showdown with Henry in Act III, Scene ii echoes the recent dispute: Henry speaks for the company management, and the wriggling Wolsey allows Harris his moments of hypocritical humility, staging the language of a reconciliation bought on his terms alone:

KING:　　　　　　　　　　　Have I not made you
　　　　　The prime man of the state? I pray you tell me
　　　　　If what I now pronounce you have found true:
　　　　　And if you may confess it, say withal
　　　　　If you are bound to us, or no. What say you?
WOLSEY: My sovereign, I confess your royal graces,
　　　　　Showered on me daily, have been more than could
　　　　　My studied purposes requite, which went
　　　　　Beyond all men's endeavours. My endeavours
　　　　　Have ever come too short of my desires,
　　　　　Yet filed with my abilities; mine own ends
　　　　　Have been mine so that evermore they pointed
　　　　　To th'good of your most sacred person, and
　　　　　The profit of the state. For your great graces
　　　　　Heaped upon me, poor undeserver, I
　　　　　Can nothing render but allegiant thanks,
　　　　　My prayers to heaven for you, my loyalty
　　　　　Which ever has and ever shall be growing,
　　　　　Till death, that winter, kill it.

　　　　　　　　　　　　　　　　　　　　　　　(III.ii.161–79)

Are you 'bound to us, or no', asks Betterton, and Harris, the 'ayery' man, replies that his fault was always in wanting more than he could accomplish. When Wolsey bids his farewell later in the scene, he speaks the conventional language of resignation while acknowledging that he owes everything he once had to royal favour:

> O how wretched / Is that poor man that hangs on princes' favours!
> There is betwixt that smile we would aspire to,
> That sweet aspect of princes, and their ruin,
> More pangs and fears than wars or women have;
> And when he falls, he falls like Lucifer,
> Never to hope again.
>
> (iii.ii.366–72)

Just so had Harris emerged from his dispute with Davenant; without the Duke's intervention, ruin awaited him. Playing with the parallel universe in which he might have ended up with nothing, he expresses to Cromwell his feeling of utter destitution outside the world of royal and divine protection:

> Had I but served my God with half the zeal
> I served my king, he would not in mine age
> Have left me naked to mine enemies.
>
> (iii.ii.454–7)

Harris's summer machinations had ensured that there was no chance of that happening. On 22 December 1663, the King and Duke came to the opening to enjoy the subtext for themselves.[59]

Another echo sounded for Betterton at the end of the play, when the infant Elizabeth I is blessed by the court and made the subject of a stirring prophecy by Cranmer. 'Never before / This happy child did I get anything', responded Betterton as Henry (v.iv.64–5). Thomas and Mary Betterton, the leading Macbeths of their age, would have no children until in 1668 they fostered Anne Bracegirdle, later the 'unspotted lily' of the English stage; it is conjectured that a false pregnancy may explain Mary's premature designation as 'Mrs Betterton' in 1661.[60] Fatherless and childless as 1663 drew to a close, the Bettertons found family in one another and in their company.

Genealogy had always been a feature of *Henry VIII*, which brought unprecedented financial gains. Downes distributed honours evenly while showing what the success meant to Davenant: even more closely involved than usual in rehearsals, and again anxious to show everyone that Betterton bore the torch of tradition:

This play, by order of Sir William Davenant, was all new clothed in proper habits: the King's was new, all the lords, the cardinals, the bishops, the doctors, proctors, lawyers, tipstaves, new scenes. The part of the King was so right and justly done by Mr Betterton, he being instructed in it by Sir William, who had it from old Mr Lowin that had his instructions from Mr Shakespeare himself, that I dare and will aver, none can or will come near him in this age in the performance of that part. Mr Harris's performance of Cardinal Wolsey was little inferior to that, he doing it with such just state, port and mien that I dare affirm, none has hitherto equalled ... Every part by the great care of Sir William being exactly performed, it being all new clothed and new scenes, it continued acting 15 days together with general applause.[61]

This time, the dates match. John Lowin had joined the King's Men from Worcester's troupe in 1603 and was still active in 1637, when Davenant's career as a playwright was well underway.[62] The reference to 'Every part' implies that Davenant taught the entire cast some stage history, yet Downes's descriptions of Betterton's Henry and Harris's Wolsey are invitingly different.

Betterton's performance, both 'right' and 'just', was accurate in relation to Davenant's instructions, to the part as written, and to some superordinate idea of kingliness; its 'just' quality was the outcome of sustained deliberation. Harris's 'state, port and mien' were personal qualities he alone could bring to his role. Downes's grammar says it: Betterton was subordinated to his role by the passive mood, Harris elevated by the active; Betterton the complete professional, Harris a charismatic presence; the learned graces versus the natural. It is pertinent that while Harris had himself painted as Wolsey, Betterton owned a painting of Henry VIII, said to be the work of Holbein.[63] Political analogies to the Downes passage should not, therefore, obscure its performance inflections: '[i]n testifying to these theatrical begats, Downes imagines a line of legitimate succession descending from an originary moment of canonical authority like a royal dynasty',[64] writes Joseph R. Roach, as if Downes were celebrating a practice inimical to true performance. But the 'authenticity' in question meant different things to different actors within the context of professional discipline: a spectrum of activity ranging from Betterton's 'done by' to Harris's 'doing'. Typically, such discipline served Betterton for decades to come, and he was still playing Henry in 1707.[65]

The success of *Henry VIII* appears to have reconciled Harris to the company, and while there is no indication of further ructions, repertory evidence suggests that the management went on exploiting the quarrel.[66] One Shakespeare–Fletcher collaboration alerted Davenant to another. In

September 1664 the company produced his adaptation of *The Two Noble Kinsmen*, reworked to ensure a happy resolution to the quarrel of Palamon and Arcite over the beautiful Emily. In the new play, *The Rivals*, both survive and are reconciled. Betterton's character, Philander, transfers his affections from Heraclia, the object of his dispute with Harris's Theocles, to a second woman, Celania. Concluding the play, Betterton shakes virtual hands with Harris:

> My quarrel here with Theocles shall end,
> I lose a rival and preserve a friend.[67]

Celania was played by Pepys's former maid, Winifred Gosnell, and at one point in the play she and Harris had to sing a duet; when she went out of tune, he followed her to rescue the occasion.[68] It was the gesture of an accomplished singer but also, when all was said, a good trouper.

Individual performances were not enough to keep the theatre afloat, especially when there was no certainty as to how audiences would respond to older plays, whether by Shakespeare, Davenant or both. From 1664, whatever its sense of history, the company was united in trying to expand its repertoire and discover new theatrical forms to go with new performance styles. Dozens of new scripts would be required every year. There were rewards for ambitious playwrights – if a play lasted beyond two performances, the profits of the third went to the author – but many early Restoration playwrights were gentlemen more interested in prestige than money. The two major new Duke's Company plays of 1664 were by a baronet and an earl: Sir George Etherege's *The Comical Revenge* and the Earl of Orrery's *Henry V*, in which Harris finally got his chance to play the king to Betterton's Owen Tudor.[69] For Orrery, writing plays was a way of assuaging his guilt at having served the Cromwellian regime; his Henry is 'a romanticized portrait of Charles II – handsome and adventuresome'.[70] Not for nothing does Henry marry a foreign princess called Katherine, or overcome his past wildness in emulating the grace of his late father. Orrery's self-flagellation struck a chord and the play ran for ten successive days. Another servant of the old regime, Samuel Pepys, enjoyed it but thought its success hinged on the performances of the Bettertons and Harris, for all its 'raptures of wit and sense'.[71]

Etherege's *The Comical Revenge* is very much a first play, with too many plot lines, changes of style, and stereotypes: an honourable lover speaking couplets of unintentionally comic regularity (Betterton – 'The man indeed I ne'er did see / But have heard wonders of his gallantry');[72] his cousin, a blundering, gambling drunk called Sir Frederick Frollick (Harris); and Frollick's French valet, a Restoration Inspector Clouseau. Etherege's playful francophobia was well received, and according to Downes the play earned £1000 in a month;[73] it was the most successful comedy the company had yet performed. Allusions to the contrasting gentilities of Betterton and Harris persisted. When Sir Frederick joins his cousin in Act IV, he has Betterton's sobriety down to a tee: 'What, my lord, as studious as a country vicar on a Saturday in the afternoon? I thought you had been ready for the pulpit.' Beaufort's riposte has the frisson of past quarrels, as Harris is reminded of his good fortune in sharing in the ceaseless action of repertory theatre: 'I am not studying of speeches for my mistress; 'tis action that I now am thinking on, wherein there's honour to be gained; and you, cousin, are come luckily to share it.'[74]

If, in 1664, the Duke's Company had little time for the squabble which nearly led to Harris's departure, there was nothing it could do about the following year's catastrophe. Its work was gathering momentum, while the King's Company was struggling to match its scenic innovation and company discipline. Davenant could point to new and successful plays in the repertory, revivals of favourites from the past three years, and new productions such as *Macbeth*, which opened in the autumn to exploit the play's association with the Gunpowder Plot. The triumvirate of the Bettertons and Harris, as Macduff, was the core of its success. In the spring of 1665, Orrery provided another tragedy, *Mustapha*, in which Betterton repeated his exotic turn as Solyman the Magnificent, and the scenery from *The Siege of Rhodes* came out of storage. Harris played the title role of his son, presumably enjoying the tone of martyrdom that linked the sufferings of Mustapha to those of Charles I.[75]

Then, on 5 June 1665, fate: no acting 'in this tyme of Infection of the Plague'.[76] Seventeen fallow months ensued. What did the company do? The records are silent except for indications that the court continued to provide for actors.[77] Previous London companies had attempted to tour the provinces at times of plague, but there were restrictions on travel.[78] Betterton may have maintained a bookselling business in Westminster as the plague pits of Tothill Fields filled up; the mortality bills suggest that the worst was over in the west of the city by the end of July. For such times the adaptability of the Flowerdews served him well. The other actors, too, may have returned to their first trades, although business was meagre with better-off Londoners in flight. The King's Company improved their building, causing Pepys to wonder on 19 March 1666 when 'they will begin to act again'. It is remarkable how little the personnel and buildings of the two companies were affected by the twin disasters of plague and fire. Robert Nokes apart, there is no record of a performer dying in 1665 and the theatres were untouched in 1666, although John Leake's map of the devastated area indicates that they had a narrow escape.[79] Since Davenant and some of his actresses lived on the premises, they probably spent those few days in September 1666 as other tradesmen did, standing guard at their premises with buckets.

The next two years would prove almost as difficult for the Bettertons. Before the reopening of the theatres, plays were permitted at court. Whitehall saw a performance on 29 October 1666 of *The Comical Revenge*. Pepys was there, admiring the ladies, bemoaning the acoustics and noticing a casting oddity – no Mary Betterton, and no Thomas. They had both featured in the original production; this was precisely the time when the theatres would look to recover as quickly as possible from the disasters of plague and fire, and since it was a royal performance the best actors were presumably in demand. Even if the couple had left London during the closure of the theatres, they would surely have returned for this performance in front of the king and court. This was, perhaps, the first onset of the illness which would keep Betterton from the stage for eight months from October 1667.

In the circumstances, both companies needed to act with discretion. Davenant and Killigrew had bought economic advantage with their patents but in return they needed to be careful about their pretensions to gentility. Davenant's micro-management of his company worked in his favour but Killigrew was more lax, and on April 1667 he paid for it. In Edward Howard's *The Change of Crowns*, John Lacy played a 'country gentleman come up to Court, who doth abuse the Court with all the imaginable wit and plainness'.[80] He was imprisoned briefly, quarrelled with Howard, and they fought. Pepys's source for this story, Harris's friend Rolt, was surprised that Howard did not exercise *droit du seigneur* and 'run [Lacy] through', but the actor was, after all, 'too mean a fellow to fight with'. What happened next conveys the social tensions that existed between actors and gentry. Howard did not draw his sword, but ran off to complain to the king, who – to the delight of the 'gentry' – closed the King's Theatre for becoming 'too insolent'.[81]

Mark S. Dawson's focus on social conflict between members of the audience means that he does not mention the episode, but it further complicates his account of gentility and the status of actors. The idea that 'social distinction' was elided by 'genteel performances' takes insufficient notice of performed irony.[82] The social relationship between Lacy and Howard looks straightforward enough according to the martial code Pepys invokes: Lacy was simply 'too mean a fellow to fight with'. It was both compounded and complicated by Lacy's role in the play, that of 'a country gentleman come up to Court', which meant a performance of false gentility analogous to Lacy's own pretensions as an actor in taking the role at all. But the analogy was not exact. The act of performance established the very distance from the role, the very critique of the country gentleman's performative pretensions, that the most aloof courtier could desire. In that sense, the 'genteel performance' of the actor enforced social distinctions in the moment of appearing to elide them.[83] As with Edward Kynaston's impersonation of Sir Charles Sedley, the risk was not in the performance of gentility in the abstract, but in the exact application to people or customs, a risk Betterton studiously avoided in pursuit of more general truths.

After the dust had settled, two records of performances by Betterton indicate that audiences were proving hard to attract, and that the company was overcome by professional malaise. Pepys saw productions of Orrery's *Mustapha* and a translation of Corneille's *Heraclius* on successive days in early September, and on both occasions the company principals, renowned for discipline, corpsed:

both Baterton and Harris could not contain from laughing in the midst of a most serious part, from the ridiculous mistake of one of the men on stage … they did so spoil it with their laughing and being all of them out, and with the noise they made within the Theater, that I was ashamed of it and resolve not to come thither again a good while, believing that this negligence, which I never observed before, proceeds only from their want of company in the pit, that they have no care how they act.[84]

Later in his career Betterton would be described as 'the grave Mr Betterton' who struggled to break into a smile at the most ludicrous of stage accidents.[85] In 1667, with laughing on stage, making merry in the wings, forgetting lines and half-empty houses, even the well-drilled Duke's Company was, temporarily, a shambles.

Things got worse. On 16 October 1667, Pepys went to see a favourite Duke's production, *Macbeth*, only to find that Betterton was ill; the title role was taken by a junior actor, Young ('who is but a bad actor at best'), and Pepys 'and everybody else' went off the play as a result. When he got home, he found his wife had been to the theatre and left early because of Young; still, the company thought it worth persisting with the production, which was staged again for Guy Fawkes Day. Betterton's absence proved a lengthy one and all his parts were reassigned. William Smith stood in for Porter's *The Villain*, causing Pepys to turn back.[86] Later he heard that Smith had acted 'as well or better then he; which I do not believe'. Other productions such as *The Tempest* and *The Rivals* resurfaced without him, while new plays including Etherege's second, *She Would If She Could*, had no part for him. If the Pepyses' reactions were typical the company must have struggled. The obvious commercial move – having Harris take over some of his roles – did not materialise. The experience of the early 1660s argues that Harris must have coveted a part such as Macbeth, but instead he continued in the second-string option of Macduff.

He was probably looking to the long term by using Betterton's absence to consolidate his managerial credentials. Davenant, approaching his sixty-second year, had not made a will but his widow and eldest son, still a minor, would inherit the business and decide who should run it. Betterton, with his professional standing, straight dealing and financial prudence, would surely be the front-runner. Harris had some ground to make up and it is unlikely that Davenant had forgotten the dispute of 1663. We do not know what Betterton did during the eight months' absence; as a shareholder he would continue to draw money, but Davenant probably needed extra assistance in maintaining the business. In Betterton's absence, Harris played the best part of all: not Macbeth or Prospero but the capable, trustworthy deputy.

On 7 April 1668, Davenant died. When Pepys heard the news he did not know 'who will succeed him in the mastership of that House', and there followed a period of wrangling among the surviving Davenants.[87] When they reached it, the solution must have seemed the best one for those who worked in the Duke's Company as well as those who had merely sunk money into it. As Harris later deposed, he and Betterton 'were chose by all Parties interested in the said Theatre to manage the same'.[88] The decision was logical: the two senior actors, court connections joined to financial prudence, each compensating for the other's shortcomings. They had settled into peaceful co-existence. On 6 July 1668, Harris met Pepys at Samuel Cooper's studio and told him, without trace of rivalry, that his partner had recovered; Pepys promptly went to see both men in Orrery's *Henry V*, 'glad to see Betterton'.

While Betterton returned to his gruelling schedule of acting, Harris did less and less. Although the two 'ran the company smoothly for about ten years', Betterton assumed the greater burden; while the case for joint management could not have been put with smoother persuasion than by Henry Harris, he perhaps had always seen it as a path to an easier life.[89] When Davenant had drawn up the agreement with his shareholders in

1660, Harris had been waiting in the wings, ready to seize his opportunity once the company was established, and in 1668 he repeated the trick.

On 9 April, the two men were side by side as they followed Davenant's body from Lincoln's Inn Fields to Westminster Abbey. There were, Pepys observed, many coaches, many dependent children, but also many hackneys, 'that made it look … as if it were the burial of a poor poet'.[90] Another poor poet, Richard Flecknoe, attempted to sum up Davenant's achievements:

> Now Davenant's dead the stage will mourn
> And all to barbarism turn;
> Since he it was, this later age
> Who chiefly civiliz'd the stage.
> Great was his wit, his fancy great
> As e're was any poet's yet;
> And more advantage none'er made
> O'th'wit and fancy which he had.
> Not only Daedalus art he knew
> But even Prometheus's too;
> And living machines made of men
> As well as dead ones, for the scene.[91]

Both Betterton and Harris, opposites in so many ways, owed their careers to Davenant's twofold legacy – to his immersion in England's theatrical past, to his instinct for what new technology could do for its future. Political conviction played its part: the restored monarchy must have a theatre where the extravagances of the Stuart masque could be shown to the widest audience. Although his meagre funeral gave no clue, he had left them something else: a real business opportunity, as long as they followed his example as managers of the Duke's Company.

CHAPTER 8

Actor management: running the Duke's Company

Davenant's 'grant' in 1660 had been a matter of state; when he died, the succession was his family's to decide. If that reflected a patent given him and 'his heirs', it was also a minor landmark in the evolution of a fully commercial theatre. Betterton and Harris ushered in the age of the actor-manager; Davenant's death marked the decline of the courtier-manager. John Dennis thought the change wrested control from 'Gentlemen, who had done particular services to the Crown' and handed it to 'illiterate, unthinking, unjust, ungrateful and sordid' players.[1] Written late in Betterton's career, it was a brusque assessment for someone who had acknowledged the actor's help with one of his plays – Dennis was really writing about Cibber, Wilks and Booth but spattered Betterton with the same brush – that also neglects the courtly inclinations of the Duke's Company management after 1668.[2] They were, after all, 'sworn to attend his Royal Highnesse' and would do so at state events such as the funeral of the first Duchess of York in 1671, which closed the theatres.[3] Later tradition would inscribe Betterton himself as the last courtly actor-manager.[4] His prudence in comedy told him that he would have to manage as he had acted, with a consciousness of livery. Harris's prudence was dictated by doubling as Yeoman of the Revels; he could not supervise a masque and behave like John Lacy. The Bettertons too were in demand as acting coaches to royalty.[5] More than discipline and commercial nous, the new management inherited from Davenant a fundamental sense of cultural affiliation. Too young to have 'done particular services to the Crown' during the war or its aftermath, they were, nevertheless, men of 1660.

Prudence of another order was needed. Having learned bookselling and acting from resourceful and cunning patriarchs, Thomas Betterton started working in 1668 for a resourceful and cunning woman. Davenant's third wife, Lady Mary, had been on the scene as long as scenes themselves. When Davenant returned from France in 1655 with plans for *The First Days Entertainment*, the diplomacy of his marriage soon emerged.

Henrietta Maria du Tremblay shared the queen mother's name but settled for plain English Mary. After the Restoration she adjusted to life as her husband's business partner and to the actresses' boarding house that was home. Perhaps even before she was widowed, she maintained 'a particular interest in the company accounts, seeing to it that payments for plays before royalty were routed through her'.[6] When Davenant died intestate, Lady Mary oversaw the disposal of his debts as well as the tribute to her late husband's literary talents they barely deserved, a folio of his plays.[7] In 1673 she deposed that she had had 'sole government' of the company during the minority of her son Charles, appointing 'Treasurers and Receivers, making Dividends and ordering of affairs'.[8]

Because 'sole government' and financial control are not synonymous, Lady Mary's position should not be overstated, yet Jacqueline Pearson describes her as 'a working manager', not simply 'a figurehead'.[9] Gilli Bush-Bailey even calls her 'a theatrical entrepreneur' responsible for recruiting female playwrights and discussing casting with actresses.[10] The financial details of the 1668 transition say otherwise. Lady Mary understood that she needed managers who knew their business, and she needed to pay them well; in fact, to give them the greatest incentive to take over. Davenant himself had, Harris later swore, managed 'without any salary or consideration for the same beside the share or shares he had therein'.[11] The new managers, by contrast, were given twenty shillings a week on top of their share of the profits and acting salaries. Predictably, Harris craved more – as well as pursuing his duties as Yeoman of the Revels, he petitioned for and in 1670 obtained the post of Chief Engraver of Seals, turning his drafting skills to account.[12] Most of his financial problems were solved; on only two occasions in 1668 and 1669 was he pursued for debt, but the old difficulties returned eventually. Lady Mary must have been sure of Harris's managerial talents to compensate for the risks he presented, but the success of the company from 1668 may be attributed to her *not* being another interfering Henry Herbert and Christopher Rich. Having employed two capable specialists, she was sensible enough to let them do just what Betterton preferred: get on with the job.

Stock structure after 1668 was designed to shift responsibility towards the actors as well. Davenant had held back shares to fund operating costs and new productions but also sold to outside investors, who gained excellent returns in good years and grief come fallow time. Reforms devised in 1668 transferred risk to the main performers. In future, all costs would be deducted from takings before profits were distributed, and more shares went to the principal male actors. However reassuring the presence of

Betterton and Harris, it meant a more demanding regime. No longer 'carefully sheltered children', the actors now had more responsibility for their business.[13] The days of teeny tantrums like Harris's were over. Some found the new arrangements uncongenial and Betterton duly bought out some of his colleagues, manoeuvring himself through financial acuity to the position of dominance in the company which Davenant had enjoyed by royal patent. Most people benefited, and the average annual dividend was maintained at the healthy levels set by Davenant.[14] As 1660 had marked Betterton's arrival as an actor, 1668 installed him as an entrepreneur capable of acting respectability with a view to buying it.

How did the two managers divide their duties? Carrying out 'the socializing which made important friends for the theatre at Court' fell naturally to Harris, with his two court sinecures, smooth conversation and ease in high society.[15] Decisions about artistic policy were probably shared, but Betterton continued with his former responsibility for scrutinising the accounts, along with James Nokes, although a treasurer, Thomas Cross, was inherited from Davenant's days and paid twenty-five shillings a week for record-keeping, paying all staff and capital costs, and distributing profits to shareholders. By his own recollection, Cross's records were transparent and often scrutinised by other members of the company, which is how this embezzler came to grief in November 1674, to be replaced by one of Lady Mary's sons, Alexander.[16]

Integral to everything was effective discipline. Davenant had set high standards but in different circumstances, and the new management structure must have raised expectations. If Betterton and Harris were to be in charge and therefore spending less time acting, might there not be more opportunities for second-rank players in the company? Harris acted less but Betterton carried on with the same prodigious industry as before and it was not long before Matthew Medbourne began to moan. He could look at his managers with some disrespect since he had been among those fined for kidnapping Sir Henry Herbert's servant. In December 1669 he showed he had not learned from the experience, arrested for 'refractory and disorderly [conduct] contrary to the Rules of [the] house'; it was just one of a number of cases in the three years after Davenant's death when company discipline was badly breached.[17] At times, heavy weaponry was needed. These were royal servants, and while there was a system of fines for non-attendance at rehearsal or, still worse, performance, Betterton and Harris occasionally had to go to the top, showing the zeal of new managers determined to make an impact. The Lord Chamberlain got involved in cases of persistent absence, such as those of three minor actors, Lisle, Adams and Allenson, arrested in 1670.[18] Equally, the management had discretion to give bonuses 'to such whose merits deserved it'.[19] Going to the top could be a double-edged sword. As Harris had returned to the company in 1663 following the Duke of York's intercession, so in 1681 Lord Chamberlain Arlington would instruct Betterton to take back the actress Norris, following an unspecified breach of discipline and some process of official arbitration that had both reconciled her 'unto her adversary' and established her submission 'to ye rules & Government of ye Company'.[20]

Both managers vetted new plays. A different approach was required depending on how a script had come forward – from an established author or colleague, or an unknown outsider. Pepys describes Harris's summary way with the naval storekeeper, part-time antiquary and musician, Silas Taylor.[21] *The Serenade, or Disappointment* lived up to its subtitle and Harris discarded it after reading, to Taylor's outrage, a single act. Betterton enjoyed a more fruitful if fraught relationship with Thomas Otway, who would produce a string of successes for the company from 1675. Otway lived in debt, depression or both and Betterton needed to keep him stable. So reliable was he in reaching the third, benefit performance that by one report Betterton would 'take for pawn the embryo of a play' from him so that he could both live and write. The amount would be deducted from the third day takings but it was a risky way of keeping talent on an even keel. This was 'kind Banker Batterton' at work.[22] The Tonson brothers, Otway's most regular publishers, also loaned him money, an arrangement guaranteed to cause trouble.[23] In the early 1680s, Betterton induced Otway to move to Hampshire, site of clean and cheap living, but he returned in the grip of his infatuation with Elizabeth Barry. 'My Tyrant!' he wrote, 'I endure too much Torment to be silent ... Desire makes me mad, when I am near you: and Despair when I am from you.'[24] After Otway's death in April 1685, Betterton attempted to track down the manuscript of his unfinished play about Iphigenia, on which there may have been a down payment.[25] Pity Betterton the task of managing this man and the woman on whom he was fixated. Since Otway wrote Barry's best roles he probably did not know whether it was the real or the performing woman who drove him to despair; discussion of casting was, agonisingly, part of a manager's relationship with his playwright even after the first run.[26] It would later be said of Betterton that he brought the same care, and no doubt patience, to his dealings with his actors: in Edmund Curll's words, 'he employed himself in visiting, and overlooking their Actions as a Guardian, or Father'.[27]

No such treatment was available for the scores of hopeful playwrights who failed to trouble the audience for more than a night or two, if that, even if Betterton chose to appear in their plays: names such as the Reverend Joseph Arrowsmith, Mrs Frances Boothby, Dr Nicholas Brady, the Earl of Bristol, Laurence Maidwell, Thomas St Serfe, or the unknown authors of such plays as *The Faithful General*, all of whom speak not only of the desperation of the companies to find new work, but of the culture of amateur playwriting on which they could draw.[28] Others printed plays with the addition, 'Unacted', following, in some cases, rejection by the theatres.[29] Even so, David Crauford's complaint about a later company's rehearsal of his play, *Courtship-à-la-Mode*, specifically exempts from blame Betterton, who had done Crauford 'all the justice [he] could indeed reasonably hope for'.[30] The same praise comes more grudgingly from the mouth of Sullen in the satirical *A Comparison of the Two Stages*, whose playwright friend had found that 'Mr. *Batterton* did him (as I have heard him say) greater Justice than he expected'.[31] Charles Gildon enjoyed Betterton's help with the 'Fable' of his play, *Love's Victim*, Settle the same for *Distress'd Innocence*, while Dryden acknowledged his role in re-shaping *Troilus and Cressida* and designing and describing the scenes of *Albion and Albanius*.[32] In the preface to *Liberty Asserted*, John Dennis thanked him 'for the Hints I receiv'd from him, as well as for his excellent Action'.[33] To Francis Manning this amounted to 'Judgment, clear as is the Brightest Morn', capable of discarding 'the Chaff, distinguishing the Corn', and it was said that during rehearsals he would not hesitate to consult 'e'en the most indifferent Poet' about his work; to Thomas D'Urfey, Betterton's opinion was that of 'undisputed Authority'.[34] He was keen to develop talent, able to offer artistic as well as financial help, and it was said to be the absence of those qualities among his successors that deterred his friend Pope from writing for the theatre.[35] It was in the nature of the task that not everyone appreciated him. Robert Gould mocked Betterton's pretensions to being 'a Man of parts', a self-appointed 'Judge of Wit', a mere actor pretending to the judgement of a gentleman-author who had risen from bookseller to 'prime Vizier': a dig at the actor's Eastern roles and a sign that even Betterton was not immune to conventional denigrations of actors.[36]

Judgements about new plays were based not only on dramaturgic merit but on the match between script and company, and that meant playing to the strengths and egos of the leading actors. Some casting decisions were automatic, not only for revivals but also when parts corresponded to performers' customary 'lines'. But there was also scope for experiment; when a play could be rejected by one house and be a banker at the other, when

Macbeth could be a masterpiece with Betterton and not worth seeing with Young, it was accepted that the performance influenced the conception of the piece. Sometimes an experiment would fail: Samuel Sandford, actor of villains, convinced no one in virtuous roles.[37] Under the post-1668 financial regime, in other words, the actors were under additional pressure to reconcile personal ambitions with what the audience would accept.

There was another dimension to Betterton's new managerial duties. Davenant had kept his actresses in a boarding house adjoining the Lincoln's Inn Fields Theatre, and was their manager and surrogate parent; in 1664 he had also, with Killigrew, been granted 'oversight & approbation' of an actors' nursery to be built by William Legg.[38] The job fell in 1668 to the Bettertons, and such would have been the company in which their foster daughter, Anne Bracegirdle, grew up. The discipline required of this surrogate family was as much for their protection as Betterton's benefit; Rebecca Marshall of the King's Company had been stalked, assaulted and had excrement 'clapd upon her face and haire'.[39] Where Marshall's despairing resort was to petition for the King's protection, the Duke's Company was more watchful. Training young actors of either sex was a significant responsibility for which both Bettertons were paid. When the fate of so many senior actresses befell Mary twenty years on – a lack of interesting roles – she devoted more time to it.

There were pastoral responsibilities for actors no longer able to perform. William Smith later recorded that fines levied for indiscipline might be 'disposed of in Charityes according to usuall Custome'.[40] In this, as in so much else, the theatre took its ethos from the city companies, like the Drapers' Company in which John Rhodes had grown up. An instance is provided by Philip Cademan – a slightly unusual one since he was part of the Davenant family furniture, a stepson from the old manager's second marriage. Davenant had agreed to allow him £100 a year but kept him on a minor actor's salary in minor roles, his dubious talent masked by doggedness and his unique ability to save his manager money just by being there.[41] Under Lady Mary's eye the agreement was honoured even after the accident of 9 August 1673 that finished Cademan's career during a performance of Davenant's *The Man's the Master*. During a stage fight with foils Harris caught Cademan, causing him to lose 'his memory, his speech and the use of his right eye'.[42] His thirty shillings a week was under threat when, two decades on, it attracted the attention of the lawyer-manager, Christopher Rich. It is hard not to sympathise with Rich's insistence that Cademan could at least sell tickets, or wonder how impaired his memory really was when the petition of 1696 exhibits recall of financial minutiae dating back three decades.[43] Benign patriarch that he was, Thomas Betterton over-looked such details in the name of professional and family affiliation. The habit was infectious. Some time after 1695 his senior actor John Bowman was pursued by the bailiff, William Browne. A 'bloody Fight ensu'd ... and in the Fray one Matthews a Door-Keeper, receiv'd a Wound, by a Sword, in his Breast, which could never be perfectly cur'd'. Knowing Matthews had been hurt 'in his Quarrel', Bowman gave him 'a weekly Pension, besides the Income of his Place, so long as he liv'd'.[44]

The most frequent occupation was to prepare the company for performance, with an adaptation of Webster's *Appius and Virginia* as *The Roman Virgin* among Betterton's first attempts.[45] Davenant's microscopic individual coaching and tough company discipline present a picture clouded by Tiffany Stern's panorama of nightmarish schedules and pre-modern textual practice: for new plays, perhaps a fortnight for the hectic cycle from author's first reading to private study to run-through to performance, punctuated six days a week by performances of other plays.[46] Between first reading and first performance, actors were left to their own devices or rehearsed scenes in pairs, their parts distinct from the script, described by Stern as the sum 'of patches of varying fixity'.[47] One anecdote has Betterton's Macbeth performing opposite a timid young Seyton – treated with characteristic kindliness – he had never set eyes on.[48] His ability to stay in character throughout a play was remarkable in the circumstances; little wonder either that his crafted style drew attention when spontaneity was what sometimes kept a show going. One consequence of the rehearsal regime was lamented by Aphra Behn. *The Dutch Lover* briefly saw the light of day in Betterton's company in February 1673 but was 'hugely injur'd in the Acting, for 'twas done so imperfectly as never any was before', with 'intolerable negligence [from] some that acted in it'.[49] The text diplomatically withheld the usual list of actors.

It was inevitable that new plays would be subject to such pressures. They had not been tested before an audience and companies could not afford to spend much time preparing for what might prove to be flops – first performances were in effect pre-release screenings. A complementary issue complicates Stern's picture. While theatre history defines periods by the new plays they produce, it is revivals that have always been far and away the chief business of mainstream companies, and rehearsal and performance practice must be seen in that context. Take the show that succeeded *The Dutch Lover*, opening on 18 February 1673 – a revival with new scenes and dances of *Macbeth*, which had been in the repertory for more than eight years with Matthew Locke's music and much the same cast: as the Macbeths, the Bettertons; Harris as Macduff; William Smith as Banquo; Sandford as a drag Hecate who outlived the introduction of actresses. It had become an established occasional piece for Bonfire Night and one that in 1664 had been boosted by a recent witchcraft trial.[50] In 1673, the object-ive was to blend settled performances with new scenery and set-pieces.

Settled the performances certainly were; at the Duke's Theatre the lead-ing man and lady were in each other's company all the time. Those best able to cope with the relentless assault on the memory of the Restoration repertory theatre were, like the Betterton Pepys heard described, the most 'studious' and 'sober' in every sense of both words.[51] Study, not the tavern, was the serious performer's occupation in the evening, and even a role first played nearly a decade before needed, as the actors said, 'repeating'.[52] That was where the real business of rehearsal happened, alone with a fellow actor or, just as valuable according to Gildon's Betterton, a mirror; or, best of all, a spouse who thought and felt the same way about the business. They were each other's mirror, the Bettertons, and it does not strain imagination to envisage them, during the intervals of the evening musical rehearsal that would have taken place the night before 18 February 1673, pacing their upstairs apartment at the theatre, reviving together the expressive threads of their scenes. If rehearsal was lonely, studious, instructional and scru-pulously external in its attention to the modulations of voice and gesture (most preparation time, says Stern, 'was spent in establishing, memoriz-ing, then honing down pronunciation and gesture'), the process acquired personal resonance and intensity once matched to the right performers.[53] By instructing one another, the Bettertons developed the emotional chem-istry that came of constantly repeating and performing the 'passions' of their parts. The impact of such preparation must also have been felt on the 'serious aspect' which Cibber remembered.[54] It is no accident that two of Betterton's biggest successes in Shakespeare feature soliloquies in which interaction gave way to meditation, dialogue to public address.

Hamlet welcomes his ghost, Macbeth forces his from the stage; Hamlet is the prince in waiting, Macbeth the regicide in blood; Hamlet suffers from inaction, Macbeth from action. The force of Betterton's Macbeth from 1664 to 1673 was that it enabled this symbolic king of cultural mem-ory to play history's demons. In the hours of private study, of repeating the role to and with Mary, he mastered, perhaps remembering more of Davenant's own bloody instructions, the passions, gestures and inton-ations of the regicide with all the determination of a double agent. Samuel Pepys found the play both a 'deep tragedy' and full of 'divertisement'.[55]

New scenes and dances there might be, but the success of the performance would depend on how each actor was able to articulate their passions to the audience. 'Come, give us a taste of your quality', says Hamlet to the First Player, 'come, a passionate speech' (ii.ii.423–4). Such passions were not in Shakespeare's words but in the thoughts and feelings they denoted. 'If Shakespeare were stripped', Dryden would observe, 'of all the bombasts in his passions, and dressed in the most vulgar words, we should find the beauties of his thoughts remaining; if his embroideries were burnt down, there would still be silver at the bottom of the melting-pot'.[56] This was an inheritance from the old days of the King's Men: the ability to break 'the script down into relevant "passions"' and to effect 'speedy transitions' between them.[57] The predominant passion of *Macbeth* was what for Dryden characterised Shakespeare's approach to narrative: he 'generally moves more terror' in his 'bolder and more fiery genius'.[58] Amid all the scene changes and musical embellishments, the passions of Shakespeare's design must emerge.

In Davenant's adaptation the company acted not only the 'passions' of their characters but a heightened consciousness of destiny, as if not just performers of character but commentators on their place within the narrative: '[t]heir words seem to foretell some dire predictions', says Macduff after listening to a new witches' song in Act II. It is the language of baroque theatre, the actors buoyed by a heightened state of feeling and of knowledge of their predicament. Such language serves the need actors felt for connection with the plot in an age before scripts. Davenant would rewrite Shakespeare with a consciousness of clarifying what might now be called 'objectives' for actors and audiences: he has the Macbeths recriminate with each other in Act IV – 'had not your breath / Blown my Ambition up' – before Lady Macbeth is confronted by Duncan's ghost.[59] Each actor draws the arc of the other's opposing trajectory, Mary Betterton succumbing to the supernatural as Thomas has learned to master it.

The new scenery was the instrument of the passions. It is easy to claim, in Gildon's words, that it worked 'to the Destruction of good playing'.[60] Soon after the February performances an anonymous poet complained that

> Now empty shows must want of sense supply.
> Angels shall dance, and Macbeths witches fly.[61]

Occasionally, the scenic language of medieval Scotland lapses quaintly into that of Restoration London: on the lookout for Banquo, Macbeth's three hired thugs see someone 'alight at the park gate' on their way from the 'palace'.[62] But as Barbara A. Murray has written, '[i]n all these basic settings there is potential for creating, by candlelight, a sense of unrevealed possibilities and eerie unexplored places'.[63] The freshly painted scenes provided a new medium for expressing the play's shifting world of shadows, its oscillations between the intimate and the public, the domestic and the uncanny. Such a style exercises a claim on any audience's attention equal to the white glare of *Macbeth*-à-la-Brecht.[64] While its flying witches were creatures of the sceptical Restoration, wonders wrought from physics, in their impact they mirrored Betterton's own ghostly encounters, his voice and body raised to the heights in the face of the supernatural. It was a mode he would soon revisit in a court performance of *Doctor Faustus* and continue to be enchanted by in revivals of old repertory such as *The Merry Devil of Edmonton*.[65]

If no other incentive were needed to ensure that actors and scenes worked together to produce an effect described by Pepys as 'proper and suitable', for the performance of 18 February the company was expecting royalty. A court party attended 'Mackbeth' that day, further to a court performance in 1666 and, intriguingly, a visit by the Prince of Orange for the Bonfire Night showing in 1670.[66] Yet James, the company patron, preferred the tale of exile and restitution that was the company's other Shakespearean spectacular of the 1670s, *The Tempest*, which had received five royal visits in as many months during the winter and spring of 1667–8.[67] *Macbeth* was, for the Stuarts of 1673, as ripe with equivocation as it had ever been.[68] How must the third soliloquy have sounded to an audience that feared Charles's successor could only be his Catholic brother James: 'Upon my head they plac'd a fruitless Crown, / And put a barren Sceptre in my hand …' (III.i.61–2). Betterton's professional immersion in the role, his engagement with Macbeth's passions, was a characteristic mark of political discretion.

The new scenic set-pieces were hardly free of politics either. Act IV, Scene i of the play has too much 'divertisement' to survive most modern directors. It is the moment when the complex theatrical illusion and psychological drama of Banquo's ghost turn into spectacle – illusions whose greater technological complexity risks reducing to 'empty shows'. For seventeenth-century audiences it carried the thrill of mock-liturgy, exploiting popular associations between witchcraft and Roman Catholicism – a premonition of the way the company would, in spite of its patron, exploit anti-Catholic feeling at the end of the decade.[69] In this performance Hecate descends, a cauldron sinks, witches sing and dance, and 'a shadow of eight Kings … pass by'. For once, Davenant's text has simplified the special

Illustration 5 Macbeth and the line of kings by Francois Boitard, from
Nicholas Rowe, ed., *The Works of Mr William Shakespear*, 6 vols. (London, 1709)

effects. Shakespeare's armed head, bloody child and 'child crowned, with
a tree in his hand' are banished and Hecate speaks their lines, Sandford's
grave bass and leering mouth spelling out the future:

> Macbeth shall like a lucky Monarch reign
> Till Birnam Wood shall come to Dunsinane.[70]

An illustration in Rowe's Shakespeare gives some idea of how the scene
might have looked, even though its cavernous setting naturalises the
effects achievable with Restoration scenery, and the absence of Hecate
helps to suggest that the engraver, Boitard, worked as much from a reading of Shakespeare's original as stage practice. There is the expected con-
figuration of characters: Macbeth and the witches downstage, framing the
line of kings with Banquo at their tail. But there is an oddity.

Macbeth and Banquo are Restoration aristocrats: Betterton (by inference) in his coat, hat, breeches and wig, Smith bewigged and convention-
ally ghostly in a night shirt. The 'shadow of eight kings', however, recall an

earlier period in their beards and flowing, natural hair, and the one next to Banquo looks singularly like Charles I. To represent the idea of monarchy past, the paintings of Van Dyck might be a good place to start. Although 'period' *Macbeth* was slow to emerge – Charles Macklin is credited with introducing 'old Scottish garb' to the play in 1773 – time travel had somehow to be represented.[71] Whether it was Boitard's fancy or Betterton's, it would be hard to escape from the idea that a parade of kings showing the true lineage of the Scots crown should somehow include the royal martyr himself. In Shakespeare, the last of the eight famously 'bears a glass' which shows Macbeth 'many more', perhaps an allusion to James I's supposed presence at the first performance.[72] Davenant disposes of the mirror, having found the father. It is the perfect answer to the inherent problem of the scene: at the high point of spectacle, draw on symbolism that silences criticism. To Betterton fell the line that chimed with his period's deepest trauma: 'Thy Crown offends my sight.'

The 1673 *Macbeth* was one product of a risky process. It is a sign of how confidently Betterton and Harris began in 1668 that they immediately set about planning the most daunting enterprise for any company: financing, building and occupying a new theatre. The idea was perhaps in the air when Davenant died and so informed the new share structure. Betterton and Harris's pitch to their reconstituted group of actor-shareholders must have been persuasive indeed, but their starting point would have been the limitations of Lincoln's Inn Fields, a conversion with limited technical capacity. While it had housed the first painted scenes in an English public theatre, it was too small for the effects Betterton and Harris had in mind. Crammed among houses in Portugal Row, it discouraged access by carriage – essential for attracting the highest class of patrons, especially in the winter months. Paving would not reach Portugal Row for decades.[73] Adjoining were Lincoln's Inn Fields themselves, which, although surrounded by fashionable residences, witnessed too many robberies and violent assaults for comfort, and were still being used as a place of execution and corporal punishment. One attempt to smarten it up – or perhaps simply eliminate competition – had been made in an order of April 1664 prohibiting 'puppet playes and dumb shewes in Lyncolnes Inn fields'.[74] A bigger theatre, better equipped and on a better site would allow the company to refresh the existing repertory and create new entertainment for wealthier patrons.

In the aftermath of the Great Fire, with compulsory purchase orders abounding, there was a glut of vacant sites.[75] Finding one fell to Harris and

John Roffey, a part shareholder since 1662 who would later attempt without success to sue Betterton over the status of his holding.[76] Success came through old-fashioned social networking. It was one of the company's best allies at court, the Earl of Dorset, who obliged, not without heading off other interest; twenty-six years later, he would evict the rivals who had taken it over.[77] The company agreed with Dorset's agent a site which lay just inside the fire zone: the southern end of Dorset Garden, at the top of Dorset Stairs, and therefore accessible from the river as well as down Dorset Street, leading south from Fleet Street. If Newcourt's 1658 map is any guide, 'garden' meant an orchard. On foot, the journey there was not entirely sightly. Audiences would skirt the Fleet Ditch and pass Bridewell, re-built after the fire, but it was an improvement.

The site was leased in the names of Harris and Roffey on 11 or 12 August 1670, shortly after Betterton's thirty-fifth birthday. The company was to pay £130 in annual rent on a thirty-nine year lease and the shareholders expected to raise £3000 for building costs.[78] Not everyone was pleased. Pre-war tension between theatre and city authorities surfaced when the Lord Mayor petitioned against the project, but work went ahead.[79] Evelyn saw it in construction on 26 June 1671 and wrote: 'I went home, steping in at the Theater, to see the new Machines for the intended scenes, which were indeede very costly, & magnificent.' The new machines may have been the fruit of one of Betterton's two known trips overseas. If he did, as an anecdote has it, go to Paris on the orders of the king to study the very latest in French practice, the winter of 1670–1 would have been prime time for getting the new building right, although some accounts put the visit later.[80]

Unsubstantiated tradition says that the company engaged the young Christopher Wren to design the theatre. An engraving of the river frontage made by William Dolle in 1673 exudes neo-classical elegance: three bays, a fine porch extending the sixty-foot width of the building, two storeys of apartments and dressing rooms, and a fine upper storey topped by an ogee dome, which presumably masked the more functional flying tower which was now a *sine qua non*. The arms of the Duke of York sat at the top, and Hotson reports statues of Melpomene and Thalia, the muses of tragedy and comedy. But the building Dolle drew is unlike anything else Wren designed, who in any case had been appointed in 1669 to the post of Chief Architect to the Crown, a major public office charged with seeing through the measures agreed under the two post-fire Rebuilding Acts; John Webb, whom he had beaten to the post, and who had experience of designing the theatre at Whitehall, was a more likely choice, but the consensus is that it was the work of Robert Hooke, with Grinling Gibbons engaged to carve the 'capitals, cornices and eagles'.[81] Of course, the Dolle engraving might be idealised. While it is easy to imagine the Bettertons exchanging compliments on the landing, it is too elaborate for a major public building which, once the site had been confirmed, went from design to opening in just fifteen months. Suspicions of jerry-building lingered. Wren became involved soon after the first night in November 1671, following rumours of a defective wall which the Lord Chamberlain ordered him to inspect.[82] Eighteen months later Betterton and company made a temporary return to Lincoln's Inn Fields while work was done on the stage machinery.[83] Briefly, the investment seemed precarious.

The biggest of the company's problems was the cost over-run. £3000 had been projected, and £9000 was paid. It is a familiar story – management and owners pressing for prompt completion, builders charging extra. The conditions created by the Fire played their part. Builders' wages rose steeply and carpenters, bricklayers, stone masons and glaziers poured into London to take advantage; still, there was an acute shortage of labour to deal with the crisis. The Duke's Company had mounted a new scheme of shareholding to finance the building, with one share costing £450, up to eight times the usual annual dividend, so it seems miraculous that the new building could be afforded even on the basis of its projected cost. Betterton bought a half-share, laying out £102 10s in cash and promising the rest from future revenue; he planned for a twenty-five per cent return on his investment but realised only about fifteen because of the inflated building cost.[84] Harris, prone to thinking big, bought two and three-quarter shares at a cost of more than £1200, presumably on the back of a complex borrowing arrangement. Like the Bettertons, he got free accommodation at the theatre for his pains, although he sub-let to another shareholder, Richard Middlemore, who managed the lucrative business of selling fruit in the theatre;[85] like them, too, he took advantage of the circular system of building shares. As a company shareholder, he paid rent to himself as a building sharer, after he had used his company shares as collateral in buying his building shares. No wonder the Bettertons were keen to keep an eye on the place from their apartment; as he later deposed, 'by his nearness and diligence he hath several times preserved the Playhouse from being burnt'.[86]

In later years, Betterton would be accused of loaning the company money for Dorset Garden and charging astronomic interest on the repayments, in part to pay back the loan he had taken out to fund the investment in the first place.[87] The charges were not specifically denied. Benign patriarch he may have been when it came to destitute playwrights or maimed actors, but he was also exceptionally shrewd at calculating the return he could expect from a business in which he was at once shareholder, manager, employee and accountant. A favourable gloss on the system of building shares is that it was designed to create more income for the whole company by contributing to its improved estate, but it was also risky and divisive. Whatever the box-office takings, the dividend to other shareholders, actors among them, would be restricted or potentially nullified, since the rent repayments of £7 per acting day were deducted first as costs. The effect was to align the company's financial fortunes more closely with his own, and it would work as long as he could satisfy his creditors. Others less adept at managing debt would in years to come ensure that the theatre fell into the hands of people who had only a financial interest in it. In that respect Betterton's managerial style differed from Davenant's. Where his former master had readily sold shares to generate income, Betterton concentrated his risks, confident in his ability to find and manage creditors. It was an approach based on the desire to maximise his fortune and minimise outside interference in the running of the theatre. Future disputes would end with the theatre's accounts closed even to company scrutiny, and Betterton was not disposed to give details of his financial dealings. His pre-eminence among his fellows was justification enough. If he did not, whether by temperament, company style or prevailing cultural conditions, claim the mantle of 'stardom', he made sure that he acquired its economic benefits.

In the event, the Dorset Garden project gained from two enormous slices of luck. With such complexity of debt everyone could feel grateful for the simple benefaction which came of good court connections: having 'been often there and like[d] it', the king contributed £1000 to help with costs.[88] Dorset Garden might still have failed altogether if the only rivals in town had not started to implode. They did not look like doing so in the winter of 1670–1, when Dryden's *Conquest of Granada* set new standards for heroic drama in terms of both literary respectability and box-office success.[89] Amid the swagger of success, taunts about Dorset Garden surfaced. With its 'gaudy scenes' it would be the sort of place where you might hope for Mozart but get Lloyd Webber.[90] It was management's job to look out for such tactics and respond. Betterton and Harris opened their new theatre on 9 November 1671 in low-key style, trusting to an old favourite, Dryden's *Sir Martin Mar-All*. Either the new scenic technology was not ready or they wanted a sure-fire success to recoup money; it ran for three days with full houses even though it had recently been shown at Lincoln's Inn Fields and at court.[91] Part of the same strategy was a further reliable comedy in which Betterton did not appear to best advantage, Etherege's *The Comical Revenge*.[92] It was a cautious start in which neither leading actor nor eye-catching scenery would play a significant role, Betterton's prudence as a manager characteristically outweighing his ego as an actor. But in December the time had come to match *The Conquest of Granada* with an historical spectacular of their own, John Crowne's *The History of Charles the Eighth of France*. A French subject for the new French scenery: Betterton played the title role and Downes says the production was 'all new cloath'd'.[93] But it flopped, running for no more than six intermittent performances. Not until 1673 would the theatre come into its own, with spectacular new productions such as *The Empress of Morocco* and the kind of event Betterton had dreamed of before a brick was laid: a lavish new *Hamlet* 'adorned and embellished with very curious dances between the acts'.[94]

Optimism in the King's Company was short-lived. Only two months after Dorset Garden had opened the King's Company's theatre at Bridges Street burned down, killing 'Mr Bell, one of the actors in that house'.[95] They moved temporarily to Lincoln's Inn Fields. Deep in debt, Killigrew managed to oversee the building of a new theatre. Less spacious than Dorset Garden, this first Theatre Royal Drury Lane opened on 26 March 1674 and was to prove a better venue than Dorset Garden for plays built from the core skills of writers and actors.[96] The problem was that Killigrew had a serious issue with his actors, from junior figures such as Edward Gavill, arrested in 1672 for abusing Killigrew and his colleagues 'with scandalous & reproachful Words', to senior members of the company such as Hart, Mohun and Kynaston.[97] Five years before, Killigrew had observed only half-jokingly that a house prostitute might keep them in order.[98] In a succession of disputes in 1675, he accused his troupe of numerous routine breaches of discipline, such as not turning up to rehearsals, quitting without notice, eating out or buying clothes at the company's expense, or walking off with costumes and props; and some quite ingenious ones, including sub-contracting roles to other actors, taking costumes to the pawn shop and crowding round the treasurer after the show so that no one could tell how the day's takings were divided.[99] Even on tour the difference between the two companies was obvious. When the Duke's Company erected a theatre in Oxford in 1670 it needed protection from unruly citizens; when the King's Company visited the same city four years later it was the other way round, the actors 'guilty of such great rudenesses [as] going about the

Town breakeing of windows and committing many other unpardonable rudenesses'.[100] The Duke's actor-shareholders had made the transition from childhood to business maturity while their King's counterparts were still throwing toys from the pram. There followed departures, futile royal commands and a company sword fight 'which occasioned the wounding of several'. [101]

With competitors like that, Betterton scarcely needed friends. The real surprise is that the King's Company was still able to mount the premieres of such key Restoration plays as Wycherley's *The Country Wife* and *The Plain Dealer*, and Dryden's *All for Love*. Dryden bore none of the latter commodity for the company which had staged nine of his previous plays and in 1678 he offered his next, *The Kind Keeper*, to someone who could be trusted to deal professionally with it, Thomas Betterton, and the association would last as long as Dryden's playwriting career.[102] Minor playwrights followed him.[103]

By then, in the late 1670s, Henry Harris had begun to ease himself out of his responsibilities. Joint management had worked and a smooth transition was effected to allow another senior actor, William Smith, to take over Harris's responsibilities from 1678. Again Betterton would form an effective partnership with someone of livelier social talents. Smith was of the mid-1630s generation and had trained as a barrister; he shared Harris's glamorous looks and social instincts. He had been with the company since the early 1660s. In 1666, he was reckless to a degree even Harris could not match, killing a man 'upon a quarrel in play', as Pepys wrote. Showing more concern for the perpetrator than the victim, Pepys believed that the noose was ready, 'which makes everybody sorry, he being a good actor, and they say a good man'.[104] But Smith got off and returned to acting. He became a shareholder in the Duke's Company in 1674, and on the basis of that and his management role accumulated the substantial fortune of £5300. He combined Betterton's prudence with Harris's *joie de vivre*, and when he died in 1695 his executor was charged with giving £50 to a young man whose name was to be found in a sealed trunk. Betterton he called his 'friend and oldest acquaintance' and entrusted him with the mystery man's education.[105]

There was one significant difference between Smith and his predecessor. In 1685, the year of James II's coronation, Harris's portfolio of court appointments was whittled down to the single job of Yeoman of the Revels. He did not regain favour until William and Mary were installed, when he was reconfirmed as Engraver of Seals and, a year later, chief engraver at the Mint. Court offices, as Dryden found to his cost, went with known political sympathies.[106] In 1683, when most people had accepted that James would succeed to the crown, Harris was described to Secretary of State Jenkins as 'a venomous fellow'.[107] William Smith leaned in another direction. In the will he made on 19 November 1688, days after William of Orange's announcement of invasion, Smith declared that he was to enter the army of James II 'at his own expense'; he was 'zealously attached' to the Jacobite cause. Whether he had time to join up is doubtful but he retired temporarily from acting in 1688, returning in the year of his death. Not for nothing did he specialise in roles like Willmore in Aphra Behn's *The Rover* which were readily associated with the values of the company patron.[108] When a courtier struck Smith 'in a Dispute ... behind the Scenes', the courtier was disciplined.[109]

The succession of 1678 is significant because it occurred at precisely the time when the company's identification with its patron was about to take on unprecedented controversy. For some, it had always been possible to equate the values of spectacular theatre with high-church ritual:

By the Harmony of words we elevate the mind to a sense of Devotion, as our solemn Musick, which is inarticulate Poesie, does in Churches; and by the lively images of piety, adorned by action, through the senses allure the Soul: which while it is charmed in a silent joy of what it sees and hears, is struck at the same time with a secret veneration of things Celestial, and is wound up insensibly into the practice of that which it admires.[110]

In drama as in religion, belief is multi-sensory, an act of irrational seduction. Yet, as *Macbeth* showed, such power could be used to exploit popular anti-Catholic feeling as well, and the Popish Plot years that began as Smith joined Betterton in management created serious dilemmas for the business all London knew as the Duke's Company.

CHAPTER 9

In the Company of the Duke: Betterton and Catholic politics in the 1670s

The issue came to a head on two afternoons in February 1680 that temporarily closed the Dorset Garden theatre. Audiences were already plummeting and censorship increasing when 'drunken people' crashed the auditorium mid-performance, creating 'abominable disorders', calling 'all the women whores and the men rogues' and its ducal patron a 'rascal'. As so often, the king's French Catholic mistress, the Duchess of Portsmouth, was the subject of 'several reprochfull speeches'. Lanterns and candles were thrown at the actors and by royal order the theatre went dark for a fortnight.[1] Betterton had reason to feel worried but also slightly aggrieved. Throughout the 1670s the company had squared commercial well-being with the Duke's convictions, which had long been public knowledge; at the same time, it had recently sought to capitalise on the intense public feeling that characterised the Popish Plot crisis by mounting anti-Catholic shows. If February 1680 posed a stern choice between loyalty and box-office success, it also suggested that where his patron's religion was concerned, Betterton's long mature instinct for both might be confounded.

The question of the Duke was one Betterton had had a long time to ponder. As early as 18 February 1661 Pepys had worried about 'a professed friend to the Catholiques' ascending the throne. Never the 'leader of the Catholic community in England', James did not convert formally until 1669, although he had always employed an unusual number of Catholics.[2] Come his exclusion from public office by the 1673 Test Act, followed by his renunciation in 1676 of all Anglican services, lines of political demarcation were firm enough for him to have acquired a reputation as 'a man for arbitrary power', 'heady, violent and bloody'.[3] Such qualities might make him an inspiration for drama but they did little for his profile as a patron.

It was just as well he was not inclined to do much for his company that was 'heady' or 'arbitrary', indeed, to do very much at all. James was an enthusiastic theatregoer in the decade after the Restoration, but there is little sign that he took much interest in the company named

Illustration 6 James, Duke of York, by Godfrey Kneller (1684).
Reproduced by permission of the National Portrait Gallery

for him except during the dispute with Harris, whose stage cardinals he admired. Of the thirteen performances Pepys says he attended, only four were at the Duke's: *Henry VIII* on 22 December 1663; *Love in a Tub* on 29 October 1666; *The Sullen Lovers* on 2 May 1668; and *Macbeth* on 21 December 1668. Over the period 1666–80, each company gave about the same number of performances (around 120, an average of eight per year with a decline towards the end) at court or with royalty present; the records sometimes say when the King was there, but not the Duke. With the court, substantially the most popular Duke's Company plays were Dryden's *Sir Martin Mar-All* and the Dryden/Davenant *Tempest*, which has been read as part of a trend to represent 'loyal subjects rather than powerful kings', and as a commentary on the fate of James's father-in-law, Clarendon.[4] Its ability to evoke both republican and royalist destinies, married to an unrivalled degree of spectacle, meant that it was regularly performed for royalty.

If the limit of James's profession in the early 1660s was friendship to Catholics, it extended to tolerance of their presence in the Duke's

Company. Tolerance, however, had been in short supply in Betterton's dealings with Matthew Medbourne, whose roles reflected faith and modest acting ability. Casting *Henry VIII* in 1663 had given Davenant the chance of a characteristic casting irony, doubling Medbourne as the Roman Cardinal Campeius and the English Archbishop Cranmer. Medbourne spent his lay-off during the years of plague and fire writing a fervent Catholic tragedy, *Saint Cecily or the Converted Twins*, and dedicated it in 1667 to the relation of the Duke's whom everyone knew to be of the old faith, his sister-in-law, Catherine of Braganza. If Medbourne tried to interest Davenant in it he failed; the play was never acted. Perhaps as a result, his anti-puritan version of *Tartuffe* was acted by the King's Company and dedicated to another prominent Catholic, the Earl of Castlerising.[5]

He would have cause to recall fondly a life of middling roles and rejected plays when, on 26 November 1678, he was sent to Newgate charged with high treason, having had the misfortune earlier that year of meeting, at the Pheasant Inn, a dissembler of a different order. Titus Oates swore that Medbourne intended to assassinate the King. Before he could be tried, Medbourne fell ill; unfortunate, wrote a contemporary observer, for a man 'whose good parts deserv'd a better fate than to die in prison ... through a too forward and indiscreet Zeal for a mistaken Religion'; a month later Betterton suffered the nearer loss of his brother Charles.[6] Throughout the saga there was no suggestion that the Duke's Company was, as it would be alleged of Pepys's navy office, some hotbed of Catholic sedition; on the contrary, Medbourne might easily be represented as an outsider who had earned management's mistrust.[7]

As his family background suggests, Betterton appears to have been a man of mainstream Anglican principles. The fortunes of the House of Stuart occupied significant shelf space in his household, but so did the evils of the Catholic Church. Among the ten anti-Catholic texts in his library were quartos of *An Anatomy of the French and Spanish Faction in England* and *Mysteries of State carried on by the Spanish Faction in England*, and the octavo of Thomas Bennett's three-part *Confutation of Popery*.[8] He also collected the literature of Protestant patriotism: Strype's *Cranmer's Memorials* and Hakewill's *Apology of the Power and Providence of God*.[9] He championed *Paradise Lost* before it was fashionable to do so and his painting of Henry VIII is unlikely to have been simply a memorial of his performance of the part; an anecdote casts him as the friend of Archbishop and arch anti-Catholic John Tillotson, who was curious to know why acting was more powerful than a sermon, and it was Tillotson's preaching against Catholicism in 1672 that persuaded the Duke of York to boycott the Chapel Royal.[10] A poem of 1705, admittedly as much an amused reaction to his post-Collier respectability as his religious leanings, casts him as 'pious Betterton' bent on 'the Work of Reformation ... To teach the forward Youth Morality'.[11] But just as Betterton thrived on playing such inversions of the symbolic king as Macbeth, his actor's imagination comprehended the mind of the other when it came to religion, taking in, besides such books as *Moyers pour la Conversion de tous les Heretiques*, 'Six Italian Views of St. *Peter's* Church, &c. at *Rome*'.[12] He was also a friend of Catholics such as Gildon and Pope.

So did Betterton dodge the lantern-chuckers of February 1680 with a grain of sympathy? Was the Duke's religion, after all, of professional interest to the company only as an embarrassment to be tiptoed round? The realities of repertory life suggest not, and three episodes spanning the 1670s show why. The first is the company's best documented performance outside London: at Dover, in May 1670, for representatives of the English and French courts. Although hardly anyone knew it, the future of the kingdom's religion was at stake. The second episode is the first success enjoyed by the strongly Yorkist Thomas Otway, Betterton's care for whom was not solely motivated by his commercial value to the company or his Bettertonian blend of what Gildon would call 'Nature and Propriety'.[13] An adapter of both Racine and Shakespeare, Otway appealed to Betterton's own francophile instincts by mixing French and English styles in the opportunities he gave actors to perform extremes of passion; once in print, he trumpeted his allegiance not to the company but its French-leaning (or simply French) patrons, with dedications to the Duke of York, his duchess and the Duchess of Portsmouth.[14] The apparatus of 'paratexts' encouraged playwrights to declare a political hand after the live performance; while actors and managers sometimes benefited from concealing theirs, the memorial nature of the printed text associated actors as much as authors with dedicatees.[15] Nowhere was that more the case than in the play that occupied at least ten consecutive afternoons in June 1676, *Don Carlos*.[16] Finally, this chapter returns to the violence of February 1680, reviewing the dilemmas and repertory decisions that faced Betterton during the Popish Plot crisis. The three episodes form a microcosm of Betterton's career during the 1670s, but also of the period's political theatre. Dover 1670 was akin to a court masque, with honed scripts and oblique political allusions. In 1676, court politics stepped out into the rough grandeur of popular theatre, but by 1680 the same theatre was the site of factional drama which, while it enlivened the repertory, risked silencing it altogether.

Thanks to John Downes a rich account survives of the Dover event:

[Shadwell's *The Sullen Lovers*] had wonderful success, being acted 12 days together, when our Company were commanded to *Dover*, in *May* 1670. The King with all his Court meeting his sister, the Dutchess of *Orleans* there. This Comedy and *Sir Salomon Single*, pleas'd Madam the Dutchess, and the whole Court extremely. The *French* Court wearing then excessive short lac'd coats; some scarlet, some blew, with broad wast belts; Mr. *Nokes* having at that time one shorter than the *French* fashion, to act *Sir Arthur Addle* in; *the Duke of Monmouth* gave Mr. *Nokes* his Sword and belt from his side, and buckled it on himself, on purpose to ape the French; that Mr. *Nokes* lookt more like a drest up Ape, than a *Sir Arthur:* which upon his first entrance on the stage, put the King and Court to an excessive laughter; at which the *French* look'd very Shaggrin, to see themselves ap'd by such a buffoon as *Sir Arthur*. Mr. *Nokes* kept the Duke's sword to his dying day.[17]

The company was well paid for its contribution to Anglo-French relations, even allowing for travel, board and lodging: where a performance at court usually brought in £20, and a series of performances at Windsor four years later would earn £74, for this assignment Betterton and company earned £500.[18] Presumably a similar sum was promised to the King's Company, who took over when the Duke's had finished.[19]

For Betterton, the occasion was the outcome of considerable planning with contacts at court. Sir Salomon would be a distinctive comic role for him, one that drew on his capacity for 'repressed passion' and 'potential physical threat', for his 'dextrous emotional and physical technique'.[20] It also required the self-irony that came of marrying his line in tragic tyrants to a comic, domestic setting, and the blend of registers continued to appeal to royal audiences into the eighteenth century.[21] But the significance of the role goes beyond questions of personal repertory. At Dover, the ironies generated by this symbolic king among actors played outwards to the invited and self-conscious audience.

Charles II was, as a handful of observers knew, engaged in an act of unique duplicity. Officially he was negotiating a new commercial treaty with France but on 22 May 1670 he had signed another, secret agreement to a personal conversion to Catholicism, war against the Dutch, a French subsidy which would reduce his dependence on Parliament, and French military support should any of those undertakings prove dangerously unpopular with his own people.[22] Negotiations had been going on for more than a year with the approval of Arlington and Clifford, Catholic sympathisers within Charles's 'Cabal' of senior ministers, and had been entrusted to openly Catholic members of his inner circle: the Earl of Arundell; Henry Jermyn, Viscount St Alban's and confidant of the King's mother; and Sir Richard Bellings, Queen Catherine's private secretary. The chief contact on the French side was the ambassador, Charles Colbert de Croissy, while a conduit of information was the Duchess of Orléans, sister-in-law to the French king. Her value to the enterprise outlived her. Eight days after her return to France, she died. The London theatres were silenced but a trip to Oxford, involving the erection of a temporary theatre, filled the gap for Betterton and company.[23] Grief sat well with diplomacy: the pretext for the 'official', commercial treaty was the visit of the Marquis de Bellefonds to London in July 1670 to condole with Charles on her death.

Secrecy and theatre are strange bedfellows, and while it would strain probability to imagine the actors knew what was really going on behind the scenes, there was more to *Sir Salomon* than met the eye of the prompter. For the limited facilities available at Dover, Betterton needed plays that did not require extensive scenery or music, and that meant comedy. The outstanding comic success of the previous three years had been Dryden's *Sir Martin Mar-All*, but instead the company chose Shadwell's first comedy, *The Sullen Lovers*, now two years old and not by any means a repertory staple, and *Sir Salomon Single*, so new that the Dover performance came at the end of its initial run of twelve days.[24] Both plays exemplified a rising fashion in free translations from Molière.[25] Shadwell took *The Sullen Lovers* from *Les Fâcheux* of 1661, while *Sir Salomon* exploited the success of *L'École des Femmes*, first performed on Boxing Day 1662 at the Palais Royal and repeated thirty-two times between then and Easter 1663.[26] Molière himself had created the role of Arnolphe, the middle-aged man grooming a child-bride to be sure of a faithful wife. The play was well known to members of the French diplomatic mission in 1670. It had been performed in 1663 at the house of Colbert's elder brother;[27] the dedicatee of the first edition was the Duchess of Orléans. Although *L'École des Femmes* had caused controversy for its alleged vulgarity, performing an English version of this French favourite must have seemed an embodiment of *entente cordiale* which would show the two nations' dramatic traditions to be as complementary as their royal families. For Betterton, to play the part created by the living French master was to make himself the heir of both, the master of Shakespeare in tragedy, of Molière in comedy.

While the French contingent probably did not know much about Thomas Shadwell, the author of *Sir Salomon* was familiar to them at least by repute. John Caryll had written one play for the Duke's Company, a 1667 adaptation of Shakespeare's *Richard III* called *The English Princess*. It is a defence of legitimate royal succession that deduces the inevitability of Charles II's reign from that of Richard III.[28] Betterton had taken the leading role. But it was not as a playwright that Caryll achieved distinction.[29] Born into an old Sussex family of Catholics, Caryll had returned from exile to write a defence of English Catholics, 'Not guilty, or, the plea of the Roman Catholick in England', which, though never published, was intended to contribute to Charles's emerging religious policy; its stand was moderate and firmly in favour of toleration rather than aggressive counter-reformation. His sister Mary, resident in Ghent, founded a convent in Dunkirk with the assistance of Charles II and the Duchess of York. As Abbess of Dunkirk she often provided accommodation for travellers to Dover.

Sir Salomon is the work of a man well versed in the observation of domestic politics. Molière's Arnolphe is a middle-aged bachelor anxious to avoid the misery suffered by husbands whose worldly wives deceive them – an innocent who professes experience, justly but poignantly confused by his failure to secure his wife's affection. Caryll's counterpart is more calculating but also more reckless. He has suffered in the past and has a son; he plans to disinherit the boy when he remarries but has told only his servant, Timothy, and his lawyer (for Betterton, the role drew on his line in libertines as well as tyrants). Caryll's opening scene completely refocuses Molière's play and lends it, in May 1670, a fine political edge. Where Molière stages a conversation between Arnolphe and his confidant Chrysalde on the morality of his choosing an uneducated girl, Caryll shows Sir Salomon talking to his steward, Timothy, about the legal consequences of his intended marriage. Sir Salomon's estate has been settled away from his son and onto his wife; he is advised that 'the settlement is not good in law' since Sir Salomon might be judged 'not *Compos Mentis*' to 'throw away his whole Fortune upon an unknown Woman' and at the same time disinherit his son. This is a significant departure from Molière's play, which uses its notary scene (IV.ii) as the occasion of comic buffoonery. Timothy ironically commends the 'secret Conduct of this Design' – so secret, in fact, that Salomon's wife is unaware of who he really is, because he has assumed a false name. To this Sir Salomon proclaims the beauty of secrecy: 'O Timothy: The Art of Secrecy is the Secret of the World. 'Tis the Rudder, that silently governs the whole of men's affairs. A Secret well kept, like Powder close ramm'd, does certain execution ...'[30] Again Caryll finds something in Molière to turn to his peculiar purpose. Arnolphe is a man who prides himself on his ability to expose the secrets of other men's cuckoldry to the world.[31] Timothy warns his master of the harsh judgement which awaits him in the world's eyes for his betrayal of his 'blood and estate', but Salomon defends his conduct on the basis that since children owe everything to their parents, 'when Sons Rebellious prove' the natural bond between them is cancelled.

The end of the play, which sees the cunning Salomon banished in shame, similarly presents a critical view of his underhand dealings. The father of his intended bride closes the performance by saying that everything has been concluded 'to the Satisfaction of all Parties, except *Sir Salomon Single*',

> Whose disappointed Stratagems advise,
> To shun the dangerous Sin of being too wise:
> For, as Extremes on Globes at last [do] touch,
> So Wit in Folly centres, when too much.
> Love changes Natures order: in his School
> The Young are wise; the Old Man is the Fool.[32]

This is in tune with a number of contemporary critiques of Charles's conduct, from Rochester's alleged extempore epitaph to the torrent of francophobe invective directed at his mistress of the later 1670s, Louise de Kéroualle, Duchess of Portsmouth.[33] Derek Hughes detects a similar tone in the play: '*Sir Salomon*', he argues, portrays the providential ending of tyranny based on 'arbitrary acts of exclusion: disinheritance, and denial of education'.[34] The casting of Betterton in the title role raised the stakes: Salomon is 'a fool of a different order, meaner, more powerful', and the Duke's Company's leading tragic actor increased the 'rhetorical register' of the part.[35] In Salomon he found a symbolic king prepared to cheat not only a mistress or a partner at cards, but the family of which he was, symbolically, the father – his own nation.

The play reflects the political fears of its author, a moderate Catholic anxious for extreme measures to be avoided. Translating Molière was an ideal means of clothing the message in a diplomatic language befitting the occasion. A less oblique variant of such language was used at almost exactly the same time by one of the Duke's Company's own personnel. Medbourne, fresh from his release, wrote his *Tartuffe* for production by the King's Company in 1670. He recast the anti-Jansenist slant of his original in anti-Puritan terms, giving his play the subtitle of *The French Puritan*. If *Sir Salomon* obliquely warns against taking desperate measures to restore the true faith, Medbourne's *Tartuffe* gives cruder prominence to the forces of domestic opposition. But there is also a subtler message that underlines the similarities between this play and Caryll's, and indicates its pertinence to Dover. In Hughes's words, this 'is the most obviously topical of the Molière adaptations, not only in its concern with a hypocritical zealot who threatens ... to dispossess an established family of its heritage but in its portrayal of a fundamentally decent man [Orgon] who has been compromised by association with treason'.[36] Hughes exempts the King from blame: although Medbourne could not, like Molière, represent his concluding intervention as god-like, he does envisage 'a benevolent figure to whom intercession will be made'.[37] But this underestimates the parallels between Orgon and Sir Salomon, or Orgon and Charles. The uncertainty which hangs over the exact premiere of *Sir Salomon* applies in equal measure to *Tartuffe*. Hume suggests 'Spring 1670', while Nicoll states that the premiere was at the Theatre Royal 'c. April 1670'; the title page of the first edition records that it had been 'lately acted' at the King's Theatre.[38] It was not common for Duke's actors to write plays for their rivals, and since we know that the King's Company went to Dover immediately after the Duke's, it is likely that Medbourne's *Tartuffe* was intended to complement the two other Molière translations which had just been performed there. Taken together, they offer contrasting reflections on the situation of English Catholicism, part of a conscious promotion and testing of issues relating to Catholic traditions and people.

Unless this was all an extraordinary coincidence – or Betterton and Harris are to be credited with extraordinary diplomatic insight – one of the very few people who knew about the purpose of the Dover gathering must have come up with the idea. James A. Winn argues that the *éminences grises* behind Dryden's Catholic-inspired 1669 play, *Tyrannick Love*, were Arlington and Clifford, closet Catholics and in charge of the Treaty of Dover negotiations.[39] Clifford would be the dedicatee of Dryden's *Amboyna* four years later; the dedication speaks of 'so many *Favors*, and those so great, Conferr'd on me by Your Lordship these many yeares'.[40] Arlington could be appealed to for adjudication in theatrical matters, and would become Lord Chamberlain in September 1674.[41] Although the two men shared the secret of the Dover negotiations, they brought different perspectives: Clifford as an emotional enthusiast, Arlington as a reluctant convert whose commitment was often questioned, a man accused of lacking the courage to declare his real convictions.[42] If the break-neck imagery of *Tyrannick Love* suggests Clifford's prompting rather than Arlington's, the diplomatic caution of *Sir Salomon*, whose performance at Dover connived in a plot while distancing itself from it, seems pure Arlington.

However carefully the company had prepared for its Dover visit, instructions of a different kind disturbed the performance of *Sir Salomon*. As if setting out to leaven its Catholic sympathies, Dryden had dedicated *Tyrannick Love* to the Duke of Monmouth, riskily attributing his

Illustration 7 James Scott, Duke of Monmouth, from the studio of
Godfrey Kneller (1678). Reproduced by permission of the National Portrait Gallery

attractions to some 'uncommon purpose' devised by providence.[43] At
Dover, Monmouth goaded Betterton and his actors into usurping diplomacy with the raucous laughter of cultural stereotype and rewarded them
for it. The prank was not out of character. Pepys and others on the fringes
of the court knew Monmouth as 'a most pretty spark', fond of dancing and
plays: he would take a leading role in the court masque, *Calisto*, under the
supervision of Betterton and Harris; he had appeared at court in Dryden's
The Indian Emperour, a play dedicated to his wife.[44] His intervention at
Dover succeeded by reminding the English contingent of what it meant
to be a good-natured, anti-French and anti-Catholic patriot. It also highlighted to the actors that if the Duke of York was a slightly aloof patron,
Monmouth was one of the gang. He kept his own theatre company, run
initially by Edward Bedford on the same basis as Rhodes's and Beeston's,
with licence to perform everywhere except London and Westminster.[45]
But the association between Monmouth and the Duke's Company was
so established that in 1683, when Monmouth was in hiding on suspicion
of involvement in the Rye House Plot against the king's life, an anonymous informant advanced this explanation of his whereabouts: 'I offer it as
my opinion that the Duke of Monmouth may throu Dorsets Davenants
or Bettertons meanes be Lodged in one of the two Play houses.'[46] Like *Sir
Salomon*, the episode casts Betterton as a pawn in factional politics, his

ability to manage the inherently political business of his company dictated by machinations devised and executed just, but only just, over his head.

Sir Salomon at Dover had provided Betterton and his company with extra cash to finance the new Dorset Garden theatre, but it also opened up new veins of creative, or perhaps derivative, work. French comedians had made regular appearances since the 1660s.[47] Betterton wrote his own Molière adaptation, *The Amorous Widow*, either in 1669 or 1670. In the autumn of that year the company would start performing the plays of someone who regularly drew on French sources, although whether Betterton ever co-authored plays with her is now doubtful.[48] Aphra Behn was one of the most vocal and prolific of the Duke's playwrights who supported the cause of the Duke. Her flair for expounding what Robert Markley calls 'idealized Cavalier values', while hardly socially conservative, was profoundly Yorkist, the work of a 'radical royalist'.[49]

Betterton's interest in Behn's work was, in contrast to Otway's, as a manager first and as an actor second, yet as a series of acting opportunities Behn's plays form an oblique commentary on his career. Apart from the after-piece, *The Cheats of Scapin*, Betterton had a major role in every one of Otway's ten plays, comic or tragic.[50] Some of Behn's eighteen plays have no cast lists, but in addition to the tyrant Abdelazer, the sprightly Gayman of *The Luckey Chance* and the rake Tom Wilding (described as 'a Tory') in *The City Heiress*, Betterton was often a supporting act or foil to William Smith: Alcippus to his Philander in *The Forc'd Marriage*, Belvile to his Willmore in *The Rover*, Galliard to his Fillamour in *The Feign'd Curtezans*. Where Otway's tragedies allowed Betterton the emotional range of the great Shakespearean roles in a style that mirrored the classicised dilemmas of contemporary French drama, Behn's comedies addressed the paradox of Betterton's own situation as the royal servant-actor of trade origins, showing male sexuality as 'free under aristocratic regimes' but 'debased and avaricious under bourgeois ones'.[51]

Betterton's career reached a succession of high points in the work of the other house Tory, Otway. Six years on from the performance at Dover, the company would mount a starker engagement with Catholic politics that appealed strongly to James – not surprisingly, since it was about the last Catholic King of England, Philip II of Spain. Complementing the portrait of Henry VIII in Betterton's collection was another of Philip: a memorial, perhaps, or a source to be studied for the role.[52] The play, Otway's *Don Carlos*, was premiered in June 1676, coinciding with James's complete renunciation of the Anglican religion. Betterton would tell Barton

Booth that the play succeeded in spite of itself, an example of a work as unaccountably popular as *Paradise Lost* had, at first, been undeservedly unpopular.[53] The antennae that intuited public taste did not, it seems, prevent him from deploring misunderstanding of living authors. But *Don Carlos* was mounted with political rather than aesthetic capital in mind, and succeeded.

Otway took his plot from the same source as better-known retellings by Schiller and Verdi, a prose history by César Vischard, Abbé de Saint Réal translated into English in 1674 by someone identified only as 'H.J.' Son of Philip II, Don Carlos is in love with his stepmother, a woman promised to him in marriage whom his father has taken for himself. Philip is too immersed in statecraft to be of much interest to his wife, but the feeling is not reciprocated: 'the enjoyment of her, far from diminishing his passion, did but augment it.'[54] Accordingly, Otway invited Betterton to play the sexually charged potentate:

> Hence to Loves secret Temples let's retire,
> There on his Altars kindle th'Am'rous fire,
> Then Phoenix-like each in the flame expire.[55]

'To what unwelcome joys I'm forc'd to yield', confides the Queen, but torn between love and duty, she chooses duty; H.J. told his patroness, Lady Ellis, that his aim had been to 'vindicate the Queen of Spains Vertue'. Carlos is also the object of another woman's devotion – the Princess Eboli, who schemes to unmask what she supposes to be the prince's intimacy with the Queen, ruthlessly using her aged lover Rui Gomez (another Latin role for Medbourne) to further her chances of forging an alliance with the libertine Don John of Austria. Carlos vows to defect to the rebels against Spanish rule in Flanders, and Saint Réal devotes a third of the work to the painful birth of Protestantism in France.

Verdi has Carlos rescued from assassination by the ghost of his grandfather; Saint Réal makes him die a Roman bathtub death as his father succumbs to ulcers and lice. Otway sentimentalises the ending, reconciling the prince and his father while making them both suffer: Carlos emerges from vigorous self-harming to die on his stepmother's bosom. The King goes mad, and 'runs off raving'.[56] Otway's editor, J.C. Ghosh, argues that the dramatist omitted the political dimensions of the story in order to concentrate on pathos, making the ending a 'happy innovation' calculated to draw the greatest number of tears.[57] But the play's conception is so caught up in the complex history of James's career that it is political from beginning to end.

When he published the play, Otway dedicated it to James in view of the 'mighty Encouragement I receiv'd from your Approbation of it when presented on the Stage'.[58] Many playwrights at least pretended to cringe as they wrote dedications, for all the money and favours they brought; Dryden wrote of the 'stale exploded trick of fulsome panegyrics' (but only after having just written one).[59] Otway wrote them from financial need and ideological fervour, weaving strands of his lucklessly loyal autobiography into the lives of the aristocracy. In *Don Carlos* he invokes ambition, the wish to avoid toiling 'in the same round' and shunning 'a smoother path for fear of being lost'.[60] It is the key note of the play. Don Carlos, a prince in waiting whose right in love is endlessly deferred, talks tall:

> I was born high, and will not fall less great,
> Since triumph crown'd my Birth, Ill have my Fate.[61]

The play pays other compliments to its dedicatee. In 1658, the young James had commanded a wing of the Spanish army at the Battle of the Dunes in Flanders; the army was led by none other than John of Austria, who lost to superior French forces. In 1676, England was allied with France against the Dutch, and James had been Lord Admiral in conflicts between them, which explains why, in the prologue, Otway is torn between 'the fame of France and Spain'. Out of respect to James, he makes them 'both Heroick'.[62] For all his devotion, Carlos, 'fierce as a lion … else soft as angels, charming as a God', exudes the romanticised sexuality with which another follower of James, Aphra Behn, imbued her heroes. For such a role, the Duke's Company had the perfect actor: William Smith, James's favourite.[63]

Just as *Henry VIII* had played Betterton against Harris, *Don Carlos* traded on the contrasting associations of Betterton and Smith, the Carolean against the new Jacobean. The role of Philip II blends Shakespearean influences so as to highlight Betterton's cultural dominance as a performer, but also the paradoxes of being a symbolic king. Otway opens with a bang: the Spanish court in full splendour. Philip displays political and marital confidence but, as in *Hamlet*, a dissenting voice intrudes. Otway paraphrases Shakespeare as Philip asks him, 'Why does my Carlos shroud / His joy, and when all's Sunshine wear a Cloud?'[64] The age's greatest Hamlet steps into the shoes of Claudius, clearing the floor for the favourite of the next regime. But to handle Philip's later transition from statesman to jealous husband, Otway turns to Othello:

> Meant? What should looks and sighs and pressings mean?
> No, no: I need not hear it o're again.[65]

Betterton would not play Othello until the 1680s, when company reorganisation gave him ownership of additional roles, but *Don Carlos* provided a dry run that allowed him to reconcile the naturalism of his Shakespearean style with the emotional extremes demanded by Otway; an actor's response to the dilemma posed by the company's patron.

Othello is the role of Betterton's which after Hamlet was best recorded, and some of what Steele wrote about that performance was rehearsed in Philip II:

The wonderful agony which he appeared in, when he examined the circumstance of the handkerchief ... the mixture of love that intruded upon his mind upon the innocent answers *Desdemona* makes, betrayed in his gesture such a variety and vicissitude of passions, as would admonish a man to be afraid of his own heart, and perfectly convince him, that it is to stab it, to admit that worst of daggers, jealousy.[66]

It is recognisable from Cibber: the ability to convey a conflict between opposites, to show a character's love amid anguish, or, in *Hamlet*, the 'filial reverence' that combats naked fear. Betterton's Othello further showed his ability to trace an exact emotional path through broken words:

Whoever reads in his closet this admirable scene will find that he cannot, except he has as warm an imagination as Shakespeare himself, find any but dry, incoherent and broken sentences; but a reader that has Betterton act it, observes there could not be a word added; that longer speech had been unnatural, nay impossible, in Othello's circumstances.[67]

As Betterton's acting exceeded Pepys's reading, so it supplied for Steele an organising principle of nature that connected the audience to the playwright's intentions. But if Othello was naturalised by such acting, he remained monstrous, just as Otway's Philip suffers but ends up sensationally mad. Where *Don Carlos* began with a nightmare tableau of how the English court might look on Charles II's death, Betterton's performance of its last Catholic king visited the possibility of humanising him through exploration of the most violent passions. The 'fierce flashing fire' which Cibber claimed to find in his Hotspur was subject to the English moderation that, in Anthony Aston's words, showed his passion most in the act of stifling it, 'as Fume smoaks most'; yet in principle the extremes of roles such as Philip and Betterton's dozen oriental tyrants threatened something alien and unrestrained.[68] For Joseph Roach, Betterton's Othello captured anxieties about racial otherness, but its prototype, Philip II, reflected ones played out in parliamentary debate.[69]

Don Carlos was revived under Jamesian rule in 1686 and again at the safe distance of the 1690s, but the company may have risked it in the incendiary circumstances of 1679 – months after Oates's testimony, the arrest of the Duke's chaplain, and the death of Edmund Berry Godfrey.[70] By the time the lanterns started to fly Betterton was promoting repertoire distasteful to James – now in temporary exile – and his party. One play on those afternoons may have been John Crowne's sensationalised *Henry VI* adaptation, *The Misery of Civil War*. Betterton played Warwick, a role comparable to Shaftesbury's in promoting the claims of the Duke of Monmouth. The vitality of fringe entertainments endorsed the view of Crowne's prologue that playwrights were learning to 'Damn the Pope': the Lord Mayor's Show of October 1680, with its 'plotting Papists litany'; a school play about Pope Joan that claimed to expose 'the Debaucheries and Villanies of the Popish Faction'.[71] Later, Crowne would complain that *The Misery* had been suppressed because of its own exposure of 'Popish Courts'.[72] Whatever its surface appeal to managements increasingly desperate for the kind of topical fare that would attract audiences, anti-Catholic drama was both boon and risk, as likely to draw in customers as incur the penalties of disruption, censorship or disfavour. When in June 1680 the King's Company mounted Elkanah Settle's own Pope Joan play, *The Female Prelate*, 'the Duchesse of Portsmouth to disoblige Mr Settle the Poet carried all the Court with her to the Dukes house', perhaps acting on intelligence supplied by the Catholic Duke of Norfolk, who had seen it the day before.[73] There is no evidence of further performances until after James II's removal from power.[74]

A severe drop in attendance towards the end of the 1670s concentrated minds. Decisions that once seemed incompatible with the livery were now attractive, but one rule still applied: do anything but give personal offence to anyone who could close the theatre or maim one of its actors. For all Crowne's complaints about *The Misery of Civil War*, for all the displeasure of the Duchess of Portsmouth and her allies, it was entirely possible for Betterton to capitalise on popular feeling by taking the title role in the '*mélange* of atrocities' that was Nathaniel Lee's *Caesar Borgia*; the play glories in its hostility to priests and popes without reducing its case to the particular, even if a 'religious quarrel' at the theatre followed soon after, with 'many swords … drawn' and a novice of St Omer's one of the combatants.[75] Other roles might allow Betterton to mimic square-jawed devotion to the crown – like Tate's loyal general Theocrin – or inhabit the borderlands of acceptability. Lee's *Lucius Junius Brutus*, with Betterton in the title role, was banned after three days in 1680 because of its 'Scandalous Expressions & Reflections upon ye Government'.[76] In 1681 Shadwell's equally anti-Catholic *The Lancashire Witches* passed the censor's eye only to be recalled.[77] Satire directed at those less popular at court was another matter. With dry understatement Andrew Marvell described the anonymous *Sir Popular Wisdom* of 1677 as a play 'where my Lord Shaftesbury and all his gang are sufficiently personated'; drier still, he added that 'the King will be there'.[78] For Betterton's company, the apotheosis of such satire took place on 9 February 1682, when Shaftesbury appeared as the perverted senator, Antonio, in Otway's *Venice Preserv'd*. Otway dedicated the play to the beacon of Catholic factions, the Duchess of Portsmouth.

Betterton's familiarity with Monmouth did not, any more than his wearing the Duke of York's livery, entail partisan support. He had to be the calculating observer suggested by his ownership of a volume called *The Transactions of the House of Peers concerning the Popish Plot*.[79] But in such unstable circumstances his calculations were almost bound to go awry. In July 1682 he prepared the title role of Dryden's *The Duke of Guise* only to see it banned because 'the Duke of Munmuth ... complained' of its reflections on him, although lobbying later in the year would restore the play to the repertory.[80] The play became more popular as it became more likely that James would succeed to the throne.[81] In August 1682, Aphra Behn's anti-Monmouth epilogue to the anonymous *Romulus and Hersilia* landed her and the actress who spoke it in custody, although when Betterton had uttered similar sentiments as the Duke of Guise he escaped punishment.[82] As a manager and an actor, Betterton had no shortage of opportunities to exercise his judgement about the political risks presented by new plays, but with Monmouth as with the Duke of York, he learned to push as hard as he could against the boundaries of his duty to noble patrons. Only occasionally did he push too hard, tempted by commercial advantage. In 1692, John Banks's Lady Jane Grey play, *The Innocent Usurper*, seemed an attractive prospect until it was banned, and it never made the stage.[83]

As so often in Betterton's career the structural context in which he made such decisions helped determine their outcome. *The Duke of Guise* was performed not by the Duke's Company, which had ceased to exist on 4 May 1682, but by the new United Company, which saw Betterton and his rivals at Drury Lane agreeing to join forces in the wake of falling audiences and King's Company indiscipline.[84] The Duke's shadow continued to fall across Betterton's work even when the Duke's Company had disbanded. *Venice Preserv'd* had been scurrilously anti-Whig, and the company continued in the same vein with the premiere that was being prepared as Betterton was negotiating the articles of union. Aphra Behn's *The City Heiress*, which opened in late April 1682, removes Shaftesbury from the Venetian brothel of Otway's play and puts him squarely in seventeenth-century London as Sir Timothy Treatall, a man with republican sympathies but royal ambitions who shares Sir Salomon's vanity and craft; this time Betterton played the disinherited nephew Tom Wilding, symbol of a glamourised Stuart cause. The problems that beset *The Duke of Guise* and *Romulus and Hersilia* later that summer suggest that the United Company management took the opportunity of the union to return to the loyal values of the mid-1670s, or indeed the early 1660s, no matter how vocal the political opposition (a pamphlet of 1683 complained that *The Duke of Guise* was 'intended to provoke the rabble in to tumults and disorder').[85] No longer desperate for a share of a divided audience, no longer tempted by economics into political compromise, Betterton could make his new company more truly the Duke's than it had been since 1678.

CHAPTER 10

Union: Betterton and theatrical monopoly, 1682–1695

Even without the Popish Plot crisis, the Duke's Company's rivals would have driven themselves into the ground. Years of squabbling led to a prolonged closure of the King's Theatre in 1681, the old season ending early and the new one scarcely beginning. Merger talks followed.[1] On the King's Company's side sat Charles Hart, by now trying to provide for his own retirement, and Edward Kynaston, Betterton's oldest acquaintance in the theatre world. The trust that came of old alliances was vital, for no other King's personnel knew about the talks, least of all their owner-manager, the vexed and devious Charles Killigrew.[2]

Betterton and Smith took the initiative in complete accord with their own patentee, Charles Davenant, who had inherited his right from Sir William. On 14 October 1681, Hart and Kynaston agreed startling preliminary conditions: not to act for their company or assist it, to pay the Duke's any money they received from it, and to yield all rights to King's plays and properties. They would encourage a union between the two companies and, if necessary, sue Killigrew to achieve it.[3] Hart was to be paid five shillings per acting day and Kynaston ten, but the old prohibition against actors moving companies presented an obstacle. It took months to bring the agreement into daylight: the Articles of Union were not signed until 4 May 1682.[4] In the midst of these machinations Betterton had one of his quietest winters as a performer.[5] Desperate to see a return on his investment, Charles Killigrew agreed to the deal and he did well enough from it to suggest that Hart had been pushing at an open door – fifteen per cent of the new company's profits and joint ownership with Charles Davenant. Killigrew did not stop to ask the investors who held shares in the Drury Lane theatre, so inviting a raft of unsuccessful legal challenges.[6]

How does Betterton emerge from the episode? In 1979 Judith Milhous invoked business logic: the King's Company was poorly run, a merger would improve the all-round performance of its remains, and the stronger unit that resulted would enjoy a monopoly.[7] Betterton could see what the future would bring for his rivals and offered them a better species of demise. In 2004 Milhous described the episode as 'a stumbling-block for various biographers' who, ignoring the King's Company's desperate situation, see it as a serious challenge to 'Betterton's reputation for probity'.[8] To economics she added the supposition of royal approval. Nine years after the negotiations Betterton would testify hearing from Arlington that 'it was the King's will and Pleasure that the two patentees should unite and make one Good Company' – a safe gambit, admittedly, when Arlington was long dead.[9] It is debatable whether business logic need entail commercial sabotage – Betterton did after all help create the bad future for his rivals on which the deal was predicated – or whether, restrictions on actors' movement between companies still being in force, another means could have been found to 'secure the services of two of the most knowledgeable members of the rival troupe', especially when Hart was seeking only to retire on his proceeds.[10] So, while Joseph Knight may have stumbled in describing the deal as 'one-sided and dishonest', there can be no doubt that this was an exceptionally ruthless takeover by a man for whom good business was its own defence.[11]

Even so, Betterton did not take one obvious opportunity: for managing the new company he continued to draw only the twenty shillings per week agreed in 1668; Smith drew the same. Neither man benefited from new shareholding arrangements intended to compensate Killigrew for taking on the King's Company debt. Other advantages sufficed: more plays, parts, costumes, theatres and scenery, and no competition for audiences, even though the new rental agreement for the Drury Lane theatre meant a steep increase in overheads.[12] It was a recipe for personal prosperity, and for the next decade Betterton's income swung between the substantial sums of £282 and £487 a year, which put him on a par with senior government officials.[13] As in the Dorset Garden share agreement of 1671, as long as his interests were inextricably linked to the theatre's, he need not worry about improving his salary.

Comparison with 1671 also underlines Betterton's self-confidence in personnel management. He did not flinch at the King's Company's prima donnas, pawn-shop cheats, embezzlers and hotheads. Others might have effected an instant clear-out but the new company was at first inclusive, although a small handful of actors left immediately and the chief casualties were the back-stage staff.[14] Overall, the number of performers increased from twenty-seven to forty-two, and Betterton's reputation for fatherly care was surely tested to the full. The subsequent five years tell a different story. By 1687 the acting staff had almost halved through retirements and departures north or west, with Edinburgh and Dublin proving attractive for disenchanted London actors. Betterton and Smith looked at the enlarged company of 1682 and decided that economies could be achieved by a combination of natural wastage and casting decisions designed to focus minds. The same period, Milhous notes, saw 'a very respectable return' for shareholders.[15] A potentially explosive situation was defused through cautious, non-confrontational management.

It was probably with his wife's consent that the process of trimming began close to home. The decline of Mary Betterton's acting career had begun with the emergence of Elizabeth Barry in the 1670s, a new stage lover for her husband, and while she continued to play longstanding roles such as Lady Macbeth, in new plays she frequently made only cameo appearances. A landmark – or nadir – had been Lucrece in Lee's 1680 *Lucius Junius Brutus*, whose sole scene ends in suicide at the end of Act I.[16] A union of companies that increased personnel by fifteen served to accelerate a six-year trend, so coaching younger performers became her chief activity. It was the natural option for a woman who remained, even in her professional decline, 'prudent and constant' rather than 'fond and passionate'.[17]

The most difficult cases to handle were the actors of equivalent seniority to Betterton himself. Here Betterton was largely fortunate. Hart got his pension but did not live to enjoy it, dying in August 1683.[18] Kynaston continued to act for another sixteen or seventeen years (too long, in Cibber's view) and as Betterton's old associate and co-signatory of the October 1681 agreement, he proved consistently co-operative.[19] Trouble came in the shape of someone proud of his career, outflanked by Hart and Kynaston's manoeuvrings for a union, and determined to find redress.

Of all Restoration actors Michael Mohun had the strongest royalist credentials, seeing combat in the Civil War and becoming an authentic Behnian rover afterwards. He fought with Prince James in Flanders and acted in an entertainment at Antwerp in 1658. In 1660, he said, it was the restored king's 'Sacred Pleasure ... that he should Act againe'. Details of Mohun's devotion to the royal cause come from a document he prepared after the union of 1682 – a petition to the king, no less.[20] It speaks of a longstanding enmity with Hart, always the grander of the two (according to Downes, Hart 'might teach any King on Earth how to comport himself'); by contrast, Mohun was 'a little man of mettle'.[21] Like Medbourne, he was a Catholic.[22] He had quarrelled with Hart in the past.[23] Now, in 1682, seeing his old rival with his ill-gotten pension, Mohun was outraged. He had been deprived of his share of 'ye Scenes Clothes & playes'; instead of his share, he had an offer of twenty shillings for every performance he gave, but with a catch. The new company would focus on the old Duke's repertory ('they haueing not studied Our Playes'), and he would not perform more than about twenty times a season. Two decades of King's Company quarrels were wrapped up in the plea which ends his petition: to have 'the same Conditions as Mr Hart and Mr Kinaston haue (whos Shares were all equall before)'.

Mohun's grudge was nominally against Charles Killigrew. Betterton and Smith are not mentioned in the petition, and with a few exceptions it was Hart's roles rather than Mohun's that Betterton would take over.[24] But it was managers who made repertory decisions, so if there was anything to Mohun's suspicion that he would be constructively dismissed that plan was Betterton's to devise. It never happened: Mohun won, not without foot-dragging from his new managers.[25] Arlington signed the final order, perhaps sympathising with a fellow traveller to Rome. Deals might be signed to establish a commercial basis for the newly united company, but state interference could still redraft the rules. What softened the blow was the same factor that helped to reduce the company roll during the 1680s. Betterton could always have reckoned on Mohun's age. Mohun won his pension and had the satisfaction of outliving Hart, but only by a year. He was buried in October 1684.[26] Had he lived another ten years, the company could have afforded his pension, for the average day's profit was nearly £10, which meant that one share in the company would yield about £90 a year.[27] With three shares, Charles Killigrew did well. With his share, management salary and acting fees, not to mention the money paid to his wife, Betterton was doing very well indeed, and not only financially. Union meant that the plays which had been assigned to the King's Company were now available, so a new range of major roles opened up, including Othello and Brutus.[28]

As Hamlet and Henry VIII, Betterton had worked from William Davenant's memories of pre-war performances. Faced with major new roles in Shakespeare, where did he turn? Partly to Hart, partly to reading. True to his account of Betterton's Hamlet, Cibber found in his Brutus an attention to character that derived from the text. Here again was the restrained power and critical intelligence of his earlier performance:

When the Betterton *Brutus* was provok'd in his Dispute with *Cassius*, his Spirit flew only to his Eye; his steady Look alone supply'd that Terror which he disdain'd an Intemperance in his Voice should rise to. Thus, with a settled

Dignity of Contempt, like an unheeding Rock he repelled upon himself the Foam of *Cassius*.[29]

Brutus's stoic disdain for emotional display is Betterton's; the maturity and self-command of the character turn out to be the perfect actorly accomplishment. But the real master-stroke is in finding the textual clue to the real nature of Brutus's temper, and then acting on it:

> O Cassius, you are yoked with a lamb
> That carries anger as the flint bears fire,
> Who, much enforced, shows a hasty spark
> And straight is cold again.

(IV.iii.109–12)

With this in mind, says Cibber, Betterton would 'open into that Warmth which becomes a man of virtue'. When Aston considered the performance, it was Betterton's control he remembered. Seeing his Brutus opposite the Cassius of John Verbruggen was like watching a contrast between raw talent and mature art – '*Verbruggen* wild and untaught ... *Betterton* in the Trammels of Instruction.'[30]

'Trammels of Instruction': apparently the opposite of a reasoned engagement with the text, the phrase speaks volumes about Betterton's method. His modesty lay partly in 'not presuming to understand any characters' until he had heard 'repeated instructions' from the author.[31] When he took over parts from other senior actors after the union, his instinct was to learn them from authoritative sources. The role of Alexander the Great in Nathaniel Lee's *The Rival Queens* had been one of Hart's greatest successes, and was taken on by either Goodman or Mountfort in 1685.[32] When, in turn, Betterton learned the role after Mountfort's death he strove to reproduce details from Hart's original 1677 performance:

Betterton ... acted Alexander with as much éclat as any of his other characters. This accomplished and yet modest player, when rehearsing this character, was at a loss to recover a particular emphasis of Hart, which gave a force to some interesting situation of the part: he applied for information to the players who stood near him. At last one of the lowest of the company repeated the line exactly in Hart's key. Betterton thanked him heartily and put a piece of money in his hand as a reward for so acceptable a service.[33]

The anecdote was printed years after Betterton's death, but it is true to his reputation both as a company man and as an actor. The whole group, even 'the lowest', were custodians of their performance tradition, and Betterton's impromptu bonus was the kind of gesture which would secure loyalty while making the point that it was, ultimately, 'service' that was expected. 'Hart's key' was a distinctive verbal music that needed to be captured not just for the sake of its sound, but for an inflection of meaning (it 'gave a force to some interesting situation'); evidently Betterton was a meticulous student of other actors and their roles as well as of his own, and took advantage of his very occasional afternoons off to watch the King's Company perform.[34] The ultimate performance of Alexander was Betterton's, the outcome of careful study and emotional moderation, but it could only gain from reference to the model of the actor who had created it. His respect for Hart's key derived from a respect for Nathaniel Lee's intentions. Dramatists read their works out loud at rehearsal, and Lee was such a powerful reader that he had prompted Mohun to a tantrum: 'Unless I were able to play it as well as you read it, to what purpose should I undertake it?' he protested.[35]

Betterton appears to have suffered from no such anxiety of influence. As an interpreter of the text, he could get as close as possible to the author's intentions without feeling merely inferior. Instructions were not the end of invention, but part of its *raison d'être*. The practice outlived him. In June 1710, two months after his death, Robert Wilks attempted a conscious 'exercise in succession' by picking up the mantle of Othello.[36] In lesser hands, imitation would be merely that. When Cibber recalled the Irish actor Estcourt taking over Anthony Leigh's role in Dryden's *The Spanish Fryar*, the effect was to create merely 'a dead likeness', 'like a Child's Painting upon the Face of a Metzo-tinto'.[37]

Theatrical monopoly and the glut of new roles that came with it meant that new writing suffered. In turn, this diminished the likelihood of political controversy at a time when London prepared itself for the Jamesian succession: more revivals meant more known quantities, and after *The Duke of Guise* was restored to the stage there is little sign of official interference other than the replacement in 1687 of Dryden's *The Spanish Fryar* with Fletcher and Massinger's less controversial *The Spanish Curate*, in which Betterton had first acted for Rhodes.[38] During the mid-1670s the London stage had seen an average of twenty or more new plays in each season; in the 1680s, the number dwindled to as few as three. Apart from the political risks, new plays cost time and money, and many of the established dramatists were reaching the end of their careers. Wycherley and Etherege had not written since the previous decade; Lee was confined to Bedlam; poverty-stricken Behn slowly dried up; Otway's last play premiered in July 1683; Shadwell wrote no plays between 1681 and 1688. As long as the public was content with the novelty of seeing old favourites with new casts, there was little incentive to encourage new talent, and the short-term policy was a short-term commercial success. In 1690 George Powell diagnosed the situation:

The time was, upon the uniting of the two *Theatres*, that the reviveing of the old stock of Plays, so ingrost the study of the House, that the Poets lay dormant; and a new Play cou'd hardly get admittance, amongst the more precious pieces of Antiquity, that then waited to walk the Stage.

Powell still felt able to dedicate his play to 'the Patentees and Sharers of Their Majesties Theatre', dubbing Betterton's company 'the true Maecenas of Poetry', but in the circumstances the compliment was more than usually strained.[39]

Betterton preferred other challenges: equal to the excitement of new roles, the opportunity for a bigger company to mount the multi-media spectaculars he had always thought a recipe for commercial success. The most ambitious depended on close collaboration with Dryden, the ideal talent for what would be, in effect, the last court masque of Stuart England. For the extravaganza of 1685 called *Albion and Albanius*, Betterton pulled out every stop.

From the outset the project caused astonishment. In a letter to the Countess of Rutland, Edward Bedingfield claimed £4000 had been spent on the show and that ticket prices were to be raised fourfold as a result – a guinea for a box, half a guinea for a place in the pit.[40] The annual receipts of the company were only about £10,000, while the annual production budget was a mere £3800.[41] Bedingfield was sceptical: 'the rates proposed will not take soe well', he observed. Selling the idea to the company must have been a challenge.

Betterton had done it before, the trend towards scenic spectaculars given impetus by the move to Dorset Garden. In August 1673 the Duke's Company had been observed preparing 'an Opera and great machines', with French dancers and choristers from the Chapel Royal.[42] That show was probably Shadwell's revision of Davenant and Dryden's revision of *The Tempest*, which opened in April 1674; 'not any succeeding Opera got more Money', said Downes, his adulation for once sounding an ominous note.[43] Next the company pushed the boundaries of genre further with Shadwell's florid 'English Opera', *Psyche*. February 27, 1675 saw the premiere of this cosmopolitan cornucopia, with instrumental music by an Italian and dances by a Frenchman to go with the home-grown skills of the vocal composer, Locke, scene painter, Stephenson, and the *éminence grise*, 'at whose desire [Shadwell] wrote upon this Subject', Thomas Betterton.[44] The idea had perhaps sprung from first-hand experience. Betterton may have seen the French opera with his own eyes some time between 1671 and 1673, and wanted to recreate it at Dorset Garden.[45] In 1676 he would import from France properties for Charles Davenant's *Circe*, which enjoyed sufficient success – and the customary benefit of exemption from excise – to forestall criticism.[46] Reflecting on the music for *Psyche*, Roger North described the entertainment as a 'masque' worthy of 'a vertuoso's cabanet', but others nearer to home had different concerns.[47] Elkanah Settle, who wrote for the company a *Pastor Fido* that might be described as *Psyche* on a budget, said that he had

> often heard the Players cursing at their oversight in laying out so much on so disliked a play; and swearing that they thought they had lost more by making choice of such an Opera-writer than they had gained by all his Comedies; considering how much more they might have expected, had such Entertainment had that scence in it, that it deserved.[48]

Shadwell may have credited Betterton with the idea, but Settle makes it sound like a collective decision. If anyone came out of it badly it was Shadwell, whose talents were for city comedy, while Betterton emerged unscathed. Settle agreed with Downes that the real recipe for success was obvious: 'for the future,' Settle added, 'they expect the *Tempest*, which cost not one Third of *Psyche*, will be in request when the other is forgotten.' Downes's assessment was more defensive but drew the same conclusion. *Psyche* had cost £800 – a snip compared to *Albion and Albanius*, but still more than twenty per cent of the annual production budget – yet it had run for eight successive performances and 'prov'd very Beneficial to the Company'. Still, he added, 'the *Tempest* got them more Money'.[49] The precedent set by *Psyche* had not just been about money: it focused attention on the right ingredients for big scenic shows. Foreign music *per se* was not the issue – it was the underlying thread of 'sense' in the plot and dialogue, and for that it was best to rely on English Shakespeare.

If Settle was right about the grumbling surrounding *Psyche,* it was surely with trepidation that Betterton's colleagues learned of his 1683 summer travel plans. After completing the season with the last Otway play they would see, *The Atheist*, Betterton and others went to Paris. It was a newsworthy event: 'Mr Betterton with other Actors are gone over [to France] to fetch the designe', reads a newsletter dated 14 August 1683.[50] If Gildon is to be believed, Betterton communicated easily in French (he owned two French dictionaries and a French New Testament along with a substantial collection of French plays) and presumably led his actors with as much assurance in Paris as he did in London.[51] According to Francis Manning, he learned the scenic arts from the French but then taught them how to blend the 'Soul' of acting with the 'Marble Form' of scenery'.[52] Later correspondence by the German composer, Jakob Greber, shows that his name was known to musicians across Europe, while a letter to Betterton from Etherege in May 1687 hints at a lively knowledge of music.[53] The 1683 newsletter states that he was in Paris strictly on company business: 'The Manager of the King's Theatre intends within short time to performe an Opera in like manner of it of France.' Letters from the English ambassador in Paris, however, indicate that this was an official mission, and one that involved protracted negotiation. Richard Graham, Lord Preston, refers to Betterton's visit in correspondence with the Earl of Sunderland on 25 August.[54] A month later, the English actors were still in town. They had been there, writes Preston, 'some weeks since by his Majesty's command'. The intention was 'to endeavour to carry over the Opera';[55] that is, the company run by Jean-Baptiste Lully, who by 1683 enjoyed a monopoly in Paris under Louis XIV's protection. Lully was at the high point of his success, mounting a series of major works with his librettist Philippe Quinault.[56] His company was the most prestigious, the best patronised and the largest in the world.

The scheme proved too ambitious: 'impracticable' is Preston's word for it, or perhaps for how Betterton found it. Is there a whiff of inadequate preparation, or inadequate funding, or a lack of interest in the first place? To go all the way to Paris only to find that the king's great idea was simply 'impracticable' – one letter from the English embassy to Whitehall enumerating the violins, singers and properties could have said as much. Betterton probably sensed that his company would have to bear too much of the risk and it was as well there was an alternative plan in the shape of someone who four years earlier, in fear for his life, had swapped London for Paris. On 31 March 1679, the Catalan and Catholic composer Louis Grabu had packed his threadbare bags and fled a city increasingly consumed by anti-popish violence.[57] He left behind what had been a flourishing if controversial career at court and, after his exclusion by the 1673 Test Act, a number of theatrical commissions: *Ariadne* for the King's Company in 1674; *Timon of Athens* and D'Urfey's *Squire Oldsapp* for Betterton in 1678.[58] Betterton could be sure that another old Catholic associate could help 'to represent something at least like an Opera in England for his Majesty's diversion'.[59]

First, Grabu needed some assurances. He wanted the king's protection, 'and what encouragement his Majesty shall be pleased to give him if he finds that he deserves it'. The money had been sorted, for Betterton had started to spend the £4000 which amazed Edward Bedingfield. 'He hath already assured him of a pension from the House.' No wonder he found Grabu 'very willing and ready to go over', and the idea of a pension for a single piece of work suggests that Betterton had in mind some longer-term arrangement.[60] He cannot have been too conscious of the musical opinions of people like Pepys, who disliked the Anglo-French style, but realised his theatre needed new musical talent. Locke and Banister had died in 1677 and 1679 respectively, while Purcell's official duties absorbed much of his time. Recruiting Grabu suited Betterton as much as it did the king.

The new season opened at the beginning of October 1683, and Betterton needed a librettist. Dryden was pre-eminent among playwrights at a time of generational shift, and this would be the tenth time in sixteen years he had worked with Betterton.[61] John Crowne, Elkanah Settle and Thomas Shadwell were the only credible alternatives but the latter had proved himself suspect on this territory, and Dryden's Laureateship was decisive: this was to be not simply a French opera, but one that glorified the House of Stuart. The piece evolved over more than a year, and the court sampled Dryden's text between May 1684 and the following winter, when there was a rehearsal at the apartment of Charles's French mistress, the Duchess of Portsmouth.[62]

The text affirmed values of loyalty to the Stuart dynasty which Betterton and the Duke's Company had struggled to promulgate consistently during the years of the Exclusion crisis. Its stage pictures of London, including copies of the statue of Charles I at Charing Cross and of Charles II at Windsor, recall the restorative imagery of park scenes. Dryden's preface reveals Betterton's personal investment in the project: 'The descriptions of the scenes, and other decorations of the stage I had from Mr Betterton, who has spared neither for industry, nor cost, to make this entertainment perfect, nor for invention of the ornaments to beautify it.'[63] The results were opulent without precedent. In Act II, Albion and Albanius are greeted by Apollo in all his, and the theatre's, glory: 'The farther part of the heaven opens, and discovers a machine as it moves forward, the clouds which are before it divide, and show the person of Apollo, holding the reins in his hands. As they fall lower, the Horses appear with the rays, and a great glory about Apollo.'[64] If anyone had been in any doubt about their true identity, Apollo announces that Albion and Albanius, otherwise known as Charles and James Stuart, are there by divine right:

> All hail, ye royal pair,
> The gods' peculiar care!
> Fear not the malice of your foes;
> Their dark designing,
> And combining,
> Time and truth shall once expose …[65]

It is the core masque theme – discord quashed, concord restored – applied to a situation which Betterton had been exploring with varying degrees of loyalty for ten years. Act II begins in 'a Poetical Hell' peopled by those damnable figures Zeal and Democracy, 'conceived in Heaven, but born in Hell'. Allusions abound to the illegal claims of the Duke of Monmouth, while the mythological surface is further scored with politics by the appearance in Act III of Rumbold, the one-eyed archer accused of being ring-leader of the 1683 Rye House Plot, in which the king was to have been assassinated. 'Shoot, holy Cyclop, shoot', cry the denizens of hell.[66]

Dryden's preface says that the play had been 'made' in Charles's honour, and he had been present at rehearsals, 'especially the first and third acts of it'. It was the music he loved most: the 'composition and choruses' he had thought 'more just and more beautiful than any he had heard in England' – another sign that the king's true cultural and spiritual allegiance lay beyond his own kingdom. On his death bed he finally declared himself a Catholic. In a postscript to his preface, Dryden says that the piece was 'all composed' and 'ready to have been performed' when Charles II died, in February 1685. A four-month closure of the theatres followed and Dryden returned to his play in the summer. Its message and genre had, he thought, been reinforced by the king's death. The only adjustment he thought necessary was to the ending, but that, like James's succession, disturbed what had gone before scarcely a jot: 'those very causes, which seemed to threaten us with troubles, conspired to produce our lasting happiness.'[67] The apotheosis of the play pictures what for Betterton was that quintessentially royal image, 'a walk of very high trees', this time at Windsor. Albion has risen to the clouds 'on a machine', leaving his brother to sit amid the Knights of the Garter while being entertained with 'songs of gods, and fit for gods to hear'.[68] The many spectators who failed to enjoy Grabu's songs stood condemned.

If the play spoke a kind of propaganda too few people believed, it was also upstaged by the very discord it represented: 'This play being perform'd on a very Unlucky Day, being the Day the Duke of Monmouth landed in the west: the Nation being in a great consternation, it was perform'd but six times, which not answering half the charge they were at, involv'd the company very much in debt.'[69] The dates add up. Monmouth landed at Lyme Regis on 11 June 1685;[70] Charles had died on 6 February and Dryden says he left his play for four months afterwards. Doubtless the loyal Downes was trying to deflect criticism from Betterton, but his financial summary adds to the feeling that a monumental risk had been taken. *Albion and Albanius* needed more than a dozen performances just to cover its costs at a time when some plays did not run for more than three. If Betterton had persuaded the company and shareholders to enter into it against their wishes, and with memories still fresh of the great escape called *Psyche*, they had every right to be upset.

Albion and Albanius was an embarrassing failure. An anonymous poem commends the ingenuity of the stage technology but condemns everything else, suggesting that it all came down to the foreign music:

> Each actor on the stage his luck bewailing,
> Finds that his loss is infallibly true;
> Smith, Nokes, and Leigh, in a fever with railing,
> Curse poet, painter, and Monsieur Grabu.
> Betterton, Betterton, thy decorations,
> And the machines, were well written, we knew;
> But all the words were such stuff, we want patience,
> And little better is Monsieur Grabu.
> Damme, says Underhill, I'm out of two hundred
> Hoping that rainbows and peacocks would do;
> Who thought infallible Tom could have blundered?
> A plague upon him and Monsieur Grabu![71]

Preparation for the show had been the most complex and costly of Betterton's career, yet in mounting *Albion and Albanius* 'infallible Tom' mistook the archaism of the masque for the novelty of scenic spectacle, political loyalties out-running commercial judgement.

His part in the show was probably to introduce and draw it to a close; for such signature events he stood out front.[72] Delivering prologues and epilogues was an art in itself. Either in character, stepping beyond it, or as a representative of the management, the actor had to engage specified groups of spectators while speaking the *lingua franca* of the form, heroic couplets. The implicit invitation to dialogue, the possibility of the audience talking back, had to be monitored through tone, gesture and physical presence. Like a stand-up comic, the actor needed to remain open to the audience while knowing that there was a routine to complete. Betterton's success depended on making his audience feel that they could trust him to speak truth, even when that meant playing on their doubts. In speaking prologues and epilogues, Cibber said, 'He had a natural gravity that gave strength to good sense, a tempered spirit that gave life to wit, and a dry reserve in his smile that threw ridicule into its brightest colours.'[73] What could he say to the audience of *Albion and Albanius*? His natural gravity and dry reserve must, like his 'infallible' commercial judgement, have been strained. Already nervous of the play's foreign musical idiom, the prologue jokes about the habits of the French audience:

> In France, the oldest man is always young,
> Sees operas daily, learns the tunes so long
> Till foot, hand, head, keep time with every song:
> Each sings his part, echoing from pit and box,
> With his hoarse voice, half harmony, half pox.

So far so good, but then comes a mistake. Since the French show themselves 'good subjects by their singing', the English should do likewise ('on that condition, set up every throat'), even if they opposed James's succession: 'You Whigs may sing, for you have changed your note.'[74] The only option now is to 'get by singing what you lost by roaring'. Comparably coercive, the epilogue speaks the Stuart language of divine right:

> When heaven made man, to show the work divine,
> Truth was his image, stamped upon the coin:
> And when a King is to a God refined,
> On all he says and does he stamps his mind.

James's public commitment to his faith should not be a source of faction, but of trust – 'He plights his faith, and we believe him just' – and it is the very strength of that faith which will make him as heroic a king as he had been a prince:

> The saint who walked on waves securely trod
> While he believed the beckoning of his God.

Forget the French and their music, the epilogue concludes – it is the British way to govern by 'Plain Dealing', by the consent of words mutually exchanged, and the power of the word awakens thoughts not only of divine creation, but of the divine mission of empire:

> Thus Britain's basis on a word is laid,
> As by a word the world itself was made.[75]

Albion and Albanius was Betterton's tribute to the dynasty which had always commanded his loyalty, and the grandeur of its language, iconography, ideology and financial commitment appears to embody a profound allegiance to it. But, as in the years of the Popish Plot, the story would change. Dryden gained from James's succession while Betterton carried on as before; when the three years of James's rule ended and William of Orange came to the throne, Dryden found himself ejected from his court posts while Betterton endeavoured to make himself secure. The tempered spirit and dry reserve with which he spoke a prologue may not always have guaranteed box-office success, but they were useful tools in adapting to changing political fortunes.

His attention was soon absorbed by a change closer to home, the seeds of which were planted two years after *Albion and Albanius*. He had just passed fifty-two on the day in August 1687 when Charles Davenant, joint owner of the United Company, asked him to witness a document. The business was going well. The company had recovered from Dryden's masque and boasted regular profits, a streamlined group of actors, no troublemakers, and no disputes about pensions, shares or roles – a good time for any owner to decide to cash in.[76] Davenant duly sold his interest in the company but kept it in the family, and his younger brother Alexander took over. There was nothing to worry Betterton on the surface. During the 1660s, William Davenant had traded in company shares with people who had little obvious experience of the theatre;[77] success had been built since his death on the basis of Betterton and partner managing competently. But there was a catch which did not emerge for years and when it did, it spelled trouble for everyone. Alexander Davenant could not afford his brother's shares. He had borrowed more than three-quarters of their price and then found it impossible to repay the money. Eventually Betterton would have to answer to his creditors.

For a while the crisis was obscured since company management stayed within the trusted Davenant family. Two months into his takeover, in October 1687, Alexander Davenant made Betterton an offer. Stand aside as manager but remain as senior artistic adviser, in modern parlance: the loss of managerial salary would be made good by additional shares and the equivalent of an annual bonus – in other words, same money, less bother. Co-manager William Smith would be offered severance to go quietly and off he went, when the time came, to fight for James II. Another Davenant, Thomas, would be paid to manage the company but would rely heavily on the senior actor, and during this period, a later document indicates, 'all things were done as Mr Betterton would have it'.[78] There is no hint that Betterton was unhappy. The trappings of managerial control mattered little when the substance remained. As long as he had the freedom to play the roles he desired and exercise overall artistic control – and as long as his financial interests were protected – there was no reason to object. Perhaps, at the age of fifty-two, he felt it was time to focus again on essentials, and if anything this was a return to the days in which he had risen to fame: a secure company, undisputed leading-man status, management by a Davenant.

In reality, it was Betterton who did the managing. Alexander had shown heroic faith in his twenty-three-year old younger brother, whose qualifications for running London's only licensed theatre company remain obscure. Thomas Davenant was paid well, all the same: the sum, in fact, of Betterton's and Smith's managerial salaries. References to Davenant's activities from 1687 suggest that whatever was on his job description, his daily life was more that of a finance clerk and occasional errand-boy than a manager. His known tasks include taking a list of actors to the Lord Chamberlain, hearing complaints about accounting, collecting payment for court performances, and being so rude to the playwright Dr Nicholas Brady that the company was forced by the Lord Chamberlain into performing his unrevived and unrevivable play, *The Rape*.[79] Betterton probably viewed this latest scion of the great family with kindly scepticism. Indeed, the only reason for agreeing to the deal that Alexander Davenant had offered him in October 1687 would be the thought that with such an *ingénu* in charge, things would carry on much as they had done. So they did as far as the key decisions were concerned: Betterton 'gave out which Plays he would during that time'.[80]

While his co-manager Smith departed to defend King James's indefensible interest, Betterton's habits and instincts told him to stay put and adapt. Within months of William of Orange's arrival his company had started to mount new-style comedies associated with bourgeois, constitutional values.[81] In Shadwell's *Bury Fair* Betterton played, in April 1689, a new kind of cultured, moral hero who upholds 'simple country virtues against city corruption'; overall, the play reacts against the tradition of Stuart libertinism by showing how 'morals and rationality are of crucial importance in determining ... actions and feelings'.[82] Bellamy was a part Betterton's legendary studiousness qualified him to play. The following month the company drove the point home by reviving Dryden's tragicomedy *The Spanish Fryar*, described as 'the only play forbid by the late King'. Its taboo status can only be explained by its ribald treatment of the eponymous brother Dominic, which struck a more triumphalist note in May 1689 than it had at its premiere nine years before, during the height of the Popish Plot crisis. But the main plot tells a less clear-cut story. Betterton

played Torrismond, a man who does not know that his real father is the
recently deposed king, supposed dead until a stunning Act V denouement
reveals that it was all a plot to test Torrismond's eventual bride, Queen
Leonora. In 1680, Torrismond rehearsed the old story of Charles Stuart in
exile as a way of defending the lineal rights of his brother:

> But let the bold conspirator beware,
> For heaven makes princes its peculiar care,

the play ends.[83] In 1680 it had been a prismatic affair, skilfully designed to
excite both Whig and Tory, Exclusionist and Successionist, a 'Protestant
play' by a man who converted to Catholicism five years later, however
much James disapproved of it.[84] By 1689 its bold conspirators had crystallised into the shape of Jacobites and its 'merciful king', 'loath to revenge,
and easy to forgive' had metamorphosed from Charles Stuart into William
of Orange, whose Act of Grace of May 1690 pardoned all those who had
supported James.[85]

Still, the play retained its power to shock. The performance on 28 May
1689 is known because it was attended by the new queen, Mary, and her
maids of honour. The only play 'forbid by the late King' exerted a strong
hold on the daughter who had usurped him, and in the event it was too
much for her. Mary may have approved of the political sentiments but was
so embarrassed by the way they were expressed that she hid behind her
fan, pretending to call for her 'palatine and hood' – anything to avoid the
spectacle of Elizabeth Barry's Leonora marrying Betterton's Torrismond
and assuming the throne her father had once occupied.[86]

It is tempting to feel that in deciding on this particular play in the spring
of the Glorious Revolution Betterton displayed no such embarrassment,
just tub-thumping topicality. The year 1688 had created a new appetite
for anti-Catholic feeling and the company's best financial interest was in
feeding it. In August that year, when the theatres had closed for the summer, the work went on. Constantijn Huygens visited Bartholomew Fair
and thought most people were there 'to laugh at the Pope'.[87] If Betterton
was among them, he probably reflected that for all the friendships, working relationships and loyalty he had enjoyed with Catholics, this was
good business; after Anthony Leigh's death in January 1693 he would
take the title role of *The Spanish Fryar* himself.[88] Yet the persistence of
those networks may also have informed the revival of the play. Its author
and his associate Dryden had lost his court posts as Poet Laureate and
Historiographer Royal months earlier, leaving him with no choice but to
turn back to the stage as a source of income.[89] In the early months of 1689

he was lying low in Soho. What better way of doing him a favour than staging a play known to have been so disliked by the late king? If the revival of *The Spanish Fryar* brought Dryden the possibility of a share of receipts, it also promised to help rehabilitate him in the eyes of the new Protestant regime that had curtailed his livelihood. It was a neat way of reconciling political and company loyalty, an act of political trimming worthy of Halifax himself.[90] The double act that had foisted *Albion and Albanius* on insufficient audiences and incredulous shareholders could move on in the space of four years from Stuart masque to Stuart satire. By 1701, Betterton would be playing Nicholas Rowe's *Tamerlane*, a hero publicly compared to 'the greatest Character of the present Age', William III, and he would be one of the handful of performers named as 'Comoedians in Ordinary' to Queen Anne.[91] As Stuart values faded from view his symbolic royalty became a transferable commodity, transcending dynastic affiliation.

The constitutional revolution of 1688 affected Betterton less than the managerial one that followed over the next five years. The transfer of power to Thomas Davenant had been without consequence to his leading actor's position in the company, unlike the events set in motion by a sale of stock that took place on 18 March 1690. Alexander Davenant had decided to take his turn at cashing in his shares; in return, he agreed to manage the interest thus acquired by a hard-nosed lawyer from Somerset who in years to come would challenge every assumption Betterton held about the way to run a theatre company.[92]

Few theatre people have had such negative press as Christopher Rich. Cibber devotes pages to what Milhous calls his 'tyrannical ways and pinchpenny management',[93] and that sums up the difference between two men and two managerial styles. Betterton led by example, inclusion and tradition, unafraid to lavish money when he thought the cause right and the audience enthusiastic. Rich was the first theatre manager of whom the term 'Thatcherite' might be used, although a rival, Owen Swiney, preferred 'Lewis Le Grand'.[94] He set out to undermine company hierarchies, to set young against old, to ensure that actors were paid as economically as possible in order to secure the best possible return for shareholders, and above all to isolate that bastion of company-based theatre, Thomas Betterton. Tensions were slow to emerge, but when they did, in 1693, the results were explosive.

CHAPTER 11

Back to the future: breakaway
to semi-retirement

To the stubbornness of his North Somerset community, with its history of defying both royal and parliamentary tax collectors, Christopher Rich added the brains and money required for a legal career.[1] In his late twenties he was at Gray's Inn, clerk to Sir Thomas Skipwith, Sergeant-at-Law, and falling in with Skipwith's son, also Thomas.[2] Joint business interests developed. Skipwith Junior bought a share of the Duke's Company on 31 March 1682, after the secret discussions about the United Company but six weeks before the formal agreement. There was every reason for someone with inside knowledge to believe that the new monopoly would make money, even if shares were costly.[3] But it was not quite the success Skipwith hoped for, however well the actors did from it. He and Rich looked on and wondered how long they could put up with that acquisitive yet profligate bastion of the establishment, Thomas Betterton.

Their chance came with Charles Davenant's transfer of shares to his brother Alexander in 1687. Alexander could not afford them any more than he could afford to pay Skipwith back for his help in buying them. All he could do was sign over to him the dividends and, at the end of the road, the shares themselves. Betterton acted on oblivious as, on 22 March 1688, Christopher Rich acquired his first slice of the company.[4] Alexander remained a useful front. On 18 March 1690 he became manager of Rich's interest, which now extended to one-sixth of the stock.[5]

On the surface this was a quiet month for Betterton, a fact which might not have passed Rich by. There were two premieres – John Crowne's *The English Friar* and Thomas Shadwell's *The Amorous Bigot* – but Thomas and Mary Betterton featured in neither.[6] He was busy all right, but with another spectacular. In June 1690 appeared an adaptation attributed to Betterton of Massinger and Fletcher's *The Prophetess*, 'being set out with Costly Scenes, Machines and Cloaths: The Vocal and Instrumental Musick, done by Mr Purcel; and Dances by Mr Priest; it gratify'd the Expectation of Court and City; and got the Author great Reputation.'[7] Even the treachery of another house playwright, Shadwell, could not derail the show. Exacting revenge for what he saw as Dryden's suppression of his own talents, he complained to Secretary of State Dorset about an alleged political aspersion in Dryden's prologue, which was then withdrawn.[8] The episode did not stop Dryden's even-tempered friend, Betterton, from accepting two more of Shadwell's plays. *The Prophetess* re-appeared throughout the next decade, and five years after Betterton's death, Rich's company recognised its financial success by reviving it.

The spectacle was to become an annual finale to the season. In May 1691 came Dryden and Purcell's *King Arthur*, with Betterton in the title role. May 1692 saw Purcell's *The Fairy Queen*, a musical augmentation of *A Midsummer Night's Dream* with a spectacular finale unprecedented even in Betterton's re-imaginings of Shakespeare:

a symphony is heard and the stage suddenly lights up, discovering a Chinese garden. The architecture, trees, plants, fruits, birds and animals are quite unlike those we know in our part of the world. There is a large arch through which can be seen other arches with close-set trees and an arbour. Above, a hanging garden rises in terraces surrounded by pleasant bowers, with a variety of trees and numerous strange birds circling about. From the topmost platform the water from a spurting fountain falls into a large pool.[9]

The source may have been Ogilby's *History of China and East Tartary*, which Betterton owned.[10] Naturalism and fantasy went hand in hand, and the scene illustrates a growing trend for the theatre to picture global trade; baroque display anticipated imperial grandeur.[11] It would require an outlay to match of £3000.[12] Betterton's imperial imagination ranged beyond the blacking he daubed for Othello, beyond the body of the actor, and into the environment of his acting. The commerce of the theatre, like that of trading companies, craved the broadest geographical scope, awakening the romance of empire in the meticulous detail and wondrous difference of the movable scenery that enveloped the performers and showed a world, as the stage direction put it, 'quite unlike [the one] we know'. Conversations with Charles Davenant, author of works on global trade, perhaps sustained Betterton's enthusiasm and he would have been delighted, the day before his death, to see 'Four Kings lately arriv'd from America' watching a performance of *Hamlet*.[13]

The formula for success was reflected in the formulaic approval of Downes: new scenes, new clothes, new dances, new music, although the expense was such that 'the Company got very little'.[14] That could not be overlooked in February 1692, when the accumulated debt was about £800, or about seven lots of annual returns for shareholders.

But it appears that Betterton was more intent on the popularity of his blockbusters with the town and court. They took the language of *Albion and Albanius* and made it speak of other national heroes. *King Arthur* embodied the continuity of British kingship in the shape of the symbolic actor-king, Thomas Betterton, who the following year would also play Bancroft's Henry II and, later still, lesser roles that reached deep into the nation's past; *The Fairy Queen* celebrated the pre-eminence of Shakespeare among the arts.[15] In May 1693 came the downturn. *The Prophetess* was revived because a new production was too expensive, and Betterton had had a personal taste of financial disaster amid the perils of global trade.

Just as the company was being infiltrated by money men, Betterton was himself on the verge of ruin. In 1692 he lost the savings he had invested with his friends Sir Francis Watson and Dr John Radcliffe, estimated at between £2000 and £8000, in a shipping venture to India; docking at Ireland and finding no convoy to escort it home, the ship was captured 'by the Marquis de Nesmond, with all her rich cargo, which amounted to more than 120,000*l*'.[16] An accumulator and collector by instinct, Betterton had taken a personal risk of the kind he normally saved for business. He had almost certainly thought to retire a gentleman. The misfortune was worse for Watson; his daughter Elizabeth joined the Betterton household soon afterwards with her actor-husband, John Bowman, himself not unknown to the bailiffs.[17]

1692 had been a grim year. The company was losing money while Betterton was splashing out thousands on *The Fairy Queen* and contemplating his fortune lining a Frenchman's pockets. In November one of his most bankable playwrights, Shadwell, died; then, on Friday 9 December, a worse shock. William Mountfort had worked with Betterton for fifteen years. Like Henry Harris, he was glamorous, popular with the court and gifted with the ease in comedy which had always eluded Betterton. Cibber remembered 'the wit of the Poet always [seeming] to come from him Extempore'.[18] Combining all those marketable gifts with the skills of a minor playwright, Mountfort was a major asset, for all his occasional Harris-like tantrums. In December 1692, however, he was murdered while trying to protect Anne Bracegirdle from abduction.[19] His death was marked by such loving titles as *The Ladies Lamentation for their Adonis* (1692) and *The Player's Tragedy* (1693). The latter's subtitle – *Fatal Love* – said what people thought about Mountfort's relationship with Bracegirdle; predictably enough given the marriage of John Bowman and Elizabeth

Watson, or indeed that of the Bettertons themselves, who had met under Sir William Davenant's roof.

It was a personal and professional challenge for the Bettertons. The man who might have been their adoptive son-in-law died protecting their adopted daughter, under their noses. They were approaching sixty, Thomas and Mary, and William Mountfort and Anne Bracegirdle were potential future leaders of the company. To Betterton fell the melancholy business of reviving some of Mountfort's roles.[20] It was an actor's way of dealing with grief, playing the dead to maintain a living, both awakening and erasing the memory of William Mountfort.

Just when it seemed that things could get no worse, Anthony Leigh, veteran portly clown of the Duke's Company since 1671, died four days before Christmas 1692. When the December 1692 issue of *The Gentleman's Journal* forecast that 'we are like to be without new plays this month and the next', it was accurate.[21] Not until the end of February 1693 did the company conclude that the show had to go on and was mounting premieres by Southerne and Congreve, the latter hailed by Dryden as the great young hope of British theatre at a time when a generation of post-1660 dramatists had largely disappeared: 'he never saw such a first play in his life' was Dryden's verdict on *The Old Bachelour*, which ran for fourteen consecutive performances in March 1693.[22]

By *The Double Dealer*, which followed it in October 1693, Dryden was still more impressed: this was 'the promised hour' when the 'present age of wit obscure[d] the last'.[23] The play had been circulated, read or perhaps rehearsed before its premiere 'for an audience of several Persons of the first Rank both in Wit and Quality', who gave it a more favourable response than is indicated by the eight performances it received in its first six weeks in the repertory.[24] The dense plotting and claustrophobic setting – unusually for a Restoration comedy, there are no public spaces, only the gallery of a household and rooms leading off it – derive from Congreve's wish to preserve 'the three Unities of the Drama' with 'the utmost Severity'.[25] To Betterton fell the Iago-like role of Maskwell, exploiting his association with old Stuart rakes and his 'compelling aspect' in soliloquy, a device some of Congreve's critics found as out-dated as the character's ideology. Defending it, Congreve allows a glimpse of how Betterton exposed to the audience a process of deliberation without seeming to acknowledge their presence: 'when a Man in Soliloquy reasons with himself, and *Pro's* and *Con's*, and weighs all his Designs: We ought not to imagine that this Man either talks to us, or to himself; he is only thinking, and thinking such Matter as it were inexcusable Folly in him to speak.'[26]

Like Christopher Rich, Congreve had studied law and he found fruitful material in the power of legal manoeuvring to shape social relations. His heroes succeed with the benefit of law, his villains are undone by it. Such faith would be needed by Betterton, for the new vein of writing talent offered by Congreve was a distraction from the underlying conditions facing the company and its shareholders. By January 1693, before rehearsals for *The Old Bachelour*, they had become abundantly clear to Betterton, who gave up his shareholding and, at his own request, was paid a salary instead. After the East India Company disaster, he needed to consider what was best not only for the company but for his dependants. A secure salary was better than variable dividends or none. It was the start of a period when the company he had led for the past eleven years began to fall apart. He had seen it happen to the King's Company in the 1670s, thanks to the inability of management to deal with the prima-donna behaviour of leading actors. That was a situation he would have been able to control by force of personality and reputation. But the crisis of 1693–5 put him on the other side of the fence. Dealing with managers who had no knowledge of the theatre except how much money it could be expected to yield, he would find himself cast as the uppity, irresponsible actor. His response was to divest himself of all pretence that he could mount a defence on business or even legal terms and join forces with the actors he trusted. He had started his career as a company man and he would continue that way.

Crisis was in the air by the summer of 1693. For the past eighteen months, Sir Robert Legard, Master in Chancery, had been conducting an official inquiry into the company's finances and on 27 July he published his report, clarifying shareholdings which had become confused over a period of thirty years. Alexander Davenant fled to the Canary Islands in the autumn.[27] For a while Betterton and his masters saw things the same way; he was persuaded to resume his managerial duties, even to put pressure on a handful of actors led by Thomas Doggett who thought their talents under-used. By the end of the year, the shocking denouement: the two lawyers, Thomas Skipwith and Christopher Rich, flourished a document revealing how it was that Alexander Davenant had been able to afford his shares. The two of them now controlled the company, and Rich took hold of the purse-strings. By June 1694, it was already Rich who was taking money for court performances.[28] It was a nightmarish inversion of Congreve's *The Way of the World*, in which tyranny is vanquished with one flourish of a secret deed of conveyance.[29]

Irritating economies crept in – enough to make the actors feel as if a way of life was under threat. An historic concession on the sale of fruit in the theatre disappeared; the annual new wig which was a mark of Betterton's standing in the company could no longer be afforded. Fines for indiscipline were levied with unprecedented ferocity. Then, the torrent: individual actors' benefit performances were cut back and salaries lowered. Betterton had tempted Doggett back into the company with a generous offer which, once Doggett was back through the door, turned out not to be so generous. The final insult challenged the very core of the company's working practice and corporate memory. Betterton knew from the 1682 Union that the surest way to undermine an actor was not through his pocket but his roles. Under the Rich regime, actors could be 'turned out' of their established parts 'for noe crime & without warning & ignorant insufficient fellowes putt in their places'.[30] Betterton could find no better way of describing the situation than by invoking his theatrical pedigree, but his assumptions were poignantly out of kilter with the priorities emerging around him. The new owners, he complained, were 'treating us not as we were the Kings & Queenes servants but the Claimers slaves'.[31]

In a conflict of feudalism and capitalism, Betterton's best tactic was to appeal high in the language of 'oblig'd, faithful [and] humble' servitude of which the Longleat letter indicates he was an assured user.[32] The old connections would work in his favour, and there was none more familiar than the Lord Chamberlain himself, Charles Sackville, Earl of Dorset. Dorset's friendships with theatre people went back many years and took many forms. He is the urbane Eugenius of Dryden's *Essay of Dramatick Poesie* and its dedicatee; he had sent Dryden a copy of *Paradise Lost*; he had extended the hospitality of his bedroom to Nell Gwyn, who in 1678 had reported him 'worse in thre months for he drinkes aile with Shadwell & Mr Haris at the Dukes house all day long'.[33] As Lord Chamberlain, he maintained influence over the licensing of plays and the running of the patented theatre, and he had known Betterton personally for decades.

So, in December 1694, one year after Rich had begun to alienate his best actors, after months of squabbling and a summer season by junior actors designed by the owners to show that ignorant and insufficient fellows could after all make money,[34] Betterton and fourteen of his senior colleagues marched on Dorset's office with a petition. The actors asked for nothing less than deliverance from an 'Oppression ... soe intollerable & heavy that unlesse relieved wee are not able to act any longer'.[35] Fifteen actors, fifteen grievances: in Milhous's transcription the document runs to four pages and blends general complaints with individual axe-grinding (item thirteen reads, 'Mrs Verbruggen desires 5s per weeke may be added to her Sallary', while item five bemoans the scandalous new practice of not mounting a play unless there is a viable audience). But the document was designed for higher purposes. It begins with an appeal to 'Rights', to 'agreed Methods', to 'priviledges'. This was the language of conservatism spoken by people versed in a genre familiar to Dorset – the dedicatory epistle, with its lush fields of patronal bounty and wisdom. The petition was intentionally provocative, delivered in the hope of forcing the share-holders to cut their losses and quit; Milhous concludes that it 'threatens a strike' if Dorset does not intervene.[36] There was a simpler appeal. Betterton played on the associations of his relationship with Dorset, their shared investment in a concept of natural order which was threatened by radicals like Rich. Not so much a strike, perhaps, as the retirement of England's symbolic king, the passing of a more humane order.

Dorset acted swiftly, arranging a meeting for 17 December. A week in advance (and probably only a few days after the players' petition) he received a stern response from Skipwith. In a document more than twice the length of Betterton's, Skipwith and Rich responded to talk of rights, agreed methods and privileges with a point by point demonstration of their legal claims.[37] Betterton they characterised as someone who for years had been living at the company's expense with his free apartment and shady financing of the Dorset Garden Theatre; who had suppressed younger talent, pretending at sixty to be capable of 'That which he could at 30 or 40'; who had switched from shareholder to salaried status when it suited him only to complain afterwards; who had regularly failed to attend rehearsals for plays in which he had no part, in spite of his managerial responsibility; who had been rewarded generously for his work and Mary's in running the young actors' nursery; who had misrepresented the company's situation to his fellow actors in order to further his own ends. He was, Skipwith states, a 'mutinous' ring-leader who had pressured others into joining his pro-test. To that task he had brought the intimidating weight of patriarchy. Skipwith had asked Elizabeth Bowman why she had signed the actors' petition even though she had recently had a pay rise and was expecting the child who would keep her from the stage for months. The answer was predictable: 'onely because Mr Betterton whom she calls father desired her soe to doe.' Then Skipwith listed the nineteen actors, almost all of the younger generation, who had *not* signed the petition.

The discomfort Dorset presumably felt is shared by Milhous, for whom the reply 'must raise serious questions as to [the managers'] good faith, not to mention their honesty'; but what those questions are is not clear.[38] The fact that Skipwith and Rich replied so quickly and in such detail is one sign of the plain fact that Milhous reluctantly concedes: the law was on their side, and they knew it. If they sounded abrasive or provocative, such is the way when legal minds pit themselves against wounded acolytes of custom. Skipwith and Rich suspected that Betterton had a deeper agenda and complemented their reply with a plea that no one set up a theatre in London without their permission. On 12 December they succeeded. Five days later, the scene was set for Dorset's attempt at arbitration.

They met at the chambers of one-time amateur playwright and brother-in-law of Dryden, Sir Robert Howard. Dorset presided. Rich, Skipwith and Killigrew, confident of the law but perhaps already fearing that patronal influence was against them, lined up against Betterton's contingent of senior performers. The meeting did not last long before they traded insults. Betterton and Barry sounded grand, Rich and partners pernickety. When the meeting broke up, they knew that the next step would be a battle over whether Betterton and company could start a rival theatre. But the next step was an accident. Five days later, when Thomas and Mary Betterton were celebrating their thirty-first wedding anniversary, Queen Mary fell gravely ill and the theatre was closed. On 28 December, she died.[39] The closure was extended to Easter 1695, the actors thrown back on their own means, and Betterton had already acted his last role for Rich.

The closure concentrated minds. Time away from their managers intensified the actors' dread of returning to 'oppression' and they cast around for alternatives. Dorset worked on a set of compromise proposals favouring the actors. For the managers, the closure underscored the burden of an idle or unpopular theatre, and on 11 February 1695 they put out feelers for a reconciliation based on Dorset's proposals.[40] But Betterton had inside experience of their tactics, having tempted back Doggett the previous year with false promises, and he declined a meeting. Rich could not afford competition, and Betterton was confident enough of Dorset not to be unduly worried about offending him by rejecting the compromise. By 19 March, Rich and Skipwith understood that more was at stake than legal right and they applied to Dorset for an 'amicable composure of matters'.[41] They were too late. Betterton and his friends had been busy fitting out another theatre and less than a week after Rich and Skipwith's olive branch, Dorset handed the rebel actors their licence. For the lawyer-businessmen the outcome defied belief, but they were not done yet.

Betterton was not encumbered with choice when it came to a new theatre. Where memory led his eye fell. If he and the others had had any scenery to take with them to the old tennis court at Lincoln's Inn Fields it would not have fitted, and the difficulties the new company would eventually encounter stemmed from Betterton's inability to scale down production styles forged in bigger spaces.[42] As soon as they had moved to Dorset Garden in 1671 they had begun to outgrow the old house which, empty for twenty years, now needed major refurbishment; a rival jibed that it was merely a 'booth'.[43] Unless he was suffering from historical double vision, Downes implies that it had reverted to being a tennis court in their absence: 'the House being fitted up from a Tennis-Court, they Open'd it the last day of April 1695.'[44] The fifteen plaintiffs were augmented with a mixture of old and new actors to form a company of thirty-one, and some of the stage staff from the old company were persuaded to join in. The exercise crystallised Betterton's approach to company theatre. As he neared his sixtieth birthday, he decided to start out all over again in the building which already symbolised his own links to the great tradition of English drama. Entering the building again, he stepped into the shoes of Sir William Davenant, who claimed to have heard the footfalls of Shakespeare. Moving back was a gesture of aristocratic contempt for the new money values of Rich and Skipwith, and an influential audience was primed: 'the Town was ingag'd in its favour', while 'the assistance they receiv'd from some Noble Persons did 'em eminent Credit'; the opening was characterised by 'the good Humour' of 'Noble Patrons'.[45] Amid the cat-fight of commercial competition, Betterton had cunningly activated the network of aristocratic patronage which had seen the first Lincoln's Inn Fields company into being.

Fittingly, the first new play arrived by legal manoeuvre. Congreve's *Love for Love* had been written for the old United Company. After the first reading Congreve delayed committing the play to Rich and *Love for Love* had 'a narrow Escape', presumably with strong encouragement from Betterton.[46] Not all the original actors travelled with it. Indignant that they had not been offered shares, Joseph Williams and Susannah Verbruggen defected back to Rich and the opening of 30 April 1695 became a more complex event as a result. It ran for thirteen performances and continued to be a banker for the company both at Lincoln's Inn Fields and for commissioned performances. In February 1697 there was a showing for the Princess of Denmark's visit to Whitehall, while the company celebrated their credentials in the eyes of the law with a performance at the Inner Temple in November 1697, in the presence of 'the Lord Chancellor, with divers of the Judges'.[47] The audience was 'extreamly well pleas'd', for all the moral objections to the play and its slighting depiction of lawyers.[48] Such successes were vital for Betterton's self-esteem as much as his profit projections; influential patrons helped to determine taste, and in the company of the court and the higher eminences of the professions, trade was transformed into calling.

Congreve had originally imagined Joseph Williams as the spendthrift young lover, Valentine, who has fallen out of favour with his tyrannical father, Sir Sampson, a nightmarish caricature of arbitrary power. With Betterton stepping in, the mismatch of ages became an in-joke: in the old tennis court where he had first become the best actor in the world, Betterton was multiply rejuvenated. Although one of Betterton's mistakes as a manager at the new Lincoln's Inn Fields Theatre was his failure to exploit the fashion for new, sentimental comedy, *Love for Love* offered him a role consonant with that trend which also toyed with the material contingencies of 1695. Rescued from poverty by the heiress Angelica, Valentine makes his commitment with sentimental excess, but in the language of finance: 'I intend to doat on at that immoderate rate that your Fondness shall never distinguish itself enough to be taken notice of.' Angelica's reply alludes to Rich's withered heart: 'Have a care of large Promises; you know you are apt to run more in Debt than you are able to pay.'[49]

If the lines were spoken in triumph, Rich and his fellow patentees had done everything in their power to prevent them being heard. In 1695, the Lord Chief Justice, Sir John Holt, was asked to adjudicate on a writ issued against 'Betterton and others, who had erected a Playhouse', on the grounds that 'it was a Nuisance to the Neighbourhood'.[50] Having ignored the writ, the company faced prosecution for contempt of court, but their counsel intervened to protest that the only way they could defend themselves was to be formally indicted. The case went in their favour, Holt drawing a contrast with that of the rope-dancer Jacob Hall, who in 1671 had been convicted of causing a nuisance in the public highway after erecting a stage at Charing Cross.[51] But an equally significant reason for Betterton's successful defence was the identity of his accusers: 'And in this Case, the Prosecution is carried out by the Patentees of the Old Playhouse, and not by the Inhabitants of the Place; which shews they do not think it a Nuisance, if it be one.' Rich had probably looked into the Hall case sufficiently to feel that it established a precedent. He had obtained the writ after Dorset's final approach to the rebels on 19 March, as a desperate and vindictive last resort, and presumably confident that the more spacious environs of their own Drury Lane and Dorset Garden theatres meant there was little chance they would be hoist with their own petard. Attempts at legal action continued until the end of the year.[52]

Whatever their motives, claiming nuisance against Betterton was not their only course of action. At the end of the report on the case of *R* v.

Betterton, it is noted that 'an Information against the Players of the new Playhouse' had been lodged by someone invoking the increasingly fashionable language of moral fervour: the plays acted by the breakaway troupe were denounced as 'profane and lewd'.[53] Again Betterton won, but Holt's ruling indicates that the penalties could have involved 'estreatment' or forfeiture of their licence; he was not amused by Betterton's attempt to have the case dismissed on the grounds that the plaintiffs mistook the name of the theatre. It may be no accident that *Love for Love* was later the target for informants inspired by the writings of Jeremy Collier, when successful prosecutions were brought against individual actors, Betterton included.[54] One response of the players then was an advertising innovation clarifying responsibility for the text: for a revival of Congreve's *The Double Dealer* in 1699, the company took the unusual step of publishing the author's name on the playbill while making it clear that 'several expressions' had been 'omitted'.[55] It would not be surprising if Skipwith and Rich, whose own theatrical fortunes suffered just as Betterton's were recovering, continued with their campaign after the escape to Lincoln's Inn Fields. *Love for Love*, the benchmark success of the new company, would have been a satisfying target.

Five years later, Betterton made the same play part of the theatre's defence against Collier. Both companies agreed to mount benefit performances in late June 1700 for 'the Redemption of the English now in Slavery at Machanisso in Barbary'.[56] The thought of English sailors captured by North African pirates prompted the Drury Lane management to mount *The Tempest*. Betterton's response was less imaginative but more practical. He would mount the play likely to yield the most money, however incongruous the subject. That play was *Love for Love,* part of a strategy to prove that theatres after Collier were not dissolute but charitable: 'which good example,' read *The London Post*, 'may move others to be speedy and generous.' How speedy or generous is unclear. While the Theatre Royal paid 'into the hands of the Churchwardens of St Martin's the sum of 20 £ out of the receipts of the play acted by that company', '[w]hat the other company gave I do not yet hear'.[57]

His finances uncertain, Betterton pursued other lines of work, as he had earlier in his career. When the ninth Sir John Perceval, Earl of Egmont, took up a place at 'Mr. *Demeure*'s Academy' for '*French, Latin,* Geography, Musick, Dancing, Fencing, Vaulting, Quarter-Staff, and other hardy Exercises', his guardian knew that public life demanded other talents, so he arranged private tuition with 'Mr. *Betterton*, the famous Tragedian,

[who] was employed to instruct him in those Parts of Oratory which consist of Emphasis and Action'.[58] The arrangement lasted until 1698, when Perceval enrolled at Westminster. Betterton took on other pupils such as the clergyman, Ralph Bridges, who needed help with his ordination sermon – further vindication of his professional respectability.[59] Perceval would see his old tutor play Othello in 1709.[60]

Private coaching was grounded in Betterton's work, and Mary's, with younger performers or courtiers. For Mary in particular it was almost her chief occupation. Later she would draw fifty shillings a week 'constantly pd her in Complem[t] to M[r] Betterton', in recognition of her role in training young performers, but also of her fading stage presence.[61] Betterton's teaching nudges Gildon's *Life* closer to authenticity: submitting what he did to a system of instruction, possibly drawing on texts such as Bulwer's *Chirologia*, which he owned, was a pre-requisite of dealing effectively with young actors and noblemen. His teaching was exacting but cheerful. To Barton Booth he was 'a second father' by virtue of his 'kind admonitions and friendly instructions'.[62] He had first seen Mary Porter in a Lord Mayor's pageant playing 'the Genius of Britain', and when she joined the theatre some time in the 1690s 'she was so little when first under [Betterton's] tuition, that he threatened her, if she did not speak and act as he would have her, to put her into a fruit-woman's basket and cover her with a vine-leaf'.[63] To young Perceval he played the professor of gentility, imparting through his vocation of acting the craft of acting vocations, instructing others as he had painstakingly instructed himself. The ideological disturbance created by the impersonation of gentility, its 'hollowing out' of behavioural codes, is second nature to stage historians, but in Betterton's coaching of the aristocracy lies a deeper paradox. The actor may know better than his pupil what it takes to be gentleman-like, but in telling him he merely allows him to fulfil his pre-ordained destiny. Coaching Perceval, Betterton was superior but subservient. If the experience reminded him of how far he had come by virtue of instruction, he knew too how far he had to go.

The story of the Lincoln's Inn Fields company between 1695 and the opening of the Queen's Theatre in 1705 has been told so authoritatively by Judith Milhous that a critical summary of her account, referenced to the wider context of Betterton's life, fills in what is known of him between *Love for Love* and the summer evenings in Reading evoked by Gildon.[64] Milhous divides the period three ways: the three-and-a-half seasons until 1698, when the company enjoyed relative success; four less stable years at the end of which its fortunes began to recover; then the very difficult years from the death of William III in 1702, when accusations about Betterton's financial management abounded and the suspicion arose that he was creaming off funds for his retirement.

Until 1698 the company enjoyed success in a competitive environment. Actors moved about in search of better deals, a minor industry developed in imitating Betterton and Barry – a sure sign of their rivals' desperation – and new plays felt the pressure of a climate that increasingly preferred musical, athletic or even zoological entertainment: when Christopher Rich 'started adding animal acts to his offerings he was admitting that plays alone were not enough', a trend accelerated by such novelties as Henry Winstanley's Mathematical Water Theatre, which had opened in 1696.[65] The break-up of the United Company had deprived Rich of senior professionals but also seeded tensions among the younger actors who made the switch to Lincoln's Inn Fields only to see their opportunities blocked by the old guard.[66] Oldest of them all, Betterton was as busy as ever, playing at least six new roles a season from 1695 to 1698.[67]

The new company was a gerontocracy rather than a dictatorship. The agreement made by the breakaway actors shows that Betterton was not in control of the business, merely 'first among equals', although whether even a senior figure such as Elizabeth Barry held shares – a key index of power – is unclear.[68] To Barry did fall one of the duties previously shared with Harris, that of finding new plays; one result was a crop of new writing by women, very little of which survived its first run.[69] Even the outstanding talent of the decade, Congreve, did not quite answer expectations with his last play, *The Way of the World*; its imperious dedication suggests that the company never thought it had a repeat of *Love for Love* on its hands, or a *Mourning Bride*, in which Betterton had played another Othello-like role.[70] Barry later admitted that the greatest successes were in the spectaculars which the new house was nevertheless ill-equipped to provide on the scale of its only competitor: 'we have had pretty good success in the Opera of Rinaldo and Armida where the Poet made me command the sea the earth and air', she wrote to Lady Lisburne.[71]

Barry prefaced her report by saying that the winter season had been the worst she could remember, and this was the start of a downturn. In 1699 Anne Bracegirdle voiced the company's darkest fear that the Lincoln's Inn Fields Theatre would once again reverberate to the sound of tennis balls; by August 1701 it was doubted whether both theatres made more than a 'poppet show in a country town', and music concerts helped keep them open.[72] It marked the start of a period lasting until 1702 in which the tensions inherent in the breakaway ignited – disgruntled junior actors, a poorly equipped theatre, new writing that largely failed to persuade the audience. When Gildon's Betterton sat in his Reading garden and bemoaned the poor discipline of younger actors, this was what he had in mind. Barton Booth, whose arrival in the autumn of 1700 prompted a review of the company's hierarchy, told Cibber of 'the difficulties Betterton then laboured under and complained of: how impracticable he found it to keep their body to that common order which was necessary for their support'.[73] It is a persistent metaphor in Betterton's life: the labour of managing the body to ensure order and support. Worst sin of all in the eyes of the former bookseller's boy, the younger performers relied 'too much upon their intrinsick merit', saving their efforts for personal benefit performances.[74] Intervention in November 1700 by Jersey, the new Lord Chamberlain, elevated Betterton to a position of 'sole management' designed to guarantee not artistic control but the whip-hand in dealing with those found 'negligent in their business'.[75] Another provision of the same order indicates the level of anxiety to be found among shareholders over Betterton's financial dealings. After the purchase of 'cloths, scenes &c ... for ye immediate service of ye Company', Betterton was restricted to spending a maximum of forty shillings on any item, a challenge for someone who had blown £4000 on *Albion and Albanius*.[76]

Still, he remained convinced that semi-operas such as Motteux's *The Mad Lover*, premiered in January 1701, were the way forward. His instincts as a new-style manager led him to further old-style repertory. *The Ambitious Step-mother* was an exotic play after Settle by Nicholas Rowe, who reminded people of Otway.[77] William Burnaby's *The Ladies Visiting Day* is described by Milhous as an example of 'the Carolean satiric style' which had started to go out of fashion at least a decade earlier; the dedication suggests it failed to reverse the trend.[78] Shakespeare remained in the repertory with an adaptation of *The Merchant of Venice* and performances of Tate's *King Lear*, in some of which – a sign of changing times and company pressures – George Powell took over the title role.[79] Yet Betterton maintained a more consistent record of commissioning new work than his rivals at Drury Lane, albeit from a lower base; this was a period in which he largely remained cautious, anxious to stick with established policies and successes.[80] Unfortunately he did so in the context of changing patronage, his company playing courtly repertory to an audience that could only come after working hours.[81]

Such power as Jersey's intervention gave Betterton he was able to use, and the upturn in the company's fortunes through 1701 was thanks to 'better handling of the standard repertory and improved discipline'.[82] Yet instances of his extravagance persist, as if the hope never expired that he might create one last box-office sensation. The financial conditions imposed upon him by Jersey's order were partly the result of the season given to 'Monsieur Ballon, the famous French dancing master (whose father teaches the dauphins 3 sons)' at Easter 1699, for which Ballon was paid 500 guineas, 400 of which came from the Lincoln's Inn Fields Theatre.[83] Even though the company lost money on him, Betterton repeated the stunt first in 1700, when he contracted Anthony L'Abbé for three years, and then again early in 1702, when he paid another 400 guineas to Madame Subligny of the Paris Opera, and again failed to recover costs.[84] The price was a more restricted repertory and fewer regular actors over the following year. Such extravagances followed the appointment in July 1696 of a dancing master in residence, Joseph Sorin, who was paid thirty shillings per week; the actor with clumsy feet consistently over-estimated the commercial appeal of dancing, although some contemporary observers failed to notice it in their admiration of his acting.[85] Gildon has Betterton bemoan the cost of French dancers, but the complaint rings hollow even in the context of L'Abbé's dissatisfaction with being ignored by his manager.[86]

Betterton's extravagances stemmed from his lifelong attachment to French culture. Visits to France, contacts with French diplomats, the influence of Charles II in introducing French styles to early Restoration theatre, and adapting French comedies had left a mark on him so profound that he became unable to appreciate that the London audience and – if reports of internal dissatisfaction with *Psyche* are correct – his own companies did not always share his tastes. The francophile aspirations of the early Carolean court had enjoyed dubious popularity with Londoners in the 1660s, never mind forty years later, when Louis XIV recognised the Old Pretender as King of England, but Betterton could not divest himself of them. The partiality left its mark on his collection of prints, which included such items as *Tableaux du Cabinet du Roy*, *Veues Nouvelles des plus beaux Lieux de France & d'Italie*, and even *Conquêtes de Louis le Grand Roy de France*.[87] Even Downes grumbled, while trying to place the blame on a section of the audience: 'In the space of Ten Years past, Mr Betterton to gratify the desires and Fancies of the Nobility and Gentry; procur'd from Abroad the best Dancers and Singers … who being Exorbitantly Expensive, produc'd small Profit to him and his Company, but vast Gain to themselves.'[88] Not all nobility and gentry agreed with the trend, and when the fictitious Dryden of Thomas Brown's *Dialogues* lighted on an ironic name for the actor it was no accident that he came up with 'Sieur

Batterton.[89] An habitual actor of French roles, Betterton might not have minded.[90]

Less elevated habits of the career impresario died just as hard. While he was negotiating the visit of Madame Subligny, Betterton attempted to repeat the Dorset Garden move of 1671 by offering, via the shareholder Charles Killigrew, to rent at £5 per acting day the Theatre Royal, Drury Lane, whose lease was up on 9 November 1701. The occupier, Rich, ensured that the deal stalled, while Killigrew tried to undermine him through the actors. If the manoeuvre recalled the Dorset Garden move in the search for a bigger theatre, it also reproduced the aggressive tactics Betterton had used to secure the 1682 Union. He was, at least, respectable: a deposition by Killigrew refers to his agreement with 'T. Betterton gent and John Watson Citizen and Draper of London' to lease the theatre from midsummer 1702.[91] The gentleman and the citizen draper: a small satisfaction for the former bookseller's boy. The takeover of Drury Lane came to nothing, but it was a sign not only that the gentleman-actor had faith in his company's and probably his own future, but that he had lost nothing of his business sense. Charles Killigrew had merely 'wanted his money, and he was entirely indifferent as to how he got it or from whom'.[92] Come the spring of 1702, Betterton resorted to another well-honed tactic, petitioning the recently crowned Queen Anne for a union of the companies. He invoked economics, art and morality: the audience was not large enough to support two theatres, while competitive bidding for overseas artistes forced up prices; in desperation both companies had turned to 'Tumblers, Vaulters [and] Ladder dancers' who threatened to bring the theatre down to the level of Bartholomew Fair; and – strained logic – a union would help prevent the 'Irregularitys and Indecency's' that had landed Betterton and his fellows in court several times over the past four years.[93]

The final phase of managerial responsibility in Betterton's life, from 1702 to 1705, saw a let up in his capacity for learning new roles, but none in his industry.[94] Although it taxed his ailing memory, acting was a welcome distraction from management.[95] He faced a minor revolt by the company's leading clown, Thomas Doggett, a threat of prosecution unless 'Indecencies and Abuses' of the stage were reformed (accompanied by public agitation), and two sustained assaults on his financial probity. The first was an action taken by shareholders led by Sir Edward Smith to reclaim undistributed profits; nothing was proven on its final collapse in 1708.[96] More damaging was a petition by the actor John Verbruggen, who accused Betterton and Elizabeth Barry of syphoning off profits, accumulating debts, not disclosing financial information and denying benefits to everyone except themselves.[97] The same themes and more were taken up in an anonymous play of 1705, *The Lunatick*, in which Betterton, Barry and Bracegirdle were characterised as organised cheats, keeping two sets of books, not paying debts, failing to disclose payments to foreign performers, withholding pay for junior actors, pocketing payments for court performances, taking benefit days at peak season, using the theatre as a lodging to avoid using coal at home, and acting despite 'Age, Ugliness and Gout'.[98] The outcome of Verbruggen's submission is not known. Although the words 'leave to examine ye books' and 'liberty to examine subscriptions' are written in the margins of his complaint, it is not clear whether they were notes made by the person who heard it or directions about resolving it. Milhous, forthright in her defence of Betterton's management, admits that some way was found to settle the grievance privately and so avoid having the accounts audited.[99] It was his preferred way: gentlemanly and discreet, the interests of the company perfectly aligned to his own.

The year 1705 marks the start of the period when that partial fiction could no longer be maintained. Vanbrugh and Congreve acquired a licence to run a new company in a new theatre, the Queen's at Haymarket, and promptly brought in Betterton and the Lincoln's Inn Fields actors. Betterton assigned his licence to Vanbrugh and once again the old tennis court stood empty, awaiting sale.[100] It was a good deal for all parties. Vanbrugh gained experienced and disciplined performers, who gained a better theatre and more security. They were on salaries and so protected from the vicissitudes of both the box-office and the cost of building, which did not compare badly with that of Dorset Garden.[101] The licence envisages a fresh start for the post-Collier age ('for the better Reforming the Abuses and Immorality of the Stage ... a new Company of Comedians should be Establish'd'), but it was the old actors, with their track record of prosecution for profanity, who best met the new management's commercial needs.[102] Fearing immersion in debt, Congreve withdrew after less than a year, not before Vanbrugh had started pressing for a union with Rich's company.[103]

Betterton could look on without nostalgia. He began to shed more roles while retaining a measure of influence. A poor eighteen months followed in which the company lacked direction and recycled too much Lincoln's Inn Fields stock. There was the indiscipline of George Powell, one of Betterton's successors, and with the appointment of Owen Swiney as manager in 1706 Betterton began the progress towards semi-retirement in which Gildon found him in Reading.[104] Seasons were designed to give him longer breaks and in 1707 he went for five months without performing.[105]

Drama was starting to give way to opera, and according to one report 'Betterton ... and the best of them, must give place to a bawling Italian woman, whose voice to me is less pleasing than merry-andrew's playing on the gridiron'.[106]

With Swiney a further reorganisation had taken place, and Downes poignantly marked the moment as the conclusion of his own history of the Restoration stage. Swiney had imported Drury Lane personnel. Downes lost his place to his counterpart and beheld, half in wonder, half in sadness, 'the only remains of the Duke of *York's* Servants, from 1662, till the Union in *October* 1706', otherwise known as Cave Underhill and Thomas Betterton.[107] The formal union of the companies followed two years later, but increasingly Betterton's energies were devoted not to the business of negotiating contracts, casts or shareholdings, but to the theatrical inheritance that would also be his greatest bequest. Alongside other favourites such as Montezuma and Heartwell he would play Macbeth in each of his last three seasons, Othello and Lear in two of them and, in late September 1709, at the age of seventy-four and with seven months to live, one last Hamlet. Other roles he would continue to perform up to the brink of death the following spring, but here was a final attempt to embody through Shakespeare the man he had always been: a man, as *The Tatler* said of the Prince himself, of 'great expectation, vivacity and enterprise'.[108]

In September 1709 *The Tatler* may have been amazed at how well Betterton 'acted youth' but his first Ophelia probably could not bear to watch. After her husband's death on 28 April 1710, a fortnight after his painful, slippered last performance, the same journal reported that Mary Betterton had 'long pined away with a sense of his decay, as well in his person as his little fortune'. All that prevented her from dying at the shock of bereavement was its driving her mad, her 'absence of reason ... her best defence against age, sorrow, poverty, and sickness'.[109] Interment in Westminster Abbey promised one last flourish of scenic grandeur, the symbolic berth among the English kings whose fittingness Steele would proclaim days later, but although it was an affair of 'great Decency' there was no money for a memorial stone, even of the modest variety that remembered Betterton's grandfather and uncle next door in St Margaret's: the occasion could only remind Mary – assuming she was capable of such recall – of the burial in the Abbey more than forty years before of their master Davenant, who had been treated, in Pepys's words, like 'a poor poet'.[110] Eventually friends rallied round, even royalty. A pension, a benefit night and – briefly – a salary from the theatre; from Queen Anne, remembering how an actress had coached her to move and speak like a princess, at least the promise of a further pension.[111]

The state of her late husband's affairs was a matter of real concern, although anyone who had read a pamphlet published by company treasurer Zachary Baggs in July 1709 would have been surprised to hear it. Commissioned to clear management of the charge that actors were underpaid, Baggs came up with some impressive but plausible numbers. The semi-retired Betterton was on 41s a week and Mary – almost completely retired – 11s; with his annual benefit plus occasional gifts that meant, for the preceding nine months, nearly £640 in the Betterton family kitty.[112] Yet by the time Betterton died another nine months later there was little or nothing left. Perhaps he had been paying off debts and whether through negligence or the knowledge that there was nothing to give, he made no will. A memoir published eighty years later movingly captures his sorry state – a lifetime's social ambition thwarted – but also the complex blend of qualities that meant he could not be written off as just a 'player':

Betterton died very poor; a man it is said everybody loved, in and out of the theatre; and known by courtier and peasant by the appellation of *honest Tom* – that was honour indeed as an actor and manager … but neither his genius, his labour, his excellence, fame, goodness, nor even his honesty had procured him [a] gentleman-like existence.[113]

Not until 1719 was administration of his estate granted to his elderly sister, Mrs Mary Kelly, seven years after Mary Betterton's own death, for which she had been better prepared than her husband.[114]

Amid her sister-in-law's demented grief in the spring of 1710 it fell to Mary Kelly to make a decision about Betterton's chief movable asset, piled up in his Covent Garden lodgings. A symbol of his trade beginnings and his genteel aspirations, it consisted of 200 or so paintings and prints, and more than 550 books. Missing, however, was his most famous possession, sold a while before in yet another tidy piece of business. The inaugural bequest to the National Portrait Gallery known as the Chandos Portrait of Shakespeare has since become an icon of Britain's theatrical heritage, and Thomas Betterton was among the first to appreciate and publicise its significance.

CHAPTER 12

Books and pictures: Betterton and the Chandos Portrait

Jacob Hooke, bookseller, was instructed to draw up the auction catalogue, and copies of *Pinacotheca Bettertonaeana* (Betterton's picture gallery) were left in favourite coffee-houses for friends, collectors and dealers: St James's, near the Palace, where Steele sometimes wrote *The Tatler*; Mr Ellar's at Westminster Hall, Will's in Cornhill, Mr Squire's in Fuller's Rents, where the ill-fated Medbourne had hung out.[1] The sale took place at Betterton's Russell Street lodgings on 24 August 1710, the forty-ninth anniversary of his first Hamlet. It was not an instant success, so a further sale was advertised in December.[2]

Hooke did not often deal with pictures. His six other sale catalogues of the period were named 'bibliopolii' or 'officina' for the collections of the booksellers Christopher Hussey and William Shrewsbury, and 'bibliotheca' for the libraries of gentlemen such as John Ray, FRS and Charles Bernard, the Queen's Sergeant-Surgeon.[3] Among other catalogues up to 1800, 'bibliotheca' is by far the most common term and 'pinacotheca' so rare that it features nowhere among the titles in *Eighteenth Century Collections Online*. If *Pinacotheca Bettertonaeana* signalled rarity value, it also spoke of gentility precariously poised between the trade credentials of the bookseller and the gentlemanly company of Hooke's other clients. For Hooke, Betterton was not the 'late eminent Tragedian' of Gildon's *Life*, merely 'that Celebrated Comedian, lately Deceas'd'. Yet the Longleat letter shows him as part of a network of connoisseurs that included aristocrats such as Lord Weymouth, anxious both to augment and share their collections, even with actors.[4]

Betterton's collection of more than 550 books was modestly impressive – he owned more than 150 folios – but it was not that of a conventional gentleman, and he may have owed some of it to trade connections. With no education in the classics, he had translations from Greek and Latin (he had subscribed to Dryden's Virgil, produced by his old associate Jacob Tonson) but no originals.[5] French literature and drama are better

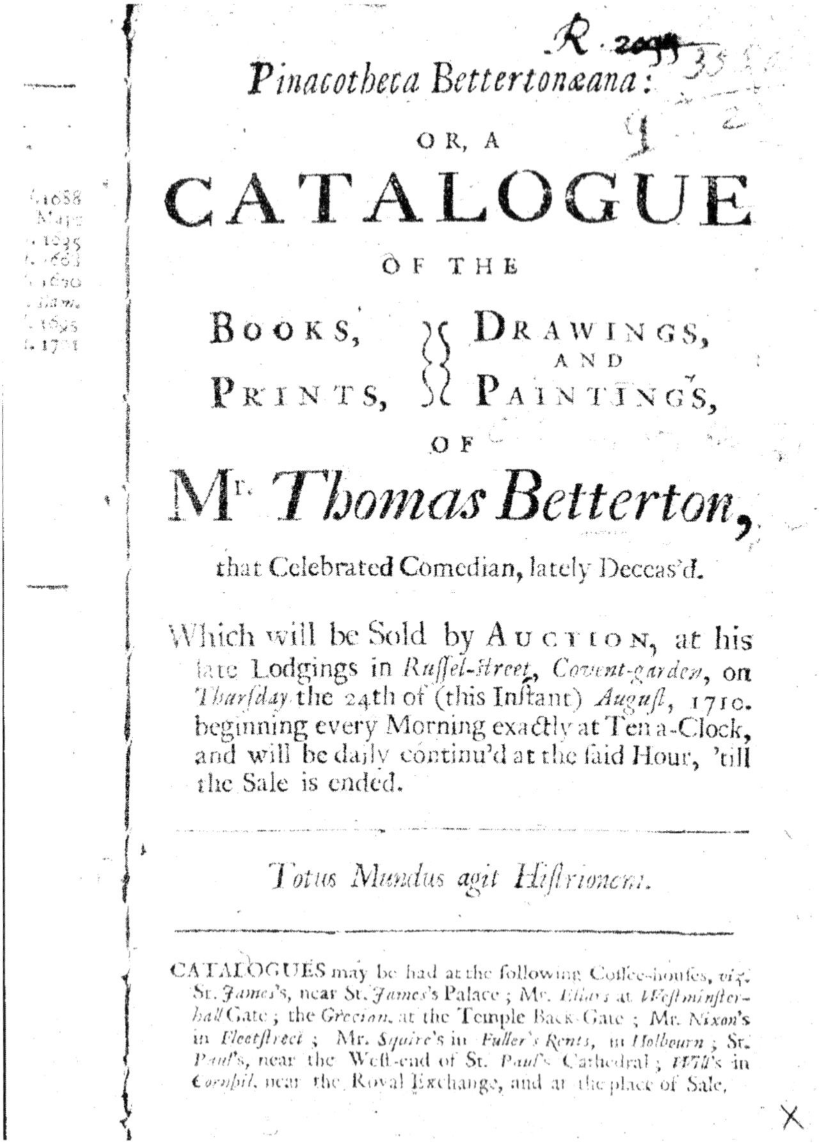

R. 20

Pinacotheca Bettertonæana:

OR, A

CATALOGUE

OF THE

BOOKS, DRAWINGS,
AND
PRINTS, PAINTINGS,

OF

Mr *Thomas Betterton,*

that Celebrated Comedian, lately Deceas'd.

Which will be Sold by AUCTION, at his late Lodgings in *Ruffel-ftreet, Covent-garden,* on *Thurfday* the 24th of (this Inftant) *Auguft,* 1710. beginning every Morning exactly at Ten a-Clock, and will be daily continu'd at the faid Hour, 'till the Sale is ended.

Totus Mundus agit Hiftrionem.

CATALOGUES may be had at the following Coffee-houfes, *viz.* St. *James's,* near St. *James's* Palace; Mr. *Elliot's* at *Weftminfter-hall* Gate; the *Grecian,* at the Temple Back-Gate; Mr. *Nixon's* in *Fleetftreet;* Mr. *Squire's* in *Fuller's Rents,* in *Holbourn;* St. *Paul's,* near the Weft-end of St. *Paul's* Cathedral; *Will's* in *Cornhil,* near the Royal Exchange, and at the place of Sale.

Illustration 8 The sale catalogue for Betterton's collection: Jacob Hooke's *Pinacotheca Bettertonaeana* (1710)

represented. History, royal biography and travel books feature prominently but not English plays, where memory or scripts sufficed. Some future
scholar will be fortunate to discover the first item in Hooke's supplementary list of 'Eleven Bundles of Plays and Parts of Plays, each containing
24 – MSS', which may indicate the real scope of Betterton's repertoire: 264
roles, compared to the 183 for which Milhous found evidence.[6] The most
striking gap concerns the man who had been a constant reference point in
Betterton's career. Leaving aside speculation about how many items were
withheld from auction, it is remarkable how little his generation's definitive Hamlet had collected under the heading, 'William Shakespeare'.

It was hardly for want of interest in the history of English poetry and
drama. He had folio editions of Beaumont and Fletcher and Ben Jonson
to add to his volumes of Chaucer, Spenser, Milton and Dryden; among
his picture collection, according to the Longleat letter, were 'heads' of
Fletcher, Suckling and Chaucer, to modernised versions of whose poetry
his name is linked. In the 1712 *Miscellaneous Poems and Translations by
Several Hands* he is credited with translations of the Prologue (retitled
'Chaucer's *Characters*') and the Reeve's Tale, recast as 'The Miller of
Trompington'. Alexander Pope, represented elsewhere in the same volume, wrote that he had helped them into print.[7] The list of Chaucer attributions had grown by 1739, when George Ogle's edition included versions
of the Doctor of Physick, Seaman and Plowman allegedly by Betterton;
in the 1741 edition the list ballooned to eighteen attributions. The 1740s
Betterton revival was partly responsible, but the 1712 edition is another
matter. Betterton's known writing habits suggest a man who readily
translated French verse but only into English prose, so the idea that Pope
took his sketches and turned them into verse is plausible.[8] Pope's friendship extended to painting a copy of Kneller's portrait of Betterton, now
at Scone Palace.

Betterton prepared at least one acting edition of Shakespeare in the shape
of the 1700 *Henry IV*, but on the evidence of *Pinacotheca Bettertonaeana* he
did not own either a Shakespeare folio or any quartos. A single unnamed
Shakespearean play is found in an arbitrary lot of eleven by other authors
in the supplementary list. The only substantial Shakespearean item among
his books is Nicholas Rowe's six-volume set of 1709, 'with Cuts' or engravings, some of which probably featured his own performances.[9] Since Rowe
also acknowledged Betterton's help in researching Shakespeare's life, it
might have been a complimentary copy that spared the actor the thirty
shilling outlay: Betterton had visited Warwickshire 'on purpose to gather
up what Remains he could of a Name for which he had so great a Value'.[10]

Shakespeare was so much a part of the actor's professional life that his works need only be represented by all those 'Parts of Plays'.

Hooke's list of 155 prints and drawings and sixty-seven paintings does little more than his list of folios to persuade us that Betterton had been an avid Shakespearean collector. He owned three portraits of himself as a Turk (presumably including the Greenhill portrait of him in *The Siege of Rhodes*), with 'the Bayes on his Head' (as if to confirm Cibber's view that a great actor is the equal if not the superior of a great author), and in the domestic happiness he enjoyed with Mary, but none represents him in a Shakespearean role.[11] Drawings of 'Scarramouches and other Antick Figures' are, the Turk aside, the only explicitly theatrical items, as if the collector and the actor were separate people.

Pinacotheca Bettertonaeana therefore provides a slightly puzzling context for the Longleat letter, which mentions a 'Head' of 'Shakespeares', and for a note made nine years after Betterton's death by the antiquarian George Vertue, who had become interested in a painting owned by his barrister friend, Robert Keck:

Mr Betterton told Mr Keck several times that the Picture of Shakespeare he had, was painted by one John Taylor a Player, who acted for Shakespear and this John Taylor in his will left it to Sir Willm. Davenant. & at the death of Sir Will Davenant. – Mr Betterton bought it, & and at his death Mr. Keck bought it in whose poss[ession] it now is.[12]

This was the Chandos Portrait.[13] It had taken Vertue at least two attempts to get the story straight. First, he referred to 'the only Original' picture of Shakespeare that belonged to Keck, who had bought it for forty guineas from an actor whose name Vertue could not instantly recall, so he later hazarded a guess and in the margin wrote 'Richard Burbridge'. The actor had bought the painting from Sir William Davenant, who in turn had 'had it' of the man he called – at the very least – his godfather, Shakespeare. It had been, says Vertue, painted by 'one Taylor', described as a 'Player and painter' who was Shakespeare's 'intimate friend', which appears to confuse Joseph Taylor the actor with John Taylor, later master of the Painter-Stainers' Company. At the second attempt, Vertue thought better of describing the picture as the 'only original' and went instead for the more modest 'one original', which has encouraged scholars to believe that the Chandos Portrait was 'an uncollected commission, or a rejected version, or even an early studio copy of another picture'.[14] Vertue was accustomed to thinking carefully about such things. His memorial in

Illustration 9 'Besides Shakespeares': William Shakespeare, attributed to
John Taylor. The Chandos Portrait (*c*.1610). Reproduced by
permission of the National Portrait Gallery

Westminster Abbey, in the opposite cloister to Betterton's grave, attributes
to him 'all the Genius of the graphic Art', and he had studied with Michael
Vandergucht, whose engraving of the Chandos Portrait featured in the
frontispiece to Rowe's Shakespeare.

Betterton's buyer was clearly a willing listener and E.A. Greening
Lamborn, in spite of adding extra stages to the lineage spelled out by
Vertue, made perfect sense of how a young lawyer got talking to an old
actor about a picture of Shakespeare.[15] Robert Keck was twenty-four when
Betterton died, far from suspiciously young, even if the last of the several
times he heard about the portrait must have been up to fifteen years before
Vertue wrote his notes. Keck's father Anthony, according to Lambourn,
was 'a very rich Money Scrivener' who did not see eye to eye with his son.

Robert was 'an excellent Antiquary' with a substantial collection of books and 'curiosities' which ate up a good deal of his living allowance in the eleven years between his matriculation at Oxford and his entry to the bar in 1713.[16] When Nicholas Rowe recalled Betterton's Warwickshire excursion he was describing exactly the kind of activity that enthused Keck.

For his prize purchase, Keck would need all the enthusiasm he could summon. Forty guineas was a hair-raising amount for someone yet to make his way in the world: not far off the cost of a coach, and significantly more than the £30 Samuel Cooper, painter of kings, charged Pepys.[17] It is a fair guess that it was more, too, than Betterton had paid in 1668, when forty guineas was not far off half his annual salary.[18] Other figures underline the point. In 1706 Godfrey Kneller was charging £15 for a bust-sized portrait; in 1720 Jonathan Richardson charged twenty guineas for the same; while in 1741 Joseph Highmore observed that 'the price of a Copy is always half that of an original', and that for the past eighteen years he had charged ten guineas for bust portraits.[19] Whether the Chandos Portrait was the 'only' original or 'one' original, it was priced as if it were the finest specimen of an 'only' original. Antiquarians less cautious than Keck might well have needed reassuring 'several times' that it was worth so much, particularly when Shakespeare had yet to be declared the 'National Poet'.[20] Yet it had always been clear that the Chandos Portrait had a singular claim to authenticity. Thanks to Ben Jonson, at least a few hundred owners of a Shakespeare Folio had learned to be sceptical about the Droeshout engraving:

> This Figure, that thou here seest put,
> It was for gentle Shakespeare cut;
> Wherein the Graver had a strife
> with Nature, to out-do the life.[21]

What was needed to convey the Chandos Portrait's superior credentials was the very assurance that Betterton supplied: that it was the work of someone truly 'intimate' with his subject. In the context of Betterton's wider collection it would require his particular advocacy, his 'several times' of telling. Nearly two thirds of the paintings Hooke lists are by a named artist, while almost all the portraits identify their subjects. A dark, unsigned, half-finished picture of an unnamed early-seventeenth-century man might fade into yet greater obscurity amid a collection advertised as including four Brueghels and two Holbeins.[22]

The Longleat letter shows that Betterton kept the portrait at Reading in a house he was evidently keen to dignify with the trappings of cultural

Illustration 10 'Look not on his picture': William Shakespeare, by
Martin Droeshout. From *Mr William Shakespeares Comedies,
Histories, & Tragedies*. The First Folio (1623)

history: not just Shakespeare's 'Head', but Chaucer's, Fletcher's and
Suckling's.[23] There, it was very much private property, but Tarnya Cooper
speculates that it had not always been so, attributing its unusually worn
surface to either over-zealous cleaning or the over-frequent handling that
would come of its having hung in the theatre.[24] Davenant had lived on the
premises at Lincoln's Inn Fields; Betterton would do the same at Dorset
Garden. Come the rupture of 1695, he would surely be anxious to rescue
anything of financial or sentimental value from the unworthy Christopher
Rich. At Reading it was saved for the eyes of fellow connoisseurs. Since
none of the other literary portraits features in *Pinacotheca Bettertonaeana*,
they too may have undergone the same journey.

When he wrote the Longleat letter in May 1704 Betterton showed little
sign of wanting to sell, although the interest of Lord Weymouth raised
the prospect and eventually the financial realities of semi-retirement in
Reading must have forced his hand. Did he embellish the credentials of
the portrait to obtain the best possible price? There is no doubting his
business acumen, but the similarity between the history of the portrait
and the dubious genealogy of the role of Hamlet – Taylor to Davenant to

Betterton – is not necessarily suspicious. As Samuel Schoenbaum writes, 'That Davenant once owned the canvas does not strain credulity', any more than his claims to familiarity with Shakespeare's colleagues.[25] As a former King's Men playwright, Davenant was well placed to pass on any amount of theatrical memorabilia and in John Rhodes, Betterton had had another source capable of puncturing any tall stories told by Davenant. A still closer associate could make other connections. Assuming he had been a Painter-Stainers' apprentice in the 1650s, Henry Harris must have known of the company master and likely painter of the Chandos Portrait, John Taylor. Such grains of authority helped form the glue of the company structure in which Betterton had always worked and thrived. Cibber observed that he was 'a man of Veracity' when it came to anecdotes and he had little to gain from misrepresenting the authenticity of the Chandos Portrait to a man such as Thomas Thynne, Lord Weymouth, a Privy Councillor since June 1702.[26]

The same may be said for another associate with a strong interest in the Chandos Portrait. Jacob Tonson, the leading publisher of his day and convenor of the Kit-Cat Club which supported the 1695 breakaway and the building of the Queen's Theatre in 1705, was responsible for Rowe's Shakespeare, with its engraving of the Chandos Portrait. Months after Betterton's death, he moved to premises in the Strand called the Shakespeare's Head, the sign of which may well have reproduced the same image. Some of his best clients – Dryden, Otway, Steele, Pope and Congreve – were known to Betterton, who was on friendly terms with other members of the Kit-Cat Club such as Richard Norton, whose Southwick house he visited.[27] Why Betterton, painted by Kneller in perfect Kit-Cat style and upheld as a model of Kit-Cat ideals, never joined the club is unclear, but no doubt a combination of allegiance to Queen Anne, back history with James II, friendship with the arch-Tory Bolingbroke, lost fortune and less than clubbable manner played their part.[28] In many ways his double, Tonson – a clumsily formed bookseller with high aspirations – tolerated no one else from his own background: about two-thirds of the Kit-Cat members were knights at least.

The triangular relationship between Betterton, Tonson and the image of Shakespeare probably began in 1679, when Tonson bought the copy of Dryden's *Troilus and Cressida*. The show had begun with Betterton delivering a prologue in the person of Shakespeare's ghost, and the opening lines could have made sense in performance only if the actor's appearance approximated to some image of Shakespeare:

SEE, my lov'd *Britons*, see your *Shakespeare* rise,
An awful ghost confess'd to human eyes!
Unnam'd, methinks, distinguish'd I had been
From other shades, by this eternal green,
About whose wreaths the vulgar Poets strive,
And with a touch, their wither'd Bays revive.
Untaught, unpractis'd, in a barbarous Age,
I found not, but created first the Stage.
Like fruitfull *Britain*, rich without supply.[29]

That image could have been the one most circulated: the Droeshout engraving, even though Betterton had no copy of it. But it could have been the Chandos Portrait, hanging somewhere in the Dorset Garden theatre. The existence of any pictures of Shakespeare in 1679 makes Michael Dobson's turn to the deconstructive seem a little too sharp when he says of the prologue that it deduces a Shakespeare 'from his own oeuvre as a dramatic character in order to authorise the revival of his plays', as if Dryden and Betterton conspired in a merely textual act of fantasy.[30] Shakespeare was a visual presence as well as a textual one, already 'embodied' in pictures before the actor's intervention, and authenticating the degree to which, as an actor, Betterton himself embodied the idea of a Shakespearean tradition, the 'ghost' present in the contours of his performances. For his benefit night in 1709 Nicholas Rowe spelled out the consequences of a thin house:

Had you with-held your Favours on this Night,
Old SHAKESPEAR'S Ghost had ris'n to do him right.[31]

Betterton as Hamlet faced his father's ghost with, in Cibber's words, 'an impatience, limited by filial reverence'.[32] His legendary ability to act encounters with the supernatural signalled humility in the face of the past, an act of possession by its prior claim to cultural authority. Seeing the picture of Shakespeare – the image, ghost-like, outliving the presence – he saw the thread to the past that informed and justified his professional existence.

Recent scholarship on early theatrical biography has understandably represented that emergent form as something done *to* actors rather than *by* them, but the signs are that Betterton participated actively in the efforts of John Downes and Charles Gildon to record his life for posterity.[33] It is easy to overlook the obvious fact that Downes published *Roscius Anglicanus* in 1708, during the twilight of Betterton's career; also that the volume is as much a tribute to the actor designated by its title as an exercise in stage

history. The extent of personal details about Betterton, from his upbringing to the death of his younger brother William in a swimming accident,
shows that the book is centred on the actor and to some extent dependent
on his own memories as well as Downes's. The likelihood is that Downes
started writing the book after being made redundant in 1706, talking to his
old master as he went. For all its inventions, Gildon's *Life* also has a basis
in biographical fact. In the face of actors who craved money and applause
at the expense of refining their art, of the twin evils of Christopher Rich
and the performing artistes who threatened to overwhelm serious drama, a
theatrical genealogy stretching back to Shakespeare constituted the greatest dignity affordable by a man who belonged to a profession still short,
for all Gildon's efforts, of respectability. Shakespeare's father had craved
his coat of arms; having none, Betterton sought the dignity of professional
ancestry and the portraiture that figured it.[34] While he believed it to be
true, he was also predisposed by temperament and ambition to tell the sort
of story he told Keck about the Chandos Portrait.

But, as throughout his life, this theatrical innovator and die-hard trad-
itionalist appears to have had a strong grasp of the commercial value of
his assets. In *A Comparison Between the Two Stages*, the character Ramble
recalls how many new plays failed in the late 1690s, with 'every fresh
Author being in hast to be damned with those that went before'. His inter-
locutor, Sullen, describes the solution devised by the 'cunning old Fox'
Betterton: perform more Shakespeare, but not before consulting him
directly. Betterton 'enters his Closset, and falls down on his Knees, and
Prays':

> O Shakespear, Shakespear! What have our Sins brought upon us! We have
> renounc'd the wayes which thou hast taught us, and are degenerated into Infamy
> and Corruption: Look down from thy Throne on Mount Parnassus, and take
> commiseration on thy Sons now fallen into Misery: Let down a Beam of thy
> brightness upon this our forlorn Theatre; let thy Spirit dwell with us, let thy
> Influence be upon our Poets, let the Streams of thy Helicon glide along by
> Lincolns-Inn-Fields, and fructifie our Soil as the Waters of the Nile make fruitful
> the barren Banks of Egypt.

Comforted, he chose 'two or three' of Shakespeare's plays to put on
and blessed 'the Relickes of this Saint' as 'more precious than those at
Loretto'.[35] The context for the story is accurately described in that performance records indicate revivals of *Henry IV* and *Measure for Measure* in
January and February 1700.[36] It is also true in spirit to Betterton. As with
the Chandos Portrait, veneration for Shakespeare went with the financial acuity to be expected of an old fox: 'a Penny that comes in from so

pious a Shrine', reflects Sullen's Betterton, 'must needs prosper'. Talking to Shakespeare was from the outset a route to the genteel retirement of which his books and pictures were the vivid but failed symbol, a way of getting 'rid of this beggarly Trade' by, the allegation runs, keeping third-night profits for himself instead of handing them to a new author.[37] Sullen adds that Christopher Rich followed suit and started praying to a picture of Ben Jonson, determined that a 'Heathen Player' should have no 'more Religion than a Lawyer'.[38]

If, as Mark S. Dawson notes, 'the importance of lineage to claims of gentility' was in decline during Betterton's lifetime, it was a fresh and reassuring concept for an actor to place alongside the new discourse of gentility through refined manners which any professional observer of human conduct was well placed to embody.[39] But lineage itself was, Dawson adds, 'a cultural construct', and that is true in a direct sense of Betterton and his longstanding relationship to a theatre company that took its bearings from a world before the war. Through its folklore as much as its hierarchy, company life brought out in him a quality which the smallest handful of his contemporaries mistook for pomposity, but which for theatre history must crystallise his significance: a fitting pride in his professional ancestry and an assurance of his own place in it.

Notes

I INTRODUCTION

1 Judith Milhous calculates 131 new roles and fifty-two in older plays. See 'An Annotated Census of Thomas Betterton's Roles, 1659–1710', *Theatre Notebook*, vol. 29 (1975), 33–45 (part 1), and 85–94 (part 2), 33; hereafter 'Census'. She adds that this is probably an under-estimate. In Jacob Hooke's *Pinacotheca Bettertonaeana* (London, 1710), the sale catalogue of the actor's books and pictures (hereafter PB), are itemised 'Eleven bundles of Plays and Parts of Plays, each containing 24 – MSS', which might indicate up to 264 roles (22). PB is available in microfilm copy at the British Library: S.C. 246 (9).

2 Milhous argues that only two of the twelve plays attributed to Betterton are by him. See her 'Thomas Betterton's Playwriting', *Bulletin of the New York Public Library* 77 (1974), 375–92.

3 *The Diary of Samuel Pepys*, ed. Robert Latham and William Matthews, 11 vols. (London: Bell and Hyman, 1971–83), 4 November 1661; hereafter *Diary*.

4 *Gazetteer and London Daily Advertiser*, 22 October 1756, no.4715.

5 Some recent studies are Jean Benedetti, *David Garrick and the Birth of Modern Theatre* (London: Methuen, 2001); George Winchester Stone and George M. Kahrl, *David Garrick: A Critical Biography* (Carbondale: Southern Illinois University Press, 1979); Jeffrey Kahan, *The Cult of Kean* (Aldershot: Ashgate, 2006); Herschel Clay Baker, *John Philip Kemble: The Actor in His Theatre* (London and New York: Greenwood Press, 1970); Alan S. Downer, *The Eminent Tragedian: William Charles Macready* (Cambridge, Mass.: Harvard University Press, 1966); Jeffrey Richards, *Sir Henry Irving: A Victorian Actor and His World* (London: Continuum, 2006). Roger Lewis, *The Secret Life of Laurence Olivier* (New York and London: Applause Books, 1997), x, counts fourteen other biographies of Olivier.

6 R.W. Lowe, *Thomas Betterton* (London, 1891). For Betterton the manager, see Judith Milhous, *Thomas Betterton and the Management of Lincoln's Inn Fields 1695–1708* (Carbondale: Southern Illinois University Press, 1979); hereafter *Management*. See also Jane Milling, 'Thomas Betterton and the Art of Acting', in Martin Banham and Jane Milling, eds., *Extraordinary Actors: Essays on Popular Performers* (Exeter: University of Exeter Press, 2004),

21–35; Joseph Roach, 'Betterton's Funeral', in his *Cities of the Dead. Circum-Atlantic Performance* (New York: Columbia University Press, 1996), 73–117; and the same author's *The Player's Passion: Studies in the Science of Acting* (Newark: University of Delaware Press, 1985). C.R. Rathke's 1976 Tulane University doctoral thesis is entitled 'The Career of Thomas Betterton as a Shaping Force of the Restoration Playhouse and the Restoration Drama'.

7 Cited in Hal Burton, ed., *Acting in the Sixties* (London: BBC Books, 1970), 69.

8 Cited in Lewis, *Secret Life of Laurence Olivier*, 59.

9 Anthony Holden, 'Why We Should Give Larry a Standing Ovation', *The Observer*, Review, 27 May 2007, 7. See also Alexander Leggatt, 'Richard Burbage: A Dangerous Actor', in Banham and Milling, eds., *Extraordinary Actors: Essays on Popular Performers* (Exeter: University of Exeter Press, 2004), 8.

10 William King, *Useful Miscellanies* (London, 1712), 4. The quotation appears in a publisher's preface to the tragicomedy *Joan of Hedington*. 'Batterton' and 'Baterton' were common spellings before 1750.

11 Judith Milhous, 'Thomas Betterton', *New Dictionary of National Biography*, ed. Laurence Goldmann, 60 vols. (Oxford: Oxford University Press, 2004), V.558.

12 Betterton's Letter to Colonel Finch, Thynne Papers XXV f.268 (see frontispiece). Hereafter referred to as the Longleat letter.

13 Richard Holmes, *Sidetracks. Explorations of a Romantic Biographer* (London: HarperCollins, 2000), 371.

14 Ibid., 371.

15 Ibid., 369–71.

16 Guy Davenport, *The Hudson Review*, vol. XXIII (1970), cited in Lewis, *Secret Life of Laurence Olivier*, x.

17 PB 22.

18 Pepys, *Diary*, 4 and 5 September 1667, objected to Betterton and Harris laughing and 'being all of them out'.

19 Holmes, *Sidetracks*, 374.

20 His mythological or ancient historical roles included Mark Antony in two different plays, Sedley's *Antony and Cleopatra* (1677) and Dryden's *All for Love* (1685?), Orestes in Charles Davenant's *Circe* (1677) and Dennis's *Iphigenia* (1699), Achilles in Banks's *The Destruction of Troy* (1678), Aecius in Rochester's *Valentinian* (1684), Regulus in Crowne's *Regulus* (1692), Alexander in Lee's *The Rival Queens* (1683?), Agamemnon in Granville's *Heroick Love* (1697), Ulysses in Rowe's *Ulysses* (1705) and Theseus in Smith's *Phaedra and Hippolitus* (1707).

21 Richard Steele, *The Tatler* no.167, 2–4 May 1710. Such analogies were not Steele's alone. In 'To Mr Betterton Acting Oedipus King of Thebes', Francis Manning compares Betterton's pre-eminence as an actor to that of a distinguished lady at the installation of the garter ceremony at Windsor. See Manning, *Poems upon Several Occasions and to Several Persons* (London, 1701), 44.

22　Philip Clark, church plumber (d. 21 September 1707), is buried in the West Cloister. Jodocus Crull, *The Antiquities of St Peter's* (London, 1711), 188, says that Betterton 'was buried with great Decency in the Cloyster, but there is no monument as yet set up in Remembrance of him'. John Dart, *Westmonasterium, Or the History and Antiquities of the Abbey Church of St Peters Westminster*, 2 vols (London, 1742), II.139, records that Betterton was buried near Thomas Brown and Aphra Behn 'in the *East* Walk' and that his wife Mary was laid 'upon his Coffin'.

23　Laurence Olivier, *Confessions of an Actor* (London: Weidenfeld and Nicolson, 1982), 210.

24　William Van Lennep, ed., *The London Stage Part 1. 1660–1700* (Carbondale: Southern Illinois University Press, 1963), hereafter LS1; Emmett L. Avery, ed., *The London Stage Part 2. 1700–1729* (Carbondale: Southern Illinois University Press, 1961), consulted here in the ongoing revision by Robert D. Hume and Judith Milhous, available in draft form (last accessed 1 August 2009) at www.personal.psu.edu/users/h/b/hb1/London%20Stage%20 2001/lond1700.pdf and hereafter LS2; Philip H. Highfill Jr, Kalman A. Burnim and Edward A. Langhans, *A Biographical Dictionary of Actors, Actresses, Musicians, Dancers, Managers and Stage Personnel in London, 1660–1800*, 16 vols. (Carbondale and Edwardsville: Southern Illinois University Press, 1973), hereafter BDA; Robert D. Hume and Judith Milhous, *A Register of English Theatrical Documents, 1660–1737*, 2 vols. (Carbondale and Edwardsville: Southern Illinois University Press, 1991), hereafter *Register*. Also Milhous, *Management*, and her 'Census'.

25　[Charles Gildon], *The Life of Mr Thomas Betterton* (London, 1710).

26　In particular, Tiffany Stern's *The Rehearsal from Shakespeare to Sheridan* (Oxford: Clarendon Press, 2000).

27　Gilli Bush-Bailey, *Treading the Bawds. Actresses and Playwrights on the Late Stuart Stage* (Manchester: Manchester University Press, 2007). Milhous, *Management*, 81–112.

2 LOOK, MY LORD, IT COMES:
BETTERTON'S HAMLET

1　Pepys, *Diary*, 24 August 1661. Latham and Matthews record that Robert Holmes had been to West Africa (II.160 n.3); the creature was 'presumably a chimpanzee or gorilla'.

2　Pepys, *Diary*, 31 December 1660.

3　Peter Holland, *The Ornament of Action* (Cambridge: Cambridge University Press, 1979), 108.

4　Pepys, *Diary*, 31 August 1668.

5　Milhous, 'Census', 90.

6　Ibid., 40–1.

7　For dates, see Bibliography.

8　Leggatt, 'Richard Burbage', 8.

9 John Carey, Introduction to his *Faber Book of Reportage* (London: Faber & Faber, 1987), xxxii.

10 Milling, 'Thomas Betterton and the Art of Acting', 35.

11 Alexander Pope, 'The First Epistle of the Second Book of Horace Imitated', 122, in *The Poems of Alexander Pope*, ed. John Butt (London: Methuen, 1963), 640. Steele, *The Tatler* no.167, 2 May 1710.

12 Robert Wilks was playing Hamlet in the 1706–7 season (LS2 334 and 359), although Betterton was still regularly playing Brutus, another role for which there is an eye-witness account (see below, 140–1).

13 Peter Holland, 'Hearing the Dead: the Sound of Garrick', in Michael Cordner and Peter Holland, eds., *Players, Playwrights, Playhouses. Investigating Performance, 1660–1800* (Basingstoke: Palgrave, 2007), 248–70.

14 Milhous, 'Census', Part 2, 92. For the April 1709 benefit, see below, 26.

15 Ibid., 40.

16 *The Tatler* no.1, 20 September 1709.

17 Roach, *Player's Passion*, 30–1.

18 Ibid., 55–6.

19 Dene Barnett, *The Art of Gesture: the Practices and Principles of Eighteenth-Century Acting* (Heidelberg: Carl Winter, 1987).

20 Carey, *Faber Book of Reportage*, xxxii.

21 Stanley Wells, Introduction to *Shakespeare in the Theatre. An Anthology of Criticism* (Oxford: Clarendon Press, 1997), 15.

22 William Shakespeare, *Hamlet Prince of Denmark*, 1.ii.64. All quotations from Shakespeare are taken from *The Complete Pelican Shakespeare*, ed. Alfred Harbage (New York: Viking Press, 1969).

23 Donald Mullin, 'Lighting on the Eighteenth-Century London Stage: a Reconsideration', *Theatre Notebook*, 34 (1980), 74; Pepys, *Diary*, 24 August 1661.

24 Beale played Hamlet in John Caird's Royal National Theatre production (2000); West in Stephen Pimlott's Royal Shakespeare Company version (2001).

25 Colley Cibber, *An Apology for the Life of Mr Colley Cibber* (London, 1740), 70.

26 Anthony Aston, *A Brief Supplement to Colley Cibber Esq. His Lives of the Famous Actors and Actresses* (London, 1747); reprinted in *An Apology for the Life of Mr Colley Cibber*, ed. R.W. Lowe, 2 vols. (London, 1889), II.299–303.

27 For reviews of Beale's Hamlet see the Royal National Theatre's online archive, accessed 2 June 2008: www.website-archive.nt-online.org/productions/rd/more/hamlet.html.

28 Cibber, *Apology*, 66.

29 Nicholas Rowe, ed., *The Works of Mr William Shakespear*, 6 vols. (1709), v.2365.

30 Gildon, *Life*, 139. For the unreliable nature of the book, see above, 25.

31 LS1 31.

32 Jessica Munns, 'Images of Monarchy on the Restoration Stage', in Susan J. Owen, ed., *A Companion to Restoration Drama* (Oxford: Blackwell, 2001), 109.

33 LS1 225 translates BM Add. Mss.27, 962v, f.312, a newsletter by one Salvetti: 'On last Wednesday all the royal family were present at the theatre to hear the tragedy of *Hamlet*, which, for their greater entertainment, was adorned and embellished with very curious dances between the acts.' The same performance is recorded in the Lord Chamberlain's accounts transcribed in Allardyce Nicoll, *A History of Restoration Drama 1660–1700*, 4th edn (Cambridge: Cambridge University Press, 1952), 310.

34 Evelyn, *Diary*, 26 November 1661: 'the old play began to disgust this refined age; since his Majestie being so long abroad.' *The Diary of John Evelyn*, ed. Esmond S. de Beer (Oxford: Oxford University Press, 1959), 431.

35 Nancy Klein Maguire, *Regicide and Restoration. English Tragicomedy, 1660–1671* (Cambridge: Cambridge University Press, 1992), 13 and 42.

36 Deborah C. Payne, 'The Restoration Actress', in J. Douglas Canfield and Deborah C. Payne, eds., *Cultural Readings of Restoration and Eighteenth-Century English Theater* (Athens, GA: University of Georgia Press, 1995), 13–39.

37 Cibber, *Apology*, 241. According to Cibber, it was in 1696 that Christopher Rich shortened the stage of the Theatre Royal, Drury Lane. For discussion, see David Thomas and Arnold Hare, eds., *Restoration and Georgian England 1660–1788. Theatre in Europe: a Documentary History* (Cambridge: Cambridge University Press, 1989), 70–1.

38 I.ii.65. Readers impatient to correct this citation in line with Restoration principles are referred to the following page.

39 Cibber, *Apology*, 66.

40 Gildon, *Life*, 64.

41 For an account of the changes, see George C.D. Odell, *Shakespeare from Betterton to Irving*, 2 vols. (New York: Charles Scribner, 1920), II.24–6. The 1676 text was reprinted in 1703 in an edition sometimes wrongly attributed to Betterton. See Milhous, 'Playwriting', 381.

42 Thomas Sprat, *The History of the Royal-Society in London* (London, 1667), 113.

43 Gildon, *Life*, 32.

44 Cibber, *Apology*, 64.

45 See Emmet L. Avery, 'The Restoration Audience', *Philological Quarterly*, vol. 45 (1966), 54–61; Harold Love, 'The Myth of the Restoration Audience', *Komos*, vol. 1 (1968), 49–56; Allan Richard Botica, 'Audience, Playhouse and Play in English Restoration Theatre, 1660–1710', unpublished DPhil thesis, Oxford University, 1985; David Roberts, *The Ladies: Female Patronage of Restoration Drama 1660–1700* (Oxford: Clarendon Press, 1989).

46 Aston, *A Brief Supplement*, II.302.

47 Cibber, *Apology*, 66.

48 On the history of 'polite' English at this time, see David Crystal, *The Stories of English* (London: Penguin Books, 2004), 371.

49 Cibber, *Apology*, 70.
50 Shakespeare, *Troilus and Cressida*, i.iii.152–5. For Cibber's extended treatment of Betterton's way with verse, see *Apology*, 66–7.
51 Gildon, *Life*, 23.
52 John Downes, *Roscius Anglicanus* (London, 1708), cited throughout in the edition by Judith Milhous and Robert D. Hume (London: The Society for Theatre Research, 1987), 73.
53 For Davenant's career, Mary Edmond's *Rare Sir William Davenant* (Manchester: Manchester University Press, 1996).
54 David Farley-Hills considers Downes's wording in fine detail in 'Shakespeare and Joseph Taylor', *Notes and Queries* (March 1994), 58–61.
55 For the Chandos Portrait, see below, 176–7. For young Shakespeare keeping horses at the theatre, a story 'which Sir William Davenant told Mr Betterton, who communicated it to Mr Rowe; Rowe told it to Mr Pope', etc., *The Beauties of Biography*, 2 vols. (London, 1777), II.122–3.
56 See, for example, Bertram Joseph, *Elizabethan Acting* (Oxford: Oxford University Press, 1951), 80–2, 134.
57 For a good account, and some examples of instances in plays, see James R. Brandon, *Kabuki: Five Classic Plays* (Honolulu: University of Hawaii Press, 1992), 40–2.
58 See Wells, *Shakespeare in the Theatre*, 9 and 50.
59 Georg Lichtenberg, in M.L. Mare and W.H. Quarrell, eds., *Lichtenberg's Visits to England*, reprinted in Wells, *Shakespeare in the Theatre*, 24–8.
60 Shearer West, *The Image of the Actor* (New York: St Martin's Press, 1991), 50.
61 See, for example, Michael Dobson, *The Making of the National Poet* (Oxford: Clarendon Press, 1992).
62 Cibber, *Apology*, 60–1.
63 Ibid., 61.
64 Samuel Johnson, *Preface to Shakespeare*, in Arthur Sherbo, ed., *The Yale Edition of the Works of Samuel Johnson* (New Haven: Yale University Press, 1968), VII.66.
65 Milling, 'Thomas Betterton and the Art of Acting', 25.
66 Aston, *A Brief Supplement*, II.303.
67 Ibid.
68 Richard Flecknoe, *A Short Discourse of the English Stage*, in his *Love's Kingdom* (1664); EEBO 51.
69 *The Laureat* (1740), 31.
70 Joseph R. Roach, 'The Performance', in Deborah Payne Fiske, ed., *The Cambridge Companion to English Restoration Theatre* (Cambridge: Cambridge University Press, 2000), 25.
71 Aston, *A Brief Supplement*, II.303.
72 Thomas Davies, *Dramatic Miscellanies*, 3 vols. (London, 1783–4), III.32.
73 For 'invention', see Richard A. Lanham, *A Handlist of Rhetorical Terms* (Berkeley: University of California Press, 1987), 37.
74 Richard Cumberland, *Memoirs* (London, 1806), 60.

75 Walter Benjamin, 'The Work of Art in the Age of its Technological Reproducibility', in Howard Eiland and Michael W. Jennings, eds., *Walter Benjamin. Selected Writings*, 3 vols. (Cambridge, Mass.: Belknap Press, 2002), III.101–33; this is the revised 1935 version of the essay often referred to as 'The Work of Art in an Age of Mechanical Reproduction', first published in 1933. For the impact of print on theatrical culture, see Dustin Griffin, *Literary Patronage in England, 1650–1800* (Cambridge: Cambridge University Press, 1996); Julie Stone Peters, *Congreve, the Drama and the Printed Word* (Stanford: Stanford University Press, 1990) and *Theatre of the Book, 1480–1880* (Oxford: Clarendon Press, 2000).

76 Cibber, *Apology*, 71.

77 Paulina Kewes, *Authorship and Appropriation. Writing for the Stage in England, 1660–1710* (Oxford: Clarendon Press, 1998); Brean S. Hammond, *Professional Imaginative Writing in England, 1670–1740* (Oxford: Clarendon Press, 1997).

78 Cibber, *Apology*, 60.

79 *London Evening Post*, 3 October 1732, no.756.

80 For Betterton's real and imagined authorship, Milhous, 'Playwriting'. For reflections on Betterton's 'parts and capacity' as an actor and writer, see the letter dated 23 May 1712 from 'The Hon. J.C.' to Pope in *Letters of Mr Alexander Pope and Several of his Friends* (London, 1737), 78.

81 Gildon, *Life*, 88.

82 See chapter 4 of Cheryl Wanko's *Roles of Authority. Thespian Biography and Celebrity in Eighteenth-Century Britain* (Lubbock: Texas Tech University Press, 2003).

83 For a recent survey, see Ophelia Field, *The Kit-Cat Club. Friends Who Imagined a Nation* (London: Harper, 2008), 62–102.

84 Robert D. Hume, 'Before the Bard: "Shakespeare" in Early Eighteenth-Century London', *ELH*, vol. 64 (1997), 41–75.

85 Paul Langford, *A Polite and Commercial People. England 1727–1783* (Oxford: Clarendon Press, 1989), 59–121; see also his *Englishness Identified: Manners and Character 1650–1850* (Oxford: Oxford University Press, 2000).

86 Gildon, *Life*, 28.

87 Pierre Bourdieu, trans. Richard Nice, *Distinction: A Social Critique of the Judgment of Taste* (London: Routledge, 1986); original French version published in 1979.

88 Wanko, *Roles of Authority*, 44.

89 Mikhail Bakhtin, *Problems of Dostoevsky's Poetics*, trans. Caryl Emerson (Manchester: Manchester University Press, 1984), 6.

3 AN OBSTINATELY SHADOWY TITAN: BETTERTON IN BIOGRAPHY

1 Daphne Phillips, *A History of Reading* (Reading: Countryside Books, 1980). The quotations from Gildon's *Life* that follow are from pp. 1–2.

2 PB title page says that the auction of Betterton's goods was to be held 'at his late Lodgings in *Russel-street, Covent Garden*'.

3 On Betterton being 'surprised' by 'acute pains of gout' during performance, and George Powell's mimicry of them, see Davies, *Dramatic Miscellanies*, I.138.

4 Milhous, 'Census', 40. In 1707, Milhous notes, 'Although the company played a full summer season, Betterton did not appear from 28 May until 6 November'.

5 On 12 March 1709 Robert Wilks had played Valentine and he resumed the role the following season (LS2 517) before handing it on to Barton Booth (LS2 527). It had been intended that *Othello* would be Betterton's benefit play in March 1709 but the choice was changed 'At the desire of several Persons of Quality'. He played Othello on 24 March 1709 notwithstanding.

6 The best account of the occasion is in LS2 479, which notes that 'the notion that this was a "farewell" benefit is a sentimental fabrication', since Betterton subsequently acted until the end of April and into the following season until his death a year after the *Love for Love* benefit. Anne Bracegirdle, whose last known performance before this was on 20 February 1707 (LS2 344), came out of retirement to play Angelica and speak Congreve's new prologue (BDA II.90); according to one report, day tickets cost a guinea each and demand was such that the stage was crammed with spectators as well as the auditorium. Even at the tickets' face value Betterton would have earned about £154 from the performance. See also Cibber, *Apology*, 71.

7 John Weaver's *An Essay Towards an History of Dancing* appeared in 1712; *The Censor* and *The Prompter* followed in 1717 and 1734; then Curll and Oldys's *History of the English Stage* in 1741. For a valuable modern collection, see Lisa Zunshine, ed., *Acting Theory and the English Stage, 1700–1830*, 5 vols. (London: Pickering & Chatto, 2008).

8 Gildon, Preface to the *Life*.

9 Theobald, Preface of the Editor, *Double Falsehood* (London, 1767).

10 Johnson's Life of Pope says that 'a version into modern English of Chaucer's Prologues, and one of his Tales ... were believed to have been the performance of Pope himself'. His friend Elijah Fenton had 'made him a gay offer of five pounds, if he would shew them in the hand of Betterton'. Johnson, *The Lives of the English Poets*, 3 vols. (Dublin, 1780–1), II.293. On 23 May 1712 Pope's correspondent J.C. mentions Betterton's 'remains' falling into 'such hands as may render 'em reputable to [Betterton] and beneficial to [his widow]', a reference to the publication of the Chaucer versions by Lintot. See *Letters of Mr Alexander Pope and Several of his Friends*, 78. For further discussion of Betterton's supposed Chaucer, see Chapter 12.

11 Anon., *The Elegant Entertainer and Merry Storyteller* (London, 1767), 62–3. Proof of the Reading address is in the Longleat Letter (see frontispiece), which states that he kept good portraits of Shakespeare and Chaucer there.

12 Charles Gildon, Preface to *Love's Victim; or, The Queen of Wales* (London, 1701). Betterton also played Rhesus, King of Wales in the play.

13 William S. Howell, 'Sources of the Elocutionary Movement in England, 1700–1748', *Quarterly Journal of Speech*, vol. 45 (1959), 1–18, documents Gildon's reliance on a translation of La Facheur's *Essay Upon the Action of an Orator*; Roach, *Player's Passion*, 31, adds Thomas Wright's *The Passions of the Mind* (London, 1604) to the mix. Betterton did not own a copy of either but did possess a key rhetorical text of the seventeenth century, John Bulwer's *Chirologia, or the Natural Language of the Hand* (London, 1644); PB 14. The description of Gildon as merely 'a pastiche' is in Milhous, DNB V.557.

14 See Leslie Stephen's old DNB entry, VII.1226.

15 Wanko, *Roles of Authority*, 43 and 39.

16 Gildon, *Life*, 9.

17 'Theatricus', 'A Dissertation on the Theatre', *Public Advertiser*, 7 February 1764, no.9130.

18 Cibber, *Apology*, 71. LS2 561 reprints an advertisement announcing the play as 'For the benefit of Mr Betterton'. Wycherley's Letter to Pope, dated 27 April 1710, appears in *Letters of Mr Alexander Pope*, 25.

19 Pope, letter to Cromwell dated 17 May 1710 in *Letters of Mr Alexander Pope*, 55.

20 Joan Lane, *John Hall and His Patients* (Stratford-upon-Avon: The Shakespeare Birthplace Trust, 1996), 159, 213, 309 and 319.

21 Steele, *The Tatler*, 2–4 May 1710.

22 Wanko, *Roles of Authority*, 47–8, cites *Memoirs of the Life of Mr. Theophilus Keene* (1718) and Benjamin Victor's *Memoirs of the Life of Barton Booth* (1733).

23 See Oliver Lawson Dick, ed., *Aubrey's Brief Lives* (Harmondsworth: Penguin, 1982), 69–70.

24 Robert Gould, 'A Satyr against the Play-House', in *Poems, Chiefly Consisting of Satyrs and Satirical Epistles* (London, 1689), 183.

25 Wanko, 'Three Stories of Celebrity: *The Beggar's Opera* "Biographies"', *Studies in English Literature*, vol. 38 (1998), 489.

26 Aubry De La Motraye, *Travels Through Europe* (London, 1723), 143.

27 Wanko, 'Three Stories', 50.

28 Curll repeated the formula on the title page of the spurious 1741 *History of the English Stage*.

29 Milling, 'Thomas Betterton and the Art of Acting', 35.

30 Anon., 'A Session of the Poets', in George DeForest Lord, ed., *Poems on Affairs of State*, 6 vols. (New Haven: Yale University Press, 1977), 1.356: 'His wit had most worth, and modesty in't, / For he had writ plays, yet ne'er came in print.'

31 Gildon, Preface to the *Life*. *The Amorous Widow* had been a popular play during the period 1707–10, although Betterton does not seem to have performed in it then; its popularity indicates that Gildon was seeking a quick profit. See performances on 7 February 1707 (LS2 342), 19 November 1709 (LS2 522) and 29 April 1710. The latter performance, the day after Betterton's death, was advertised as a benefit for the actor William Bullock.

32 Anon., Preface to *The Amorous Widow* (London, 1706).

33 See John Mullan, *Sentiment and Sociability. The Language of Feeling in the Eighteenth Century* (Oxford: Clarendon Press, 1988), 18–56.

34 *Lloyd's Evening Post and British Chronicle*, 10 March 1758, no.101.

35 The first to develop the idea was John Harrington Smith, 'Thomas Corneille to Betterton to Congreve', *Journal of English and Germanic Philology*, vol. 45 (1946), 209–13. The title of Betterton's lost play, *The Woman Made a Justice*, hints at more genteel subversion.

36 In *A Collection of Original Poems, Translations and Imitations* (London, 1714), 24.

37 Sir George Etherege, *The Man of Mode* (London, 1676), 68; Thomas Shadwell, *The Libertine* (London, 1675); Dryden, *Amphytrion* (1690); Lee, *The Princess of Cleve* (1681); Edward Ravenscroft's *The London Cuckolds* premiered at Betterton's theatre on 22 November 1681, although he did not act in it; William Congreve, *The Way of the World* (1700); Betterton played the rakish Lovemore in Southerne's *The Wives Excuse* (1692). The association of actor and role was strong enough for Southerne's epilogue to imagine the following complaint about Lovemore's failure to conquer Mrs Friendall: 'Damn me, cries one, had I been Betterton, / … I know what I had done; / She should not ha' got clear of me so soon.'

38 Downes, *Roscius Anglicanus*, 78.

39 Cibber, *Apology*, 77, referring to Mountfort's Willmore in Behn's *The Rover* (1677).

40 Milhous, 'Census', 91. For Betterton 'rend[ing] the soul with horror and despair' as against Garrick's ability to shine in comic and tragic roles both young and old, *Gazetteer and New Daily Advertiser*, 10 November 1766, no.11757. Approximately one-third of Betterton's known roles were in comedy, for further discussion of which see below, Chapter 5. Wilks was playing Jupiter, Dorimant and Don John from 1706; see LS2 363 and 430; Powell also played Jupiter (LS2 451).

41 Wanko, *Roles of Authority*, 224 n.12, proposes Edmund Curll as the first person to publish the term in his 1731 biography of Anne Oldfield. OED gives the later date of 1779 for a reference to Garrick.

42 Milhous, *Management*, 178.

43 Mary Luckhurst and Jane Moody, eds., *Theatre and Celebrity* (London and New York: Palgrave, 2006).

44 Vivian de Sola Pinto, *English Biography in the Seventeenth Century* (London: George Harrap, 1951), 202.

45 Gildon, *Life*, 18.

46 Jeremy Collier, *A Short View of the Immorality and Profaneness of the English Stage* (London, 1698); also Yuji Kaneko, *The Restoration Stage Controversy*, 6 vols. (London: Routledge Thoemmes, 1996), Joseph Wood Krutch, *Comedy and Conscience after the Restoration* (New York, 1924) and Michael Cordner, 'Playwright versus Priest: Profanity and the Wit of Restoration Comedy', in Payne Fiske, ed., *The Cambridge Companion to English Restoration Theatre*, 209–25.

47 Gildon, *Life*, 19.
48 Narcissus Luttrell, *A Brief Relation*, 10 and 12 May 1698, IV.378–9, in LS1
    LXV and 495: 'The justices of Middlesex did not only present against the
    playhouses, but also Mr Congreve, for writing the Double Dealer; Durfey,
    for Don Quixot; and Tonson and Brisco, booksellers, for printing them.'
    Betterton had been appearing as Maskwell – another Stuart schemer – in
    The Double Dealer since its premiere in October 1693. He had no role in
    Don Quixote, which had opened in May 1694, but was in charge of the
    company.
49 Recorded in Luttrell, V.111 and cited in *Register* no.1674. A further indictment
    in October 1700 is reported in Krutch, *Comedy and Conscience*, 170, and cited
    in LS2 8.
50 *The Post Man*, 17–19 February 1702, reprinted in *Register* no.1681. Gallingly for
    Betterton, actors from the rival company were acquitted of the same charge
    later in the month (*Register* no.1683). There were further cases in October
    1706, by which time the 'Information' was deemed 'frivolous'; MS newsletter
    in LS2 321.
51 Gildon, *Life*, 19. The unused prologue ('He from the Stock the Prostitute
    transplants, / And swells the humble Whore with Buskin'd Rants') is in
    Poems on Affairs of State, from 1640 to This Present Year 1704, 3 vols. (London,
    1704), III.417.
52 John Dennis, *A Large Account of the Taste in Poetry and the Causes of the
    Degeneracy of it* (London, 1702) reprinted in Edward Niles Hooker, *The
    Critical Works of John Dennis*, vol. 1 (Baltimore: The Johns Hopkins Press,
    1939), 289–94.
53 Dennis, *Critical Works*, 294.
54 All three works were published in 1698; PB 10.
55 LC 7/3, fol.159, reprinted in Krutch, 178. In the spring of 1702 Betterton
    and others petitioned against further prosecutions on the grounds that
    the plays in question had already been licensed. LC 7/3, fol.166, in *Register*
    no.1696.
56 Davies, *Dramatic Miscellanies*; Edmund Malone, ed., *The Plays and Poems
    of William Shakespeare*, 11 vols. (London, 1790), II.250–5, and *An Historical
    Account of the Rise and Progress of the English Stage* (London, 1800), 320–2 and
    325–6.
57 John Genest, *Some Account of the English Stage from the Restoration in 1660
    to 1830*, 10 vols. (Bath, 1832). Joseph Knight, 'Thomas Betterton', DNB ed.
    Leslie Stephen and Sidney Lee, 22 vols. (Oxford: Oxford University Press,
    1917), II.434–41; first published in London, 1885.
58 John Doran, 'Frozen-Out Actors', *The Cornhill Magazine* (1862), 167–77.
59 Lowe, *Thomas Betterton*, 56. For Milhous on Lowe, 'Census', 33.
60 Knight, DNB, II.439. Lord Macaulay's *Critical and Historical Essays*, first
    published in 1843, included a celebrated condemnation of Restoration play-
    wrights and championed Collier as heroically righteous. For Victorian criti-
    cism and Restoration comedy, see Robert D. Markley, 'The Canon and its

Critics', in Payne Fiske, ed., *The Cambridge Companion to English Restoration Theatre*, 226–42.

61 Arthur P. Stanley, *Historical Memorials of Westminster Abbey* (London, 1886), 287; Sir Walter Besant and G.E. Mitton, *The Fascination of London. Holborn and Bloomsbury* (London: Adam and Charles Black, 1903), 24.

62 Leslie Hotson, *The Commonwealth and Restoration Stage* (Cambridge, Mass.: Harvard University Press, 1928); Nicoll, *Restoration Drama*.

63 In particular, Elizabeth Howe, *The First English Actresses* (Cambridge: Cambridge University Press, 1992), and Bush-Bailey, *Treading the Bawds*.

64 Michael Caines, Paul Goring, Nicola Shaughnessy and Robert Shaughnessy, eds., *Lives of Shakespearian Actors, Part I: David Garrick, Charles Macklin and Margaret Woffington by Their Contemporaries*, 3 vols. (London: Pickering and Chatto, 2008).

65 *Stage Beauty*, dir. Richard Eyre (London: Lions Gate Films, 2004). The script is an adaptation by Jeffrey Hatcher of his own play, *Compleat Female Stage Beauty*.

66 *The Libertine*, dir. Laurence Dunmore (London: Mr Mudd Films, 2005). This too is an adaptation of a play, Stephen Jeffreys's *The Libertine* (London: Nick Hern Books, 1994), in which Betterton does not appear.

67 Baroness Orczy, *His Majesty's Well-Beloved. An Episode in the Life of Mr Thomas Betterton as Told by His Friend John Honeywood* (London: Hodder and Stoughton, 1919), 119.

68 Orczy, *His Majesty's Well-Beloved*, 21 and 232.

69 Pepys, *Diary*, 7 April 1668.

70 See Luckhurst and Moody, *Theatre and Celebrity*, 59.

71 Gildon, *Life*, 57.

72 Francis Manning, *An Essay on the Vicious Bent and Taste of the Times* (London, 1737). For Manning's celebration of Betterton's Oedipus, see 185 n.21.

73 Davies, *Dramatic Miscellanies*, II.131. The reference is to the role in Dryden's *All for Love*.

74 The Epilogue to John Banks's *Cyrus the Great* (1696) reads: 'The Curtain's dropt, and [Betterton] is glad he's gone; / The Poet too, has loaded him so sore, / He scar[c]e has breath enough for one word more.'

75 Powell, Epilogue to *The Fatal Discovery* (1698); for Aston, see above, p. 14; Car Scroope, 'In Defence of Satire', in *The Poetical Works of the Earls of Rochester, Roscommon and Dorset*, 2 vols. (London, 1737), I.61.

76 *The Female Wits*, III.i, in Fidelis Morgan, ed., *The Female Wits. Women Playwrights of the Restoration* (London: Virago, 1981), 423.

77 Anon., *A Satyr on the Players* (c.1682–5), MS 'Satyrs and Lampoons', BL Harley 7317, 96.

78 Milling, 'Thomas Betterton and the Art of Acting', 33.

79 Pepys, *Diary*, 27 February 1668.

80 Gildon, *Life*, 36 and 139.

81 Advertisement for *The Maid's Tragedy*, 13 April 1710, reprinted in LS2 561. For the uses of Betterton's picture collection, see Milhous, NDNB, 558.

82 Gildon, *Life*, 6.

83 For T.S. Eliot on the dissociation of sensibility, 'The Metaphysical Poets', reprinted in Frank Kermode, ed., *Selected Prose of T.S. Eliot* (London: Faber, 1975), 59–67; Walter J. Ong, *Orality and Literacy. The Technologizing of the Word*, 2nd edn (London: Methuen, 1982), 71.

84 A process recently documented by David Bevington, *This Wide and Universal Theater: Shakespeare in Performance, Then and Now* (Chicago: University of Chicago Press, 2007).

85 *Connoisseur*, 21 November 1754, XLIII, 5.

86 *The Censor* no.90, 3 vol. edn (London, 1717), III.202–3.

87 Mark S. Dawson, *Gentility and the Comic Theatre of Late Stuart London* (Cambridge: Cambridge University Press, 2005), 238.

4 AN ACTOR OF LONDON: EARLY YEARS, 1635–1659

1 *Miscellany Poems* (London, 1708), 150, has a prologue to the University of Oxford, 'Spoke at the last Act by Mr Betterton, 1703'. For Dover, France and Warwickshire see chapters 9, 10 and 12 respectively. John Le Neve, *The Lives and Characters of the Most Illustrious Persons British and Foreign* (London, 1713), 534–5, contains an extraordinary glimpse of actors and gentry sharing a social world in the summer months: 'Mr Norton's [taste] was led by the *Dramma*, in which he perform'd himself as [Anthony Henley] did, having for that purpose a little Theatre in his House at *Southwick*, where Mr Betterton, Mr Booth, Mr Mills, Mr Wilks, Mrs Barry, Mrs Bracegirdle, Mrs Oldfield, and the most noted Players in Town, have been entertain'd for Two or Three Months in the Vacation, and acted Comedies and Tragedies, in which the Owner of the House has frequently had a Part; the Gentlemen and Ladies coming thither from the Country Twenty Miles about, and a Band of Musick always attending. The Scenes, and all other Dramatick Representations were in Form.' See Robert Jordan, 'Richard Norton and the Theatre at Southwick', *Theatre Notebook*, vol. 38 (1984), 105–15. William J. Burling, *Summer Theatre in London, 1661–1820* (Madison and London: Fairleigh Dickinson University Press, 2000), 29, concludes that summer touring took place until the company union of 1682, when hirelings were employed to do it.

2 Milhous, 'Census', 89, explains the likely volume of Betterton's appearances and the difficulty of counting them.

3 On the date of Agas's map, Christopher Hibbert and Ben Weinreb, eds., *The London Encyclopaedia* (London and Basingstoke: Macmillan, 1983), 510.

4 See Edward Walford, *Old and New London*, vol. 4 (London, 1878), 14–15, and Hibbert and Weinreb, *The London Encyclopaedia*, 892.

5 Walford, *Old and New London*, vol 4, 16. Pepys, *Diary*, 18 July 1665.

6   See Lawrence Stone, 'The Residential Development of the West End of London in the Seventeenth Century', in Barbara C. Malament, ed., *After the Reformation* (Manchester: Manchester University Press, 1980), 167–212. Oliver's map is reproduced in Peter Whitfield, *Cities of the World. A History in Maps* (London: British Library, 2005), 108–9.

7   A suspicion voiced by Liza Picard, *Restoration London* (London: Weidenfeld and Nicolson, 1997), 6.

8   Guildhall Library, Christ's Hospital MSS.

9   I owe this observation to H.E. Paston-Bedingfield, York Herald at the College of Arms, correspondence dated 17 September 2008.

10   BDA 11.77 gives details of Matthew Betterton's will.

11   BDA 11.73.

12   Roger Wakefield, *Wakefield's Merchant and Tradesman's General Directory* (London, 1789), 22, lists a Francis Betterton of Southwark as a 'dealer in English wine, brandy and rum'.

13   Details are from G.E. Aylmer, *Rebellion or Revolution? England from Civil War to Restoration* (Oxford: Oxford University Press, 1986), 29.

14   *A History of the English Stage*, 2.

15   Anne Crawford, *A History of the Vintners' Company* (London: Constable, 1977), 51.

16   Barton Booth, who joined the Lincoln's Inn Fields company in 1700 after a period of acting in Dublin, had attended Westminster School for six years. See his letter to Lord Lansdowne of 1712, cited in Judith Milhous and Robert D. Hume, eds., *Vice Chamberlain Coke's Theatrical Papers 1706–1715* (Carbondale: Southern Illinois University Press, 1982), 195.

17   Gildon, *Life*, 17.

18   PB 18.

19   Anonymous, cited in William A. Armstrong, 'Actors and Theatres', *Shakespeare Survey*, vol. 17 (1964), 197.

20   Hotson, *Commonwealth and Restoration Stage*, 17–31. For flogging, see J.M. Beattie, *Crime and the Courts of England* (Princeton: Princeton University Press, 1986), 461–4.

21   Gildon, *Life*, 2.

22   *A History of the English Stage*, 5.

23   *Account*, 7.

24   *Biographia Britannica*, 5 vols. (London, 1747), 11.286. Hereafter BB.

25   Betterton played leading roles in four of Southerne's plays (dates are for his first performances): Alphonso in *The Disappointment* (1684), Lovemore in *The Wives Excuse* (1691), Villeroy in *The Fatal Marriage* (1694) and Virginius in *The Fate of Capua* (1700).

26   Philip Gaskell, *A New Introduction to Bibliography* (Oxford: Clarendon Press, 1972), 180.

27   Stationers' Company Court Book G, f.117r, in Alison Shell and Alison Emblow, eds., *An Index to Stationers' Company Court Books E, F and G. 1689–1717* (Oxford: Oxford University Press for the Bibliographical Society, 2007).

28 H.R. Plomer, *A Dictionary of the Booksellers and Printers Who Were at Work in England, Scotland and Ireland from 1641 to 1667* (London: Bibliographical Society, 1907). No Betterton is listed in D.F. McKenzie's authoritative *Stationers' Company Apprentices 1641–1700* (Oxford: Oxford Bibliographic Society, 1974).

29 Cited in Paula R. Backscheider, 'Behind City Walls: Restoration Actors in the Drapers' Company', *Theatre Survey*, vol. 45, no.1 (May 2004), 77.

30 Andrew Gurr, *The Shakespearian Playing Companies* (Oxford: Oxford University Press, 1996), 388.

31 Backscheider, 'Behind City Walls', 76.

32 Backscheider, 'Behind City Walls', 79.

33 See Backscheider, *Spectacular Politics* (Baltimore: Johns Hopkins University Press, 1993), 25–42.

34 Middlesex County Records, III.282, cited in *Register* no.1.

35 The spectre of two different John Rhodeses is examined in G.E. Bentley, *The Jacobean and Caroline Stage*, 7 vols. (Oxford: Oxford University Press, 1941–68), II.544–6.

36 Jonathan Richardson, *Explanatory Notes and Remarks on Milton's* Paradise Lost (London, 1734), xc.

37 P.M. Handover, *Printing in London from Caxton to Modern Times* (London: Allen and Unwin, 1960), 65.

38 For its textual history, see Nigel Smith, ed., *The Poems of Andrew Marvell*, rev. edn (Harlow: Pearson, 2007), 23–5.

39 Marvell, 'Upon the Death of the Lord Hastings', 57–8, in Smith, *Poems of Andrew Marvell*, 23.

40 Lois Potter, *Secret Rites and Royal Writing* (Cambridge: Cambridge University Press, 1990).

41 A dozen items in *Pinacotheca Bettertonaeana* betray this interest, including *The Works of K. Charles I, with His Life and Martyrdom* (PB 1), Clarendon's *History of the Rebellion* (PB 4), James Heath's *Chronicle of the Civil Wars of England* (PB 4) and *The Life and Death of Prince Rupert* (PB 14). Betterton also owned portraits of Charles I, Charles II and Queen Mary (PB 19 and 20).

42 Gould, 'A Satyr against the Play-House', 183. For a comprehensive study of parliamentary elections and associated practices in this period, see David Hayton, Eveline Cruikshanks and Stuart Handley, *The House of Commons 1690–1715* (Cambridge: Cambridge University Press, 2002).

43 Richardson, *Explanatory Notes*, xc.

44 BB II.286.

45 Milhous, NDNB, 553.

46 Edmond, *Rare Sir William Davenant*, 103–20.

47 BB II.286, note A(5).

48 Davies, *Dramatic Miscellanies*, III.397.

49 PRO E179/146/394c.

50 Cibber, *Apology*, 72; Downes, *Roscius Anglicanus*, 46. See the portrait of Kynaston by Mary Beale reproduced by Jennifer Renee Danby, 'Portraits of

Restoration Actors Michael Mohun and Edward Kynaston: New Evidence',
Theatre Notebook, vol. 59, issue 1 (2005), 2–18.

51 See Pepys, *Diary*, 16 June 1663 for Sedley's antics outside the Cock Inn.
52 As does BDA ii.73.
53 Walford, *Old and New London*, vol. 4, 15.

5 A WALK IN THE PARK: BETTERTON AND THE SCENE OF COMEDY

1 Milhous, 'Census', lists sixty-three out of 183 roles that can be described as comic; he created 131 roles.
2 Milhous, 'Census', 92. Betterton first played the *Henry IV* Falstaff in 1700, and appeared in *The Merry Wives* for a court performance in April 1704; LS2 163. The former was a signature role, featuring in his 18 May 1704 benefit, although his adaptation, *King Henry IV, with the Humours of Sir John Falstaff* (1700) includes little to suggest he saw the show as a star vehicle; see Milhous, 'Playwriting', 387. For the significance of his Falstaff to Kit-Cat members, see Field, *The Kit-Cat Club*, 74.
3 Dates for these roles are given in the Bibliography. Betterton had experimented with a harshly satirical character, Railmore, in Motteux's 1696 *Love's a Jest*.
4 Milhous 'Census', 91. Dryden's *Feign'd Innocence, or Sir Martin Mar-All* was a long-running success that opened on 15 August 1667. Dryden 'adapted the Part purposely for the Mouth of Mr Nokes' (Downes, *Roscius Anglicanus*, 62). For Betterton and Behn, see below, 184–5. Milhous adds that Betterton did appear in the farce *Squire Trelooby* 'to oblige Congreve and Vanbrugh' in March 1704, but he may also have been attracted by another adaptation of French comedy; the play is based on Molière's *Monsieur de Pourceaugnac*.
5 Peter Holland, 'Farce', in Payne Fiske, ed., *The Cambridge Companion to English Restoration Theatre*, 109.
6 *The Tatler* no.10, 30 April 1709.
7 Nicoll, *Restoration Drama*, 67. Such roles included Filamor in Stapylton's *The Step-Mother* (1663), Mr Art in Orrery's *Mr Anthony* (1669), Lovemore in his own *The Amorous Widow* (1670?), Townlove in Payne's *The Morning Ramble* (1672), Bevil in Shadwell's *Epsom Wells* (1672), Ramble in Crowne's *The Countrey Wit* (1676), Dorimant in Etherege's *The Man of Mode* (1676), Lord Bellamour in D'Urfey's *Madam Fickle* (1676), Longvil in Shadwell's *The Virtuoso* (1676), Wittmore in Behn's *Sir Patient Fancy* (1678), Welford in D'Urfey's *Squire Oldsapp* (1678), Galliard in Behn's *The Feign'd Curtezans* (1679), Beaugard in Otway's *The Atheist* (1683), Gayman in Behn's *The Luckey Chance* (1686), Polidor in Crowne's *The Married Beau* (1694), Bellair in Dilke's *Lover's Luck* (1695), Bellamour in Granville's *The She-Gallants* (1695), Woodvil in Doggett's *The Country-Wake* (1696), Grammont in Motteux's *The Novelty* (1697), Courtine in Burnaby's *The Ladies Visiting-Day* (1701), and Bevil in Boyle's *As You Find It* (1703). The style he learned from revivals of pre-war repertory including

Suckling's *Aglaura* (1659/60), Fletcher's *The Mad Lover*, *A Wife for a Month*, *Rule a Wife and Have a Wife*, *The Tamer Tamed* and *The Wild Goose Chase* (all 1659/60), Davenant's *The Unfortunate Lovers* (1659/60), Fletcher and Rowley's *The Maid in the Mill* (1659/60) and Shirley's *The Grateful Servant* (1661/2).

8   Gildon, *Life*, 140; for his poor dancing, Aston, *A Brief Supplement*, II.301.
9   Cibber, *Apology*, 76.
10 Gildon, *Life*, 2 and 80.
11 On the commercial value of comedy over tragedy, LS1 cxxix.
12 PB 4.
13 Nicoll, *Restoration Drama*, 182.
14 See Holland, *Ornament*, 19–54.
15 Nicoll, *Restoration Drama*, 43.
16 Ibid., 67.
17 For the benefit, advertisement dated 4 June 1711 recorded in LS2 643. For Wilks, see, for example, the performance of 16 November 1706 listed in LS2 322.
18 Betterton owned a copy of Hobbes's *Elements of Philosophy* and a portrait of him. PB 6 and 20.
19 Amanda Vickery, *In Pursuit of Pleasure* (Milton Keynes: Open University Press, 2001), 47.
20 In January 1669 the King's Company actress Katherine Corey was imprisoned for impersonating Lady Harvey but 'Charles II reportedly returned to the play and refused all demands that Corey apologize to Lady Harvey or that the actors be prevented from satirising members of the court'. MS letters of 11 and 21 January 1669 in *Register* nos.474 and 478.
21 Gildon, *Life*, 6.
22 Manning, 'To Mr Betterton', 45.
23 Gildon, *Life*, 48.
24 Etherege, *The Man of Mode*, 49.
25 Congreve, *The Way of the World*, 23.
26 Pepys, *Diary*, 11 and 28 February 1666.
27 Lewis Mumford, *The City in History: Its Origins, its Transformations and its Prospects* (London: Penguin Books, 1961), 424.
28 Eduardo E. Lozano, *Community Design and the Culture of Cities: The Crossroad and the Wall* (Cambridge: Cambridge University Press, 1990), 261–2.
29 Thomas Dekker, *The Wonderfull Yeare* (London, 1603), D1r.
30 Reproduced as the frontispiece to Ronald Hutton, *Charles II, King of England, Scotland and Ireland* (Oxford: Clarendon Press, 1989).
31 Anna Keay, *The Magnificent Monarch: Charles II and the Ceremonies of Power* (London: Continuum, 2008).
32 Yi-Fu Tuan, 'Space and Context', in Richard Schechner and Willa Appel, eds., *By Means of Performance: Intercultural Studies of Theatre and Ritual* (Cambridge: Cambridge University Press, 1990), 127.
33 Gildon, *Life*, 27.

34 Reproduced in Thomas and Hare, *Restoration and Georgian England*, 87–91.

35 Jean I. Marsden, 'Spectacle, Horror, and Pathos', in Payne Fiske, ed., *The Cambridge Companion to English Restoration Theatre*, 179.

36 Simon Schama, *Landscape and Memory* (London: Fontana, 1996), 570. Rochester, 'A Ramble in St James's Park', in *Complete Poems and Plays*, ed. Paddy Lyons (London: Dent, 1993), 46.

37 Betterton, *The Amorous Widow*, 13.

38 Cynthia Wall, *The Literary and Cultural Spaces of Restoration London* (Cambridge: Cambridge University Press, 1998), 149.

39 Cited in ibid., 153.

40 Roy Strong, *The Artist and the Garden* (New Haven: Yale University Press, 2000), 119.

41 See David Norbrook, *Writing the English Republic: Poetry, Rhetoric and Politics, 1627–1660* (Cambridge: Cambridge University Press, 1999), 12, 37–8, 48, 55.

42 Suetonius, *The Twelve Caesars*, trans. Robert Graves (Harmondsworth: Penguin, 1989), 51.

43 Martial, *Liber de Spectaculis*, 2.12.

44 Shakespeare, *Julius Caesar*, III.ii.249–54.

45 Stephen Gosson, *Plays Confuted in Five Actions* (London, 1582), G7v.

46 Martin Butler, *Theatre and Crisis, 1632–1642* (Cambridge: Cambridge University Press, 1984), 179.

47 Edward, Earl of Clarendon, *The History of the Rebellion and Civil Wars in England*, ed. W. Dunn Macray, 6 vols. (Oxford: Clarendon Press, 1888), I.135.

48 Evelyn, *Diary*, 11 April 1653.

49 Schama, *Landscape and Memory*, 159.

50 Keith Thomas, *Man and the Natural World: Changing Attitudes in England, 1500–1800* (Harmondsworth: Penguin, 1983), 209.

51 Downes, *Roscius Anglicanus*, 109.

52 Evelyn, *Silva: Or, a Discourse of Forest-Trees, and the Propagation of Timber in His Majesty's Dominions*, 5th edn (1729), facsimile edition (London: Stobart and Son, 1979), 262; Maguire, *Regicide and Restoration*, 14.

53 John Milton, *The Tenure of Kings and Magistrates* (London, 1649); Robert Filmer, Preface to *Observations upon Aristotle's Politiques* (London, 1652).

54 Edmund Waller, 'On St James's Park, as Lately Improv'd by His Majesty', in G. Thorn Drury, ed., *The Poems of Edmund Waller*, 2 vols. (London: George Routledge and Sons, 1893), II.44, ll. 69–72.

55 *Silva*, xxviii; for more on druids, Schama, *Landscape and Memory*, 161.

56 Rochester, 'A Ramble in St James's Park', ll. 19–20.

57 Reproduced in Hutton, *Charles II*, 275. The illustration is from *A True Narrative of the Horrid Hellish Popish Plot. The Second Part (1679)*.

58 Christopher Thacker, *The History of Gardens* (London: Croom Helm, 1979), 144. For Mollet, see Kenneth Woodbridge, *Princely Gardens: the Origins and Development of the French Formal Style* (London: Thames and Hudson, 1986).

59 Martin Lister, *A Journey to Paris in the Year 1698* (London, 1699), 37.
60 Strong, *The Artist and the Garden*, 119.
61 Thomas and Hare, *Restoration and Georgian England*, 107.

6 IN THE DUKE'S COMPANY, 1660–1663

1   Chancery 7/100/68, in *Register* no.2. In January 1661 Davenant purchased adjoining land to enlarge the theatre premises (Chancery 7/100/68, *Register* no.57); his right to the entire site was disputed in January 1662 (Chancery 7/455/70, *Register* no.120).
2   Beeston was granted a licence to act at the Salisbury Court in June 1660; see BL Add. MS 19,256, fol.100, in *Register* no.6. George Jolly claimed to have had agreements with both Beeston and Davenant but was ordered to cease playing on 13 November 1661; see LC 5/137, p. 333, *Register* no.104.
3   See above, 52. For Evelyn, *Diary*, 29 May 1660.
4   John Ogilby, *The Relation of His Majesties Entertainment Passing through the City of London* (London, 1661).
5   John Parton, *Some Account of the Hospital and Parish of St Giles in the Fields, Middlesex* (London: Luke Hansard & Sons, 1822), 236, in *Register* no.9. On this evidence Rhodes's company probably performed forty-three times up to 28 July 1660. For an order 'against Disturbing the Cockpitt by soldiers', BL Egerton MS 2542, fols.405–6, *Register* no.21.
6   BL Add MS 19256, fol.46v. Herbert ordered the playhouses to pay Rogers for 'guarding [them] from all molestations'. Cited in *Register* no.17. In December 1663 the Lord Chamberlain issued an order to control those who 'rudely presse & with evill Language & blowes force their wayes into the two Theatres'. See LC 5/138, p. 459, *Register* no.260. As late as 1708 there appears an order against the trouble caused by 'persons coming behind the Scenes and Standing upon the Stage during the Performances'. LC 5/154, p. 320, *Register* no.1959.
7   An order of 25 February 1665 is aimed at controlling the 'great disorders in ye Attyring-house [of the Duke's Theatre] to ye hindrance of ye Actors & interruption of ye scenes'. State Papers 44/22, p. 32; *Register* no.306. For a decree that spectators should pay for entry to the theatres, see the proclamation of 23 July 1670 in *Register* no.567; on the nuisance caused by servants, State Papers 44/36, p. 138, *Register* no.730.
8   State Papers 44/5, pp. 158–60 and 29/8, no.1, in *Register* nos.7 and 8.
9   *Register* includes nearly 100 references to regulations or disputes about acting in Norwich.
10 Herbert's protest to the King, dated 4 August 1660, is in BL Add. MS 19256, fol.48; *Register* no.13.
11 Financial details are from PRO CP 40/2751, rot.317, in *Register* no.16. For L'Estrange, State Papers 29/78, no.96, *Register* no.237.
12 BL Add. MS 37157, fol.64 and two printed letters of 8 and 9 October 1660 show correspondence between Herbert and the Mayor of Maidstone, Kent, who disputed Herbert's authority to license plays beyond the court of

St James; cited in *Register* nos.31, 33 and 34. Well into 1662 Herbert was going to law against Davenant for defying his jurisdiction: BL Add. MS 19256, fols.101 and 106, in *Register* nos.91–2, and Chancery 40/2753, rot.1190, *Register* no.122. The temporary suspension of the company's acting in September 1661 may have been the result of Herbert's legal manoeuvres; LC 5/184, fol.127v., in *Register* no.94.

13 State Paper 29/10, no.169, in *Register* no.18. The King's grant to Davenant and Killigrew, BL Add. MS 19256, fol.47, is reproduced in Thomas and Hare, *Restoration and Georgian England*, 11–12.

14 BL Add. MS 19256, fol.50, in *Register* no.32.

15 For Mohun, manuscript dated 13 October 1660 in *Register* no.35. Mohun's petition to the King, BL Add. MS 19256, fol.71, is no.36. For Beeston, warrant dated 29 August 1663 in LC 5/185, fol.70v, in *Register* no.241. A further arrest warrant against Beeston was issued in September 1664; LC 5/186, fol.13, in *Register* no.293.

16 A draft order reprinted in LS1 13 refers to daily performances at three named theatres as late as 20 August 1660.

17 Thomas Middleton and William Rowley, *The Changeling* (London, 1653), EEBO 12.

18 Downes, *Roscius Anglicanus*, 45.

19 Pepys, *Diary*, 18 August 1660.

20 Milhous, *Management*, 8.

21 LC 5/138, p. 91, in *Register* no.252, shows Rhodes being paid £20 for a court performance on 1 November 1662.

22 LC 5/138, p. 387, reprinted in Nicoll, *Restoration Drama*, 278, n.5 and cited in *Register* no.265.

23 *Register* records five summonses against Rhodes between April 1663 and July 1669.

24 State Papers 44/9, 247–50; *Register* no.188.

25 LC 5/137, p. 332–3; *Register* no.29.

26 Between March and September 1661 Davenant sold shares or part shares to five people, one of them in trust to a further investor; *Register* nos.66–9, 76–7 and 95.

27 For the Dublin monopoly, State Papers 63/304, no.171, in *Register* no.47. The grant was initially made but revoked in March 1661 after protests by the incumbent, John Ogilby.

28 Calculated by Botica, 'Audience, Playhouse and Play', 35.

29 Gildon, *Life*, 15.

30 Aaron Hill, *The Prompter*, no.51, Tuesday 6 May 1735.

31 The document is reprinted in Nicoll, *Restoration Drama*, 285–6, n.10.

32 On 30 August 1660 the bookseller Humphrey Moseley denied to Herbert that he had entered into any agreement with Rhodes about rights to plays printed by him. Harvard Theatre Collection TS 992.31.7F, in *Register* no.22. According to LC 5/137, pp. 343–4, in *Register* no.50, Davenant was given the right to perform his own plays and *The Tempest, Measure for Measure, Much*

Ado about Nothing, Romeo and Juliet, Twelfth Night, Henry VIII, The Sophy, King Lear, Macbeth, Hamlet and *The Duchess of Malfi*, as well as temporary rights to a further six including a previous success of Betterton's, *Pericles*.

33 Milhous, *Management*, 3.

34 Substantial sections of the document, BL Add. Charter 9295, are in Thomas and Hare, *Restoration and Georgian England*, 33–5.

35 Note added to LC 5/137, 343–4, in *Register* no.50.

36 Herbert proceeded against Betterton in May 1662 (BL Add. MS 19256, fol.104, *Register* no.134). Betterton was one of a number of actors fined for assaulting Herbert's messenger on 4 July 1662 (Middlesex County Records, III, 322–3, reprinted in *Register* no.144); see below, 92.

37 On 26 January 1681 John Roffey claimed that Betterton denied him redemption on a half-share in the Dorset Garden Theatre. Chancery Suit 7/575/62, in *Register* no.1122.

38 Ronald Hutton, *The Restoration* (Oxford: Oxford University Press, 1987), 290.

39 Backscheider, 'Behind City Walls', 76.

40 LC 3/73, fols.100v–101, 113, in *Register* no.24.

41 Milhous, *Management*, 3.

42 See Alice Clark, *The Working Life of Women in the Seventeenth Century* (London, 1917).

43 As an actor-manager later in life Betterton championed work by women even when there was obvious prejudice against it. He appeared in Susannah Centlivre's *The Platonick Lady* in 1706; according to the author's dedication, her bookseller reported customers refusing to buy it because of its authorship. In her preface to *Almyna, or The Arabian Vow* (London, 1707), Mary Delariviere Manley notes 'Mr Betterton's unwearied care, (who is desired to accept the Author's acknowledgements for so faithfully discharging the Trust that was repos'd in him)'. For his relationship with a female manager, Lady Mary Davenant, see below, 102–3. His other roles in plays by women included Sir Charles in Pix's *The Innocent Mistress* (1697), Melito Bondi in Pix's *The Deceiver Deceiv'd* (1697), Gramont in Trotter's *Fatal Friendship* (1698), Lovewell in Centlivre's *The Gamester* (1705) and Arwide in Trotter's *The Revolution of Sweden* (1706). For Betterton and Aphra Behn, see below, 130.

44 George Savile, Marquess of Halifax, 'The Lady's New Year's Gift; or, Advice to a Daughter', in J.P. Kenyon, ed., *Halifax. Complete Works* (Harmondsworth: Penguin, 1969), 311.

45 BDA IV.222 and VI.364.

46 Davies, *Dramatic Miscellanies*, III.196. For commentary, see Gilli Bush-Bailey, 'Revolution, Legislation and Autonomy', in Maggie B. Gale and John Stokes, ed., *The Cambridge Companion to the Actress* (Cambridge: Cambridge University Press, 2007), 27.

47 For more on the social background of Restoration actresses, see Deborah C. Payne, 'The Restoration Actress', in Owen, *Companion*, 72–7.

48 Anthony Hamilton, *Memoirs of the Comte de Gramont*, trans. Horace Walpole (London: The Folio Society, 1965), 178–9.

49 PB 20.

50 Downes, *Roscius Anglicanus*, 53.

51 From the Articles of Agreement between Davenant and the Duke's Company, BL Add. Charter 9295, partially reprinted in Thomas and Hare, *Restoration and Georgian England*, 33–5.

52 Successive warrants stipulate material for cloaks and capes: 'foure yards of bastard scarlet cloath and one quarter of a yard of veluett for [performers'] liueries'. LC 5/137, p. 31 and others, reprinted in Nicoll, *Restoration Drama*, 325–6. See also the order of 6 March 1672 issued for the King's Company players Mohun, Hart and Kynaston. LC 7/1 and 5/140, p. 5, cited in *Register* no.677.

53 Milhous, *Management*, 14. For a survey of actors' salaries, and a great deal else besides, see Robert D. Hume, 'The Economics of Culture in London, 1660–1740', *Huntington Library Quarterly*, vol. 69, no.4, 487–533. Picard, *Restoration London*, 246–57, summarises Restoration prices.

54 See 'Finances', in the Companion to Pepys, *Diary*, x.130.

55 For example, in April 1662 the company was paid £270 for plays presented before royalty, either in the theatre or at court. LC 5/137, p. 110; *Register* no.130. In June 1662 fifteen performances brought in £300 (LC 5/137, p. 389; *Register* no.212).

56 Pepys, *Diary*, 22 October 1662.

57 For Davenant, LC 5/185, fol.29v, *Register* no.209; for Rhodes, see above, 72; for Harris, see below, 87.

58 Milhous, 'Playwriting', 379, notes that one of the booksellers named on the title page was Chetwood, who had his apprenticeship with Edmund Curll, publisher of Betterton's supposed *History of the English Stage*. Chetwood also published the 1722 reissue of Massinger's *The Roman Actor*, sometimes attributed to Betterton.

59 Philip Massinger, *The Bondman* (1638 edn), EEBO 40.

60 See Dryden's 'Of Heroic Plays', Essay Preface to *The Conquest of Granada Part 1* (London, 1672). On heroic plays and Stuart government, J. Douglas Canfield, *Heroes and States. On the Ideology of Restoration Tragedy* (Lexington: University of Kentucky Press, 2000); Derek Hughes, *English Drama 1660–1700* (Oxford: Clarendon Press, 1996).

61 Betterton's 'Eastern' and 'Indian' roles, including a number of tyrants, included Cambyses in Settle's *Cambyses* (1671), Crimalhaz in Settle's *The Empress of Morocco* (1673), Solyman in Settle's *Ibrahim* (1676), Abdelazer in Behn's *Abdelazer* (1676), Orontes in Pordage's *The Siege of Babylon* (1677), Mithridates in Lee's *Mithridates* (1685?), Montezuma in Dryden's *The Indian Emperour* (1691?), Cyrus in Banks's *Cyrus the Great* (1695), Osman in Manley's *The Royal Mischief* (1696), Attabanus in Cibber's *Xerxes* (1699), Iopano in Oldmixon's *The Governor of Cyprus* (1703), Mahomet in Trapp's *Abra-Mule* (1704) and the Old Emperor in Dryden's *Aureng-Zebe* (1706?).

62 The unknown author of *A Satyr on the Players* wrote, 'being chief, each Playing Drab to Swive / He takes it as his just Prerogative. / Methinks I see him mounted, hear him Roar / And foaming cry; God's blood you little whore / Zounds how I fuck, I fuck like any Moor' (99). Robert Gould's 'A Satyr against the Play-House' drew the same parallel: 'Witness Millbank, where Osmin keeps his Trulls / With what, by sharing, he exacts from Fools' (183). It is a sign of his equanimity that Betterton owned a copy of Gould's works, published in 1709; the only indication that Gould hit the mark is also in Betterton's library in the shape of *A General History of Whoring* (1697), PB 12.

63 Davenant, *The Siege of Rhodes. The First and Second Part* (1663), 12.

64 Richard Jeffree, *Mr Cartwright's Pictures: A Seventeenth-Century Collection* (London: Dulwich Picture Gallery, 1987), 13.

65 PB 19. Betterton owned a number of books relating to Turkey, including Richard Knolles's *General History of the Turks* (1638 edn) and Aaron Hill's *The Present State of the Ottoman Empire* (1710). See PB 1 and 3.

66 Milhous, 'Census', 91.

7 EQUAL WITH THE HIGHEST: THOMAS BETTERTON AND HENRY HARRIS, 1663–1668

1 Davenant's agreement document of 5 November 1660 (BL Add. Charter 9295), in James Orchard Halliwell, *A Collection of Ancient Documents* (London, 1870), 27–32.

2 Harris's name is not in the Freedom Register 1658–81 (Guildhall Library MS 5668) or the index to the Court Minute Book (MS 5667/1) of the Painter-Stainers' Company. However, no Freedom Registers survive for the period before 1658, while the apprentice binding books do not begin until 1666, both too late for Harris.

3 BL Add. Charter 9295, in Thomas and Hare, *Restoration and Georgian England*, 34.

4 Pepys, *Diary*, 20 February 1667.

5 For *Julius Caesar*, see the letter from Katherine Phillips to Lady Temple, 3 March 1664, cited in LS1 74; in *Register* no.267, the date is given as 22 January 1664.

6 Pepys, *Diary*, 3 February 1664.

7 See above, 71–2.

8 Dryden, Letter to Jacob Tonson dated August 1684, in E.C. Ward, ed., *The Letters of John Dryden* (New York: AMS Press, 1965), 23–4.

9 Gould, 'A Satyr against the Play-House', 183.

10 Thomas Brown, *Amusements Serious and Comical* (London, 1702), 52.

11 Motraye, *Travels Through Europe*, 143.

12 Pepys, *Diary*, 24 January 1667.

13 Ibid., 6 January 1668; also 29 May 1667.

14 Ibid., 7 January 1668. The play had been published in 1667 as *Love Tricks*.

15 Pepys, *Diary*, 30 March 1668.

16 Ibid., 26 April 1668.

17 First performed in 1664.

18 Pepys, *Diary*, 29 April 1668. Pepys and 'the wits' were privileged: an order of three years before had forbidden entry to 'ye Attyring house' of the Duke's Theatre to anyone 'of what quality soever' who did not belong to the company. See 202 n.7.

19 Pepys, *Diary*, 11 May 1668.

20 The *Register* lists 24 occasions on which Harris was sued by private individuals, starting with William Watkins's suit of 23 April 1667; see LC 5/186, fol.137, in *Register* no.379.

21 Orrery's *The History of Henry the Fifth* was first acted by the Duke's Company in August 1664. For the portrait, *Diary*, 5 September 1668.

22 Pepys, *Diary*, 30 March 1668.

23 For Anne Harris, LC 5/190, fol.134, *Register* no.956, and LC 5/190, fol.183, *Register* no.1029; for Emma Worcester, LC 5/190, fol.174, *Register* no.1009.

24 Dawson, *Gentility and the Comic Theatre*, 238.

25 Pepys, *Diary*, 22 October 1662.

26 Chancery document 66/3009; *Register* no.186.

27 LC 5/185, fol.46; *Register* no.216.

28 State Papers 44/15, p. 141, *Register* no.232.

29 LC 5/138, p. 388, cited in Nicoll, *Restoration Drama*, 329. An order of 16 March 1665 charges Harris with making sure that the private theatre at Whitehall is in good order. LC 5/138, p. 425, cited in *Register* no.311.

30 See above 74–5, and below, 92.

31 The patent was not awarded until 1 June 1667, following a stop on the process in April. For the patent, PRO C66/3090, no.13; for the stop, LC 5/138, p. 369. *Register* nos. 387 and 375.

32 Treasury Papers 29/1, p. 270; *Register* no.410.

33 Pepys, *Diary*, 24 October 1663.

34 Pepys, *Diary*, 22 July 1663.

35 LS1 31.

36 Ibid., 39.

37 Pepys, *Diary*, 7 September 1661. For further information see Latham and Matthews, *The Diary of Samuel Pepys*, II.174 n.1. The performance is listed in LS1 39.

38 For *Bartholomew Fair*, 7 September 1662; for *Twelfth Night*, 11 September 1662. He had already seen the revival of Jonson's play on 8 and 22 June of the same year. On 20 January 1669 he described *Twelfth Night* as 'one of the weakest plays that ever I saw on the stage'.

39 Downes, *Roscius Anglicanus*, 52. Loans and gifts of royal clothing were not uncommon. On 11 December 1667 Pepys reported that the King had given his company £500 for sixteen scarlet robes to be worn in Jonson's *Catiline*.

40 Downes, *Roscius Anglicanus*, 52.

41 Pepys, *Diary*, 4 November 1661.
42 Edwin Chappell, ed., *Shorthand Letters of Samuel Pepys* (Cambridge: Cambridge University Press, 1933), 22.
43 LS1 44.
44 Pepys, *Diary*, 1 March 1662.
45 Downes, *Roscius Anglicanus*, 53.
46 LS1 44. The same designation occurs in the cast list for Thomas Porter's *The Villain*, which opened on 18 October 1662; see LS1 56.
47 *The Spanish Fryar* (London, 1681), 13.
48 Davies, *Dramatic Miscellanies*, III.397.
49 BDA II.96.
50 Cibber, *Apology*, 96.
51 See above, 80.
52 Pepys, *Diary*, 22 October 1662.
53 Gildon, *Life*, 7.
54 Ibid., 15.
55 Pepys, *Diary*, 1 February 1664: Pepys notes that Anne Marshall's voice was 'not so sweet' as Mary Betterton's.
56 PB 20. PB 19 also records a crayon drawing of Mary Betterton by Greenhill.
57 *Middlesex Sessions Books*, III.322; *Register* no.144. The other actors involved were the Nokes brothers, Turner, Lillieston, Medbourne, Underhill, Sandford, Dixon, Price and Pavy.
58 Pepys, *Diary*, 22 December 1663.
59 Ibid.
60 BDA II.97 and Milhous, *Management*, 28.
61 Downes, *Roscius Anglicanus*, 55–6.
62 Andrew Gurr, *The Shakespearean Stage 1574–1642*, 3rd edn (Cambridge: Cambridge University Press, 1992), 44 and 62.
63 PB 19.
64 Roach, 'The Performance', 32–3.
65 For *Henry VIII*, the performances of 15 and 27 February 1707 recorded in LS2 343 and 346. By then a later rival, John Verbruggen, had taken over Wolsey.
66 On 1 January 1664 Pepys complained that the 'so-much cried up play of *Henry the 8th*' was 'so simple a thing, made up of a great many patches'.
67 Davenant, *The Rivals*, in *The Works of Sir William Davenant* (London, 1673), 117.
68 Pepys, *Diary*, 10 September 1664.
69 Betterton played the same role more than thirty years later in Mary Pix's *Queen Catharine* (1698).
70 Maguire, *Regicide and Restoration*, 175.
71 Pepys, *Diary*, 13 August 1664.
72 Etherege, *The Comical Revenge* (London, 1664), 20.
73 Downes, *Roscius Anglicanus*, 56–7.

74 *The Comical Revenge*, 49.
75 Maguire, *Regicide and Restoration*, 178.
76 LC 5/138, p. 417, reprinted in Nicoll, *Restoration Drama*, 286–7 n.8.
77 *Register* nos.335, 338 and 339.
78 See Paul Slack, *The Impact of Plague in Tudor and Stuart England* (Oxford: Oxford University Press, 1985).
79 BL Maps, Crace I.50, reproduced in Whitfield, *Cities of the World*, 106–7. For Nokes, see above, 76.
80 Pepys, *Diary*, 15 April 1667.
81 Pepys, *Diary*, 20 April 1667.
82 Dawson, *Gentility and the Comic Theatre*, 112–41 and 238.
83 Ibid., 238.
84 Pepys, *Diary*, 4 September 1667. *Heraclius* was acted the following day.
85 See the account of Rowe's *The Fair Penitent* (1703), in which George Powell called for his dresser Warren while the latter was playing his corpse: 'Even the grave Mr Betterton *Smil'd in the Tumult, and enjoy'd the Storm*'. Recorded in Chetwood's *A General History of the Stage*, 253–4, and reprinted in LS2 93.
86 Pepys, *Diary*, 24 October 1667.
87 Milhous, *Management*, 27.
88 Deposition of Harris in Killigrew vs. Davenant, 17 October 1691, C24/1144; *Register* no.1401.
89 Milhous, *Management*, 27.
90 Pepys, *Diary*, 9 April 1668.
91 From Richard Flecknoe's *Sir William D'Avenant's Voyage to the Other World*, cited in Hotson, *Commonwealth and Restoration Stage*, 223. Hotson, 224–6, also reprints a more eulogistic elegy on Davenant which shows him joining the English dramatic greats, including Jonson and Shakespeare 'in a Sphere / Of those great souls who once admir'd him here'. *Register* no.440 cites a printed broadside 'Elegy Upon the Death of Sir William Davenant' that optimistically compares him to Shakespeare and many other Renaissance dramatists.

8 ACTOR MANAGEMENT: RUNNING THE DUKE'S COMPANY

1 John Dennis, 'The Causes of the Decay and Defects of Dramatick Poetry', in Hooker, ed., *The Critical Works of John Dennis*, II.277–8.
2 For Betterton's assistance with Dennis's play *Liberty Asserted* see below, 106. Betterton also played Miramont (1704), Rinaldo in Dennis's *Rinaldo and Armida* (1698), Orestes in his *Iphigenia* (1699) and Virginius in his *Appius and Virginia* (1709).
3 The oath is repeated in lists of company members, for example LC 3/25, p. 162, *Register* no.155. For the Duchess of York's death in 1671 and the theatre closure, LC 5/12, p. 302, *Register* no.617.

4 'A Discourse on Operas', in Francesco Vanneschi's *Fetonte* (London, 1747), observes that 'Betterton and his Wife' were 'the last Actors employ'd in instructing' princes and princesses to act (iv).

5 LC 5/141 records Harris's role in producing John Crowne's *Calisto* at court in 1674–5; the Bettertons coached the Princesses Mary and Anne (*Register* nos.891–917). See also Eleanor Boswell, *The Restoration Court Stage* (Cambridge, Mass.: Harvard University Press, 1932).

6 BDA IV.167; warrant of 3 January 1671 for plays acted between 16 November 1668 and 20 June 1670 in Harvard fMS Thr 57 (1); *Register* no.594. Further examples, *Register* nos.679 and 1071.

7 *Register* no.445. A principal creditor called John Alway was named as the administrator after Lady Mary had renounced responsibility, but only on paper. This Alway is the 'John Otway' once thought to have owned the Chandos Portrait of Shakespeare; see below, 230, n.15.

8 Chancery Lawsuits C8/299/134 and C24/1144/1; *Register* no.780.

9 Jacqueline Pearson, *The Prostituted Muse: Images of Women and Women Dramatists 1642–1737* (Hemel Hempstead: Harvester Wheatsheaf, 1988), 32.

10 Bush-Bailey, *Treading the Bawds*, 29.

11 Chancery suit C24/1144 of 17 October 1691; *Register* no.1401.

12 See W.W. Wroth, rev. C.E. Challis, 'Henry Harris', NDNB, 25.427–8.

13 Milhous, *Management*, 27–8.

14 Ibid., 14 and 31.

15 Ibid., 30.

16 Ibid., 29.

17 For Medbourne, LC 5/187, fol.187; *Register* no.532.

18 For Jeremiah Lisle, LC 5/188, fol.3v; *Register* no.554. For Adams and Allenson, arrested for 'absenting themselfes from ye Dukes house Theatre', LC 5/188, fol.36v; *Register* no.570.

19 PRO C6/316/21, cited in Milhous, *Management*, 30.

20 Letter from Arlington to Betterton dated 7 May 1681 in LC 5/144, p. 114 and *Register* no.1128.

21 Pepys, *Diary*, 7 May 1669.

22 'A Satyr against Poetry', in Vincent de Voiture, *Familiar Letters of Love, Gallantry, and Several Occasions*, 2 vols. (London, 1718), 1.92.

23 A document in the Osborne Collection at Yale University dated 24 June 1680, in *Register* no.1113, records a loan of £11 made by Jacob Tonson the elder to Otway. Richard Tonson, Jacob's brother and business partner, published *Don Carlos* (1676), *Titus and Berenice* (1677) and *Friendship in Fashion* (1678). However, Otway's next four plays, starting with *Caius Marius* in 1680, were published by three different booksellers, one of whom, Richard Bentley, was the unusual dedicatee of *The Souldiers Fortune* (1681), where he was said to 'pay honestly for the Copy' (sig. A2). By the time Otway published his last play, *The Atheist*, in 1684, Bentley and Jacob Tonson had decided to share the risks and benefits of working with him.

24 Otway, 'Love-Letters written by the late most ingenious Mr Thomas Otway', in J.C. Ghosh, ed., *The Works of Thomas Otway*, 2 vols. (Oxford: Clarendon Press, 1932), II.475.

25 The *London Gazette* of 25–29 November 1686: 'Whereas Mr Thomas Otway some time before his Death made Four Acts of a Play, whoever can give Notice in whose Hands the Copy lies, either to Mr Thomas Betterton, or Mr William Smith at the Theatre Royal, shall be well Rewarded for his Pains.' The advertisement was repeated in *The Observator* of 27 November–4 December 1686.

26 See, for example, Dryden to Tonson, BL Egerton MS 2869, fol.30, *Register* no.1233, on his discussions with Betterton about casting revivals of *All for Love* and *The Conquest of Granada*, previously King's Company plays.

27 Cited in BDA II.81.

28 Joseph Arrowsmith, *The Reformation* (1673); Frances Boothby, *Marcelia* (1669); Nicholas Brady, *The Rape* (1692); George Digby, Earl of Bristol, *Elvira* (1663); Laurence Maidwell, *The Loving Enemies* (1679); Thomas St Serfe, *Tarugo's Wiles* (1667); anon., *The Faithful General* (1706). Dates indicate first performances. Betterton played Gunderic in Brady's play, Lorenzo in Maidwell's and Marus in *The Faithful General*.

29 For example, John Dover, *The Roman Generals* (1667); Alexander Green, *The Politician Cheated* (1663); Thomas Rymer, *Edgar, or the English Monarch* (1678); Edward Sherburne, *Troades, or the Royal Captives* (1679); J. Talbot, *Troas* (1686).

30 David Craufard, Preface to *Courtship-a-la-Mode* (1700).

31 *A Comparison Between the Two Stages* (London, 1702), 11. The reference is to a play performed by the breakaway Lincoln's Inn Fields company after 1695.

32 For Gildon, see above, 25–6; for Settle, Preface to *Distress'd Innocence* (London, 1691); for Dryden, *Troilus*, see his Preface to the 1679 text (EEBO 5) and for *Albion* see below, 146–7.

33 Dennis, Preface to *Liberty Asserted*, in *Critical Works*, I.324. For Dryden discussing the casting of *Don Sebastian* with Betterton, see Ward, *Letters*, 23–4.

34 Manning, 'To Mr Betterton', 46; Gildon, *Life*, 16; D'Urfey, Dedication to *The Intrigues at Versailles* (London, 1697), A2.

35 Owen Ruffield, *The Life of Alexander Pope, Esq.* (London, 1769), 25, notes: '[Pope] had a strong propensity to the tragic drama, and should certainly have made it his principal study, had not the moral and intellectual characters of the players of his time, so different from that of Betterton, always deterred him.' Ruffield, 26, also notes that even Betterton could not persuade Pope to turn his poem 'Alcander' into a tragedy.

36 Gould, 'A Satyr against the Play-House', 183.

37 Cibber, *Apology*, 79.

38 State Papers 29/95, no.102; *Register* no.270.

39 State Papers 29/142, no.160 and 29/191, no.31, in *Register* nos.318 and 368.

40 PRO C6/316/21, cited in Milhous, *Management*, 30.

41 BDA III.4.

42 LC 7/3, reprinted in Nicoll, *Restoration Drama*, 329–30. Downes, *Roscius Anglicanus*, 66–7, also reports the incident. LS1 207, reprints an entry from the diary of Thomas Isham, who thought that the play was *Macbeth*, with Harris as Macduff and Cademan covering Betterton's absence.

43 LC 7/3, in Nicoll, *Restoration Drama*, 330.

44 Alexander Smith, *The Comical and Tragical History of the Lives and Adventures of the Most Noted Bayliffs in and about London and Westminster* (London, 1723), 45–6.

45 Milhous, 'Playwriting', 384, argues that the play came to be referred to as Betterton's adaptation on the basis of minor cuts and changes to the original for the 1669 production.

46 Stern, *Rehearsal*, 124–94.

47 Stern, 'Re-patching the Play', in Peter Holland and Stephen Orgel, eds., *From Script to Stage in Early Modern England* (Basingstoke and New York: Palgrave Macmillan, 2004), 170.

48 Thomas Davies, *Memoirs of the Life of David Garrick, Esq.* (London, 1780), 20–1.

49 Aphra Behn, Preface to *The Dutch Lover* (London, 1673), EEBO 6.

50 Pepys first saw the play on 5 November 1664. On the relationship of play and plot, see Gary Wills, *Witches and Jesuits* (Oxford: Oxford University Press, 1996). For Sir Matthew Hale's trial of two witches in 1664, and his careful reasoning as to their existence, see Picard, *Restoration London*, 272. For the identity of Betterton's choreographer, probably Joseph rather than Josias Priest, see Jennifer Thorp, 'Dance in Late 17th-century London: Priestly Muddles', *Early Music* (May 1998), 198–210.

51 Pepys, *Diary*, 22 October 1662.

52 Stern, *Rehearsal*, 151–5.

53 Ibid., 160.

54 Cibber, *Apology*, 66.

55 Pepys, *Diary*, 7 January 1667.

56 Dryden, Preface to *Troilus and Cressida* (London, 1679), EEBO 12.

57 Stern, *Rehearsal*, 75.

58 Dryden, Preface to *Troilus*, EEBO 11.

59 *Macbeth, A Tragedy*, adap. Davenant (London, 1674), 53–4.

60 Gildon, *Life*, 6.

61 Epilogue to *The Ordinary*, in *A Collection of Poems Written upon Several Occasions by Several Persons* (1673), 167.

62 *Macbeth, A Tragedy*, 37.

63 Barbara A. Murray, *Restoration Shakespeare. Viewing the Voice* (New York and London: Associated University Presses, 2001), 52.

64 As for example, in Howard Davies's 1982 production for the Royal Shakespeare Company.

65 LS1 239 lists a court performance of Marlowe's *Faustus* for 28 September 1675. *The Merry Devil of Edmonton*, first published in 1608, has been attributed to

Drayton, Dekker and others. Betterton played Sir Ralph Jerningham from 1689.

66 For Pepys, *Diary*, 7 January 1667. For the 18 February 1673 perform-ance, LC 5/141, p. 2, reprinted in Nicoll, *Restoration Drama*, 309; for 17 December 1666, LC 5/139, p. 125, in Nicoll, 308; for the Prince of Orange, LS1 176.

67 LC 5/139, p. 125, in Nicoll, *Restoration Drama*, 308–9. For contrasting views of *The Tempest*'s significance for the Stuarts, see James A. Winn, *John Dryden and His World* (New Haven and London: Yale University Press, 1987), 188, and Maguire, *Regicide and Restoration*, 131–6. There is no direct evidence that Betterton played Prospero, and this was the period of his eight-month illness.

68 For an account of the fissures in the play's historiography, see David Norbrook, '*Macbeth* and the Politics of Historiography', in Kevin Sharpe and Stephen N. Zwicker, eds., *The Politics of Discourse. The Literature and History of Seventeenth-Century England* (Berkeley: University of California Press, 1987), 78–116.

69 On music and supernatural scenes from the period see Steven E. Plank, '"And Now About the Cauldron Sing": Music and the Supernatural on the Restoration Stage', *Early Music*, vol. XVIII, no. 3 (1990), 393–407.

70 *Macbeth, A Tragedy*, 48

71 See Thomas and Hare, *Restoration and Georgian England*, 329.

72 H.N. Paul's *The Royal Play of Macbeth* (New York: Scribner and Sons, 1950) develops more fully than any other account – and not without con-troversy – the idea that the play was conceived for performance before James I and his brother-in-law, Christian IV of Denmark, in August 1606. Boitard's illustration is in Rowe, *The Works of Mr William Shakespear*, v.2298.

73 *The London Encyclopaedia*, 634.

74 LC 5/185, fol.148v; *Register* no.280.

75 Picard, *Restoration London*, 27–32.

76 For Roffey's half share, bought from Richard Bayly, see Guildhall MS 7842; *Register* no.154. For the dispute with the Bettertons, Chancery 7/575/62 and 7/581/135; *Register* nos.1122 and 1172.

77 On 26 September 1669, John Cressett wrote to him to say that two men had asked about the site and whether 'the Players' had an interest in it. Kent Archives Office U269.C93/10; *Register* no.517. On the eviction see Milhous, *Management*, 121. For details of negotiations over the site, see Hotson, *Commonwealth and Restoration Stage*, 229.

78 Chancery 5/284/40, reprinted in *Register* no.571. As part of the original agree-ment the lease was reassigned first to John Baker and Thomas Franklin, then back to the Davenant family through Lady Mary's youngest son, Nicholas, and his partner John Atkinson.

79 Nicoll, *Restoration Drama*, 289, citing Richard Baxter, *Reliquiae Baxterianae* (London, 1696), III.89.

80 Lowe, *Thomas Betterton*, 113.

81 See Diana de Marly, 'The Architect of Dorset Garden Theatre', *Theatre Notebook*, vol. 29 (1975), 119–24. For Gibbons, Horace Walpole, *Anecdotes of Painting in England*, 4 vols. (London, 1786), III.150.

82 Although the order in LC 5/14, p. 73, refers to the 'Duke's Theatre in Salisbury Court', that is presumed to confuse new and old sites; *Register* no.659.

83 Milhous, *Management*, 43–4.

84 BDA II.78. A Chancery document of 18 July 1674 lists the sharers in the Dorset Garden building with the proportion of the £7 daily rent they were to receive. Of the eleven shareholders, five were actors: Betterton, Harris, Nokes, Smith and Underhill. Lady Mary Davenant and Thomas Cross had a longstanding connection with company administration, while the remainder were outsiders; *Register* no.853.

85 Later contested by Christopher Rich; *Register* nos.1218, 1305, 1476, 1785, etc. For Harris's shares, BDA VII.129.

86 Deposition in Chancery suit C24/1144 of 17 October 1691; *Register* no.1401.

87 'The Reply of the Patentees', Article 1, LC 7/3, reprinted in Nicoll, *Restoration Drama*, 335. The rate cited is twenty per cent.

88 BL Add. MS 36,916, fol.233; *Register* no.657.

89 According to LS1 177–80, it opened in December 1670 and was still playing in mid-February 1671.

90 Dryden, Prologue to *Marriage à la Mode* (London, 1673). The assault continued in Dryden's other works, especially *Notes and Observations on the Empress of Morocco* (London, 1674).

91 Downes, *Roscius Anglicanus*, 68.

92 Ibid., 69.

93 Ibid., 69.

94 Newsletter for December 1674 cited in LS1 225.

95 *The Bulstrode Papers*, I, 217, cited in LS1 192, which lists other accounts of the fire of 25 January 1672. See also *Register* nos.669 and 670.

96 The first play was Fletcher's *The Beggar's Bush*; LS1 214.

97 This section draws on the calendar of events presented by Milhous, *Management*, 31–5. As early as 1667 Mohun was having pay docked for absences from the theatre. See LC 5/138, p. 411; *Register* no.409. For Gavill, LC 5/189, fol.104v; *Register* no.740.

98 Pepys, *Diary*, 24 January 1669.

99 See the order dated 19 April 1678 in LC 5/143, p. 69; *Register* no.1051.

100 For the Duke's Company in Oxford, Order in the Oxford City Council Book, 29 June 1670, *Register* no.564; for the King's Company, letter dated 28 July 1674 in Add. MS 28,929, fol.1v, *Register* no.859.

101 LC 7/1, fol.5, cited in LS1 242. Newdigate Newsletter, 21 March 1682, cited in LS1 307.

102 LS1 269 dates the premiere as 11 March 1678. For the protest of King's Company shareholders against Dryden's desertion, see *Register* no.1059.

Among other roles in Dryden's plays Betterton acted in *An Evening's Love* (1685–6), Dorax in *Don Sebastian* (1689), Cleomenes in *Cleomenes* (1692) and Alphonso in *Love Triumphant* (1693).

103 John Leanerd had written two plays for the King's Company but in 1678 offered *The Counterfeits* to Betterton, who played Vitelli.

104 Pepys, *Diary*, 14 November 1666. Cibber, *Apology*, 52, lists Smith with Betterton, Mountfort and Bracegirdle as being 'irreproachable in his Personal Morals, and Behaviour'.

105 BDA ii.86.

106 For Dryden's fall from grace after 1688, see Winn, *John Dryden and His World*, 381–421.

107 BDA vii.130.

108 For discussion of these 'Tory Comedies', see Robert Markley, '"Be Impudent, Be Saucy, Forward, Bold, Touzing, and Leud": The Politics of Sexuality and Feminine Desire in Behn's Tory Comedies', in J. Douglas Canfield and Deborah C. Payne, eds., *Cultural Readings of Restoration and Eighteenth-Century English Theater* (Athens, GA: University of Georgia Press, 1995), 114–40.

109 Cibber, *Apology*, 49.

110 Dryden, Preface to *Tyrannick Love* (1670), EEBO 3. A similar defence of theatre is found in the Catholic writer Richard Flecknoe's *A Discourse of the English Stage* (1664).

9 IN THE COMPANY OF THE DUKE:
BETTERTON AND CATHOLIC POLITICS IN THE 1670S

1 Three sources reprinted in LS1 284: *The True News; or Mercurius Anglicanus*, 4–7 February 1679/80; and two letters from the Dowager Countess of Sunderland to Henry Sidney dated 6 January 1679/80 (probably a misdating for February) and 19 February 1679/80. LS1 284 suggests that performances had recommenced by 19 February. Five court performances are recorded from 11 to 27 February 1680, perhaps as compensation.

2 John Kenyon, *The Popish Plot* (Harmondsworth: Pelican Books, 1974), 37.

3 Kenyon, *The Popish Plot*, 39, citing J.R. Jones, *The First Whigs* (Oxford: Oxford University Press, 1966), 67–8.

4 Maguire, *Regicide and Restoration*, 137. Maguire notes that the play opened only three weeks before Clarendon's flight to France. See also above, 213 n.67.

5 Matthew Medbourne, *Tartuffe, or the French Puritan* (London, 1670).

6 For Medbourne, BDA x.165. BDA ii.73 gives the date of Charles Betterton's burial as 20 December 1678.

7 For Pepys's dangerous situation during the Exclusion Crisis, see Richard Ollard, *Pepys* (Oxford: Oxford University Press, 1974), 245–61.

8 PB 7 and 14.

9 PB 21.

10 For *Paradise Lost*, see below, 131 n.53. Tillotson (1630–94) became Archbishop of Canterbury in 1691. For his conversation with Betterton, George Whitefield, *The Works of the Reverend George Whitefield*, 7 vols. (London, 1771–2), IV.339. For the Duke of York and Tillotson see Alexander Gordon, 'John Tillotson', DNB XIX.875.

11 *The Oxford Treatment of their Cambridge Friends* (London, 1705), 9.

12 PB 8 and 18.

13 Charles Gildon, Preface to *Love's Victim* (1701), ECCO 7.

14 *Don Carlos* (1676) is dedicated to the Duke, *The Orphan* (1680) to the Duchess, and *Venice Preserv'd* (1682) to the Duchess of Portsmouth. His *Titus and Berenice* (1677) is a version of Racine's *Bérénice*, and his *The History and Fall of Caius Marius* (1680) an adaptation of *Coriolanus*. On Otway and passions, see anon., *A Comparison Between the Two Stages*, 96–7, which judges that Nicholas Rowe was 'ambitious of following *Otway* in his Passions; but Alas! how far off?' Betterton encouraged Rowe and appeared in his *The Ambitious Step-Mother* (1700), *Tamerlane* (1702), *The Fair Penitent* (1703) and *Ulysses* (1706).

15 Gerard Genette, *Paratexts: Thresholds of Interpretation*, trans. Jane E. Lewin (Cambridge: Cambridge University Press, 1997). For studies of 'paratexts' in the Renaissance and Restoration, see David M. Bergeron, *Textual Patronage in English Drama, 1570–1640* (Aldershot and Burlington: Ashgate, 2006), and Deborah C. Payne, 'The Restoration Dramatic Dedication as Symbolic Capital', *Studies in Eighteenth-Century Culture*, vol. 20 (1990), 27–42.

16 According to LS1 245, the play opened on 8 June 1676 and was still playing on 19 June.

17 Downes, *Roscius Anglicanus*, 64.

18 Nicoll, *Restoration Drama*, 289 n.1, citing *The Calendar of State Papers, Treasury Books, 1669–72*, 495; Nicoll lists payments for court performances on 305–14. The payment had not been made by 17 August 1670, when the Secretary of the Treasury noted that the sum of £500 was owing; see PRO T29/625, fol.131; *Register* no.572. For the Windsor performances of 1674, see Chancery suit C8/299/134; *Register* no.856.

19 BL Add. MS 36916, fol.182: '[the Duke's Company having] beene there all the time past came up yesterday and the kings goe downe this day'; *Register* no.556.

20 Milling, 'Thomas Betterton and the Art of Acting', 26.

21 The play was given for Prince George's birthday on 28 February 1704; see LS2 152.

22 This account is drawn chiefly from Ronald Hutton, 'The Making of the Secret Treaty of Dover, 1668–1670', *The Historical Journal*, vol. 29, no.2 (1986), 297–318, and from David Ogg, *England in the Reign of Charles II*, 2nd edn (Oxford: Oxford University Press, 1961), 337–43.

23 Oxford City Council Book, 29 June 1670; *Register* no.564.

24 *The Sullen Lovers* opened on 2 May 1668 according to Pepys, who found it 'tedious' and lacking 'design'. LS1 records six performances between then

and May 1670. LS1 169 gives April 1670 as the premiere of *Sir Salomon* but then gives only a date of 9 May 1670 before a Dover performance of 19 or 20 May. Downes, *Roscius Anglicanus*, 65, says that 'the Play being Singularly well Acted, it took 12 Days together'.

25 Performances of Molière adaptations had been common for the past three years: Dryden's *Sir Martin Mar-All* (1667, from *L'Étourdi* of 1655) and *An Evening's Love* (1668, from *Le dépit amoureux* of 1656); Lacy's *The Dumb Lady* (1669? from *Le Médecin Malgré Lui* of 1666); Shadwell's *The Hypocrite* (1669? from *Tartuffe* 1664) and *The Sullen Lovers* (1668, from *Les Fâcheux* of 1661); and Davenant's *The Playhouse to be Let* (1663, from *Les Précieuses Ridicules* of 1659). Others followed immediately after, such as Betterton's own *The Amorous Widow* (*c.*1670), and, also in 1670, Medbourne's *Tartuffe*, then Shadwell's *The Miser* in 1672.

26 Gérard Sablayrolles, Introduction to Molière, *L'École des Femmes* (Paris: Larousse, 1970), 9–10. Caryll's play also includes elements of Molière's *L'École des Maris* (1661).

27 Sablayrolles, Introduction, 10. The appointment of Colbert de Croissy as ambassador to the Court of St James did not take place until 1667, so it is possible that he saw both *L'École* and *Sir Salomon*.

28 Robert D. Hume, *The Development of English Drama in the Late Seventeenth Century* (Oxford: Oxford University Press, 1976), 251; Pepys, *Diary*, 7 March 1667.

29 Details of Caryll's life are taken from Howard Erskine-Hill, 'John Caryll, Jacobite, First Baron Caryll of Durford', NDNB, x.454–6.

30 John Caryll, *Sir Salomon Single* (London, 1671), 3.

31 *L'École des Femmes*, 1.i.19–20. Chrysalde says to Arnolphe, 'vos plus grands plaisirs sont, partout ou vous êtes, / De faire cent éclats des intrigues secrètes'.

32 Caryll, *Sir Salomon Single*, 91.

33 Rochester's 'Here lies a Great and Mighty King' is in *Complete Poems and Plays*, 86. On the Duchess of Portsmouth, and how Dryden dealt with her status, see Ann A. Huse, 'Cleopatra, Queen of the Seine: The Politics of Eroticism in Dryden's *All for Love*', *Huntington Library Quarterly*, vol. 63 (2000), 23–46.

34 Derek Hughes, *English Drama 1660–1700*, 119.

35 J. Douglas Canfield, *Tricksters and Estates: On the Ideology of Restoration Comedy* (Lexington: University Press of Kentucky, 1979), 68.

36 Hughes, *English Drama 1660–1700*, 119.

37 Ibid., 119–20.

38 Hume, *Development*, 263; Nicoll, *Restoration Drama*, 367.

39 Winn, *John Dryden and His World*, 202.

40 Dryden, 'To the Right Honourable the Lord Clifford of Chudleigh', *Amboyna, or the Cruelties of the Dutch to the English Merchants* (London, 1673), A2.

41 For example, in a plea by the city of Norwich to restrict the activities of players there: State Papers 29/269, no.113/2; *Register* no.536. Arlington's appointment as Lord Chamberlain is recorded on the cover of LC 3/28; *Register* no.866.

42 Ronald Hutton, 'Thomas Clifford, First Baron Clifford of Chudleigh', NDNB, xii.115–19; Alan Marshall, 'Henry Bennet, First Earl of Arlington', NDNB, v.101–5.

43 Dryden, 'To His Highness the Duke of Monmouth', *Tyrannick Love* (London, 1672), EEBO 3.

44 The words are Pepys's, *Diary*, 7 September 1662; on his personal charms, see Evelyn, *Diary*, 15 July 1685. For *Calisto*, Nicoll, *Restoration Drama*, 320; for the court performance of *The Indian Emperour*, Pepys, *Diary*, 14 January 1668.

45 For Bedford, LC 5/12, p. 185; *Register* no.530. For the company's appearance in Norwich under John Perin, Mayor's Court Book (Norwich), 1666–7, fol.262v; *Register* no.816.

46 Deposition of 13 July 1683 in State Papers 29/428, no.108; *Register* no.1212. The Davenant is Charles.

47 Royal address in LC 5/12, p. 252; *Register* no.525.

48 LS1 263. Genest began speculation that *The Counterfeit Bridegroom*, an adaptation of Middleton's *No Wit, No Help, Like a Woman's*, was the work of Betterton and Behn. Milhous, 'Playwriting', 379, quashes the idea.

49 Markley, 114 and 120.

50 Betterton played the title role in *Alcibiades* (1675); King Philip in *Don Carlos* (1676); Titus in *Titus and Berenice* (1676); Goodvile in *Friendship in Fashion* (1678); the title role in *The History and Fall of Caius Marius* (1679) and then Marius Sr (1706/7); Castalio in *The Orphan* (1680); Beaugard in *The Souldier's Fortune* (1680); Jaffeir in *Venice Preserv'd* (1682); and Beaugard again in *The Atheist* (1683).

51 Kate Aughterson, *Aphra Behn. The Comedies* (Basingstoke: Palgrave, 2003), 199.

52 PB 19.

53 Letter from Barton Booth to Aaron Hill, 19 June 1732, no.53 in *A Collection of Letters, Never Printed Before: Written by Alexander Pope; and Other Ingenious Gentlemen, to the Late Aaron Hill, Esq* (London, 1751), 82.

54 *Don Carlos, or An Historical Relation of the Unfortunate Life and Tragical Death of That Prince of Spain* (London, 1674), 20.

55 Otway, *Don Carlos* (London, 1676), 2.

56 Ibid, 66.

57 Ghosh, *The Works of Thomas Otway*, 1.41.

58 Otway, 'To His Royal Highness the Duke', *Don Carlos*, A2.

59 Dryden, 'To the Right Honourable John, Lord Haughton', *The Spanish Fryar* (1681), EEBO 4.

60 Otway, 'To His Royal Highness', A2.

61 Otway, *Don Carlos*, 33.

62 Otway, 'The Prologue', *Don Carlos*, EEBO 4.

63 Cibber, *Apology*, 49.

64 Otway, *Don Carlos*, 2.

65 Ibid., 21.

66 Steele, *Tatler* no.167, 2–4 May 1710. Milhous, 'Census', 37 notes that there is no firm evidence that Betterton played Othello until 1689.

67 *Tatler* no.167.

68 Cibber, *Apology*, 62; Aston, *A Brief Supplement*, II.5, but Milhous, 'Census', 41, doubts whether Betterton ever played Hotspur.

69 Roach, *Cities*, 115.

70 LS1 342, 440 and 272. The events of the plot are related in Kenyon, 80–149.

71 Crowne, Prologue to *The Misery of Civil War* (London, 1680), EEBO 2. Thomas Jordan, *London's Glory; or, The Lord Mayor's Show* (London, 1680); *The History of Pope Joan*, unpublished but performed 'by Scholars of a Latin School in Cannon Street' in December 1679; both cited in LS1 292 and 283.

72 Crowne, 'To the Right Honourable William, Earl of Devonshire', *The English Frier: or, The Town Sparks* (London, 1690), EEBO 4.

73 Newdigate Newsletter of 3 June 1680 cited in LS1 287.

74 LS1 368 speculates that the 1689 reprinting of the play marked a theatrical revival.

75 The description of Lee's play is Hume's, in *Development*, 348. The play opened in May 1679; the epilogue contains approving references to Pope-burning and the trial of Father David Lewis, executed at Usk in August. For the quarrel, Letter of John Verney to Sir R. Verney, 23 June 1679, cited in LS1 277. Lee was capable of writing less controversial roles for Betterton, such as Varanes in *Theodosius* (1680) and Crispus in *Constantine the Great* (1683).

76 LC 5/144, p. 28 cited in LS1 293. Nahum Tate's *The Loyal General* opened in December 1679 (LS1 282).

77 When the play was printed in 1682, Shadwell's preface 'To the Reader' described how the play was 'licenc'd … at first with little alteration' until an 'Alarm' caused it to be recalled and censored.

78 Letter to Sir Edward Harley dated 17 November 1677, cited in LS1 265. The play was not printed but the performance is recorded at LC 5/145, p. 120.

79 PB 11.

80 Letter from John Drummond to the Marquis and Duke of Queensbury, 26 July 1682, cited in LS1 310, which also prints newsletters on the same subject. For the play's reinstatement in November 1682 see Newdigate Newsletter of 28 November 1682, cited in LS1 317. For discussion of the play's topicality, and Dryden's disingenuous denials, see Hume, *Development*, 223–4.

81 A revival on 24 May 1684 is recorded in the Newdigate Newsletter of that date; cited in LS1 327.

82 Newdigate Newsletter of 15 August 1682, cited in LS1 311.

83 John Banks, *The Innocent Usurper* (London, 1694). Betterton is listed as intended for the role of Lord Gilford Dudley. He had played Piercy in Banks's Anne Boleyn play of even more controversial times, *Vertue Betray'd* (1682).

84 LS1 309.

85 The author was Thomas Hunt, cited in *Register* no.1183. A further vindication of Monmouth followed in *Sol in Opposition to Saturn. Or a Short Return*

to a Late Tragedy Call'd the Duke of Guise (London, 1683). Dryden's own *Vindication of the Duke of Guise* was published two months later.

10 UNION: BETTERTON AND THEATRICAL MONOPOLY, 1682–1695

1   LS1 299 records a suspension of acting from late spring 1681 until October.
2   For a detailed account of the negotiations and their consequences see Milhous, *Management*, 37–43.
3   From a lost manuscript summarised in Gildon, *Life*, 8–9; *Register* no.1134.
4   The agreement is in BL Add. MS 20,726, fols.10r–13v; *Register* no.1151.
5   Milhous, 'Census', 36, lists only three new roles for the 1681–2 season.
6   See *Register* nos.1153, 1171, 1176, 1185, 1208.
7   Milhous, *Management*, 37.
8   Milhous, NDNB, v.555.
9   PRO C24/1197, no.56, cited by Milhous, NDNB, v.555. Betterton's testimony was in 1691 and Arlington died in 1685.
10 Milhous, NDNB, v.555.
11 Knight, DNB, 437.
12 Milhous, *Management*, 39–40.
13 Milhous, 'United Company Finances, 1682–1692', *Theatre Research International*, vol. 7 (1981–2), 37–53.
14 Milhous, *Management*, 41.
15 Ibid., 42.
16 *Lucius Junius Brutus*, 12.
17 Davies, *Dramatic Miscellanies*, III.397.
18 A printed broadside of 31 August 1683 laments the death of 'that Worthy and Famous Actor, Mr Charles Hart'; *Register* no.1215.
19 Cibber, *Apology*, 76.
20 LC 5/191, fol.102v, reprinted in Nicoll, *Restoration Drama*, 327–8; *Register* no.1169.
21 Downes, *Roscius Anglicanus*, 42.
22 His letter of 1678 to Secretary of State Joseph Williamson pleaded exemption from the ten-mile recusant exclusion zone around London. See State Papers 29/408, no.64; *Register* no.1068.
23 Pepys, *Diary*, 7 December 1667.
24 Two notable exceptions were Leontius in Beaumont and Fletcher's *The Humorous Lieutenant* and Melantius in their *The Maid's Tragedy*, which Betterton probably first played in 1686; see LS1 342.
25 An order of 23 November 1682 is in LC 5/191, fol.103, and another of 5 December 1682 in fol.105 of the same; *Register* nos.1170 and 1175.
26 Date given in John H. Astington, 'Michael Mohun', NDNB, 38.513.
27 Milhous, *Management*, 42. See also Edward A. Langhans, 'New Restoration Theatre Accounts, 1682–1692', *Theatre Notebook*, vol. xvii (1963), 118–34.

28 Hart is first recorded as playing Othello in January 1675 (see LS1 227) and Brutus in January 1672 (LS1 191).

29 Cibber, *Apology*, 62–3.

30 Aston, *A Brief Supplement*, ii.300.

31 Davies, *Dramatic Miscellanies*, iii.399.

32 See LS1 344, performance of 19 December 1685.

33 Davies, *Dramatic Miscellanies*, iii.271–2. Cibber, *Apology*, 65–6, also writes about Betterton's Alexander in Lee's *The Rival Queens*, which had premiered on 17 March 1677; LS1 255. Betterton also took over Hart's role, Manly, in Wycherley's *The Plain Dealer* and Arbaces in Beaumont and Fletcher's *A King and No King*. For a similar anecdote about Betterton's managerial style and the young Cibber, see Davies, *Dramatic Miscellanies*, iii.417–18.

34 Davenant and Killigrew's original patents included an agreement to make seats available for each other.

35 Cibber, *Apology*, 68.

36 LS2 506.

37 Cibber, *Apology*, 174. Cibber was probably referring to the performance on 18 October 1704; LS2 189.

38 LS1 356.

39 Powell, 'The Epistle Dedicatory', *The Treacherous Brothers* (London, 1690), A2; Powell's reflections on the dearth of new plays are in the Preface, EEBO 3.

40 HMC, 12th Report, Appendix, Rutland MSS., Part v, vol. ii, p. 85, cited in LS1 334. Milhous examines the claim in 'The Multimedia Spectacular on the Restoration Stage', in Shirley Strum Kenny, ed., *British Theatre and the Other Arts, 1660–1800* (Washington: Folger Books, 1984), 55–6.

41 Milhous, *Management*, 259.

42 Letter dated 22 August 1673 from Vernon to Williamson in State Papers 29/336, no.273; *Register* no.794.

43 LS1 215–16; Downes, *Roscius Anglicanus*, 74.

44 LS1 229–30. The composer was Giovanni Battista Draghi and the choreographer St André. Shadwell's Preface to the 1675 edition credits Betterton with the inspiration as well as 'great industry and care' (EEBO 6).

45 See Murray Lefkowitz, 'Shadwell and Locke's *Psyche*: the French Connection', *Proceedings of the Royal Musical Association*, vol. 106 (1979–80), 42–55.

46 *Circe* premiered in May 1677 and according to Downes, *Roscius Anglicanus*, 77, 'answer'd the Expectation of the Company'. A warrant issued by the Earl of Danby on 7 December 1676 permits 'the import, Customs free, of certain particulars consigned from Calais to Thomas Betterton … to be used in the new Tragedy not yet acted called Circe' (PRO 30/32/38, fol.154r, in *Register* no.985). It was customary not to charge excise from the movement of French actors, musicians, dancers and their materials, although they might be searched; see, for example, PRO 30/32/50, p. 65, *Register* no.860.

47 *Roger North on Music*, ed. John Wilson (London, 1959), 306–7.

48 Settle, Preface to *Ibrahim the Illustrious Bassa* (London, 1676), cited in LS1 230. Settle's *Pastor Fido* featured Betterton as Sylvano and opened in December 1676.

49 Downes, *Roscius Anglicanus*, 75.

50 Cited in LS1 320.

51 For Gildon see above, 43. PB 3 and 6 lists the dictionaries of Cotgrave and Miège; for the French New Testament, PB 8. For plays by numerous French writers including Racine, Molière, Quinault and both Corneilles, PB 22.

52 Manning, 'To Mr Betterton', 45.

53 Greber letter from Johann Sigismund Cousser's Commonplace Book (1704), cited in *Register* no.1788; the letter from Etherege at Ratisbon is dated 16/26 May 1687 and the relevant section is reprinted in BDA II.84. Betterton's contribution to London music is summarised in Curtis Price and Margaret Laurie's 'Thomas Betterton', *New Grove Dictionary of Music and Musicians*, 29 vols. (Oxford: Oxford University Press, 2003), III.494; see also references in Price's seminal *Henry Purcell and the London Stage* (Cambridge: Cambridge University Press, 1984).

54 HMC, VII, Appendix, p. 288, *Register* no.1214.

55 Letter from Lord Preston to the Duke of York, HMC, VII, Part III, p. 290, *Register* no.1216. The letter is dated 22 September 1683.

56 Jérôme de la Gorce, 'Jean-Baptiste Lully', in *New Grove*, XV.295.

57 See Peter Holman, 'Louis Grabu', *New Grove*, X.242–3.

58 For Pepys's dislike of Grabu's music and his friend Banister's jealousy over Grabu's appointments, *Diary*, 20 February 1667. For *Ariadne*, *Timon* and *Squire Oldsapp*, LS1 215, 266 and 270.

59 Preston, letter of 22 September 1683.

60 Ibid.

61 The Duke's Company had staged *Sir Martin Mar-All* and *The Tempest, or the Enchanted Island* in 1667, *Marriage-à-la-Mode* in 1671, *The Assignation* in 1672, *Amboyna* in 1673, *The Kind Keeper* and *Oedipus* in 1678, *Troilus and Cressida* in 1679 and *The Spanish Fryar* in 1680.

62 For discussion of scheduling, see Milhous, 'Multimedia Spectacular', 51–2.

63 Dryden, Preface to *Albion and Albanius*, 2nd edn (London, 1691), EEBO 6.

64 *Albion and Albanius*, 1st edn (London, 1685), 18.

65 Ibid., 18.

66 Ibid., 10 and 26.

67 Dryden, Postscript to the Preface, *Albion and Albanius*, 2nd edn, EEBO 5.

68 *Albion and Albanius*, 1st edn, 29.

69 Downes, *Roscius Anglicanus*, 84.

70 David Ogg, *England in the Reigns of James II and William III* (Oxford: Clarendon Press, 1955), 145.

71 Printed in Sir John Hawkins, *A General History of the Science and Practice of Music*, 5 vols. (London, 1776), IV.396.

72 For example, Dryden's 'Prologue to the King and Queen, at the Opening of their Theatre, Spoken by Mr. *Batterton*' (London, 1683).

73 Cibber, *Apology*, 158.
74 In this respect Milhous's view of the show is questionable: its 'French prece-
    dents are of interest to the scholar, but they would have had no bearing on the
    response of most audience members in 1685.' See 'Multimedia Spectacular',
    52.
75 Dryden, Epilogue to *Albion and Albanius*, 1st edn, EEBO 8.
76 Milhous, *Management*, 42–3.
77 Hotson, *Commonwealth and Restoration Stage*, 220–1, records share or part-
    share sales to Richard Alchorne, Sir William Russell, Mrs Olive Porter (in
    trust), Robert Garter, Richard Viscount Lumley, Richard Cheston, George
    Porter, William Ashburnham and Richard Bayley. One person who acquired
    a part-share from Davenant and did have obvious knowledge of the theatre
    was the playwright and poet Abraham Cowley.
78 Chancery suit C24/1144 of 17 October 1691; *Register* no.1401.
79 Milhous, *Management*, 56–8. Shadwell, a friend of Brady's, protested to the
    Earl of Dorset (the Lord Chamberlain) about Thomas Davenant's dismissive
    attitude towards the play, which was put on in 1692 with almost the strongest
    cast available to the company. Thomas and Mary Betterton did their bit to
    try to make it work.
80 From Article 6 of LC 7/3, fols.2–4 ('The Petition of the Players'), cited in
    Milhous, *Management*, 58.
81 See Hume, *Development*, 381–431.
82 Ibid., 390.
83 Dryden, *The Spanish Fryar*, 83.
84 See Winn, *John Dryden and His World*, 335. In his preface to John, Lord
    Haughton, Dryden describes *The Spanish Fryar* as 'a Protestant play for a
    Protestant patron' (EEBO 4).
85 Ogg, *England in the Reigns of James II and William III*, 241.
86 Account by Daniel Finch, Earl of Nottingham, cited in LS1 371.
87 *The Journal of Constantijn Huygens*, cited in LS1 371–2.
88 On 18 March 1707 Betterton played the part in a benefit performance for
    himself; other recorded performances were on 13 November 1706 and 29
    January 1707. See LS2 350.
89 Winn, *John Dryden and His World*, 434–5.
90 For Halifax's 'Character of a Trimmer', *Complete Works*, 49–104.
91 Rowe's Epistle Dedicatory to the 1702 text says 'There are many Features, 'tis
    true, in [Tamerlane's] Life, not unlike His Majesty' (ECCO 6). For the swear-
    ing in of Betterton, Barry, Bracegirdle and John Verbruggen as 'Comoedians
    in Ordinary', LC 5/166, p. 151, cited in LS2 126, which attributes the small
    number to 'Anne's lack of interest in the theatre'.
92 Milhous, *Management*, 53; BL Add. Charters 9298 and 9299 in *Register*
    no.1369.
93 Milhous, *Management*, 51.
94 Letter from Owen Swiney to Colley Cibber in the Osborn Collection, Yale,
    and reprinted in LS2 317.

11 BACK TO THE FUTURE: BREAKAWAY
TO SEMI-RETIREMENT

1   David Underdown, *Revel Riot and Rebellion. Popular Politics and Culture in England, 1603–1660* (Oxford: Oxford University Press, 1987), 77.
2   Judith Milhous, 'Christopher Rich', NDNB, 46.661. Much of what follows is indebted to Milhous, *Management*, 51–79; the timeline she presents on 52–5 is recommended as a clear narrative of events.
3   According to Folger Z.c. 22 (43), in *Register* no.1418, a half-share in 1691 went for £495.
4   BL Add. Charter 9301; *Register* no.1320.
5   BL Add. Charters 9298 and 9299; *Register* no.1369. The full articles of agreement, dated 26 March 1691, are in BL Add. Charter 9302; *Register* no.1393.
6   Casting details in LS1 380–1.
7   Downes, *Roscius Anglicanus*, 89, who describes the play as 'wrote by Mr. Betterton'. Milhous, 'Playwriting', 385, argues that like *The Roman Virgin* this was more a case of cutting and pasting on Betterton's part.
8   In *The Muses' Mercury* (January 1707), cited in LS1 382.
9   *The Fairy Queen*, sometimes attributed to Settle but possibly Betterton's own work, from the libretto for the recording directed by William Christie (Arles: Harmonia Mundi, 1989), 69.
10 In the 1671 edition; PB 2.
11 See Canfield, *Heroes and States*, 144.
12 Luttrell, *A Brief Historical Relation*, 11.435; *Register* no.1428.
13 Advertisement cited in LS2 566. Among other works Charles Davenant published *An Essay on the East India Trade* (1697).
14 Downes, *Roscius Anglicanus*, 89.
15 Other roles set in Ancient Britain from the later period of Betterton's career include Cassibelan in Charles Hopkins's *Boadicea Queen of Britain* (1697) and Caelius in Granville's *The British Enchanters* (1706).
16 Joseph Towers, 'The Life of Dr John Radcliffe', *British Biography*, 10 vols. (Sherborne, 1766–7), VII.256–7. Watson remains a mystery.
17 BDA 11.84. For bailiffs, see above, 108.
18 Cibber, *Apology*, 76. Cibber goes on to note that when Mountfort played in Behn's *The Rover* at court, 'Queen Mary was pleas'd to make in favour of Montfort, notwithstanding her disapprobation of the play'.
19 LS1 416. Mountfort wrote four plays, the best of which is *Greenwich Park*, performed in 1691. Betterton played Rheusanes in his 1688 play, *The Injur'd Lovers*. For details of the case, see Albert S. Borgman, *The Life and Death of William Mountfort* (Cambridge, Mass.: Harvard University Press, 1935).
20 Cibber, *Apology*, 76.
21 Cited in LS1 417.
22 *Memoirs Relating to Mr Congreve Written by Mr Thomas Southern*, cited in LS1 419.

23 Dryden, 'To my Dear Friend Mr Congreve on his comedy call'd *The Double Dealer*', in Congreve, *The Double Dealer* (London, 1694), n2.

24 For the pre-performance success, see Congreve's dedication of the play 'To the Right Honourable Charles Mountague, One of the Lords of the Treasury', in *The Double Dealer*, A2. For performance history between late October and early December 1693, see LS1 428, citing a letter of Dryden's dated 12 December 1693.

25 Congreve, 'To the Right Honourable Charles Mountague', *The Double Dealer*, EEBO 3.

26 Ibid., EEBO 4.

27 Milhous, *Management*, 232, Appendix B, notes that after the Legard report 'both sides ... filed Exceptions which are not yet argued'. The Legard report is in Chancery Papers C38/246; *Register* no.1454.

28 Warrant of 30 June 1694; LC 5/151, p. 369; *Register* no.1475. Rich claimed £221 for eleven performances since January 1690.

29 Congreve, *The Way of the World* (London, 1700), 87.

30 'The Petition of the Players', cited in Milhous, *Management*, 61 and reprinted in full as Appendix A to the same; also ibid., 59.

31 Ibid., 61.

32 See Frontispiece.

33 Winn, *John Dryden and His World*, 161–2, 210. For Dorset's drinking, see a letter presumed to be of June 1678 from Nell Gwyn to Laurence Hyde; *Register* no.1056.

34 LS1 436.

35 'The Petition of the Players', in Milhous, *Management*, 226.

36 Milhous, *Management*, 62.

37 PRO LC 7/3, transcribed by Milhous, *Management*, 230–46.

38 Milhous, *Management*, 62.

39 The closure was announced in a newsletter of 29 December 1694; *Register* no.1491.

40 Lost MS described in a letter from the patentees to the Lord Chamberlain and cited in *Register* no.1495.

41 LC 7/3, fols.62–3, cited in *Register* no.1498.

42 Milhous, *Management*, 48.

43 The subtitle to George Powell's Prologue to his *The Fatal Discovery* (London, 1698) refers to 'Betterton's Booth in *Little-Lincoln's Inn Fields*' (EEBO 3).

44 Downes, *Roscius Anglicanus*, 91–2.

45 *A Comparison Between the Two Stages*, 10. Cibber, *Apology*, 126, reports Halifax as being 'a great Favourer of Betterton's Company'.

46 Cibber, *Apology*, 115.

47 For the Whitehall performance, *The Post Boy*, 2–4 and 6–9 February 1697, in LS1 474; for the Inner Temple, *The Post Boy*, 30 October–2 November 1697, cited in LS1 488.

48 John Oldmixon, *Reflections on the Stage* (London, 1699), 69.

49 Congreve, *Love for Love* (London, 1695), 91.

50 *A Report of All the Cases Determined by Sir John Holt, Knt. from 1688 to 1710* (London, 1738), 538. But see also Judith Milhous and Robert D. Hume, 'New Documents about the London Theatre 1685–1711', *Harvard Library Bulletin*, vol. xxxvi, no.3 (summer 1988), 260–1, i.e. 260–1; eighteen residents brought a remonstrance against the theatre, citing 'the throng of Coaches' and the danger of being 'Knock'd Downe, and Robb'd, if not alsoe murthered'.

51 *The Fourth and Last Part of Modern Reports. Being a Collection of Several Special Cases Argued and Adjudged in the Court of King and Queen's Bench* (London, 1703), 237.

52 Milhous and Hume, 'New Documents', 264.

53 *A Report ... Sir John Holt*, 538.

54 See above, 32.

55 Dryden, in a letter to Mrs Steward of 4 March 1699, says that 'the printing of an author's name, in a play bill, is a new manner of proceeding, at least in England'. See Dryden's *Letters*, 113.

56 *The London Post*, 28 June–1 July 1700, cited in LS1 530.

57 Ibid.

58 James Anderson, *A Genealogical History of the House of Yvery*, 2 vols. (London, 1742), II.404.

59 The Reverend Ralph Bridges sang Betterton's praises as a tutor to Sir William Trumbull; see Milhous, NDNB, v.557, citing a letter in the Downshire MSS. In *Novus reformator vapulans* (London, 1691), 5, Tom Brown lamented the tendency of preachers to think of themselves as actors, adding that it would be 'to Mr Betterton's loss' if the pulpit became as exciting as the stage.

60 LS2 512. Perceval remarked to Elizabeth Stockwell that 'they who cannot be moved at Othello's story so artfully worked up by Shakespeare, and justly played by Betterton, are capable of marrying again before their husbands are cold, of trampling on a lover when dying at their feet, and are fit to converse with tigers only.'

61 'The Reply of the Patentees', 10 December 1694, Article 15, reproduced in Nicoll, *Restoration Drama*, 340. See also BDA II.98.

62 Davies, *Dramatic Miscellanies*, III.403.

63 Ibid., 464.

64 Milhous, *Management*, 80ff.

65 Ibid., 112. For Winstanley, see Evelyn, *Diary*, 20 June 1696.

66 Milhous, *Management*, 82, citing *A Comparison Between the Two Stages*, 7.

67 For his roles in this period, Milhous, 'Census', 38.

68 Milhous, *Management*, 83. For the question of Barry's share-ownership, see Milhous and Hume, 'New Documents', 267 n.47.

69 Milhous, *Management*, 112.

70 *The Way of the World* opened on 5 March 1700 and ran for no more than a week; see LS1 525–6. Congreve's dedication to the Earl of Mountague discloses pleasant surprise, 'for but little of it was prepar'd for that general taste which seems now to be predominant in the palates of our audience'

(EEBO 4). Congreve's tragedy *The Mourning Bride* opened on 20 February 1697 and according to Downes ran for thirteen days; see LS1 474–5. Betterton played Osmyn, a noble prisoner whose language frequently echoes Othello's.

71 Elizabeth Barry to the Right Hon. Lady Lisburne, 5 January 1699, cited in LS1 507. The work referred to is John Dennis's *Rinaldo and Armida*, premiered at Lincoln's Inn Fields in November 1698. There is a satirical account of the same production in *A Comparison*, 38.

72 For Bracegirdle, the epilogue to Henry Smith, *The Princess of Parma* (London, 1699), 48; for puppet shows, letter from William Morley to Thomas Coke, 2 August 1701, Cowper MSS, HMC Report, Part II, vol. II, 434, cited in LS2 I; for music see, for example, Nicola Cosimi's seven concerts at Lincoln's Inn Fields in July 1702, cited in LS2 64.

73 Cibber, *Apology*, 179–80.

74 Ibid., 180.

75 'Orders for ye Play house in Lincoln's Inn Fields', PRC LC 5/153, fol.23, reprinted in Milhous, *Management*, 115; *Register* no.1655.

76 LC 5/153, p. 23; *Register* no.1655.

77 The play opened in December 1700 (see LS2 15); for Rowe, Otway and Betterton, see above, 216 n. 14.

78 'To His Grace the Duke of Ormond', in the 1701 edition, A2; Burnaby complains that 'Expectation ... ruin'd the Reputation' of his play. Milhous, *Management*, 144.

79 For George Granville's *The Jew of Venice*, premiered probably in December 1700, LS2 12; for Powell as Lear in January 1701, LS2 17.

80 Milhous, *Management*, 146, shows nine new Lincoln's Inn Fields plays in 1695–6 compared with the same number in 1699–1700; across the same period the Drury Lane repertory showed a decline from seventeen to eight.

81 *The Post Boy*, 5–7 December 1700, cited in LS2 13, states that the starting time for plays was confirmed as 5 p.m. in spite of 'the Inconveniency to the Gentry of Playing so late at Night'. Examples of Betterton's courtly roles in this period include Zoilus in Charles Hopkins's *Friendship Improv'd* (1699), Doria in Henry Smith's *The Princess of Parma* (1699) and Clorimon in Orrery's *Altemira* (1701).

82 Milhous, *Management*, 117.

83 Luttrell, *A Brief Relation*, IV.502–3, cited in LS1 510. Luttrell adds that Lord Cholmley paid the dancer a further 100 guineas.

84 For details of Madame Subligny, see Robert D. Hume, 'A Revival of *The Way of the World* in December 1701 or January 1702', *Theatre Notebook*, vol. 26 (1971), 30–6. For Anthony L'Abbé, see Moira Goff, *The Incomparable Hester Santlow* (Aldershot: Ashgate, 2007), 7–9.

85 An agreement between Sorin and Betterton survives in LC 7/3, fol.75; *Register* no.1535. *A Satyr against Dancing. By a Person of Honour* (London, 1702), 5, lamented the stupidity of audiences in failing to notice Betterton's acting when there was so much dancing on offer: 'The Fair thus wave what *Batterton* will say, / And only talk how finely danc'd L'abbee'.

86 Gildon, *Life*, 155. The dancer complained in a letter to Sir John Stanley that Betterton had seemed to ignore him. LC 7/3, fols.29–30; *Register* no.1750.

87 PB 16.

88 Downes, *Roscius Anglicanus*, 96–7.

89 Thomas Brown, *A Collection of All the Dialogues Written by Mr Thomas Brown* (London, 1704), 41. For objections by 'a young Lady' to singing and dancing in *Julius Caesar*, see John Dennis, Postscript to *An Essay on the Opera's after the Italian Manner* (London, 1706), cited in LS2 287; for evidence of singing and dancing Shakespeare requested by patrons, the performance of *Hamlet* on 25 April 1706 listed in LS2 296.

90 His French roles included Brisac in Porter's *The Villain* (1662), Charles VIII in Crowne's *Charles the Eighth of France* (1671), the Duke of Nemours in Lee's *The Princess of Cleve* (1681), the Admiral of France in Lee's *The Massacre at Paris* (1689), and the Duke de Sanserre in D'Urfey's *The Intrigues at Versailles* (1697). Betterton also had a line in haughty Spaniards, apart from Philip II: Rodrigo in Rutter's *The Valiant Cid* (1662); Iberio in Stapylton's *The Slighted Maid* (1663), Don Henrique and Don Antonio in Tuke's *The Adventures of Five Hours* (1663 and 1706 respectively), Perez in Fletcher's *Rule a Wife and Have a Wife* (1682), Don Vincentio in Motteux's *Beauty in Distress* (1698), Don Alvarez in Vanbrugh's *The Mistake* (1705).

91 PRO C10/261/51, Killigrew *et al.* vs. Skipwith and Rich, cited in Milhous, *Management*, 122.

92 Milhous, *Management*, 123.

93 LC 7/3, fol.177; *Register* no.1689. For court appearances, see above, 30.

94 Milhous, 'Census', records between two and five new roles per season during this time, but with revivals of a significant number of favourite roles including Henry VIII, Othello, Falstaff, Dorimant, Brutus and Oedipus.

95 *A Comparison Between the Two Stages*, 198, claimed that his 'Memory begins to die'.

96 Milhous, *Management*, 152–9. Doggett gave six months' notice on 29 November 1703; LC 7/3, fol.85, cited in LS2 130. For Queen Anne's January 1704 order to act nothing 'contrary to Religion, or Good Manners', see LC 5/153, p. 434, reproduced in LS2 139. Later the same month anti-theatrical literature was distributed outside churches; see *The Post Man*, 20–22 January 1704. *The Observator* of 16–19 February 1704, cited in LS2 145, denounced the performance of *All for Love* which had marked the Queen's birthday on the 7th.

97 Undated PRO LC 7/3 and reprinted in Milhous, *Management*, 252–4.

98 'Franck Telltroth', Dedication to *The Lunatick* (London, 1705), ECCO 4–5.

99 Milhous, *Management*, 161.

100 For the licence, Downes, *Roscius Anglicanus*, 98–9; for the sale of Lincoln's Inn Fields, the advertisement in the *London Gazette*, 19–22 February 1705, reprinted in LS2 212. It was used again in July 1705 when the Haymarket Theatre needed further building work (LS2 233).

101 A report attached to *The Post Man*, 29–31 August 1704, cited in LS2 178, says that the theatre will be 'ye largest in Europe' at 60 by 132 feet and reports subscriptions totalling 3000 guineas.

102 LC 5/154, p. 35, dated 14 December 1704 and cited from Thomas and Hare, *Restoration and Georgian England*, 22.

103 On 19 July 1705 Vanbrugh lodged proposals for a union described in LS2 181 as 'outrageously self-serving', and they were rejected by Rich.

104 Downes, *Roscius Anglicanus*, 100, says that the Haymarket opened with 'half a Score of old Plays, Acted in old Cloaths'. An order of 14 November 1705 demands Powell's arrest for 'refusing to act his Part by which means the Audience were dismist'. LC 5/154, p. 119, reprinted in LS2 254. Ten days later Powell was forbidden to join the Drury Lane company; see 124 of the same document, in *Register* no.1826.

105 Milhous, 'Census', indicates a break from 28 May to 6 November 1707.

106 Fragment of a letter cited in LS2 299.

107 Downes, *Roscius Anglicanus*, 105.

108 'Census', 40–1. *The Tatler* no.70, 20 September 1709.

109 *The Tatler*, no.167, 2–4 May 1710. For Betterton's last performance, see above, 26.

110 Pepys, *Diary*, 9 June 1668. Gildon, *Life*, 9, refers to the funeral; for the Flowerdew monument, see above, 42; for Steele, above, 4.

111 BDA 11.99.

112 Baggs, *Advertisement Concerning the Poor Actors, Who under Pretence of Hard Usage from the Patentees, are about to Desert their Service* (London, 1709). The same figures were later used to argue that Betterton was a paragon of self-restraint compared with Garrick and Macklin. See *London Daily Post and General Advertiser*, 15 October 1743, no.2782.

113 Tate Wilkinson, *Memoirs of His Own Life* (Dublin, 1791), 158.

114 BDA 11.92. Details of Mary Betterton's will are given in BDA 11.99. She left money for mourning rings to a number of actors including Bracegirdle, Barry and Doggett. Her 'dear husband's picture' went to her executrix, Frances Williamson.

12 BOOKS AND PICTURES: BETTERTON
AND THE CHANDOS PORTRAIT

1 PB, title page. Three other coffee houses are named.

2 See *The Daily Courant*, 7–15 December 1710.

3 Jacob Hooke, *Bibliopolii Husseyani, pars prima* (London, 1707); *Officina Shrewsburiana* (London, 1707); *Bibliotheca Rayana* (London, 1708); *Bibliotheca Bernardiana* (London, 1711).

4 See Frontispiece.

5 Dryden, *The Works of Virgil* (London, 1697) lists Betterton, Barry and Bracegirdle among the secondary subscribers.

6 PB 22. Milhous, 'Census', 33.

7 See above, 191 n.10; Davies, *Dramatic Miscellanies*, III.400–1, represents Elijah Fenton as the instigator of an attempt to bribe Pope to forge Betterton's handwriting.

8 A view advanced by Betsy Bowden in *Chaucer Aloud* (Philadelphia: University of Pennsylvania Press, 1987), 221–4, and in *Eighteenth-Century Modernizations of* The Canterbury Tales (Cambridge: Boydell and Brewer, 1991), 3.

9 PB 10. Rowe's Shakespeare is lot 135 in the list of octavo books.

10 Rowe, *The Works of Mr William Shakespear*, I.xxxiv. For the cost of the edition, LS2 496.

11 For the Greenhill sketch and portrait, see above, 82; Cibber, *Apology*, 60.

12 For a facsimile reproduction, see Tarnya Cooper, *Searching for Shakespeare* (London: National Portrait Gallery, 2006), 54–5.

13 For information about Keck, see E.A. Greening Lamborn, 'Great Tew and the Chandos Portrait', *Notes and Queries*, 19 February 1949, 71–2. The best account of Vertue's notes is Mary Edmond, 'The Chandos Portrait: a Suggested Painter', *The Burlington Magazine*, vol. cxxiv, no.948 (March 1982), 146–9.

14 Cooper, *Searching for Shakespeare*, 55.

15 Lamborn, 'Great Tew and the Chandos Portrait'; for a critique of his additions of John Otway (really Alway) and Elizabeth Barry, see Edmond, 'The Chandos Portrait'.

16 Lamborn, 'Great Tew and the Chandos Portrait', 71.

17 Picard, *Restoration London*, 146–7, lists prices. For Pepys and Samuel Cooper, *Diary*, 30 March 1668. Cooper painted a miniature of Charles II.

18 Milhous, *Management*, 14 and 27–8.

19 Highmore quotation from a letter to James Harris, part of the Malmesbury Collection (9M73) in the Hampshire Record Office, cited in Hume, 'The Economics of Culture in London, 1660–1740', (2006), 518.

20 Kewes, *Authorship and Appropriation*, 180–224.

21 Ben Jonson, 'To the Reader', frontispiece caption to *Mr William Shakespeares Comedies, Histories, & Tragedies* (London, 1623).

22 PB 19–20. For the tendency of auctions of the time to talk up the provenance of paintings, see Iain Pears, *The Discovery of Painting: the Growth of Interest in the Arts in England, 1680–1768* (New Haven and London: Published for the Paul Mellon Centre for Studies in British Art by Yale University Press, 1988).

23 Katherine Duncan-Jones, *The Times Literary Supplement*, 21 August 2009, 6, argues that this 'Head' might have been a sculpture, but *Pinacotheca Bettertonaeana* repeatedly uses the term 'Head' to describe portraits or engravings and contains no reference to sculptures.

24 Cooper, *Searching for Shakespeare*, 59.

25 S. Schoenbaum, *Shakespeare's Lives*, 2nd edn (Oxford: Clarendon Press, 1991), 205.

26 Cibber, *Apology*, 80. For Thynne, DNB xix.848–9.

27 See above, 43 n.1.

28 In *Philosophical Works*, 5 vols. (1754), II.325, Henry St John, Viscount Bolingbroke, Secretary at War in 1704, wrote 'I knew Betterton and Mrs Barry off the stage, as well as on it'.

29 John Dryden, 'The Prologue Spoken by Mr Betterton, representing the Ghost of Shakespear', *Troilus and Cressida* (London, 1679), EEBO 12.

30 Dobson, *The Making of the National Poet*, 74.

31 Reprinted in Gildon, *Life*, xiii.

32 Cibber, *Apology*, 61.

33 Wanko, *Roles of Authority*, 50.

34 On Shakespeare's father and the coat of arms, E.K. Chambers, *William Shakespeare: A Study of Facts and Problems*, 2 vols. (Oxford: Clarendon Press, 1930), II.20.

35 *A Comparison Between the Two Stages*, 41–2.

36 LS1 522–3.

37 *A Comparison Between the Two Stages*, 41–2.

38 Ibid., 43.

39 Dawson, *Gentility and the Comic Theatre*, 13.

Bibliography

Place of publication is London except where indicated otherwise and all dates are new style.

PLAYS

The date of the first print publication is given after the short title. Square brackets indicate uncertain attribution. Where Betterton is known to have appeared in the play, his role and date of his likely first performance, where known, appear to the right. For pre-1660 plays is cited the most recent edition for Betterton (for Shakespeare that sometimes means the 1664 folio, for Beaumont and Fletcher the 1647 folio) or the one that most nearly reflects Restoration performance practice, such as the 1673 Davenant folio. The roster of Betterton's roles makes minor adjustments to Milhous's 'Census'.

Anon.	*The Fairy-Queen* (1692)	
	Variously attributed to Elkanah Settle and/or Thomas Betterton	
	The Faithful General (1706)	Marus (1706)
	The Female Wits, in Morgan, F., ed., *The Female Wits. Women Playwrights of the Restoration* (1981)	
	The Lunatick (1705)	
	The Merry Devil of Edmonton (1655)	Sir Ralph (1689?)
Arrowsmith, J.	*The Reformation* (1673)	
[Bancroft, J.]	*Henry II* (1693)	Henry II (1692)
Banks, J.	*Cyrus the Great* (1696)	Cyrus (1695)
	The Destruction of Troy (1679)	Achilles (1678)
	Vertue Betray'd (1682)	Piercy (1682)

Beaumont, W. and Fletcher, J.	*A King and No King* (1676)	Arbaces (1685/6)
	The Humorous Lieutenant (1647)	Leontius (1684?)
	The Maid's Tragedy (1650)	Melantius (1686/7)
Behn, A.	*Abdelazer* (1677)	Abdelazer (1676)
	Sir Patient Fancy (1678)	Wittmore (1678)
	The City Heiress (1682)	Wilding (1682)
	The Dutch Lover (1673)	
	The Feign'd Curtezans (1679)	Galliard (1679)
	The Forc'd Marriage (1671)	Alcippus (1670)
	The Luckey Chance (1687)	Gayman (1686)
	The Rover Part 1 (1677)	Belvile (1677)
Betterton, T.	*The Amorous Widow* (1706)	Lovemore (1670?)
	The Roman Virgin (1679)	Virginius (1669)
Boothby, F.	*Marcelia* (1670)	
Boyle, C.	*As You Find It* (1703)	Bevil (1703)
Brady, N.	*The Rape* (1692)	Gunderic (1692)
Bristol, G. Digby, Earl of	*Elvira* (1667)	
Burnaby, W.	*The Ladies Visiting Day* (1701)	Courtine (1701)
Caryll, J.	*Sir Salomon* (1671)	Sir Salomon (1670)
	The English Princess (1667)	Richard III (1667)
Centlivre, S.	*The Gamester* (1705)	Lovewell (1705)
	The Platonick Lady (1707)	Sir Thomas (1706)
Cibber, C.	*Xerxes* (1699)	Attabanus (1699)
Congreve, W.	*Love for Love* (1695)	Valentine (1695)
	The Double Dealer (1694)	Maskwell (1693)
	The Mourning Bride (1697)	Osmyn (1697)
	The Old Batchelor (1693)	Heartwell (1693)
	The Way of the World (1700)	Fainall (1700)
Congreve, W., Vanbrugh, J. and Walsh, W.	*Squire Trelooby* (1734)	Lovewell (1704)
Cowley, A.	*Cutter of Coleman-Street* (1663)	Colonel Jolly (1661)
	The Guardian (1650)	
Crowne, J.	*Henry the Sixth* (1681)	Duke Humphrey (1681)
	Juliana (1671)	Ladislaus (1671)
	Regulus (1694)	Regulus (1692)
	The Countrey Wit (1675)	Ramble (1676)
	The History of Charles the Eighth of France (1672)	Charles VIII (1671)
	The Married Beau (1694)	Polidor (1694)
	The Misery of Civil War (1680)	Warwick (1680)
Davenant, C.	*Circe* (1677)	Orestes (1677)

Davenant, W.	*Love and Honour* (1673)	Alvaro (1661)
	The Play-House to be Lett (1673)	
	The Rivals (1673)	Philander (1664)
	The Siege of Rhodes. The First and Second Part (1663)	Solyman (1661)
	The Unfortunate Lovers (1673)	not known (1660)
	The Wits (1673)	Elder Palatine (1661)
Dennis, J.	*Appius and Virginia* (1709)	Virginius (1709)
	Iphigenia (1700)	Orestes (1699)
	Liberty Asserted (1704)	Miramont (1704)
	Rinaldo and Armida (1699)	Rinaldo (1698)
Dilke, T.	*The Lover's Luck* (1696)	Bellair (1695)
Doggett, T.	*The Country-Wake* (1696)	Woodvill (1696)
Dover, J.	*The Roman Generals* (1667)	
Dryden, J.	*All for Love* (1678)	Marc Antony (1685?)
	Amboyna (1673)	
	Amphitryon (1690)	Jupiter (1690)
	An Evening's Love, or the Mock Astrologer (1671)	not known (1685/6)
	Aureng-Zebe (1676)	Old Emperor (1706?)
	Cleomenes, the Spartan Hero (1692)	Cleomenes (1692)
	Don Sebastian (1690)	Dorax (1689)
	King Arthur (1691)	Arthur (1691)
	Love Triumphant (1694)	Alphonso (1693)
	Marriage à la Mode (1673)	
	Sir Martin Mar-All, or the Feign'd Innocence (1668)	
	The Indian Emperour (1667)	Montezuma (1691?)
	The Spanish Fryar (1681)	Torrismond (1680)
	Tyrannick Love (1670)	
Dryden, J. and Lee, N.	*Oedipus* (1679)	Oedipus (1678)
	The Duke of Guise (1683)	The Duke (1682)
D'Urfey, T.	*Madam Fickle* (1677)	Lord Bellamour (1676)
	Squire Oldsapp (1679)	Welford (1678)
	The Intrigues at Versailles (1697)	Duke de Sanserre (1697)
Etherege, G.	*The Comical Revenge* (1664)	Lord Beauford (1664)
	The Man of Mode (1676)	Dorimant (1676)
Field, N.	*Woman is a Weathercock* (1612)	not known (1666?)
Fletcher, J.	*A Wife for a Month* (1647)	not known (1660)
	Rule a Wife and Have a Wife (1647)	not known (1660)
		Michael Perez (1682)
	The Loyal Subject (1647)	Archas (1660)

	The Mad Lover (1647)	The Mad Lover (1660)
	The Tamer Tamed (1647)	not known (1660)
	The Wild Goose Chase (1652)	not known (1660)
Fletcher, J. and	*The Prophetess* (1690)	not known (1690)
Massinger, P.		
	The Spanish Curate (1647)	not known (1660)
Fletcher, J. and	*The Maid in the Mill* (1647)	not known (1660)
Rowley, W.		
Gildon, C.	*Love's Victim* (1701)	King Rhesus (1701)
Granville, G.	*Heroick Love* (1698)	Agamemnon (1697)
	The British Enchanters (1706)	Caelius (1706)
	The Jew of Venice (1701)	Bassanio (1701)
	The She-Gallants (1696)	Bellamour (1695)
Green, A.	*The Politician Cheated* (1663)	
Hopkins, C.	*Boadicea Queen of Britain* (1697)	Cassibelan (1697)
	Friendship Improv'd (1700)	Zoilus (1699)
Jonson, B.	*The Silent Woman* (1620)	Morose (1684/5?)
Lacy, J.	*The Dumb Lady, or, The Farrier Made Physician* (1672)	
Leanerd, J.	*The Counterfeits* (1679)	Vitelli (1678)
Lee, N.	*Caesar Borgia* (1680)	Caesar Borgia (1679)
	Constantine the Great (1684)	Crispus (1683)
	Lucius Junius Brutus (1681)	Lucius (1680)
	Mithridates (1678)	Mithridates (1685?)
	The Massacre of Paris (1690)	Admiral of France (1689)
	Theodosius (1680)	Varanes (1680)
	The Princess of Cleve (1689)	Nemours (1681)
	The Rival Queens (1677)	Alexander (1693?)
Maidwell, L.	*The Loving Enemies* (1680)	Lorenzo (1679)
Manley, M.	*Almyna* (1707)	Almanzor (1706)
	The Royal Mischief (1696)	Osman (1696)
Marlowe, C.	*Doctor Faustus* (1604)	Faustus (1675?)
Massinger, P.	*The Bondman* (1624)	Pisander (1660)
Medbourne, M.	*Tartuffe, or the French Puritan* (1670)	
Middleton, T., and	*The Changeling* (1653)	De Flores (1660)
Rowley, W.		
Molière, ed.	*L'École des Femmes* (Paris, 1970)	
Sablayrolles, G.		
Motteux, P.	*Beauty in Distress* (1698)	Don Vincentio (1698)
	Love's a Jest (1696)	Railmore (1696)
	The Novelty (1697)	Grammont (1697)
Mountfort, W.	*The Injur'd Lovers* (1688)	Rheusanes (1688)
Oldmixon, J.	*The Governor of Cyprus* (1703)	Iopano (1703)

Orrery, Roger Boyle, Earl of	*Altemira* (1702)	Clorimon (1701)
	Henry the Fifth (1668)	Owen Tudor (1664)
	Mr Anthony (1690)	Mr Art (1669)
	Mustapha (1668)	Solyman (1665)
Otway, T.	*Alcibiades* (1675)	Alcibiades (1675)
	Don Carlos (1676)	King Philip (1676)
	Friendship in Fashion (1678)	Goodvile (1678)
	The Atheist (1684)	Beaugard (1683)
	The History and Fall of Caius Marius (1680)	Caius Marius (1679)
		Marius Sr. (1706/7)
	The Orphan (1680)	Castalio (1680)
	The Souldier's Fortune (1681)	Beaugard (1680)
	Titus and Berenice (1677)	Titus (1676)
	Venice Preserv'd (1682)	Jaffeir (1682)
Payne, H.N.	*The Morning Ramble* (1673)	Townlove (1672)
Pix, M.	*Queen Catharine* (1698)	Owen Tudor (1698)
	The Deceiver Deceiv'd (1698)	Melito Bondi (1697)
	The Innocent Mistress (1697)	Sir Charles Beauclair (1697)
Pordage, S.	*The Siege of Babylon* (1678)	Orontes (1677)
Porter, T.	*The Villain* (1663)	Brisac (1662)
Powell, G.	*The Treacherous Brothers* (1690)	
Rochester, John Wilmot, Earl of	*Valentinian* (1685)	Aecius (1684)
Rowe, N.	*Tamerlane* (1701)	Tamerlane (1701)
	The Ambitious Step-mother (1701)	Memnon (1700)
	The Biter (1705)	Sir Timothy (1704)
	The Fair Penitent (1703)	Horatio (1703)
	Ulysses (1706)	Ulysses (1705)
Rutter, J.	*The Valiant Cid* (1663)	Rodrigo (1662)
Rymer, T.	*Edgar, or the English Monarch* (1678)	
St Serfe, T.	*Tarugo's Wiles* (1668)	
Sedley, C.	*Antony and Cleopatra* (1677)	Antony (1677)
Settle, E.	*Cambyses King of Persia* (1671)	Cambyses (1671)
	Distress'd Innocence (1691)	
	Ibrahim the Illustrious Bassa (1677)	Solyman (1676)
	Pastor Fido (1677)	Sylvano (1676)
	The Empress of Morocco (1673)	Crimalhaz (1673)
Shadwell, T.	*Bury-Fair* (1689)	Lord Bellamy (1689)
	Epsom Wells (1673)	Bevil (1672)

	Psyche (1675)	
	The Libertine (1676)	Don John (1675)
	The Miser (1672)	
	The Sullen Lovers (1668)	
	The Virtuoso (1676)	Longvil (1676)
Shakespeare, W.	*Hamlet* (Davenant, adap., 1676)	Hamlet (1661)
	Henry VIII (1664)	Henry VIII (1663)
	Julius Caesar (1684)	Brutus (1683?)
	King Henry IV (Betterton, adap., 1700)	Falstaff (1700)
	Macbeth (Davenant, adap., 1674)	Macbeth (1664)
	Measure for Measure (Gildon, adap., 1700)	Angelo (1699)
	Othello (1687)	Othello (1690?)
	Pericles (1635)	Pericles (1660)
	Richard III (1634)	Edward IV (1691/2)
	Romeo and Juliet (1637)	Mercutio (1662)
	The History of King Lear (Tate, adap., 1681)	Lear (1681)
	The Merry Wives of Windsor (1664)	Falstaff (1703/4)
	Timon of Athens (Shadwell, adap., 1678)	Timon (1678)
	Troilus and Cressida (Dryden, adap., 1679)	Troilus (1679)
		Thersites (1708/9)
	Twelfth Night (1664)	Sir Toby Belch (1661)
Sherburne, E.	*Troades, or the Royal Captives* (1679)	
Shirley, J.	*Hyde Park* (1632)	
	The Grateful Servant (1660)	not known (1661/2)
	The School of Compliments (1667, as *Love Tricks*)	not known (1666/7)
	The Witty Fair One (1633)	not known (1666/7)
Smith, E.	*Phaedra and Hippolitus* (1707)	Theseus (1707)
Smith, H.	*The Princess of Parma* (1699)	Doria (1699)
Southerne, T.	*The Disappointment* (1684)	Alphonso (1684)
	The Fatal Marriage (1694)	Villeroy (1694)
	The Fate of Capua (1700)	Virginius (1700)
	The Wives Excuse (1692)	Lovemore (1691)
Stapylton, R.	*The Slighted Maid* (1663)	Iberio (1663)
	The Step-mother (1664)	Filamor (1663)
Suckling, J.	*Aglaura* (1646)	not known (1660)
Talbot, J.	*Troas* (1686)	

Tate, N.	*The Loyal General* (1680)	Theocrin (1679)
Trapp, J.	*Abra-Mule* (1704)	Mahomet (1704)
Trotter, C.	*Fatal Friendship* (1698)	Gramont (1698)
	The Revolution of Sweden (1706)	Arwide (1706)
Tuke, S.	*The Adventures of Five Hours* (1663)	Don Henrique (1663)
		Don Antonio (1706)
Vanbrugh, J.	*The Mistake* (1706)	Don Alvarez (1705)
	The Provok'd Wife (1697)	Sir John Brute (1697)
Vanneschi, F.	*Fetonte* (1747)	
Webster, J.	*The Duchess of Malfi* (1657)	Bosola (1662)
Wycherley, W.	*The Plain Dealer* (1677)	Manly (1683/4)

OTHER PRIMARY SOURCES AND EARLY PRINTED MATERIAL

Anon., *A Collection of Original Poems, Translations and Imitations* (1714)

A Comparison Between the Two Stages (1702)

An Account of the Life, Conversation, Birth, Education, Pranks, Projects, and Exploits, and Merry Conceits, of the Famously Notorious Matt. Coppinger (1695)

An Account of the Life of That Celebrated Tragedian Mr Thomas Bettertor (1747)

A Perfect Diurnall of Some Passages in Parliament (29 January–5 February 1648/9)

A Report of All the Cases Determined by Sir John Holt, Knt. From 1688 to 1710 (1738)

A Satyr against Dancing. By a Person of Honour (1702)

'A Satyr against Poetry', in Voiture, V. de, *Familiar Letters of Love, Gallantry, And several Occasions*, 2 vols. (1718), I.92

A Satyr on the Players (c.1682–5), MS 'Satyrs and Lampoons', BL Harley 7317, 96

'A Session of the Poets', in Lord, G. deF., ed., *Poems on Affairs of State*, 6 vols. (New Haven, 1977), I.356

Biographia Britannica, 5 vols. (1747)

Connoisseur (21 November 1754)

Daily Post and General Advertiser (15 October 1743)

Evening Post (3 October 1732)

Gazetteer and Daily Advertiser (22 October 1756)

Gazetteer and New Daily Advertiser (10 November 1766)

Lloyd's Evening Post and British Chronicle (10 March 1758)

Public Advertiser (7 February 1764)

Sir Walter Rawleigh's ghost (1651)

Sol in opposition to Saturn. Or a short return to a late Tragedy call'd The Duke of Guise (1683)

The Beauties of Biography, 2 vols. (1777)

The Censor, 3 vols. (1717)

The Daily Courant (7–15 December 1710)

The Elegant Entertainer and Merry Storyteller (1767)

The Fourth and Last Part of Modern Reports. Being a Collection of Several Special Cases argued and adjudged in the Court of King and Queen's Bench (1703)

The Gazette (25–9 November 1686)

The Observator (27 November–4 December 1686)

The Oxford Treatment of their Cambridge Friends (1705)

The Post-Man (6–19 September 1710)

Anderson, J., *A Genealogical History of the House of Yvery*, 2 vols. (1742)

Aston, A., *A Brief Supplement to Colley Cibber Esq. His Lives of the Famous Actors and Actresses* (1747), reprinted in *An Apology for the Life of Mr Colley Cibber*, ed. R.W. Lowe, 2 vols. (London, 1889), ii.299–303

Aubrey, J., *Brief Lives*, ed. O.L. Dick (Harmondsworth, 1982)

Baggs, Z., *Advertisement Concerning the Poor Actors, Who under Pretence of Hard Usage from the Patentees, Are about to Desert their Service* (1709)

Betterton, T., Letter to Colonel Finch, 25 May 1704. Thynne Papers, vol. xxv f.268

Bolingbroke, Henry St John, Viscount, *Philosophical Works*, 5 vols. (1754)

Brown, T., *Novus reformator vapulans* (1691)

Amusements Serious and Comical (1702)

A Collection of All the Dialogues Written by Mr Thomas Brown (1704)

Cibber, C., *An Apology for the Life of Mr Colley Cibber* (1740)

Clarendon, Edward Hyde, Earl of, *The History of the Rebellion and Civil Wars in England*, ed. W.D. Macray, 6 vols. (Oxford, 1888)

Collier, J., *A Short View of the Immorality and Profaneness of the English Stage* (1698)

Crouch, J., *A Mixt Poem ... upon the Happy Return of His Sacred Majesty Charles the Second* (1660)

The Muses Joy for the Recovery of that Weeping Vine, Henrietta Maria (1661)

Crull, J., *The Antiquities of St Peter's* (1711)

Curll, E. and Oldys, W., attr. Betterton, T., *A History of the English Stage* (1741)

Cumberland, R., *Memoirs* (1806)

Dart, J., *Westmonasterium, Or the History and Antiquities of the Abbey Church of St Peters Westminster* (1742)

Davies, T., *Memoirs of the Life of David Garrick, Esq.* (1780)

Dramatic Miscellanies, 3 vols. (1784)

Dekker, T., *The Wonderful Yeare* (1603)

Dennis, J., *The Critical Works of John Dennis*, ed. E.N. Hooker, 2 vols. (Baltimore, 1943)

Downes, J., *Roscius Anglicanus*, ed. J. Milhous and R.D. Hume (1987)

Dryden, J., 'Of Heroic Plays', Essay Preface to *The Conquest of Granada Part 1* (1672)

Notes and Observations on The Empress of Morocco (1674)

Prologue to the King and Queen, at the Opening of their Theatre. Spoken by Mr. Batterton (1683)

The Vindication of the Duke of Guise (1683)

'To my Dear Friend Mr Congreve on his Comedy Call'd The Double Dealer', in *The Letters of John Dryden*, ed. E.C. Ward (New York, 1965)

Elderfield, C., *The Civil Right of Tythes* (1650)

Evelyn, J., *The Diary of John Evelyn*, ed. E. de Beer, 4 vols. (Oxford, 1955)

Silva: Or, a Discourse of Forest-Trees, and the Propagation of Timber in His Majesty's Dominions, 5th edn (1729)

Filmer, R., *Observations upon Aristotle's Politiques* (1652)

Flecknoe, R., *A Discourse of the English Stage* (1664)

Genest, J., *Some Account of the English Stage from the Restoration in 1660 to 1830*, 10 vols. (Bath, 1832)

[Gildon, C.], *The Life of Mr Thomas Betterton* (1710)

Gosson, S., *Plays Confuted in Five Actions* (1582)

Gould, R., 'A Satyr against the Play-House', in *Poems, Chiefly Consisting of Satyrs and Satirical Epistles* (1689)

Halifax, George Savile, Marquess of, 'The Lady's New Year's Gift; or, Advice to a Daughter', in Kenyon, J.P., ed., *Halifax. Complete Works* (Harmondsworth, 1969)

Hall, J., *The Balm of Gilead* (1650)

Halliwell, J.O., *A Collection of Ancient Documents* (1870)

Hamilton, A., trans. H. Walpole, *Memoirs of the Comte de Gramont* (1965)

Harbage, A., *The Complete Pelican Shakespeare* (New York, 1969).

Hawkins, Sir J., *A General History of the Science and Practice of Music*, 5 vols. (1776)

Hill, A., *The Prompter*, no. 51, Tuesday 6 May 1735

Hooke, J., *Bibliopolii Husseyani, pars prima* (1707)

Officina Shrewsburiana (1707)

Bibliotheca Rayana (1708)

Pinacotheca Bettertonaeana (1710)

Bibliotheca Bernardiana (1711)

Johnson, S., 'Preface to Shakespeare', in Sherbo, A., ed., *The Yale Edition of the Works of Samuel Johnson* (New Haven, 1968)

The Lives of the English Poets, 3 vols. (Dublin, 1780–1)

Jonson, B., 'To the Reader', frontispiece caption to *Mr William Shakespeares Comedies, Histories, & Tragedies* (1623)

King, W., *Useful Miscellanies* (1712)

Le Neve, J., *The Lives and Characters of the Most Illustrious Persons British and Foreign* (1713)

Lister, M., *A Journey to Paris in the Year 1698* (1699)

Malone, E., ed., *The Plays and Poems of William Shakespeare*, 11 vols. (1790)

An Historical Account of the Rise and Progress of the English Stage (1800)

Manning, F., *Poems upon Several Occasions and to Several Persons* (1701)

Marvell, A., 'Upon the Death of the Lord Hastings', in Smith, N., ed., *The Poems of Andrew Marvell* (Harlow, 2007)

Milton, J., *The Tenure of Kings and Magistrates* (1649)

Motraye, A. De La, *Travels Through Europe* (1723)

North, R., *Roger North on Music*, ed. J. Wilson (1959)

Ogilby, J., *The Relation of His Majesties Entertainment Passing through the City of London* (1661)

Otway, T., 'Love-Letters Written by the Late Most Ingenious Mr Thomas Otway', in Ghosh, J.C., ed., *The Works of Thomas Otway*, 2 vols. (Oxford, 1932)

Pepys, S., *The Diary of Samuel Pepys*, ed. R. Latham and W. Matthews, 11 vols. (1971–83)

    Shorthand Letters of Samuel Pepys, ed. E. Chappell (Cambridge, 1933)

Pope, A., 'The First Epistle of the Second Book of Horace Imitated', in Butt, J., ed., *The Poems of Alexander Pope* (1963)

    Letters of Mr Alexander Pope and Several of his Friends (1737)

    A Collection of Letters, Never Printed Before: Written by Alexander Pope; and Other Ingenious Gentlemen, to the Late Aaron Hill, Esq (1751)

Quarles, F., *Gods love and mans unworthiness* (1651)

Richardson, J., *Explanatory Notes and Remarks on Milton's* Paradise Lost (1734)

Rochester, John Wilmot, Earl of, 'A Ramble in St James's Park', in *Rochester. Complete Poems and Plays*, ed. Paddy Lyons (1993)

    The Poetical Works of the Earls of Rochester, Roscommon and Dorset, 2 vols. (1737)

Rowe, N., ed., *The Works of Mr William Shakespear*, 6 vols. (1709)

Ruffield, O., *The Life of Alexander Pope, Esq.* (1769)

Sandoval, P. de., trans. Anon., *The Civil Wars of Spain* (1652)

Shell, A., and Emblow, A., eds., *An Index to Stationers' Company Court Books E, F and G. 1689–1717* (Oxford, 2007)

Smith, A., *The Comical and Tragical History of the Lives and Adventures of the Most Noted Bayliffs in and about Westminster* (1723)

Sprat, T., *The History of the Royal Society* (1667)

Steele, R., *The Tatler*, 30 April 1709 and 2–4 May 1710

Suetonius, trans. R. Graves, *The Twelve Caesars* (Harmondsworth, 1989)

Theobald, L., *Double Falsehood* (1767)

Thomas, T., *The Life of the Late Famous Comedian, Jo Hayns* (1701)

Towers, J., 'The Life of Dr John Radcliffe', *British Biography*, 10 vols. (Sherborne, 1766–7)

Vischard, C., Abbé de Saint Réal, trans. H.J., *Don Carlos, or An Historical Relation of the Unfortunate Life and Tragical Death of That Prince of Spain* (1674)

Wakefield, R., *Wakefield's Merchant and Tradesman's General Directory* (1789)

Waller, E., 'On St James's Park, as lately Improv'd by His Majesty', in Drury, G.T., ed., *The Poems of Edmund Waller*, 2 vols. (1893)

Walpole, H., *Anecdotes of Painting in England*, 4 vols. (1786)

Weaver, J., *An Essay Towards an History of Dancing* (1712)

Whitefield, G., *The Works of the Reverend George Whitefield*, 7 vols. (1771–2)

Wilkinson, T., *Memoirs of his Own Life* (Dublin, 1791)

REFERENCE WORKS

Avery, E.L., ed., *The London Stage Part 2. 1700–1729* (Carbondale, 1961) [consulted here in the revision by R.D. Hume and J. Milhous (1 August 2009) at www.personal.psu.edu/users/h/b/hb1/%20Stage%202001/lond1700.pdf

Goldmann, L., ed., *The Dictionary of National Biography*, 60 vols. (Oxford, 2004)

Hibbert, C., and Weinreb, B., eds., *The London Encyclopaedia* (1983)

Highfill, P.H., Jr, Burnim, K.A. and Langhans, E.A., *A Biographical Dictionary of Actors, Actresses, Musicians, Dancers, Managers and Stage Personnel in London, 1660–1800*, 16 vols. (Carbondale and Edwardsville, 1973)

Hume, R.D. and Milhous, J., *A Register of English Theatrical Documents, 1660–1737*, 2 vols. (Carbondale and Edwardsville, 1991)

McKenzie, D.F., *Stationers' Company Apprentices 1641–1700* (Oxford, 1974)

Milhous, J. and Hume, R.D., *Vice Chamberlain Coke's Theatrical Papers 1706–1715* (Carbondale, 1982)

Plomer, H.R., *A Dictionary of the Booksellers and Printers Who Were at Work in England, Scotland and Ireland from 1641 to 1667* (1907)

Sadie, S., and Tyrrell, J., eds., *The New Grove Dictionary of Music and Musicians*, 29 vols. (Oxford, 2003)

Stephen, L., and Lee, S., eds., *The Dictionary of National Biography*, 22 vols. (Oxford, 1917)

Thomas, D. and Hare, A., eds*., Restoration and Georgian England 1660–1788. Theatre in Europe: a Documentary History* (Cambridge, 1989)

Van Lennep, W., ed., *The London Stage, Part 1. 1660–1700* (Carbondale, 1963)

SECONDARY SOURCES

Aughterson, K., *Aphra Behn. The Comedies* (Basingstoke, 2003)

Avery, E.L., 'The Restoration Audience', *Philological Quarterly*, vol. 45 (1966), 54–61

Aylmer, G.E., *Rebellion or Revolution? England from Civil War to Restoration* (Oxford, 1986)

Backscheider, P.R., *Spectacular Politics* (Baltimore, 1993)
  'Behind City Walls: Restoration Actors in the Drapers' Company', *Theatre Survey*, vol. 45, no. 1 (May 2004), 75–87

Baker, H.C., *John Philip Kemble: The Actor in His Theatre* (1970)

Bakhtin, M., trans. Caryl Emerson, *Problems of Dostoevsky's Poetics* (Manchester, 1984)

Barnett, D., *The Art of Gesture: the Practices and Principles of Eighteenth-Century Acting* (Heidelberg, 1987)

Beattie, J.M., *Crime and the Courts of England* (Princeton, 1986)

Benedetti, J., *David Garrick and the Birth of Modern Theatre* (2001)

Benjamin, W., 'The Work of Art in the Age of its Technological Reproducibility', in Eiland, H. and Jennings, M.W., eds., *Walter Benjamin. Selected Writings*, 3 vols. (Cambridge, Mass., 2002)

Bentley, G.E., *The Jacobean and Caroline Stage*, 7 vols. (Oxford, 1941–68)

Bergeron, D., *Textual Patronage in English Drama, 1570–1640* (Aldershot and Burlington, 2006)

Besant, Sir W., and Mitton, G.E., *The Fascination of London. Holborn and Bloomsbury* (1903)

Bevington, D., *This Wide and Universal Theater: Shakespeare in Performance, Then and Now* (Chicago, 2007)

Borgman, A.S., *The Life and Death of William Mountfort* (Cambridge, Mass., 1935)

Boswell, E., *The Restoration Court Stage* (Cambridge, Mass., 1932)

Botica, A.R., 'Audience, Playhouse and Play in English Restoration Theatre, 1660–1710', Unpublished DPhil thesis, Oxford University, 1985

Bourdieu, P., trans. R. Nice, *Distinction: A Social Critique of the Judgment of Taste* (1986)

Bowden, B., *Chaucer Aloud* (Philadelphia, 1987)

    Eighteenth-Century Modernizations of The Canterbury Tales (Cambridge, 1991)

Brandon, J., trans., *Kabuki: Five Classic Plays* (Honolulu, 1992)

Burling, W.J., *Summer Theatre in London, 1661–1820* (Madison, 2000)

Burton, H., ed., *Acting in the Sixties* (1970)

Bush-Bailey, G., *Treading the Bawds. Actresses and Playwrights on the Late Stuart Stage* (Manchester, 2007)

    'Revolution, Legislation and Autonomy', in Gale, M.B. and Stokes, J., eds., *The Cambridge Companion to the Actress* (Cambridge, 2007)

Butler, M., *Theatre and Crisis, 1632–1642* (Cambridge, 1984)

Caines, M., Goring, P., Shaughnessy, N., and Shaughnessy, R., eds., *Lives of Shakespearian Actors, Part I: David Garrick, Charles Macklin and Margaret Woffington by Their Contemporaries*, 3 vols. (2008)

Canfield, J.D., *Tricksters and Estates. On the Ideology of Restoration Comedy* (Lexington, 1979)

    Heroes and States. On the Id eology of Restoration Tragedy (Lexington, 2000)

Carey, J., ed., *The Faber Book of Reportage* (1987)

Chambers, E.K., *William Shakespeare: A Study of Facts and Problems*, 2 vols. (Oxford, 1930)

Clark, A., *The Working Life of Women in the Seventeenth Century* (1917)

Cooper, T., *Searching for Shakespeare* (2006)

Cordner, M., 'Playwright versus Priest: Profanity and the Wit of Restoration Comedy', in Fiske, D.P., ed., *The Cambridge Companion to English Restoration Theatre* (Cambridge, 2000), 209–25

Crawford, A., *A History of the Vintners' Company* (1977)

Crystal, D., *The Stories of English* (2004)

Danby, J.R., 'Portraits of Restoration Actors Michael Mohun and Edward Kynaston: New Evidence', *Theatre Notebook*, vol. 59, issue 1 (2005), 2–18

Dawson, M.S., *Gentility and the Comic Theatre of Late Stuart England* (Cambridge, 2005)

Dobson, M., *The Making of the National Poet* (Oxford, 1992)

Doran, J., 'Frozen-Out Actors', *The Cornhill Magazine* (1862), 167–77

Downer, A.S., *The Eminent Tragedian: William Charles Macready* (Cambridge, Mass., 1966)

Edmond, M., 'The Chandos Portrait: a Suggested Painter', *The Burlington Magazine*, vol. CXXIV, no. 948 (March 1982), 146–9
  Rare Sir William Davenant (Manchester, 1996)

Eliot, T.S., 'The Metaphysical Poets', in Kermode, F., ed., *Selected Prose of T.S. Eliot* (1975)

Farley-Hills, D., 'Shakespeare and Joseph Taylor', *Notes and Queries* (March 1994), 58–61

Field, O., *The Kit-Cat Club. Friends Who Imagined a Nation* (2008)

Gaskell, P., *A New Introduction to Bibliography* (Oxford, 1972)

Genette, G., trans. J.E. Lewin, *Paratexts: Thresholds of Interpretation* (Cambridge, 1997)

Goff, M., *The Incomparable Hester Santlow* (Aldershot, 2007)

Greening Lamborn, E.A., 'Great Tew and the Chandos Portrait', *Notes and Queries*, vol. 19 (February 1949), 71–2

Griffin, D., *Literary Patronage in England, 1650–1800* (Cambridge, 1996)

Gurr, A., *The Shakespearian Stage 1574–1642*, 3rd edn (Cambridge, 1992)
  The Shakespearian Playing Companies (Oxford, 1996)

Hammond, B., *Professional Imaginative Writing in England, 1670–1740* (Oxford, 1997)

Handover, P.M., *Printing in London from Caxton to Modern Times* (1960)

Hayton, D., Cruikshanks, E., and Handley, S., *The House of Commons 1690–1715* (Cambridge, 2002)

Holden, A., 'Why We Should Give Larry a Standing Ovation', *The Observer*, Review, 27 May 2007, 7

Holland, P., *The Ornament of Action* (Cambridge, 1979)
  'Farce', in Fisk, D.P., ed., *The Cambridge Companion to English Restoration Theatre* (Cambridge, 2000), 107–26
  'Hearing the Dead: the Sound of Garrick', in Cordner, M. and Holland, P., eds., *Players, Playwrights, Playhouses. Investigating Performance, 1660–1800* (Basingstoke, 2007), 248–70

Holmes, R., *Sidetracks. Explorations of a Romantic Biographer* (2000)

Hotson, L., *The Commonwealth and Restoration Stage* (Cambridge, Mass., 1928)

Howe, E., *The First English Actresses* (Cambridge, 1992)

Howell, W.S., 'Sources of the Elocutionary Movement in England, 1700–1748', *Quarterly Journal of Speech*, vol. 45 (1959), 1–18

Hughes, D., *English Drama 1660–1700* (Oxford, 1996)

Hume, R.D., 'A Revival of The Way of the World in December 1701 or January 1702', *Theatre Notebook*, vol. 26 (1971), 30–6

The Development of English Drama in the Late Seventeenth Century (Oxford, 1976)

'Before the Bard: "Shakespeare" in Early Eighteenth-Century London', *ELH*, vol. 64 (1997), 41–75

'The Economics of Culture in London, 1660–1740', *Huntington Library Quarterly*, vol. 69, no.4 (2006), 487–533

Huse, A.A., 'Cleopatra, Queen of the Seine: The Politics of Eroticism in Dryden's *All for Love*', *Huntington Library Quarterly*, vol. 63 (2000), 23–46

Hutton, R., 'The Making of the Secret Treaty of Dover, 1668–1670', *The Historical Journal*, vol. 29, no. 2 (1986), 297–318

The Restoration (Oxford, 1987)

Charles II, King of England, Scotland and Ireland (Oxford, 1989)

Jeffree, R., *Mr Cartwright's Pictures: A Seventeenth-Century Collection* (1987)

Jeffreys, S., *The Libertine* (1994)

Jordan, R., 'Richard Norton and the Theatre at Southwick', *Theatre Notebook*, vol. 38 (1984), 105–15

Joseph, B., *Elizabethan Acting* (Oxford, 1951)

Kahan, J., *The Cult of Kean* (Aldershot, 2006)

Kaneko, Y., *The Restoration Stage Controversy*, 6 vols. (1996)

Keay, A., *The Magnificent Monarch: Charles II and the Ceremonies of Power* (2008)

Kenyon, J., *The Popish Plot* (Harmondsworth, 1974)

Kewes, P., *Authorship and Appropriation. Writing for the Stage in England, 1660–1710* (Oxford, 1998)

Krutch, J.W., *Comedy and Conscience after the Restoration* (New York, 1924)

Lane, J., *John Hall and his Patients* (Stratford-upon-Avon, 1996)

Langford, P., *A Polite and Commercial People. England 1727–1783* (Oxford, 1989)

Englishness Identified: Manners and Character 1650–1850 (Oxford, 2000)

Langhans, E.A., 'New Restoration Theatre Accounts, 1682–1692', *Theatre Notebook*, vol. XVII (1963), 118–34

Lanham, R.A., *A Handlist of Rhetorical Terms* (Berkeley, 1987)

Lefkowitz, M., 'Shadwell and Locke's Psyche: the French Connection', *Proceedings of the Royal Musical Association*, vol. 106 (1979–80), 42–55

Leggatt, A., 'Richard Burbage: A Dangerous Actor', in Banham, M., and Milling, J., eds., *Extraordinary Actors: Essays on Popular Performers* (Exeter, 2004)

Lewis, R., *The Secret Life of Laurence Olivier* (1997)

Love, H., 'The Myth of the Restoration Audience', *Komos*, vol. 1 (1968), 49–56

Lowe, R.W., *Thomas Betterton* (1891)

Lozano, E.E., *Community Design and the Culture of Cities: the Crossroad and the Wall* (Cambridge, 1990)

Luckhurst, M., and Moody, J., eds., *Theatre and Celebrity* (2006)

Maguire, N.K., *Regicide and Restoration. English Tragicomedy, 1660–1671* (Cambridge, 1992)

Markley, R.D., '"Be Impudent, Be Saucy, Forward, Bold, Touzing, and Leud": The Politics of Sexuality and Feminine Desire in Behn's Tory Comedies', in Canfield, J.D., and Payne, D.C., eds., *Cultural Readings of Restoration and Eighteenth-Century English Theater* (Athens, GA, 1995), 114–40

'The Canon and its Critics', in Fisk, D.P., ed., *The Cambridge Companion to English Restoration Theatre* (Cambridge, 2000), 226–42

Marly, D. de, 'The Architect of Dorset Garden Theatre', *Theatre Notebook*, vol. 29 (1975), 119–24

Marsden, J.I., 'Spectacle, Horror, and Pathos', in Fisk, D.P., ed., *The Cambridge Companion to English Restoration Theatre* (Cambridge, 2000), 174–90

Milhous, J., 'Thomas Betterton's Playwriting', *Bulletin of the New York Public Library*, vol. 77 (1974), 375–92

'An Annotated Census of Thomas Betterton's Roles, 1659–1710', *Theatre Notebook*, vol. 29 (1975), 33–45 (part 1), and 85–94 (part 2)

Thomas Betterton and the Management of Lincoln's Inn Fields 1695–1708 (Carbondale, 1979)

'United Company Finances, 1682–1692', *Theatre Research International*, vol. 7 (1981–2), 37–53

'The Multimedia Spectacular on the Restoration Stage', in Kenny, S.S., ed., *British Theatre and the Other Arts, 1660–1800* (Washington, 1984), 41–66

Milhous, J. and Hume, R.D., 'New Documents about the London Theatre 1685–1711', *Harvard Library Bulletin*, vol. XXXVI, no. 3 (Summer 1988), 260–1

Milling, J., 'Thomas Betterton and the Art of Acting', in Banham, M., and Milling, J., eds., *Extraordinary Actors: Essays on Popular Performers* (Exeter, 2004), 21–35

Mullan, J., *Sentiment and Sociability. The Language of Feeling in the Eighteenth Century* (Oxford, 1988)

Mullin, D., 'Lighting on the Eighteenth-Century London Stage: A Reconsideration', *Theatre Notebook*, vol. 34 (1980), 74

Mumford, L., *The City in History: Its Origins, its Transformations and its Prospects* (1961)

Munns, J., 'Images of Monarchy on the Restoration Stage', in Owen, S.J., ed., *A Companion to Restoration Drama* (Oxford, 2001), 109–25

Murray, B.A., *Restoration Shakespeare. Viewing the Voice* (2001)

Nicoll, A., *A History of Restoration Drama 1660–1700*, 4th edn (Cambridge, 1952)

Norbrook, D., '*Macbeth* and the Politics of Historiography', in Sharpe, K., and Zwicker, S.N., eds., *The Politics of Discourse. The Literature and History of Seventeenth-Century England* (Berkeley, 1987), 78–116

Writing the English Republic: Poetry, Rhetoric and Politics, 1627–1660 (Cambridge, 1999)

Odell, G.C.D., *Shakespeare from Betterton to Irving*, 2 vols. (New York, 1920)

Ogg, D., *England in the Reign of Charles II*, 2nd edn (Oxford, 1961)
  England in the Reigns of James II and William III (Oxford, 1955)
Olivier, L., *Confessions of an Actor* (1982)
Ollard, R., *Pepys* (Oxford, 1974)
Ong, W.J., *Orality and Literacy. The Technologizing of the Word*, 2nd edn (1982)
Orczy, B., *His Majesty's Well-Beloved. An Episode in the Life of Mr Thomas Betterton as Told by His Friend John Honeywood* (1919)
Orrey, L., rev. R. Milnes, *Opera* (1987)
Paul, H.N., *The Royal Play of Macbeth* (New York, 1950)
Payne, D.C., 'The Restoration Dramatic Dedication as Symbolic Capital', *Studies in Eighteenth-Century Culture*, vol. 20 (1990), 27–42
  'The Restoration Actress', in Canfield, J.D., and Payne, D.C., eds., *Cultural Readings of Restoration and Eighteenth-Century English Theater* (Athens, GA, 1995), 13–39
  'The Restoration Actress', in Owen, S.J., ed., *A Companion to Restoration Drama* (Oxford, 2001)
Pears, I., *The Discovery of Painting: the Growth of Interest in the Arts in England, 1680–1768* (1988)
Pearson, J., *The Prostituted Muse: Images of Women and Women Dramatists 1642–1737* (Hemel Hempstead, 1988)
Peters, J.S., *Congreve, the Drama and the Printed Word* (Stanford, 1990)
  Theatre of the Book, 1480–1880 (Oxford, 2000)
Phillips, D., *A History of Reading* (Reading, 1980)
Picard, L., *Restoration* London (1997)
Pinto, V. de S., *English Biography in the Seventeenth Century* (1951)
Plank, S.E., '"And Now About the Cauldron Sing": Music and the Supernatural on the Restoration Stage', *Early Music*, vol. XVIII, no. 3 (1990), 393–407
Potter, L., *Secret Rites and Royal Writing* (Cambridge, 1990)
Price, C., *Henry Purcell and the London Theatre* (Cambridge, 1984)
Randall, D.R., *Winter Fruit: English Drama 1642–1660* (Lexington, 1995)
Richards, J., *Sir Henry Irving: A Victorian Actor and His World* (2006)
Roach, J.R., *The Player's Passion: Studies in the Science of Acting* (Newark, 1985)
  Cities of the Dead. Circum-Atlantic Performance (New York, 1996)
  'The Performance', in Fisk, D.P., ed., *The Cambridge Companion to English Restoration Theatre* (Cambridge, 2000)
Roberts, D., *The Ladies: Female Patronage of Restoration Drama 1660–1700* (Oxford, 1989)
Salter, H.E., *Surveys and Tokens* (Oxford, 1923)
Schama, S., *Landscape and Memory* (1996)
Schoenbaum, S., *Shakespeare's Lives*, 2nd edn (Oxford, 1991)
Slack, P., *The Impact of Plague in Tudor and Stuart England* (Oxford, 1985)

Smith, J.H., 'Thomas Corneille to Betterton to Congreve', *Journal of English and Germanic Philology*, vol. 45 (1946), 209–13

Stanley, A.P., *Historical Memorials of Westminster Abbey* (1886)

Stern, T., *The Rehearsal from Shakespeare to Sheridan* (Oxford, 2000)
    'Re-patching the Play', in Holland, P., and Orgel, S., eds., *From Script to Stage in Early Modern England* (Basingstoke and New York, 2004)

Stone, G.W. and Kahrl, G.M., *David Garrick: A Critical Biography* (Carbondale and Edwardsville, 1979)

Stone, L., 'The Residential Development of the West End in the Seventeenth Century', in Malament, B.C., ed., *After the Reformation* (Manchester, 1980), 167–212

Strong, R., *The Artist and the Garden* (New Haven, 2000)

Thacker, C., *The History of Gardens* (1979)

Thomas, K., *Man and the Natural World: Changing Attitudes in England, 1500–1800* (Harmondsworth, 1983)

Thorp, J., 'Dance in Late 17th-century London: Priestly Muddles', *Early Music* (May 1998), 198–210

Tuan, Y.F., 'Space and Context', in Schechner, R., and Appel, W., eds., *By Means of Performance: Intercultural Studies of Theatre and Ritual* (Cambridge, 1990)

Underdown, D., *Revel, Riot and Rebellion. Popular Politics and Culture in England, 1603–1660* (Oxford, 1987)

Vickery, A., *In Pursuit of Pleasure* (Milton Keynes, 2001)

Walford, E., *Old and New London* (1878)

Wall, C., *The Literary and Cultural Spaces of Restoration* (Cambridge, 1998) London

Wanko, C., 'Three Stories of Celebrity: The Beggar's Opera "Biographies"', *Studies in English Literature*, vol. 38 (1998)
    Roles of Authority. Thespian Biography and Celebrity in Eighteenth-Century Britain (Lubbock, 2003)

Wells, S., ed., *Shakespeare in the Theatre. An Anthology of Criticism* (Oxford, 1997)

West, S., *The Image of the Actor. Verbal and Visual Representations in the Age of Garrick and Kemble* (New York, 1991)

Whitfield, P., *Cities of the World. A History in Maps* (2005)

Wills, G., *Witches and Jesuits* (Oxford, 1996)

Winn, J.A., *John Dryden and His World* (1987)
    'John Dryden', in Backscheider, P.R., ed., *Dictionary of Literary Biography, vol. 80, Restoration and Eighteenth-Century Dramatists*, First Series (Detroit, 1989)

Woodbridge, K., *Princely Gardens: the Origins and Development of the French Formal Style* (1986)

Yeowell, J., 'Sir Francis Watson, Bart', *Notes and Queries*, Series III (13 June 1863), 470

Zunshine, L., ed., *Acting Theory and the English Stage, 1700–1830*, 5 vols. (2008)

ELECTRONIC SOURCES

RNT Archive: www.website-archive.nt-online.org/productions/rd/more/hamlet.
html

FILMS

Stage Beauty, dir. Richard Eyre (2004)
The Libertine, dir. Laurence Dunmore (2005)

Index

N.B. Plays in which Betterton appeared are generally listed under 'Betterton, Thomas, roles'